FROMMER'S
EasyGuide
TO

Provence &
the French Riviera

by

Kathryn Tomasetti & Tristan Rutherford

Easy Guides are ✦ Quick To Read ✦ Light To Carry
✦ For Expert Advice ✦ In All Price Ranges

FrommerMedia LLC

Published by
FROMMERMEDIA LLC

ISBN 978-1-62887-114-2 (paper), 978-1-62887-115-9 (e-book)

Editorial Director: Pauline Frommer
Editor: Elizabeth Heath
Production Editor: Lindsay Conner
Cartographer: Andrew Murphy
Cover Design: Howard Grossman

Front cover photo: Luxury resort and bay of Villefranche-sur-Mer near Nice and Monaco © liligraphie
Back cover photo: Lavender fields near Valensole © Victor Zastolskiy

For information on our other products or services, see www.frommers.com.

Frommer Media LLC also publishes its books in a variety of electronic formats. Some content that
appears in print may not be available in electronic formats.

Manufactured in the United States of America

5 4 3 2 1

A foreword TO THIS EASYGUIDE TO PROVENCE & THE FRENCH RIVIERA

BY
ARTHUR FROMMER

Friends:

Provence. The Riviera. Simply to utter those words is to imagine Pleasure, sheer Pleasure. It's to visualize a world of resplendent casinos (one apiece in Nice, Cannes, and Monaco), of broad, graceful boulevards flanking the sea, of beaches with light blue umbrellas, of stunning vacationers in bikinis or the like, and of the French on vacation.

It's often been said that no one knows better than the French how to enjoy themselves. I witnessed that condition once, most indelibly, at a giant Mediterranean Club Med where a planeload of French vacationers had just arrived. Within 3 minutes of alighting from the airport buses, the entire planeload was gyrating on the dance floor and dashing to the bar for bouts of wine and worse. Within 3 minutes.

You'll have another experience of the French enjoying themselves at the exquisite lunchtime buffets on the beach in front of grand hotels like the Negresco in Nice or the Carlton or Martinez in Cannes. Never in your life will you ever have such a buffet lunch, a repast to rival the gourmet meals in many famed restaurants.

And you'll encounter such pleasures not simply in Nice, which you should definitely visit (the railroad station hotels there are unusually cheap), but also to the west of Nice in Cannes, Cap d'Antibes. St. Tropez and Juan les Pins, and to the east of Nice in Eze-Village and Monaco. There's no need for a car. Trains go along the sea, and it's usually about half an hour by rail to reach whatever you're seeking.

From the Riviera north through Provence is another sort of Pleasure, one of the most visually awesome areas of France so beautifully depicted by 19th-century impressionists from Cezanne to van Gogh. When I think of it, I think of fields of lavender stretching on into the distance, of university towns like Aix-en-Provence, of sites of Roman ruins like Avignon, of the ancient Arles on the River Rhône where van Gogh painted his famous *Night Café* and numerous Provencal landscapes.

Of additional importance in this EasyGuide is its treatment of Marseille, the second largest city in France—and for those readers who have earlier been there and been disappointed, it's time to revisit a metropolitan area where giant new investments in infrastructure, new architecture, and improved culture have literally transformed the famous port and place. Our authors have carefully surveyed the new Marseille, with its dozens of museums, theaters, galleries, and shopping areas, and they have also provided you with their recommendations for that top thrill in gastronomy: bouillabaisse (we're anxious to hear from our readers about their own discoveries of the world's finest fish stews). Although Marseille hasn't always been regarded as a part of the French Riviera, it is today—and well-practiced travelers will want to include it in their European trip.

But I need to cut short these additional images of Pleasure for fear of trespassing on the better descriptions from our authors. And who are they?

Tristan Rutherford and Kathryn Tomasetti are a married and much-published couple (who often lecture on travel journalism at major universities) who live full-time in the city of Nice, on the Riviera. Who better to write this *EasyGuide to Provence & the French Riviera,* of which we're justifiably proud? Our Frommer travel books have always made use of top journalistic talents, and Tristan and Kathryn are simply the latest in a large corps of travel experts who have written for us over the years. They share not only their knowledge, but also their wonderful zeal for guiding the reader to the best in travel.

Bon Voyage! Bon Plaisir!

Arthur Frommer

CONTENTS

ABOUT THE AUTHOR

U.S.-born, Italian-raised **Kathryn Tomasetti** writes travel and food stories for the likes of "The Guardian" and "The Times." Her library of holiday photos—snapped from as far afield as China, Albania, and Chile—has been published by "National Geographic" and "Time Out." Kathryn's favorite places in Provence are the pavement cafes of Avignon and the art-filled city of Arles.

Tristan Rutherford has been a freelance travel writer since 2002. His lucky first assignment took him to Nice and he's been based there ever since. He has visited more than 60 countries and written about 20 of them for "The Independent" and the "Sunday Times Travel Magazine." Tristan also lectures in travel journalism at London's Central Saint Martins.

ABOUT THE FROMMER TRAVEL GUIDES

For most of the past 50 years, Frommer's has been the leading series of travel guides in North America, accounting for as many as 24% of all guidebooks sold. I think I know why.

Though we hope our books are entertaining, we nevertheless deal with travel in a serious fashion. Our guidebooks have never looked on such journeys as a mere recreation, but as a far more important human function, a time of learning and introspection, an essential part of a civilized life. We stress the culture, lifestyle, history, and beliefs of the destinations we cover, and urge our readers to seek out people and new ideas as the chief rewards of travel.

We have never shied from controversy. We have, from the beginning, encouraged our authors to be intensely judgmental, critical—both pro and con—in their comments, and wholly independent. Our only clients are our readers, and we have triggered the ire of countless prominent sorts, from a tourist newspaper we called "practically worthless" (it unsuccessfully sued us) to the many rip-offs we've condemned.

And because we believe that travel should be available to everyone regardless of their incomes, we have always been cost-conscious at every level of expenditure. Though we have broadened our recommendations beyond the budget category, we insist that every lodging we include be sensibly priced. We use every form of media to assist our readers, and are particularly proud of our feisty daily website, the award-winning Frommers.com.

I have high hopes for the future of Frommer's. May these guidebooks, in all the years ahead, continue to reflect the joy of travel and the freedom that travel represents. May they always pursue a cost-conscious path, so that people of all incomes can enjoy the rewards of travel. And may they create, for both the traveler and the persons among whom we travel, a community of friends, where all human beings live in harmony and peace.

Arthur Frommer

THE BEST OF PROVENCE & THE FRENCH RIVIERA

The ancient Greeks left their vines, the Romans their monuments, but it was the 19th-century Impressionists who most shaped the romance of **Provence** today. Cézanne, Gauguin, Chagall, and countless others were drawn to the unique light and vibrant spectrum brought forth by what van Gogh called "the transparency of the air." Modern-day visitors will delight in the region's culture, colors, and world-class museums. And they will certainly dine well, too.

Provence, perhaps more than any other part of France, blends past and present with an impassioned pride. It has its own language and customs, and some of its festivals go back to medieval times. The region is bounded on the north by the Dauphine River, on the west by the Rhône, on the east by the Alps, and on the south by the Mediterranean. Provence's topography varies starkly, from the Camargue's salt marshes to the Lubéron's lavender fields, and on to the vertiginous Alpine cliffs of Haute Provence.

That fabled real estate of Provence known as the **French Riviera**, also called the Côte d'Azur, ribbons for 200km (125 miles) along the sun-kissed Mediterranean. Chic, sassy, and incredibly sexy, the region has long attracted artists and jetsetters alike with its clear skies, blue waters, and carefree cafe culture.

A trail of modern artists captivated by the region's light and setting has left a rich heritage: Matisse at Vence, Léger at Biot, Renoir at Cagnes, and Picasso at Antibes and seemingly everywhere in between. The finest collection of modern artworks is at the Foundation Maeght in St-Paul-de-Vence. Lesser-visited museums dedicated to Jean Cocteau in Menton and Pierre Bonnard near Cannes offer an equally vivid introduction to the Riviera's storied art scene.

A century ago, winter and spring were considered high season on the Riviera. In recent decades, July and August have become the most crowded months, and reservations are imperative. The region basks in more than 300 days of sun per year, and even December and January are often pleasant and sunny.

Together, Provence and the French Riviera present visitors with an embarrassment of riches—you may find yourself overwhelmed by all the choices. We've tried to make the task easier by compiling a list of our favorite experiences and discoveries in the region. In the following pages, you'll find the kind of candid travel advice we'd give our closest friends.

THE best AUTHENTIC EXPERIENCES

o **Sipping Pastis in Provence:** Pastis is synonymous with Provence. This anise-flavored liquor is sipped at sundown on every town square, from Arles to the Italian border. Beware: The Provençal are seriously brand-conscious. Order a "51" if you want to look like a local, or a "Janot" for the region's favorite organic offering. Impress the barman by ordering a *tomate* (pastis with a dash of grenadine) or a *perroquet* (literally a parrot, which is pastis with a splash of green mint syrup).

o **Breaking the Bank at Monte-Carlo:** The **Casino de Monte-Carlo** has been the most opulent place to have a flutter for over 150 years. Its creation, built in 1863 by architect Charles Garnier (of Paris Opera House fame), turned the tables for Monaco by transforming a provincial port into a world-class tourist destination. Expect frescoed ceilings and wealthy, well-dressed clientele from as far afield as China, Russia, and the U.S. See p. 218.

o **Ogling the Pomp of the Pope's Medieval Party Pad:** Those medieval popes knew a thing or two about interior design. Avignon's **Palais des Papes,** or Pope's Palace, is a moneyed medley of Gothic architecture and vast banqueting halls. The Châteauneuf-du-Pape papal vineyards just north of Avignon still produce some of the most noted wine in France. See p. 47.

o **Buying Your Daily Bread:** That cute little boulangerie just down the street? Depending on where you are, there's likely to be another—or several—a short stroll away. The daily baguette run is a ritual for many French people. Get your coins ready (one euro, give or take 10 centimes) and join the queue. To really fit in, ask for your baguette chewy *(pas trop cuite)* or crusty *(bien cuite).*

o **Shopping at a Market:** Markets offer one of the best ways to explore French towns like a local. We recommend the open-air market in **Arles,** one of Provence's most authentic destinations. A colorful line of vendors sells olives, fresh bread, cheese, and local ham underneath the city ramparts, a few blocks from the town's Roman amphitheater. See p. 59. Alternatively, French covered markets are time machines— visiting one is like taking a trip back through the centuries. Both Avignon's **Les Halles** (see p. 49) and Cannes' **Marché Forville** (see p. 150) offer high-quality artisanal treats to take home, like olive *tapenade,* as well as great things to snack on while you shop, such as vegetable-stuffed *fougasse* bread, Mara des Bois strawberries, and wedges of Cavaillon melon.

THE best RESTAURANTS

o **Le Môle,** Marseille: Chef Gérard Passédat's newest restaurants, La Table and La Cuisine (under the banner Le Môle), offer Michelin-quality cuisine at atop Marseille's MuCEM museum. And while La Table takes a classic approach to haute cuisine (elegant service, sea views, tasting menus), next door's La Cuisine dishes up similar top-notch dishes via a friendly multi-course buffet—and at just a fraction of the price. Unmissable. See p. 114.

o **Oustau de Baumanière,** Les Baux: The cinematic setting of the ancient fortress of Les Baux had troubadours singing in its streets during the Middle Ages. Today it is no less romantic. Several picturesque hideaways are tucked into the hills surrounding the village, including this double-Michelin-starred restaurant housed in a 16th-century farmhouse. See p. 60.

o **La Poissonnerie,** Cassis: The place to dine on Mediterranean fish that are literally fresh off the boat. Owned and operated by the Giannettini family for more than 75 years, this quayside eatery is half *poissonnerie* (fishmonger), half restaurant. Expect expertly prepared octopus, sardines, and red mullet so assuredly fresh that they're practically swimming. See p. 123.

o **L'Atelier Jean-Luc Rabanel,** Arles: Fixed-price tasting menus—no à la carte allowed—are becoming increasingly popular. If you're ready to put yourself in the hands of one of France's most talented chefs, try Jean-Luc Rabanel's sublime creations. This culinary genius cultivates most of his organic ingredients himself. Truly an amazing experience. See p. 64.

o **La Merenda,** Nice: Utterly unpretentious, this snug bistro doesn't take reservations or credit cards. But it remains one of the Riviera's top spots for sampling traditional Niçois cuisine. Try slow-cooked beef *daube, petits-farcis* (stuffed vegetables), and *pissaladière,* a pizzalike local flatbread topped with caramelized onions. See p. 185.

o **Le Louis XV,** Monaco: Superchef Alain Ducasse oversees this iconic restaurant—regularly rated as one of the finest in the world—located in Monte-Carlo's Hôtel de Paris. Dining is extravagant, with fare steeped in lavish ingredients, from white truffles to foie gras, and served in an ornate, golden dining room. Yet many dishes of elegant simplicity are equally magnificent. Best for serious epicureans. See p. 217.

THE most unforgettable HOTELS

o **C2 Hotel,** Marseille: One of the region's newest hotels, stylish C2 has already made a name for itself. It could be the minimally designed rooms. Or maybe the on-site spa. But we think it's probably the hotel's own beach club, perched offshore on the private Mediterranean island of Île Degaby. See p. 112.

o **La Cabro d'Or,** Les Baux: Spilling out from an original 18th-century farmhouse, La Cabro d'Or makes a luxurious Provençal bolthole. The labyrinthine grounds are undoubtedly some of the loveliest in France. Expect to stumble across walled gardens, bubbling fountains, and flower-strewn courtyards. See p. 60.

o **Mama Shelter,** Marseille: The work of legendary designer Philippe Starck, this contemporary hotel is located in the hip Cours Julien neighborhood. On the ground floor, there's a courtyard pastis bar, perfect for sampling the city's favorite aperitif. See p. 113.

o **Château Saint-Martin,** Vence: Perched on a hilltop just 20 minutes from Nice, Château Saint-Martin is one of the Riviera's most splendid hotels. The gardens are sprinkled with wildflowers. The infinity pool quite literally goes on forever. And a truly exquisite spa is onsite. Lucky guests can gaze at the Mediterranean from bed. See chapter 12, p. 173.

o **Hôtel Belles-Rives,** Juan-les-Pins: Once a vacation villa to Zelda and F. Scott Fitzgerald, the Hôtel Belles-Rives still maintains a flamboyant, 1920s feel. Sip a sundowner on the hotel's sea-facing terrace, or try waterskiing at the hotel's aquatic club, the very spot where the sport was invented almost a century ago. See p. 159.

o **Hôtel Napoléon,** Menton: This sea-facing property takes inspiration from Menton's most famous "honorary citizen," Jean Cocteau. The multi-talented author and film-maker's artworks decorate the guestrooms, many of which possess their own private terrace peeking out over the town's beachfront promenade. Best of all, even during the summer season Napoléon's rates remain refreshingly reasonable. See p. 223.

secret **PROVENCE & THE FRENCH RIVIERA**

o **Cycling in the Countryside:** The country that hosts the Tour de France offers thousands of options for bike trips, all of them ideal for leaving the crowds far behind. You're even welcome to take your bike aboard most trains in France, free of charge. For cycling through Provence's vineyards and past pretty hilltop villages, check out **Vélo Loisir en Luberon**'s downloadable routes. See p. 92. (And if all that pedaling sounds too much like hard work, you could opt to rent an electric bike in Bonnieux instead! See p. 92.)

o **Hunting for Antiques:** The 18th- and 19th-century French aesthetic was gloriously different from that of England and North America. Many objects bear designs with mythological references to the French experience. France has some 13,000-plus antiques shops throughout the country. Stop where you see the sign ANTIQUAIRE or BROCANTE.

o **Traveling First Class:** France's TGV rail network is arguably the world's fastest. Yet these trains are not just high-speed. When routes are booked in advance, they're wallet-friendly too. Throw in decor by Christian Lacroix and PlayStation Portables available to rent, and you're looking at the classiest public transport on the planet. See chapter 14.

o **Discovering secret beaches between Monaco and Roquebrune-Cap-Martin:** The Riviera's rippling coastal path turns up plenty of hidden surprises. Head east out of Monaco, passing the Monte-Carlo Beach Hotel. The trail then meanders along the Mediterranean shoreline. Aleppo pines and fig trees part to reveal the tiniest turquoise coves. Be sure to pack your swimming suit. See p. 220.

o **Staking out a private stretch of sand on the Iles de Lérins:** The Iles des Lérins may lie just a 20-minute ferry ride from Cannes, yet these two car-free islands attract just a fraction of the visitors. Take a picnic lunch and a good book, and get ready to leave the crowds back on the coast. See p. 151.

o **Rambling the Sentier des Ocres de Roussillon:** Located in the heart of the Luberon, Roussillon once possessed some of the world's most important ochre quarries. Today this landscape is just as brilliantly hued, and can be explored via a picturesque hiking trail. See p. 96.

best **FOR FAMILIES**

o **Getting Medieval in the Hilltop Town of Les Baux:** The age-old hilltown of **Les Baux** commands views over hundreds of miles of Provençal countryside. The film-set location, including the hilltop ruins of its "ghost village," plus a volley of great restaurants, have made it a retreat for France's rich and famous. Kids will love its car-free medieval streets and awesome views, not to mention the daily display of a siege engine catapult. See chapter 5.

o **Making the Most of Modern Art in Antibes:** The **Musée Picasso** (Picasso Museum) in Antibes highlights some of the most accessible art in France. The Spanish painter set up shop in the atmospheric old quarter of Antibes's Chateau Grimaldi some 70 years ago. In such relaxed surroundings, children can appreciate the color, vibrancy, and playfulness that made Picasso one of the greats of the 20th century. The far-out sculptures and sunny views of the surrounding coastline will please non-art fans, too. See p. 165.

o **Joining the Cowboys in the Camargue:** Riding a sturdy Camarguais horse and with a local cowboy to guide you, make your way through the marshes of these beautiful, remote wetlands. Spot pink flamingos and watch the *gardians* with their large felt hats rounding up black bulls bred for the bullrings of the south. If the children don't ride, then slow boats, bicycles, and Jeeps make great alternatives. See chapter 5.

o **Exploring the Calanques:** The **Parc National des Calanques** became France's newest national park in 2012. This stunning series of limestone cliffs and tumbling fjords stretch along the coast for some 30km (18 miles) southeast of Marseille. Serious hikers can trek the Calanques' rocky promontories. Families with children can take in the coastline from aboard one of the many tour boats that depart from Marseille's port. See p. 124.

o **Savoring a Screening under the Stars:** An alfresco cinema perched on the edge of the Mediterranean Sea? Only in Monaco. This unforgettable outdoor movie amphitheater is tucked under the cliffs that trim the Principality's Old Town. And as of 2014, the summer season has been extended, so visitors can take in blockbuster original language films from June through September. See p. 220.

THE best BEACHES

o **Plage de Pampelonne,** St-Tropez: Any blonde feels like Brigitte Bardot in sunny St-Tropez. And the scantily clad satyrs and nymphs splashing in the summertime surf at Plage de Pampelonne can perk up the most sluggish libido. The real miracle here is that the charm of this 5km (3-mile) crescent of white sand still manages to impress, despite its celebrity hype and hordes of A-list visitors. See p. 132.

o **Hi-Beach,** Nice: A day along the Riviera seaside may be a little different from home: Most beaches here feature private clubs with mattresses, parasols, and chilled Champagne on demand. Nice's Hi-Beach certainly offers all of the above. Yet its contemporary design, organic restaurant, and stellar cocktails set it apart from the crowd. See p. 191.

o **Paloma Plage,** Cap Ferrat: Tucked into one of Cap Ferrat's sheltered bays, petite Paloma Plage is part chic beach club and part family-friendly stretch of pebbly shoreline. In the afternoon, fragrant Aleppo pines shade much of the beach. Brad and Angelina have been known to stop by for drinks. See p. 212.

o **The beaches of Juan-les-Pins:** In the resort that invented waterskiing, it's little surprise that all the summertime action centers around Juan-les-Pins' golden shores. Spread your towel on central **Plage de Juan-les-Pins.** Or follow the locals to the unnamed sandy suntrap of beach pinched between the Hôtel Belles-Rives and Port Gallice. See p. 161.

o **Calanque d'En Vau:** Nestled into the heart of Parc National des Calanques, Calanque d'En Vau wouldn't look out of place in the tropics: Imagine an ice-white pairing of pebbly sands and transparent turquoise waters. Sitting at the base of a limestone cliffs, it's accessible only on foot (for experienced hikers) or by kayak or boat. See p. 124.

o **Plage des Marinières,** Villefranche-sur-Mer: A seemingly endless sweep of honey-hued sand, this popular beach sits at the base of a giant sun-kissed bay. It's perfect for families, as the sea shelves slowly and waves are seldom seen. See p. 204.

o **Plage de la Garoupe,** Cap d'Antibes: The sun rises at dawn over the Cap d'Antibes' most mythical beach. Views pan out over Antibes to the Alps beyond; beach bars served chilled rosé behind. And a coastal footpath around the secluded peninsula starts to your right. What more could you possibly want? See p. 161.

o **The 12 beaches of Le Lavandou:** Snaking along the coastline west of St-Tropez, Le Lavandou's dozen beaches range from family friendly (Grand Plage) to utterly exclusive (Plage du Cap Nègre—summer getaway for France's former First Lady, Carla Bruni). All boast fine golden sands and Blue Flag quality waters. See p. 135.

THE best FREE THINGS TO DO

o **Photographing Provence's rolling fields of lavender:** Sure, we've all seen those shots of iridescent Provençal hills cloaked with purple lavender. But it's another thing entirely to get out and snap these stunning—and fragrant—fields in person. Lavender's peak blooming season is usually between mid-June and mid-July; the area concentrated around Plateau de Valensole is particularly vibrant.

o **Touring Marseille's brand-new waterfront:** Following a prominent year as European Capital of Culture 2013, much of Marseille boasts an all-new appearance. Head down to the city's J4 Esplanade for unbeatable views over the Vieux Port, 12th-century Fort Saint-Jean, and Rudy Ricciotti's ultra-contemporary MuCEM. See p. 118.

o **Hiking the Caps:** The Riviera's *sentier du littoral* is an almost continuous coastal footpath that winds its way along the country's seductive southern shores. Leave the coastal hubbub behind and spend a day wandering between the wealthy private mansions and the sparkling sea on Cap Ferrat or Cap d'Antibes. See chapter 11.

o **Soaking up history and culture in Nice** (Riviera): Nice boasts more museums than any city outside of Paris. Better yet, almost all of them are free. Revel in the 17th-century opulence of Palais Lascaris (see p. 188), peek into the creative mind of an artistic genius at the Musée Matisse (see p. 189), or learn about Nice's time-honored multiculturalism at the Musée Masséna (see p. 188).

o **Visiting a wine estate:** Most of Provence and the French Riviera's prestigious vineyards welcome visitors for free tours and tastings. Just keep an eye out for signs as you drive past. Superb AOC wines are scattered throughout the region, including Côtes du Rhône (around Avignon), Côtes de Provence (through much of the South of France), Côtes du Luberon (north of Aix), and Nice's tiny AOC Bellet, west of the city center. See p. 47.

PROVENCE & THE RIVIERA IN CONTEXT

S ay 'the South of France' and a dozen images spring to mind: glitz, glamour, history, sunshine, celebrity. One could recall Cézanne in Aix, Picasso in Antibes, or Matisse in Nice. Modern day movers and shakers are also synonymous with this fabled stretch of shore: Carla Bruni near Canadel, Brad and Angelina near St Tropez, and Scarlett Johansson on the red carpet in Cannes. What's truly astonishing is that such heady culture is packed into a region just 242km (150 miles) across.

And what an easy region it is to explore. Local taxes may be high, but it affords the South of France one of the finest public transport and road networks in the world. High-speed TGV trains zip between its main cities of Avignon, Marseille, and Nice, and then connect the region to Paris, London, and beyond. Buses, boats, and new electric share-cars run to even the tiniest town. Drivers may follow in the tire tracks of Cary Grant (in *To Catch a Thief*), Robert De Niro (in *Ronin*), or Sebastien Vettel (around the Monaco Grand Prix circuit). Passengers of any persuasion may stop off and gaze at paradise anywhere they wish.

This guide is meant to help you decide where to go in Provence and the French Riviera. But ultimately the most gratifying experience will be your own serendipitous discoveries—sunflowers in the Luberon, a picnic on a Mediterranean island, an hour spent chatting with a small winemaker—whatever it is that stays in your memory for years to come.

THE SOUTH OF FRANCE TODAY

France is the most visited nation in the world by some margin. The country's sun-kissed southern regions of Provence (which includes the historic towns of Avignon, Aix-en-Provence, and Marseille) and the French Riviera (which runs from the glamorous enclave of St Tropez, through Cannes, Antibes, and Nice, to the Principality of Monaco) are the country's crown jewels. The South of France can inspire a work of genius—and has on countless occasions. Visit the brand new MuCEM in Marseille for a delicious taste of contemporary local culture; it pairs an architecturally astounding museum with a Michelin-star chef's restaurant.

Indeed, art attracts millions of visitors here each year. More importantly, France's socialist mores dictate that its masterpieces are accessible to rich and poor alike. Nice boasts more museums than any other French city outside Paris; and almost all of them are free. In St Tropez, you can view paintings by Paul Signac and Raoul Dufy inside the Musée de l'Annonciade, before stepping outside the museum into the port to see where those very canvases were made. But let's not forget what attracted these artists south in the first place: wine, beaches, color, and a sunny *joie de vivre*. Those same lures pull in visitors today.

As for style, it has always been foolhardy to try to compete with the French on their terms. On the Croisette seafront promenade in Cannes or along the beaches of the Cap-d'Antibes, locals seem effortlessly cool, tanned, and at ease. If you can't beat them, join them. Don a pair of shades and order a glass of rosé: after all, locals like Brigitte Bardot found fame alongside the region's glorious coastline. France's southern shores became Hollywood royalty in their own right in 2014 with the release of two hit movies: Woody Allen's *Magic in the Moonlight*, and *Grace of Monaco* starring Nicole Kidman. All the more reason to combine a cultural, food, or wine tour with a few days on the beach.

Newcomers have commented (often adversely) on the cultural arrogance and linguistic rigidity of Paris. Well, you can leave those worries behind in the South of France. The region has soaked up more immigrants and political exiles than almost anywhere else in the world, from Jewish émigrés escaping persecution to American writers fleeing Prohibition.

Moreover, the French Riviera in particular has been the globe's most cosmopolitan go-to destination for over a century. Additionally, the region was liberated from Nazi rule by American troops. The South of France has long welcomed the world to its palaces, parks, beaches, and UNESCO World Heritage sites. And if those millions of guests spend a few euros—and soak up a little local culture while they're here—that's all the better.

THE HISTORY OF PROVENCE & THE FRENCH RIVIERA

EARLY PROVENCE   French civilization started in the South of France. Human traces from 27,000 years ago—including cave paintings of horses and bison—are to be found in the Calanques cliffs near the resort of Cassis. The caves around Menton, the Vallée des Merveilles, and the Gorges du Verdon all boast traces of prehistoric habitation. And perhaps that's no surprise. The region's temperate climate, verdant valleys, and fish-stocked seas shelter manifold forms of life today.

Some 2,500-years-ago, while Northern France was still living in mud huts, their cousins in the south were enjoying the high life. Residents in the Greek colony of Marseille (ancient Massalia) and Nice (named after the Greek goddess *Nike*) were sipping wine and trading with the entire ancient world. Half a millennia later came the Romans. Antibes and Aix-en-Provence were on the Roman roads that stretched from Italy to their empire in Spain. Emperor Augustus later tamed the Ligurian tribes above Monte Carlo (the Trophy of the Alps monument in the town of La Turbie crowns this glory) to bring the entire French Riviera under Roman rule.

As the Roman Empire declined, its armies retreated to the flourishing colonies that had been established along a strip of the Mediterranean coast. Among others, these included Orange, Arles, and Marseille, which today retain some of the best Roman monuments in Europe.

Provence

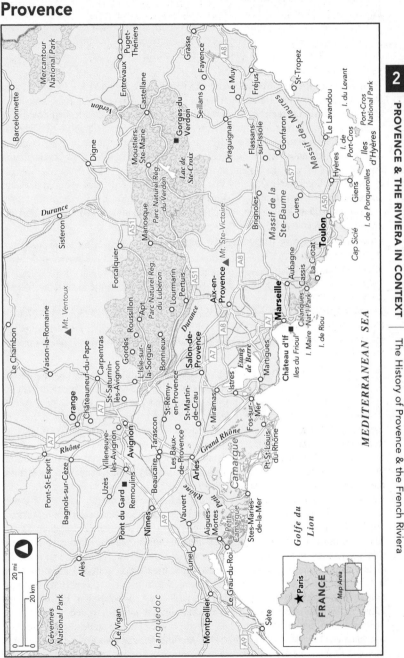

Lonely monk Saint Honoratus arrived in Cannes in AD 410 and went to meditate in peace on one of the Lérins Islands just offshore. But news of paradise travels fast. Soon the saint was joined by dozens of other co-religionists. From these humble roots, French Catholicism spread. A form of low Latin that was the common language at this time slowly evolved into the archaic French that the more refined language is based upon today.

PROVENCE IN FLAMES   As the Roman Empire foundered, a power vacuum plunged Provence back into the dark ages. Aqueducts and amphitheaters were left to ruin. Goths and Franks harassed from the north. Saracens attacked from the sea. Little wonder that so many villages in the region are built on rocky redoubts—like Eze, Les Baux, and Roquebrune—with a 360° panorama to oversee danger in every direction. Despite its eventual abuses, the church was the only real guardian of civilization during the anarchy following the Roman decline.

From the wreckage of the early first millennium emerged a new dynasty: the Carolingians. One of their leaders, Charles Martel, halted a Muslim invasion of northern Europe at Tours in 743. He left a much-expanded kingdom to his son, Pepin, who also threw the Saracen hordes out of Provence.

THE MIDDLE AGES   When the Carolingian dynasty died out, the hectic, migratory Middle Ages officially began. Normans from Sicily and Muslims from North Africa harried from the coast. Enough was enough for local count William of Arles. His united Provençal forces beat back the Saracen tide at the Battle of Tourtour near St Tropez in 973.

Relative peace lulled the South of France out of the dark ages. Temples and monasteries, like the Cathedral of Aix-en-Provence and the Abbaye de Sénanque near Gordes, heralded more settled times. The marriage of the Counts of Provence into the French royal family ushered in several centuries of prosperity.

FOREIGN INCURSION PART 1   The rising wealth of what is now the French Riviera did not go unnoticed. The trading powers of Pisa and Genoa set up shop on the coast, most notably in Villefranche-sur-Mer, which boasts two sublime castles overlooking the sea. One local Italian family also pined for a piece of the action. In 1297, the Rock of Monaco was seized by Francesco Grimaldi. Monaco has been under de facto Grimaldi rule ever since.

The 80-year relocation of the Papacy from Rome to Provence brought further wealth inland. As those who have visited Avignon's Palais des Papes will attest, those 14th century popes lived in serious style.

Alas, Provence's burgeoning wealth and power was checked by the Black Death, which began in the summer of 1348. The plague may well have arrived in Marseille via a trading ship from the east. What's certain is that it killed an estimated 33% of Europe's population, decimating the population of the South of France. A financial crisis, coupled with a series of ruinous harvests, almost bankrupted the region.

Most importantly, the newly wrecked region wasn't safe from their overlord to the north: Paris. After centuries of Franco-Provençal rule, conniving King Louis XI incorporated Provence into France 'proper,' with a forcible 'Act of Union' in 1486. Subsequent decrees that all births, deaths, and marriages must be notarized in French rang the death knell on local dialects and customs. France was here to stay.

Unfortunately, the ruling dynasty became more inept with every passing Louis. Louis XIV brought only pomp and taxes. Louis XV cared little for Provence. And Louis XVI ended up clueless (and headless) as the French Revolution cleared out the royals for good.

The French Riviera

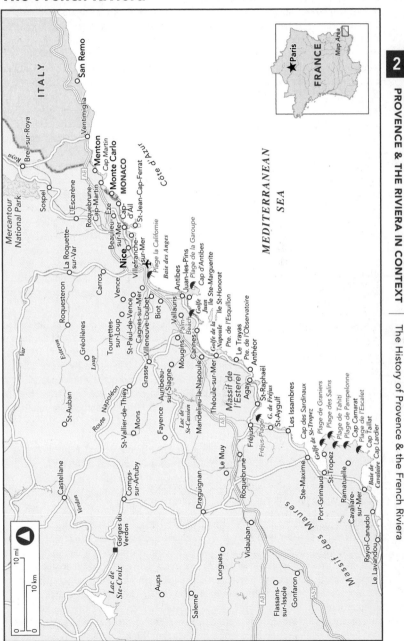

THE REVOLUTION & THE RISE OF NAPOLEON

On August 10, 1792, troops from Marseille, aided by a Parisian mob, threw the dimwitted Louis XVI and his tactless Austrian-born queen, Marie Antoinette, into prison. After months of bloodshed and bickering among violently competing factions, the two thoroughly humiliated monarchs were executed.

France's problems got worse before they got better. In the ensuing bloodbath, both moderates and radicals were guillotined in full view of a bloodthirsty crowd. Only the militaristic fervor of Corsica-born Napoleon Bonaparte could reunite France and bring an end to the revolutionary chaos. A political and military genius who appeared on the landscape at a time when the French were thoroughly sickened by the anarchy following their revolution, he restored a national pride that had been severely tarnished. In 1799, at the age of 30, he entered Paris and was crowned first consul and master of France.

But Napoleon's victories made him overconfident—and made the rest of Europe clamor for his demise. Just as he was poised to conquer the entire continent, his famous retreat from Moscow during the winter of 1812 reduced a once invincible army to tatters. As a plaque in the Lithuanian town of Vilnius once told the tale: "NAPOLEON BONAPARTE PASSED THIS WAY IN 1812 WITH 400,000 MEN"—and on the other side are the words "NAPOLEON BONAPARTE PASSED THIS WAY IN 1812 WITH 9,000 MEN".

Napoleon was exiled on the island of Elba, but not for long. He escaped with a band of followers to land on the long sandy beach at Juan-les-Pins, between Cannes and Antibes. His march to Paris through Antibes, Grasse, and Digne is commemorated in the Route Napoléon driving trail. After 100 days of terrorizing Europe, he finally met his Waterloo in 1815 at the hands of a combined British and Prussian army.

THE BOURBONS & THE SECOND EMPIRE

In 1814, following the destruction of Napoleon and his dream of Empire, the Congress of Vienna redefined the map of Europe. The Bourbon monarchy was reestablished, with reduced powers for Louis XVIII, an archconservative. After a few stable decades, Napoleon I's nephew, Napoleon III, was elected president in 1848. Appealing to the property-protecting instinct of a nation that hadn't forgotten the violent upheavals less than a century before, he initiated a repressive right-wing government in which he was awarded the totalitarian status of emperor in 1851. Steel production was started, Indochinese colonies were established, and a railway system was begun.

It was the railway that finally brought Provence under central control. A link to Marseille connected custom with ports as far away as Vietnam and Polynesia, and with it prosperity. The rail route to Nice and Monte-Carlo in the 1860s brought goods of a different kind: English gentlemen. These early tourists escaping the British winter, including Queen Victoria herself, ushered in the trade in restaurants, hotels, casinos, and beach clubs, which continues in earnest today.

FOREIGN INCURSION PART 2

Provence has always been attractive to foreigners. Some might argue too attractive, given the cosmopolitanism found in resorts like Nice and Cannes over a century ago. Direct trains delivered Russian aristocrats from Moscow. English-language newspapers shared Riviera scandals. And wealthy American *bon viveurs* brought with them their taste for beaches, hedonism, and, crucially, summer tourism. International rivalries, lost colonial ambitions, and conflicting alliances led to World War I, which, after decisive German victories for 2 years, degenerated into the mud-slogged horror of trench warfare. Mourning between four and five million casualties, Europe was inflicted with psychological scars that never healed. In 1917, the United States broke the European deadlock by entering the war.

The First World War, then the Great Depression in the late 1920s, devastated France. But Provence, insulated from the global economy by its traditional industries of wine production and farming, was spared from the worst. The French Riviera simply carried on partying. American property developers like Frank Jay Gould turned sleepy seaside towns, such as Juan-les-Pins, into rocking summer resorts. Expatriate writers, among them Ernest Hemingway and F. Scott Fitzgerald, enjoyed the dollar exchange rate and relative freedoms while they could. Artists like Matisse, Dufy, and Signac moved south to capture such heady scenes on canvas.

Crisis struck on June 14, 1940, just as an ocean liner full of American film stars were docking in Cannes for the resort's inaugural Film Festival. Hitler's armies arrogantly marched down the Champs-Elysées, and newsreel cameras recorded French people openly weeping. Under the terms of the armistice, the north of France was occupied by the Nazis, and a puppet French government was established at Vichy under the authority of Marshal Pétain. The immediate collapse of the French army is viewed as the most significant humiliation in modern French history. In Europe, Britain was left to counter the Nazi threat alone.

Pétain and his regime cooperated with the Nazis in unbearably shameful ways. Not the least of their errors included the deportation of more than 75,000 French Jews to German work camps. Pockets of resistance fighters *(le maquis)* waged small-scale guerrilla attacks against the Nazis throughout the course of the war, particularly in Provence and Corsica.

The scenario was radically altered on June 6, 1944, when the largest armada in history—a combination of American, British, and Canadian troops—successfully established a beachhead on the shores of Normandy, in northern France. An additional southern wave of Allied liberators swept up the beaches of St Tropez and Ste-Maxime on August 15. Marseille was taken on August 28, and a third of all Allied supplies eventually arrived through its port.

THE POSTWAR YEARS The South of France emerged from World War II a shadow of its former self. Its population has been decimated, and foreign guests were in no mood for a holiday on its sunny southern coast. After suffering a bitter defeat in 1954, France ended its occupation of Vietnam. It also granted self-rule to Tunisia, Algeria, and Morocco. Such changes brought in a wave of North African and Asian immigration that changed the region's ethnicity, culture, and even cuisine. In melting pots like Marseille, one may dine on Cameroonian *ndolé* while listening to Franco-Arab rap, and sipping Cambodian rice wine.

Prosperity returned to Provence by way of a new airport in Nice, high-speed train links to Paris, and heavy investment in tourism infrastructure. Glamorous cover shots of The Beatles, Grace Kelly, and The Rolling Stones enjoying the Riviera high life helped, too.

Most French believe that Jacques Chirac ran a solid presidency from 1995 to 2007. But shortly before leaving office, a rotten core was exposed. Decades of pent-up resentment felt by the children of African immigrants exploded into an orgy of violence and vandalism in 2005. Riots began in Paris and spread around the country to the suburbs of Marseille. Most of the rioters were the sons of Arab and black African immigrants, Muslims living in a mostly Catholic country. The reason for the protests? Leaders of the riots claimed they live "like second-class citizens," even though they are French citizens. Unemployment is 30% higher in the ethnic ghettos of France.

Against a backdrop of discontent regarding issues of unemployment, immigration, and healthcare, the charismatic Nicolas Sarkozy swept into the presidential office in 2007. 'Sarko' steadied the ship and reveled in his love for the French Riviera. He was regularly photographed cycling along Nice's Promenade des Anglais.

In the ensuing years, Sarkozy deepened his affection for the region by marrying glamorous model-turned-singer, Carla Bruni, who maintained a holiday home next to the Presidential retreat near Rayol-Canadel. The tabloids had a field day with Bruni, whose former lovers include Mick Jagger, Eric Clapton, and Donald Trump.

> ### Impressions
>
> *The sea is blue, but bluer than any one has ever painted it, a color entirely fantastic and incredible. It is the blue of sapphires, of the peacock's wing, of an Alpine glacier.*
>
> —Henri Matisse,
> French artist and Nice resident

Sadly for him, Sarkozy's marriage to Bruni and his holidays with the rich and famous earned him the title of the "bling bling president." In a show of how divided France was over his administration, he lost the 2012 presidential election to socialist challenger François Hollande by a whisker.

Hollande promised a government of hard-working technocrats. Alas, "Monsieur Normal" proved anything but. The nail in Hollande's claim to run a scandal free administration came in 2014 when a president's private life once again became front-page news. Not content with family ties to his first girlfriend, Ségolène Royale, or his current mistress-turned-First Lady, Valérie Trierweiler, he embarked on another relationship with actress Julie Gayet. His method of courting Miss Gayet (which essentially involved turning up to her apartment on the back of his bodyguard's scooter) was deemed tacky by the French press. He also wined and dined his new squeeze in hilltop town of Mougins . . . in the very same restaurant where he had entertained his previous lovers.

Nearly 10 years of celebrity scandal seemed to tickle tourists and locals alike. Neither presidential flings nor a global recession put off visitors to this fabled playground of France. Passenger numbers through Nice Cote d'Azur Airport rose every year through the financial crisis. Some 13 million yearly visitors now disembark and hop into a helicopter, limo, taxi, free bike, or airport bus, depending on the depth of their pockets. With new airport terminals, train links, cruise ports, and cultural attractions planned for 2020, the South of France's cosmopolitanism looks set to continue.

ART

With its stunning scenery and the particularly vibrant quality of its light, the South of France has been luring the world's most famous artists to its shores for centuries. It may have been **Claude Monet** (1840–1926) who kick-started the trend, wintering in Antibes in 1888 and portraying dozens of versions of the local landscape. But other prominent painters soon followed.

Important post-Impressionist **Paul Cézanne** (1839–1906) was born, raised, and lived most of his life in Aix-en-Provence. He adopted the short brush strokes, love of landscape, and light color palette of his Impressionist friends, eventually creating artworks that laid the foundations for Cubism.

Iconic Dutch painter **Vincent van Gogh** (1853–90) spent 2 years based in Arles, combining a touch of Japanese influence with this thick, short strokes. He worked together with **Paul Gauguin** (1848–1903) for a part of this period—their relationship culminating in a drunken argument followed by Van Gogh's dramatic ear-slicing incident—before transferring his home to nearby St-Rémy. The final year of his life was spent creating what are now world-famous paintings, (although unrecognized during his lifetime) such as *Starry Night* (1889), at the Monastère Saint-Paul de Mausole.

Pierre-Auguste Renoir (1841–1919) moved south to Cagnes-sur-Mer in 1903, living out the remainder of his life in this coastal town. His paintings and sculptures, created at his home and studio Les Collettes (now the Musée Renoir, see p. 177), demonstrate the inspiration he took both from the Riviera's landscapes as well as the female form.

Henri Matisse (1869–1954) is best known for his leading role in the early 20th-century **fauvist** movement (a critic described those artists who used the style as *fauves*, meaning "wild beasts"). But from his first visit to Nice in 1917, until his death almost four decades later, Matisse worked diligently to reflect the local light, landscapes, and people in his artworks. Vence's Chapelle du Rosiare is considered his masterpiece.

Málaga-born **Pablo Picasso** (1881–1973) painted objects from all points of view at once, rather than using such optical tricks as perspective to fool viewers into seeing "cubist" three dimensions. Perhaps the world's most famous artist as well as a brilliant and bold character, Picasso partied and painted all along the southern French coast, his final four decades spent bouncing among residences in Antibes, Juan-les-Pins, Vallauris, and Mougins. Scores of the artist's works were created here, many of them now on show at Antibes' Musée Picasso (see p. 165).

Dreamy Russian painter **Marc Chagall** (1887–1985) fell under the South of France's spell from his first visit in 1925—and it endured through his final years based in St-Paul-de-Vence. The shimmering sunshine and lush Mediterranean landscapes seemed only to enhance his renowned whimsical style, as displayed in his paintings at the Musée National Marc Chagall (see p. 189) in Nice.

Scores of other artists found Provence and the French Riviera equally inspiring, from **Paul Signac** (1863-1935) in St-Tropez (a selection of his works are exhibited at the town's Musée de l'Annonciade, see p. 131) and **Raoul Dufy** (1877-1953), to **Amedeo Modigliani** (1884-1920) and **Pierre Bonnard** (1867-1947; celebrated at Cannes' Musée Bonnard, see p. 148).

And the South of France's manifold architecture? Yep, it's just as prolific and varied. Regional highlights encompass Roman ruins, such as Orange's **Théâtre Antique** (see p. 50) and Gothic cathedrals—the most prominent being at Avignon's **Palais des Papes** (see p. 44)—as well as Belle Époque palaces like Nice's **Hôtel Negresco** (see p. 182), and a variety of cutting-edge contemporary buildings, including Marseille's new **MuCEM** (see p. 117).

> ### Impressions
>
> *The sun is so terrific here that is seems to me as if the objects were silhouetted not only in black and white, but in blue, red, brown, and violet.*
>
> —Paul Cézanne, French artist and Aix-en-Provence native

THE SOUTH OF FRANCE IN POPULAR CULTURE

Books

For a taste of Southern French culture before you travel, we recommend you load a half-dozen titles on your iPad or Kindle. You'll be spoiled for choice. More has been written about this fabulous region that almost anywhere else in the world.

No book better captures the coastline's glamorous history that *Inventing the French Riviera*, by Mary Bloom. Lucid backgrounds to the seaside's most famous cities include *High Season in Nice*, by Robert Kanigel, and *The Rise and Rise of the Côte d'Azur*, by Jim Ring. The feather boas and masked balls of yesteryear are also conjured up in *Queen Victoria and the Discovery of the Riviera*, by Michael Nelson. For a beguiling literary history of coast, look no further than *The French Riviera: A Literary Guide for Travellers*, edited by Ted Jones. In a similar genre *The Riviera Set: From Queen Victoria to Princess Grace*, by Lita-Rose Betcherman (Kindle only) charts coastal fashions and passions by way of F. Scott Fitzgerald and Brigitte Bardot. *Chasing Matisse*, by James Morgan, follows the in the footsteps Riviera's greatest painter from St Tropez to Corsica to Nice.

Provence's more earthy culture requires a different reading list. The pleasures, and pitfalls, of living in the bucolic countryside are catalogued with charm and candor in *The Olive Farm*, by Carol Drinkwater, and *A Year in Provence*, by Peter Mayle. The latter author also penned the wickedly illuminating *Provence A-Z: A Francophile's Essentials Handbook*. *Pig in Provence*, by Georgeanne Brennan, offers culinary adventures in the Provençal heartland. The region's cuisine is best indulged by *At Home in Provence*, by Patricia Wells, an American chef who also runs a cooking school in the area.

A wealth of novels elucidates the South of France myth. On the French Riviera, *Tender is the Night*, by F. Scott Fitzgerald, describes his only crazy, drunken sojourn in Juan-les-Pins, with interludes at the Hotel du Cap and Hotel Belles-Rives. *Garden of Eden*, a novel unfinished by Ernest Hemingway at the time of his passing, is set in the same time, same place. *Super-Cannes*, by J.G. Ballard, describes a similar hedonistic scene eight decades on.

The olive groves, lavender fields, and rolling hills of Provence are deftly described in *The Man Who Planted Trees*, by Jean Giono, a childrens' book with an adult theme. *Jean de Florette*, by Marcel Pagnol, describes the same magnificent countryside, as does *The Count of Monte Cristo*, by Alexandre Dumas, albeit with a brief incarceration on Marseille's Chateau d'If, a former prison island now on many visitors' itineraries. Marseille's rough and ready underworld is highlighted in *Total Chaos*, by Jean-Clause Izzo, along with several other locally set novels. Cavaillon detective Inspector Daniel Jacquot, a fictional creation by Martin O'Brien, solves crimes in the countryside in *The Dying Minutes*, and other books.

Films

The world's first filmmakers were Provence-born brothers Auguste and Louis Lumière. One of their first works, "The Arrival of a Train at La Ciotat Station" in 1895, made an entire movie theater jump from their seats lest they by run down by the locomotive on the screen. Later, Charles Pathé and Léon Gaumont, both of whom had deep roots in the region, were the first to exploit filmmaking on a grand scale.

By the mid-1950s, French filmmaking ushered in the era of enormous budgets and the creation of such frothy potboilers as director Roger Vadim's "And God Created Woman," which helped make Brigitte Bardot a celebrity around the world, contributing greatly to the image in America of France as a kingdom of sexual liberation. Alfred Hitchcock's "To Catch a Thief" in 1955 placed Cary Grant in the driving seat in a Riviera romp from Cannes to Monaco. In a similar vein, Frank Oz's "Dirty Rotten Scoundrels" shows the humorously undignified underbelly of the French Riviera. John Frankenheimer's "Ronin" starring Robert De Niro and Jean Reno, is far more serious, as they battle criminals through Nice, Eze, and Arles.

As French's second city, Marseille has formed the backdrop for several hit movies. Gérard Pirès's "Taxi" in 1998 is a blazing road movie written by Luc Besson. The 2002 locally-filmed action flick "The Transporter," starring musclebound Englishman Jason Statham was also penned by Besson.

Provence was custom-made to be captured on celluloid. From Marcel Pagnol's "La Femme du Boulanger" to Claude Berri's "Manon des Sources," it's one long bucolic playground. Foreign-funded movies sum up the region in similar grand style. Lawrence Kasdan's "French Kiss" pairs uptight American Meg Ryan with devious Frenchie Kevin Kline. The Lubéron's natural charms are showcased in Ridley Scott's "A Good Year," starring Russell Crowe and Marion Cotillard.

The big French movie of 2014 was a Woody Allen number, "Magic in the Moonlight." This romantic comedy stars Colin Firth and Emma Stone against the sun-kissed backdrop of the French Riviera. Also in 2014, "Grace of Monaco" starring Nicole Kidman, shone a light on the marriage of American actress Grace Kelly into Monaco's Grimaldi family.

Music

Music has long been synonymous with the South of France. Troubadours with their ballads traveled all over Provence in the Middle Ages. **Claude-Joseph Rouget de Lisle** (1760–1836) immortalized the region in 1792 when he wrote La Marseillaise, the French national anthem, which was sung by troops marching north from Marseille.

Rising regional wealth in the mid-1800s, coupled with the arrival tens of thousands of idyll tourists from abroad, brought grand performances to France's southern coast. Opera houses in Marseille, Nice, and Monaco are a legacy of this rococo period. All offer a fine way to while away an evening today.

Alas, music heard along the coast today—be it rap, reggae, contemporary, or classical—owes its heart to the conservatoires and colleges of Paris. That said, Nice-local **Yves Klein** (1928–62) shook up the capital's stuffy music scene in 1960. His "The Monotone Symphony" using three naked models, became a notorious performance. For 20 minutes, he conducted an orchestra on one note.

Artists with immigrant backgrounds are often the major names in the modern Southern French music scene, with influences from French Africa, the French Caribbean, and the Middle East. Along with rap and hip-hop, these sounds rule the nights in the boîtes of the region's biggest cities. **Khaled** (b. 1960), from Algeria, has become known as the "King of Raï." The most influential French rapper today is **MC Solaar** (b. 1969); born in Senegal, he explores racism and ethnic identity in his wordplays.

Music festivals celebrating sounds from across the globe remain ever popular in the South of France. Given the heady climate and liberal local populace, this is perhaps to be expected. The most famous festivals are Nice's weeklong jazz extravaganza (see

p. 20) and Avignon's 3-week summer festival (see p. 20), both in July. More offbeat shows include October's Fiesta des Suds urban rock jam in Marseille (see p. 21) and the region-wide Fête de la Musique street party on June 21.

EATING & DRINKING IN PROVENCE

As any French person will attest, French food is the best in the world. That's as true today as it was during the 19th-century heyday of the master chef Escoffier. A demanding patriarch who codified the rules of French cooking, he ruled the kitchens of the Ritz in Paris, standardizing the complicated preparation and presentation of *haute cuisine.*

Such cuisine is found on the top tables of the South of France. After all, the region has a century-old legacy of high-end tourism, and it boasts more Michelin stars than almost any other geographical area on the globe. Experimental fine dining ranges from the 500€ dinners in Monaco's Louis XV (see p. 217) to local cuisine specialists in the Provence countryside like La Cabro d'Or (see p. 60), where lunches can cost one-twentieth of that price.

However good classic dining gets, it is the earthly pull of Provençal flavors that attracts foodie pilgrims from across the planet. The South of France was originally colonized by Greeks and Romans, and has accepted several recent waves of Italian immigration. Thus a liberal splash of olive oil, wild herbs, and fresh vegetables goes into every dish.

Furthermore, Provence was once a poor cousin of Paris. Locals couldn't afford the butter, foie gras, and fillet steak of their northern brethren. Instead, local ingredients like pigeon, pigs' cheeks, and beef skirt accompany eggplant, zucchini, and lashings of tomatoes in many a dish. Not only that, the southern coast has had an enviable supply of fresh fish since time began. Local red mullet, sea bass, bream, and grouper meld with mussels, oysters, and sea urchins on most coastal menus.

Regional must-eats are a delight. Bouillabaisse, an exquisite fish soup claimed to have been invented by Venus, is Marseille's best-known dish. Between Avignon and Aix-en-Provence expect lamb from the Sisteron hills, truffles from the Lubéron, and trout plucked fresh from the river. *Sanglier* (wild boar) makes it onto the menu in more mountainous areas as well as in Corsica. French Riviera specialties include *daube* (slow-cooked beef stew), *soupe au pistou* (vegetable soup with basil), and *salade Niçoise* (traditionally made with tomatoes, olives, radishes, scallions, peppers, and tuna or anchovies). All are best served with a glass of ice-cold *rosé* in the afternoon sun.

Finally, the region has scores of ways for food lovers to get closer to the cuisine they adore. A swath of new cooking courses and market tours (see individual chapters for details) covers the entire South of France. But nothing beats breakfast or lunch purchased from a daily market. These colorful additions to every town run year-round and are stocked high with olives, cheeses, pâtés, *saucisson* air-dried sausages, free-range roast chickens, baguettes, tapenades, and much, much more. *Bon appétit.*

To accompany such cuisine, let your own good taste—and your wallet—determine your choice of wine. In the best restaurants, wine stewards, called *sommeliers,* are there to help you in your choice, and only in the most dishonest of restaurants will they push you toward the most expensive selections. Of course, if you prefer only bottled water, or perhaps a beer, then be firm and order your choice without embarrassment.

Some restaurants include a beverage in their menu rates *(boisson compris),* either as part of a set tasting menu in ritzy restaurants or as part of a fixed-price formula in cheaper places. Some of the most satisfying wines we've drank in France came from unlabeled house bottles or carafes, called a *vin de la maison.* In general, unless you're a real connoisseur, don't worry about labels and vintages. When in doubt, you can rarely go wrong with a good Côtes du Rhône, Coteaux d'Aix-en-Provence, or Côtes du Provence, the region's largest AOC *appellations.*

WHEN TO GO

Anytime is a good time to visit Southern France. Summer (July–Aug) is one long salvo of festivals, fairs, and fireworks. In spring (April–June) and fall (Sept–Nov) the weather is still gorgeous, and the coastline is warm enough for both swimming and sunbathing. As the Riviera is averages 300 days of sun per year, winter (Dec–March) can also be splendid. Furthermore, with hardly a tourist in sight, you'll be welcomed as an honorary local. Prices of hotels and restaurant menus fall out of season, sometimes dramatically.

Inland it's a slightly different story. Many museums, stores, and hotels shut up shop entirely from November until Easter. Provence in particular dreads *le mistral* (an unrelenting wind), which most often blows in the winter for bouts of a few days at a time, but can also last up to 2 weeks. That said, cities like Avignon and Aix-en-Provence are at their most hauntingly beautiful during that chilly period. Cool weather also slathers snow across the ski resorts north of Nice.

France Calendar of Events

JANUARY

Monte Carlo Motor Rally (Le Rallye de Monte Carlo). The world's most venerable car race. Mid-January. www.acm.mc.

FEBRUARY

Carnival of Nice. Parades, music, fireworks, and "Les Batailles des Fleurs" (Battles of the Flowers) are all part of this celebration. The climax is the burning the Carnival king effigy. Late February to early March. www.nicecarnaval.com.

Fête du Citron, Menton. Two-week celebration of the local lemon industry in France's sunniest town. Expect mega lemon sculptures and song. www.feteducitron.com.

Fête du Mimosas. Mandelieu-La Napoule. Seven-day party dedicated the region's yellow mimosa flowers, with parades, street

parties, and beauty pageants. www.ot-mandelieu.com.

MARCH

Napoleon's arrival, Golfe-Juan. Reimagining of Bonaparte's beachy arrival in the South of France on March 1, 1815. Celebration especially important for the 2015 bicentennial anniversary of his march to Paris. www.vallauris-golfe-juan.fr.

Le Paris-Nice, French Riviera. The nation's second most important cycle race is a precursor to the Tour de France. Route runs through Provence countryside and finishes on Nice's promenade des Anglais. Mid-March. www.letour.com.

MAY

Saintes-Maries-de-la-Mer Gypsy Festival, Camargue. Annual gypsy festival where tens of thousands of faithful walk into the waves in praise of the Black Sarah. Mid-May. www.saintesmaries.com.

Cannes Film Festival (Festival International du Film). Movie madness transforms this Mediterranean town into a media circus. Admission to films and parties is by invitation. Other films play 24 hours a day. Mid-May. www.festival-cannes.com.

Monte-Carlo Rolex Masters, Monaco. Rafael Nadal and Novak Djokovic play this clay court tournament as the Mediterranean shimmers beyond. Mid-May. www.atpworldtour.com.

Monaco Formula 1 Grand Prix. The world's most high-tech cars race through Monaco's narrow streets in a blizzard of hot metal and ritzy architecture. Late May. www.formula1.com.

Lubéron Jazz Festival. Saxophones, double bases, and guitars take over every municipal space in the village of Apt. Late May. www.luberonjazz.net.

JUNE

Fête de la Mer et des Pêcheurs, Martigues. Local fishing fleets perform boat-to-boat jousting contests. The consumption of unholy amounts of seafood is de rigueur. Late June. www.martigues-tourisme.com.

Fête de la Musique, across region. Nationwide festival of sound on the longest evening of the year. Expect drummers and DJs on every street corner. June 21.

Nice Ironman Triathlon, Nice. An incredible sight as thousands of swimmers dive into the Mediterranean. Followed by a full marathon. And an Alpine bike ride. Late June. www.ironman.com.

JULY

Les Chorégies d'Orange, Orange. One of southern France's most important lyric festivals presents oratorios, operas, and choral works in France's best-preserved Roman amphitheater. Early July to early August. www.choregies.fr.

Festival de Lacoste. One of Provence's prettiest villages becomes an open-air theatre for ballet and classical recital. Mid-July. www.festivaldelacoste.com.

Tour de France. The world's most hotly contested bicycle race sends crews of wind-tunnel-tested athletes along an itinerary that detours deep into the Alps, Provence, and French Riviera. First 3 weeks of July. www.letour.fr.

Festival d'Avignon. This world-class festival has a reputation for exposing new talent to critical scrutiny and acclaim. The focus is usually on avant-garde works in theater, dance, and music. Many of the performances take place in the 14th-century courtyard of the Palais des Pâpes. Last 3 weeks of July. www.festival-avignon.com.

Avignon OFF. Month-long fringe event packed with street theatre, comedy, and music. www.avignonleoff.com.

Bastille Day. Celebrating the birth of modern-day France, the nation's festivities reach their peak with country-wide street fairs, fireworks, and feasts. July 14.

Les Suds Arles. Seven-day cultural and world music show within the Roman amphitheaters and city walls of ancient Arles. Mid-July. www.suds-arles.com.

Nice Jazz Festival. The most prestigious jazz festival in Europe. Concerts begin in the afternoon and go on until late at night (sometimes all night) in the Jardin Albert 1er, overlooking Nice's promenade des Anglais. Mid-July. www.nicejazzfestival.fr.

Festival d'Aix-en-Provence. A musical event *par excellence*, with everything from Gregorian chants to operas composed on synthesizers. Recitals are in the medieval cloister of the Cathédrale St-Sauveur. Expect heat, crowds, and loud sounds. July. www.festival-aix.com.

Réncontres d'Arles. The prettiest town in Provence hosts a citywide photography festival. Prepare to be wowed. July to September. www.rencontres-arles.com.

Marseille Ironman Triathlon, Marseille. Ironman returned to Marseille in 2014. See thousands of swimmers line up on the Plages du Prado, before they cycle 40km then run a final 10km. Late July. www.ironman.com.

Jazz à Juan, Juan-les-Pins. Key international jazz, reggae, and blues festival. Take a place

Visitors can purchase tickets for almost every music festival, soccer game, or cultural event in France online. Try the official website first, or log onto **FNAC** (www.fnactickets.com), France's largest music chain, which offers both a digital reservation service as well as in-store ticket booths.

on an alfresco stage with the sea and setting sun behind. Late July. www.jazzajuan.fr.

AUGUST

Monte-Carlo International Fireworks Competition, Monaco. You've never seen pyrotechnics like it. The skies above Monaco are lit up twice weekly as international teams compete for the biggest bang in the business. August. www.visitmonaco.com

Festival de Musique, Menton. Outdoor seats are set up in every square and churchyard for this most genteel of classical music festivals. First 2 weeks of August. www.festival-musique-menton.fr.

Azurial Opera Festival, Cap-Ferrat. Impossibly cute 4-day opera festival in the rarified confines of the Villa Ephrussi de Rothschild on Cap-Ferrat. Late August. www.azurial opera.com.

SEPTEMBER

Les Etoiles de Mougins, Mougins. The French Riviera's premier live cooking show. Medieval Mougins is taken over by 50 top chefs for an entire weekend. Features cook-offs, interactive displays, and Michelin star standard freebies. Mid-September. www.lesetoilesdemougins.com

Journées du Patrimoine, regional. The region's grandest buildings open their doors to the public for one weekend only. Just don't pocket any souvenirs as you peek around. Mid-September. www.journeesdu patrimoine.culture.fr.

OCTOBER

Les Voiles de St-Tropez. The largest and most glamorous of the French Riviera's classic sailing regattas. Watch tens of millions of Euros worth of sail compete in the confines of the Bay of St-Tropez. Early October. www. lesvoilesdesaint-tropez.fr.

Fiesta des Suds, Marseille. No-holds-barred urban festival of African, world, and Mediterranean music in Marseille's rejuvenated docklands. Late October. www.dock-des-suds.org.

NOVEMBER

Nice-Cannes Marathon. What could be the world's prettiest marathon route runs from Nice's promenade des Anglais through the Cap d'Antibes and Juan-les-Pins. But taking part is no walk in the park. Early November. www.marathon06.com.

DECEMBER

Fête de St-Sylvestre (New Year's Eve), nationwide. In Nice, this holiday is most boisterously celebrated on the promenade des Anglais. Champagne corks fly in every other Southern French town. December 31.

RESPONSIBLE TRAVEL

From pioneering eco-friendly *autopartage* (car-sharing) programs to an unabashed enthusiasm for *biodynamique* wines, the South of France has embraced sustainability. In an age when environmental, ethical, and social concerns are becoming ever more important, France's focus on green principles—whether through traditional markets, carbon-neutral public transport, or all-natural outdoor adventure—offers visitors and residents alike plenty in the way of sustainable tourism.

Public bicycle "sharing" programs are big business in France. Nice (www.velobleu. org), Avignon (www.velopop.fr), and Marseille (www.levelo-mpm.fr) have thousands of bicycles and bike rental stations spread throughout the each town center. All offer a fast and inexpensive way to get around.

Nice introduced electronic "car sharing" scheme **Auto Bleue** (www.auto-bleue.org) in 2012. Nearly 200 eco-friendly cars with a range of 100km now ply the streets; passes for their use can be purchased by the hour, day, month, or year. More importantly, the scheme's 50 recharging points serve as charging depots for an increasing number of resident-owned electric cars.

In order to crisscross France's vast countryside, many French ditch their cars and opt instead for travel on a **TGV** (www.tgv-europe.com). This network of high-speed trains is powered by SNCF, France's government-owned rail company, which is dedicated to becoming completely carbon-neutral. TGVs run from Paris's hub to cities throughout the country, including Avignon, Aix-en-Provence, Cannes, Monaco, Nice, and Marseille.

Many hotels in France have undertaken measures to preserve the environment, and those that have are awarded with a green label. Look for hotels with the title of *La Clef Verte* (Green Key; www.laclefverte.org). The label rewards hotels that take a more environmental approach to water, energy and waste, and help raise the awareness of their guests. Even if you don't stay at a green hotel, you can still do your bit: Turn off the air-conditioning when you leave the room, request that your sheets aren't changed every day, and use your towels more than once. Laundry makes up around 40% of an average hotel's energy use.

When planning your travels, it's equally important to consider the impact your visit will have on the environment. The South of France's rippling vineyards, **Grande Randonée (GR)** hiking trails, and pristine coastline all make for enchanting (and eco-friendly) escapes.

Responsible tourism also means leaving a place in the same condition you found it. You can do this by not dropping litter and respecting the color-coded garbage recycling system. Support the local economy and culture by shopping in small neighborhood stores and at open-air markets that showcase the seasonal harvest of local, often organic *(bio)* producers. Look out for organic and *biodynamique* (biodynamic) wines, frequently sold at wine shops and farmers' markets too. And given the myriad of tiny, family-run restaurants scattered throughout France's cities, towns, and countryside, it's all too easy to dig into a home-cooked meal.

> ### Impressions
>
> *In France you cannot not have lunch. If you stopped the French from having lunch, you will have a second revolution, I can tell you.*
> —Christian Louboutin, shoe designer

SUGGESTED ITINERARIES IN PROVENCE & THE FRENCH RIVIERA

When the Frommer's guidebooks were first launched, founder Arthur Frommer cautioned his readers, "You can get lost in France." It's still an apt warning—and promise—today.

For those with unlimited time, one of the world's great pleasures is getting "lost" in France, wandering at random, making new discoveries off the beaten path. Few of us have this luxury, however, and so here we present 1- and 2-week itineraries to help you make the most of your time.

Provence and the French Riviera in particular are so treasure-filled that you may barely do more than skim the surface in a week. So relax and savor Avignon, Aix-en-Provence, St-Tropez, or Cannes—among other alluring destinations—saving the rest for another day. You might also review chapter 1, "The Best of Provence and the French Riviera," to find out what experiences or sights have special appeal to us and then adjust your itineraries to suit your particular travel plans.

The itineraries that follow take you to some major attractions and some charming off-the-beaten-track towns. The pace may be a bit breathless for some visitors, so feel free to skip a town or sight occasionally if you'd like to give yourself some chill-out time. You're on vacation, after all. Of course, you may also use these itineraries merely as a jumping-off point to develop your own custom-made trip.

PROVENCE & THE FRENCH RIVIERA IN BRIEF

Although France's 547,030 sq. km (211,209 sq. miles) make it slightly smaller than the American state of Texas, no other country has such a diversity of sights and scenery in such a compact area. Even the relatively small regions of Provence and the French Riviera—less than 300km (187 miles) from east to west—range from the Rhône's fertile Camargue wetlands, across the Lubéron's rippling vineyards, and on to the south's shimmering Mediterranean coast. Perhaps even more noteworthy are the historical and contemporary cultural differences that define each territorial area.

Destinations in Provence and the French Riviera are within easy reach of each other. **French National Railroads (SNCF)** offers fast and comprehensive service to Avignon, Aix, Marseille, Cannes, Nice, and pretty much every town in between. Speedy **Trains à Grande Vitesse (TGV)** connect most of the region's bigger cities, while slower **Transport Express Régional (TER)** chug along quieter tracks, often stopping at every heartbreakingly picturesque town en route.

You can motor along thousands of miles of Southern French roads, including a good number of well-maintained superhighways. But do your best to drive the secondary roads too: Nearly all of the region's scenic splendors are along these routes.

Despite Provence and the French Riviera's petite size, it still holds true that if you truly want to get to know this part of France, you'll probably have a more rewarding trip if you concentrate on exploring two or three areas at a leisurely pace rather than racing around trying to see everything! To help you decide where to spend your time, we've summarized the highlights of each region for you.

PROVENCE   One of France's most popular destinations stretches from the southern Rhone River to the Italian border. Long frequented by starving artists, *la bourgeoisie,* and the downright rich and famous, its premier cities are **Aix-en-Provence,** associated with Cézanne; **Arles,** famous for bullfighting and Van Gogh; **Avignon,** the 14th-century capital of Christendom; and **Marseille,** a port city established by the Phoenicians that today is the melting pot of France. Quieter and more romantic are villages such as **St-Rémy-de-Provence, Les Baux,** and **Gordes**. To the east, the Haute Provence region is home to Europe's "Grand Canyon," the Gorges du Verdon. To the west, the **Camargue** is the marshy delta formed by two arms of the Rhône River. Rich in bird life, it's famous for its grassy flats and such fortified medieval sites as **Aigues-Mortes.** For more information, see chapters 4 to 8.

THE FRENCH RIVIERA (CÔTE D'AZUR)   The resorts of the fabled Côte d'Azur (Azure Coast) still evoke glamour: **Cannes, St-Tropez, Cap d'Antibes,** and **Juan-les-Pins.** July and August are the most buzzing months, while spring and fall are still sunny but way more laid-back. **Nice** is the biggest city and most convenient base for exploring the area. The Principality of **Monaco** only occupies about 2 sq. km (¾ sq. mile) but has enough sights, restaurants, and opulence to go around. Along the coast are some sandy beaches, but many are pebbly. Topless bathing is common, especially in St-Tropez, and some of the restaurants are citadels of conspicuous consumption. Dozens of artists and their patrons have dappled the landscape with world-class galleries and art museums. For more information, see chapters 9 to 13.

FRANCE ITINERARIES
1 WEEK IN PROVENCE & THE FRENCH RIVIERA

If you budget your days carefully, 1 week provides enough time to visit the landmark towns and attractions in Provence and the French Riviera, including history-rich **Avignon,** and several resorts on the Riviera, taking in beaches, art galleries, and even the Principality of **Monaco.**

Day 1: Avignon, Gateway to Provence ★★★

Make the most of your week in the South of France by taking a flight that arrives in Paris as early as possible on Day 1. Transfer via Métro or a taxi to the Gare de Lyon, where you can board a TGV bound for Avignon (2½ hr.).

Check into your hotel in **Avignon,** one of Europe's most beautiful medieval cities. Before the day fades, you should have time to wander through the old city to get your bearings, shop for Provençal souvenirs, and see one of the smaller sights, such as the **Pont St-Bénézet** (p. 42) or the **Musée Louis Vouland** (p. 43).

Day 2: Avignon to Marseille ★★

In the morning, spend 2 hours touring the **Palais des Papes** (p. 44), the capital of Christendom during the 14th century. After lunch in one of Avignon's cozy bistros or cobblestoned outdoor cafes, hop onto one a train southwards to **Marseille** (1½ hr.). Still shimmering in the glow of its prestigious title as European Capital of Culture 2013, Marseille is awash with exceptional new cultural venues. Visit the contemporary architectural wonder that is **MuCEM** (p. 117), dive into ancient history at **Musée d'Histoire de Marseille** (p. 117), or simply stroll the perfectly picturesque **Vieux Port** (p. 110).

Day 3: Arty Aix-en-Provence ★★

Board an early train for **Aix-en-Provence** (45 min.). After checking into your hotel, shop one of the city's manifold morning **markets** (p. 85) for seasonal snacks (fresh goat's cheese, fragrant peaches, crusty baguettes) on the go. Aix is iconic artist Paul Cézanne's hometown: spend the afternoon visiting his **Atelier** (p. 82). Or get out of town and explore **Carrières de Bibémus** (p. 82), the abandoned ochre quarries that so inspired him.

Day 4: Aix to St-Tropez ★★★

Following a lazy breakfast in your hotel—or a *café crème* and a croissant at one of the sidewalk cafés along **Cours Mirabeau** (p. 82)—rent a car and drive to **St-Tropez** (p. 127). If you're feeling adventurous, you could even take a detour northwards to stop in one of the southern **Lubéron's** bucolic villages (p. 86) for lunch along the way. Upon arrival in St-Tropez, spend a good part of the early evening in one of the cafes along the harbor, indulging in that favorite French pastime of people-watching.

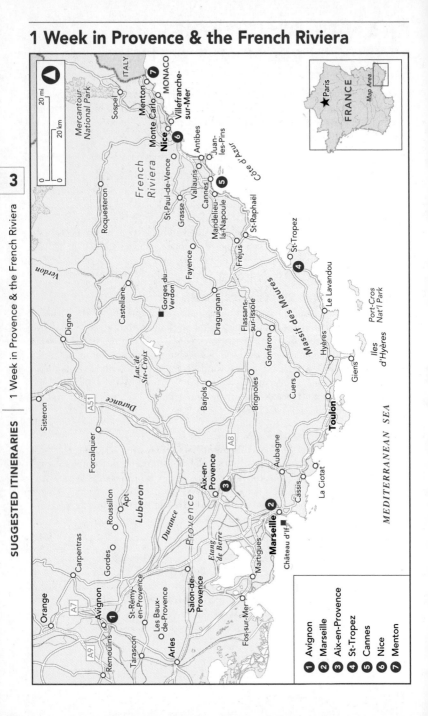

Map scale: 20 mi / 20 km

FRANCE — ★ Paris — Map Area

ITALY

Mercantour National Park

Sospel

Menton
Monte Carlo
Nice
Villefranche-sur-Mer
MONACO

7

Roquesteron

French Riviera

St-Paul-de-Vence
Grasse
Vallauris
Cannes
Mandelieu-la-Napoule
St-Raphaël
Antibes
Juan-les-Pins

Côte d'Azur

6
5

Fayence

Fréjus

St-Tropez

4

Verdon

Gorges du Verdon

Castellane

Draguignan

Flassans-sur-Issole

Massif des Maures

Le Lavandou

Port-Cros Nat'l Park

Digne

Lac de Ste-Croix

Gonfaron

Hyères

Giens

Îles d'Hyères

Bariols

Brignoles

Cuers

Toulon

A51

Durance

Sisteron

Forcalquier

Aubagne

A8

MEDITERRANEAN SEA

Roussillon
Apt
Luberon

Gordes

Aix-en-Provence

3

Cassis
La Ciotat

Provence

Durance

2

Marseille

Château d'If

Carpentras

St-Rémy-en-Provence

Salon-de-Provence

Étang de Berre

Martigues

Orange

A7

Avignon

1

Les Baux-de-Provence

Tarascon

Arles

Fos-sur-Mer

Rémoulins

A9

1 Avignon
2 Marseille
3 Aix-en-Provence
4 St-Tropez
5 Cannes
6 Nice
7 Menton

Day 5: Chic Cannes ★★★

Before leaving St-Tropez in the morning, check out the Impressionist paintings at **Musée de l'Annonciade** (p. 131). Drive 50km (31 miles) east along the coast until you reach **Cannes.**

Assuming it's summer, get in some time at the beach, notably at **Plage de la Croisette** (p. 219), and feel free to wear your most revealing swimwear. In the afternoon, take the ferry to **Ile Ste-Marguerite** (p. 161), where the "Man in the Iron Mask" was imprisoned. You can visit his cell. That evening, you may want to flirt with Lady Luck at one of the plush **casinos** (p. 151).

Day 6: Nice, Capital of the Riviera ★★★

It's only a 32km (20-mile) drive east from Cannes to **Nice,** the Riviera's largest city. After checking in to a hotel (the most affordable along the Riviera), stroll through **Vieille Ville** (p. 187), the Old Town. Enjoy a snack of *socca,* a round crepe made with chickpea flour that vendors sell steaming hot in the **cours Saleya market**. Then head for the **promenade des Anglais** (p. 186), the wide boulevard along the waterfront. In the afternoon, head for the famed hill town of **St-Paul-de-Vence** (p. 169), only 20km (12 miles) to the north. You can wander its ramparts in about 30 minutes before descending to the greatest modern-art museum in the Riviera, the **Foundation Maeght** (p. 171).

Continue on to **Vence** (p. 172) for a visit to the great Henri Matisse's artistic masterpiece, **Chapelle du Rosaire** (p. 174). From there, it's just 24km (15 miles) southeast back to Nice, where you can enjoy dinner at a typical Niçois bistro.

Day 7: Nice to Menton ★★

While still overnighting in Nice, head east for the most thrilling drive in all of France, a trip along the **Grande Corniche** highway, which stretches 31km (19 miles) east from Nice to the little resort of **Menton** (p. 224) near the Italian border. Allow 3 hours for this trip. Highlights along this road include the glitzy enclave of **Monaco** (p. 223), **Roquebrune-Cap Martin** (p. 220), and **La Turbie** (p. 209). The greatest view along the Riviera is at the **Eze Belvedere,** at 1,200m (3,936 ft.).

PROVENCE & THE FRENCH RIVIERA FOR FAMILIES

Provence and the French Riviera offer plenty of attractions for kids. Our suggestion is to begin your trip by exploring the coastline between **Nice** and **Monaco** (3 days). Then spend 2 days wandering the glittering quaysides and windswept beaches of **St-Tropez** and its peninsula, with a final 2 days spent rambling through the untamed landscape of the **Lubéron.**

Day 1: Nice ★★★

Kick off your family's French adventure in **Nice**. Here you can check into your hotel for 2 nights, as the city has the most affordable accommodation on the coast. The set out to explore this old city. There's always a lot of free entertainment in summer along Nice's seafront boardwalk, the **promenade des Anglais** (p. 186), and the people-watching on the Riviera—particularly on the beach—is likely to leave your kids wide-eyed.

In the afternoon, spend an hour or two at Nice's new **Promenade du Paillon** (p. 187) public park, where younger kids can go wild on the animal-themed playgrounds, splash around in the expanse of dancing fountains, or just run around and have fun. Parents can take turns ducking off to visit nearby attractions like the **MAMAC ★★★**, **Palais Lascaris ★**, or the **Théâtre de la Photographie et de l'Image ★**. From here, scale one of the four steep sets of stairs up to the panoramic **Colline du Château ★★**. This hilltop park is the perfect place to get a bird's-eye view over Nice's Old Town, as well as to watch the Technicolor sunset over the sea.

Day 2: St-Paul-de-Vence ★★

Today make the inland journey to the evocative hill town of **St-Paul-de-Vence** (p. 169). Children will enjoy touring the ramparts and scampering along the pedestrian-only rue Grande. After a hearty lunch at **Les Terrasses** (p. 170), it's time to explore the sculpture garden at the **Foundation Maeght** (p. 171), one of France's greatest modern-art museums. Alternatively, hop over to the nearby town of Vence. Here Matisse's **Chapelle du Rosaire** (p. 184) is bright, colorful, and—for the kids—delightfully small.

Day 3: Monaco ★★★

While still based in Nice, head for the tiny principality of **Monaco**, which lies only 18km (11 miles) east of Nice.

Children will enjoy the changing-of-the-guard ceremony at **Les Grands Appartements du Palais** (p. 218), where Prince Albert married South African swimmer Charlene Wittstock in 2011. But the best part of Monaco for kids is the **Musée Océanographique de Monaco** (p. 218), home to sharks and other exotic sea creatures.

Return to Nice for the evening and take your kids for a stroll through the Old Town, dining as the sun dips over the Mediterranean.

Days 4 & 5: St-Tropez ★★★

Hire a car and drive 110km (69 miles) southwest to the oh-so-chic village of **St-Tropez**. Although the coastal road takes a little longer than traveling via the A8, this route offers a myriad of opportunities for picnics and swims (particularly in the protected **Esterel** parkland, p. 141) along the way.

Once you've arrived, teens should make a beeline for St-Tropez's **Vieux Port** (p. 137): In summertime, there is plenty of celebrity spotting to be had from the sidewalk cafés here. If you're travelling with tots, drive over to the south side of the St-Tropez Peninsula and spend the afternoon splashing around on family-friendly **Plage Gigaro** (p. 130).

The following morning, make a day trip to the **Domaine du Rayol Canadel** (p. 135), just west of here. These botanical gardens are a delight to explore, tumbling their way down to the Mediterranean Sea. For water babies, the park even offers guided **snorkeling tours** (p. 135).

Provence & The French Riviera for Families

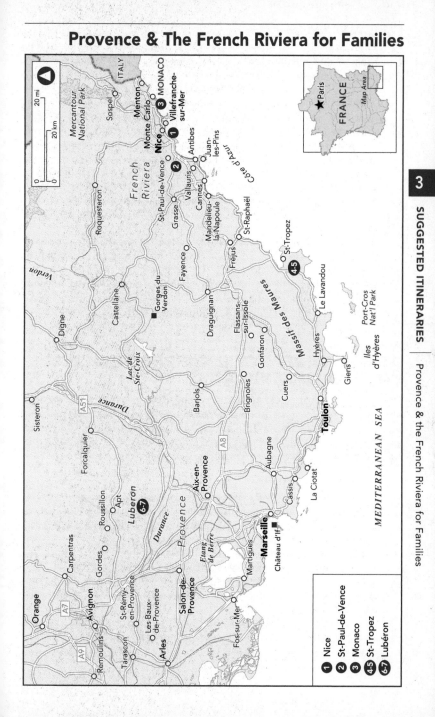

① Nice
② St-Paul-de-Vence
③ Monaco
④-⑤ St-Tropez
⑥-⑦ Lubéron

Days 6 & 7: The Lubéron ★★★

Spend the final couple of days of your trip playing around in the **Parc Naturel Régional du Lubéron** (p. 86). Wherever you may choose to base yourself—Gordes, Roussillon, Bonnieux, Lourmarin, or beyond—this verdant region is undoubtedly one of France's most beautiful.

Dedicate your first day to hiking the **Sentier des Ocres de Roussillon** (Ochre Footpath, p. 96). This easy walk winds its way through the neon orange landscape of the region's ancient ochre quarries. (Tip: Don't wear white!) If you're travelling with little ones who may not be up for the trek, visit the area by *calèche* (p. 96), or horse-drawn carriage, instead.

Between June and August, the Lubéron is cloaked in lavender fields as far as the eye can see. To learn all about the flower and its harvest, visit the **Musée de la Lavande** (p. 91) on your second day here. Or simply head up to **Sault** (p. 91), where the Tourist Office can direct you on an all-purple walking trail through the countryside.

And if your visit doesn't coincide with the lavender season, there's no need to fret: The local countryside is enchanting year round. We suggest you **rent bicycles** (p. 92) and get out and explore it. The Lubéron's "Le Calavon" road—28km (18 miles) of smooth, car-free cycling paths—is particularly well suited to families.

On your final morning, you can drop your hire car at Aix TGV station, and make your way homewards via train from here.

ART LOVERS' TOUR OF PROVENCE & THE FRENCH RIVIERA

From post-Impressionist art in Aix to 20th-century masters along the coast, the South of France is infused with art. Aficionados can experience an unforgettable trip taking in **Aix-en-Provence** (1 day), **St-Tropez** (1 day), and then the Riviera between **Antibes** and **Menton** (5 days). Museum visits can be interspersed with wonderful meals, sunbathing, and stops at the area's architectural and artistic highlights.

Day 1: Aix-en-Provence ★★

Start your art tour in Aix, the hometown of world-renowned artist Paul Cézanne. If you're arriving from Paris, jump aboard one of the many TGV trains that head south each day. The journey takes around 3 hours.

Begin your day at Cézanne's **Atelier** (p. 82), almost perfectly preserved, as it was when the great artist worked here more than a century ago. There are regularly scheduled English-language tours of the site. Afterward, a visit to the city's famed **Musée Granet** (p. 83)—one of the region's most superb modern-art museums—is a must.

Aix's plane-tree-shaded **cours Mirabeau** is almost a work of art in itself. Be sure to drop into **Brasserie Les Deux Garçons** (p. 82) for an aperitif: Cézanne used to drink and debate here with the famous French writer Émile Zola.

Art Lovers' Tour of Provence & the French Riviera

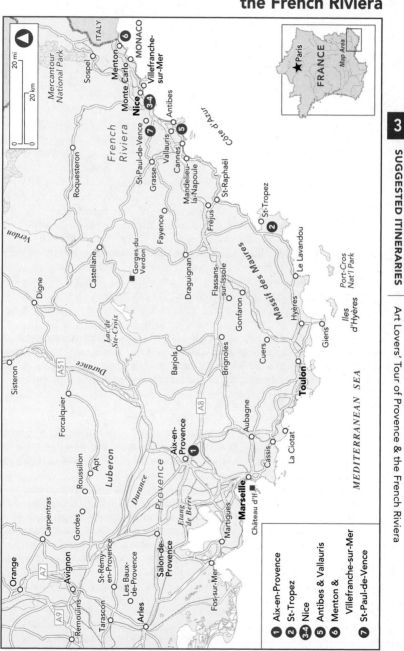

ITALY

MONACO

Menton

Monte Carlo

Villefranche-sur-Mer

Nice

Antibes

Mercantour National Park

Sospel

Roquesteron

French Riviera

St-Paul-de-Vence

Grasse

Vallauris

Cannes

Mandelieu-la-Napoule

St-Raphaël

Côte d'Azur

Fréjus

St-Tropez

Le Lavandou

Digne

Castellane

Gorges du Verdon

Fayence

Draguignan

Flassans-sur-Issole

Massif des Maures

Hyères

Port-Cros Nat'l Park

Îles d'Hyères

Giens

Verdon

Lac de Ste-Croix

Sisteron

Forcalquier

Durance

A51

Barjols

Brignoles

Gonfaron

Cuers

Aubagne

Toulon

La Ciotat

A8

Aix-en-Provence

Cassis

MEDITERRANEAN SEA

Luberon

Apt

Roussillon

Gordes

Provence

Durance

Salon-de-Provence

Martigues

Étang de Berre

Marseille

Château d'If

Carpentras

Avignon

St-Rémy-en-Provence

Les Baux-de-Provence

Orange

A7

Tarascon

Arles

Remoulins

A9

Fos-sur-Mer

FRANCE

Paris

Map Area

20 mi

20 km

1. Aix-en-Provence
2. St-Tropez
3-4. Nice
5. Antibes & Vallauris
6. Menton & Villefranche-sur-Mer
7. St-Paul-de-Vence

Day 2: St-Tropez ★★★

Rent a car bright and early, and drive to **St-Tropez** (p. 127). Since the 1890s, when painters Signac and Bonnard "discovered" this seaside town, artists and their patrons have been drawn to the French Riviera.

After lunch in one of the town's sidewalk cafés, spend the afternoon appreciating the **Musée de l'Annonciade**'s (p. 131) Impressionist paintings, many of them depicting St-Tropez and the surrounding coast. Warm evenings are best enjoyed strolling the port's pretty quays or taking in the million-dollar panoramas from the hilltop **Citadelle** (p. 131).

Day 3 & 4: Nice ★★★

The following morning, drive around 100km (62 miles) east along the coast until you reach Nice. Note that over the remainder of this itinerary, we recommend you base yourself here and make day trips to the myriad of surrounding towns that are famed for their art. (Alternatively, you may choose to stay at various villages—such as Antibes or St-Paul-de-Vence—to get a different feel for the area.) Regardless of your choice, return your rental car. Traffic-heavy roads, combined with excellent public transportation, render your own vehicle unnecessary here.

Spend the afternoon and evening getting acclimatized to Nice, strolling the promenade des Anglais, or wandering the city's atmospheric Old Town.

Outside of Paris, Nice is home to more museums than any other city in France. Begin your Day 4 citywide explorations in the neighborhood of Cimiez, where both the famed **Musée Matisse** (p. 189) and the **Musée National Message Biblique Marc Chagall** (p. 189) are located. It's possible to walk between the two (around 15 min.), but be sure to hit the Matisse Museum first—then it's downhill all the way to see Chagall's ethereal artworks.

If it's summertime, spend a couple of hours picnicking on the beach or relaxing with a glass of wine in one of the city's many sidewalk cafés. Midafternoon, make your way over the **Musée Masséna** (p. 188), where a combination of local art and history gives visitors a peek at the ritzy French Riviera of the past.

Day 5: Antibes & Vallauris ★★

Today you'll spend following in the footsteps of one of the 20th-century's modern masters: Pablo Picasso. Take one of the frequent trains from Nice to Antibes (20 min.). On the edge of the picturesque, pedestrian-friendly Old Town sits the 14th-century Grimaldi Château, now home to the **Musée Picasso** (p. 165). The Spanish artist lived and worked in this castle in 1946.

Stroll through Antibes' covered market, then—appetite piqued—stop into a small bistro, such as **Entre 2 Vins** (p. 163), for a light lunch. Next, make your way to Antibes' bus station, where frequent buses depart for Vallauris (35 min.). Picasso moved to this hilltop village during the 1950s, reviving the local ceramic-making industry and personally producing thousands of pieces of pottery. Visit Picasso's mammoth paintings in the **Musée National Picasso La Guerre et La Paix** (p. 152), the artist's tribute to pacifism.

To make your way back to Nice, it's quickest to simply reverse your route.

Day 6: Menton & Villefranche-sur-Mer ★★

Hop aboard one of the many trains heading eastwards this morning: Today you're going to be exploring artist, author, playwright, and poet Jean Cocteau's favorite seaside boltholes. Begin in **Menton** (30 min. by train from Nice). The eastern-most town on the French Riviera, Menton is home to the magnificent **Musée Jean Cocteau** (p. 226), designed by architect Rudy Ricciotti. After an hour admiring the museum's wealth of ceramics, paintings, and prints, wander the atmospheric alleyways of Menton's Old Town, perhaps stopping at **La Cirke** (p. 224) for lunch.

Early afternoon, and the sunlight is glinting off the Mediterranean waves as you head westwards to Villefranche-sur-Mer (25 min. by train from Menton). Set in a deep and sheltered bay, this medieval village is one of the coastline's most picturesque. Perched on one of the town's quays, the petite **Chapelle St-Pierre** (p. 204) was painted inside and out by Cocteau himself as homage to the town's local fishermen.

Frequent trains ply the 5-minute journey back to Nice.

Day 7: St-Paul-de-Vence ★★

Use your final day to make a day trip to the hilltop village of **St-Paul-de-Vence** (p. 169), 20km (12 miles) to the north. Wander the St-Paul-de-Vence's ramparts for half an hour, before descending to the world-class modern art on display at the **Foundation Maeght** (p. 171). En route back to Nice, stop into the **Musée Renoir** in Cagnes-sur-Mer. The artist's former home and gardens were com-pletely renovated in 2013. Note that you can either rent a car for the day or access both St-Paul-de-Vence and Cagnes-sur-Mer via frequent buses from Nice.

Spend your final night in Nice savoring a hearty Niçois dinner, paired with plenty of local wine.

FOOD & WINE LOVERS' TOUR OF PROVENCE & THE FRENCH RIVIERA

In a country that is world-renowned for its delectable food and wine, cuisine in this region counts itself among France's finest. A week's itinerary across this abundant countryside takes in local dishes that range from the hearty lamb stews of Provence to Italian-influenced recipes along the coast—with plenty of unique AOC wines to imbibe along the way.

Day 1: Avignon ★★★

The capital of the Côtes du Rhône appellation, **Avignon** is the perfect spot to begin your acquaintance with the region's fine fare. Spend your first afternoon sipping a selection of the world's most sought-after vintages on a **guided wine tour** (p. 47) through nearby Châteauneuf-du-Pape.

This evening, we recommend bedding down at the sumptuous **La Mirande** (p. 40), a gorgeous period hotel tucked just behind the Palais du Papes. It's here that Chef Jean-Claude Altmayer cooks up a four-course gourmet meal (paired with regional wines) on his ancient wood-fired oven. The action takes place in front of a dozen lucky diners at the hotel's **Table d'Hôte** (p. 49), held twice a week, so be sure to plan accordingly.

Food & Wine Lovers' Tour of Provence & the French Riviera

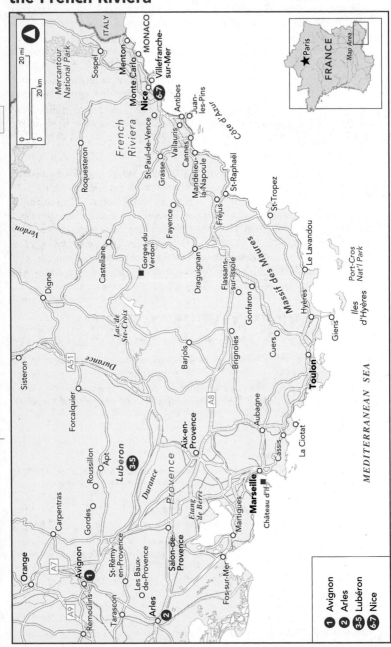

20 mi

20 km

ITALY

Mercantour National Park

Sospel

MONACO

Menton

Monte Carlo

Villefranche-sur-Mer

Nice

6-7

Antibes

Juan-les-Pins

French Riviera

Roquesteron

St-Paul-de-Vence

Vallauris

Cannes

Grasse

Mandelieu-la-Napoule

St-Raphaël

Côte d'Azur

St-Tropez

Fayence

Fréjus

Digne

Castellane

Gorges du Verdon

Draguignan

Flassans-sur-Issole

Le Lavandou

Port-Cros Nat'l Park

Massif des Maures

Verdon

Lac de Ste-Croix

Gonfaron

Hyères

Giens

Îles d'Hyères

Sisteron

Barjols

Brignoles

Cuers

Toulon

A51

Durance

Forcalquier

MEDITERRANEAN SEA

Apt

Roussillon

Luberon

3-5

Aix-en-Provence

Aubagne

A8

Carpentras

Gordes

Durance

Provence

Cassis

La Ciotat

Orange

A7

Avignon

1

St-Rémy-en-Provence

Les Baux-de-Provence

Salon-de-Provence

Étang de Berre

Martigues

Marseille

Château d'If

Remoulins

Tarascon

Arles

2

Fos-sur-Mer

A9

FRANCE

★ Paris

Map Area

1 Avignon
2 Arles
3-5 Luberon
6-7 Nice

Day 2: Arles ★★

Arles is the gateway to the **Camargue** (p. 69), an untamed land of French cowboys (as surprising as that may seem to North Americans) and indigenous wild horses.

After an afternoon of sightseeing around Arles' abundant Roman ruins, stop for an early evening aperitif at al fresco wine bar **L'Ouvre-Boîte** (p. 68). No more then a cluster of tables in a tiny, sun-dappled square, this venue's wines are regional and primarily organic.

Then—in stark contrast to the traditional meal you enjoyed last night—local super chef Jean-Luc Rabanel (**L'Atelier Jean-Luc Rabanel,** p. 64) will wow you by transforming organic ingredients from his own garden, as well as regional specialties (such as tender bull, or Camargue red rice), into a succession of ultra-contemporary dishes.

Days 3–5: Lubéron ★★★

The **Lubéron** is the heartland of true Provençal cuisine. Get to grips with the local bounty—from Carpentras strawberries and grassy green olive oil to Cavaillon melon and freshly harvested herbs—at one of the region's **daily farmers' markets** (p. 85). For a taste of how these ingredients can be transformed into traditional recipes, lunch at **Café des Poulivets** (p. 88), an authentic *bistrot de pays.*

The following day, head to **Château La Coste** (p. 83). Many of the Lubéron's best sights have an epicurean twist: Not only does the Château possess a superb Art and Architecture Walk trimmed with sculptures by modern masters, such as Alexander Calder and Tadao Andao, it's also an impressive working vineyard offering guided visits to its Jean Nouvel-designed wine cellars.

To learn more about the region's winemaking history, round out the afternoon with a visit to one of the Lubéron's wine museums, such as Ménerbes' **La Maison de la Truffe et du Vin du Lubéron** (p. 89), dedicated to wine and truffles, or Ansouis' **Musée des Arts et des Métiers du Vin** (p. 89).

On your final day in the Lubéron, we recommend relaxing and simply savoring your surroundings. Check into one of the Lubéron's more pampering places to stay, and preferably one with its own reputable restaurant. We recommend **La Coquillade** (p. 88), which is both a luxurious eco-hotel and a prestigious vineyard. Taste your way through their cellars, amble through the vines, and then dine at gastronomic Le Gourmet restaurant come evening.

Days 6 & 7: Nice ★★★

Base yourself in **Nice** for the final 2 days of your epicurean extravaganza. Spend your first day exploring the city's daily **cours Saleya market** (p. 193). Many Riviera residents opt to stock their pantries here, but if you're keen to go locals-only, head north of Nice's train station to the daily **Libération market** (p. 193) instead. Regional producers in both markets pile their fruit and vegetables high, offering plenty of seasonal samples to leisurely shoppers.

You've likely snacked your way through lunch, so simply pick a pretty sidewalk café and enjoy an afternoon glass of wine. Bellet—arguably France's smallest AOC—is the tipple of choice here, due to its location just north of Nice's airport. Round out the day with dinner at foodie favorite **La Merenda** (p. 185), where Chef Dominique Le Stanc's dishes possess more than a hint of Italian influence from just over the nearby border. But take note: The restaurant accepts neither credit cards nor reservations, so be sure to arrive early.

There's no better way to finish off your trip than by learning how to recreate these fine Provençal flavors yourself. For visitors on a budget, try **A Taste of Nice** (p. 190), which offers a 3½ hour food tour around the city. Alternatively, we recommend longtime local Rosa Jackson's cooking school, **Les Petits Farcis** (p. 190). Cordon Bleu-trained, Rosa leads market tours followed by gourmet cooking lessons and a four-course lunch in her 17th-century apartment in Nice's Old Town.

AVIGNON

AVIGNON ★★★

691km (428 miles) S of Paris; 83km (51 miles) NW of Aix-en-Provence; 98km (61 miles) NW of Marseille

In the 14th century, Avignon was the capital of Christendom. What started as a temporary stay by Pope Clement V in 1309, when Rome was deemed too dangerous even for clergymen, became a 67-year golden age. The cultural and architectural legacy left by the six popes who served during this period makes Avignon one of Europe's most alluring medieval destinations.

Today this walled city of some 95,000 residents is a major stop on the route from Paris to the Mediterranean. In recent years, it has become known as a cultural center, thanks to its annual international performing-arts festivals and wealth of experimental theaters and art galleries.

Essentials

ARRIVING Frequent TGV **trains** depart from Paris's Gare de Lyon. The ride takes 2 hours and 40 minutes and arrives at Avignon's modern TGV station, located 6 minutes from town by a brand-new speedy rail link. The one-way fare is around 80€ depending on the date and time, although it can also be as cheap as 25€ if booked well in advance. Regular trains arrive from Marseille (trip time: 70 min.; 20.80€ one-way) and Arles (trip time: 20 min.; 7.50€ one-way), arriving at either the TGV or Avignon's central station. Hourly trains from Aix-en-Provence (trip time: 20 min.; 25€ one-way) shuttle exclusively between the two towns' TGV stations. For rail information, visit www.voyages-sncf.com or call ✆ **36-35.** The regional **bus** routes (www.info-ler.fr; ✆ **08-21-20-22-03**) go from Avignon to Arles (trip time: 1 hr., 10 min.; 7.10€ one-way) and Aix-en Provence (trip time: 1 hr., 15 min.; 17.40€ one-way). The bus station at Avignon is the **Gare Routière,** 5 av. Monclar (✆ **04-90-82-07-35**). If you're **driving** from Paris, take A6 south to Lyon, and then A7 south to Avignon.

VISITOR INFORMATION The **Office de Tourisme** is at 41 cours Jean-Jaurès (www.avignon-tourisme.com; ✆ **04-32-74-32-74**).

CITY LAYOUT Avignon's picturesque Old Town is surrounded by 14th-century ramparts. Within the walls is a mix of winding roads, medieval townhouses, and pedestrianized streets. To the west of the city is the Rhône River, and beyond, Villeneuve les Avignon. Just south of the Old Town sits the Gare d'Avignon Centre train station.

SPECIAL EVENTS The international **Festival d'Avignon** (www.festival-avignon.com; ✆ **04-90-14-14-14**), held for 3 weeks in July, focuses on avant-garde theater, dance, and music. Tickets are 17€ to 40€. Prices for rooms skyrocket during this period, so book yours well in advance. An edgier alternative festival, the **Avignon OFF** (www.avignonleoff.com;

Avignon

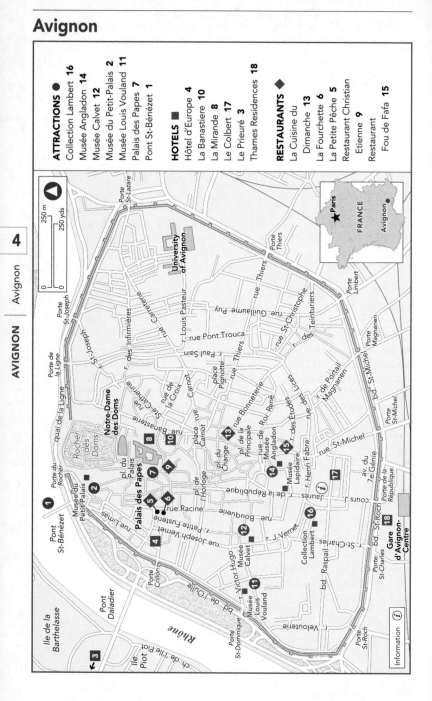

ATTRACTIONS ●

Collection Lambert **16**
Musée Angladon **14**
Musée Calvet **12**
Musée du Petit-Palais **2**
Musée Louis Vouland **11**
Palais des Papes **7**
Pont St-Bénézet **1**

HOTELS ■

Hôtel d'Europe **4**
La Banastiere **10**
La Mirande **8**
Le Colbert **17**
Le Prieuré **3**
Thames Residences **18**

RESTAURANTS ◆

La Cuisine du
Dimanche **13**
La Fourchette **6**
La Petite Pêche **5**
Restaurant Christian
Etienne **9**
Restaurant
Fou de Fafa **15**

$\mathcal{C}$ **04-90-85-13-08**), takes place almost simultaneously in July, with theater performances in various improbable venues.

International rose enthusiasts descend upon Avignon in late May for **Altera Rosa** (www.alterarosa.com), sponsored by the Société Française des Roses. Expert gardeners from all over Europe deck the Palais des Papes' Benoît XII Cloister with thousands of rose bushes, including both traditional and new breeds. Admission is 7€, 5€ for children 7 and under.

Between mid August and late September, the Palais des Papes' cour d'Honneur is illuminated by **Les Luminessences d'Avignon** (www.lesluminessences-avignon. com), a total-immersion 3-D light and sound show. Shows are held every night from mid August to mid October. Admission is 10€, 8€ for students, seniors over 60, and children from 8 to 17 years old, and free for children 7 and under.

For additional special events in the city, Avignon's **Office de Tourisme** launched the inspirational website **Ce Weekend On Aime . . .** (www.ceweekendonaime.com), or "This Weekend We Love . . ." in 2014. Around four different seasonal events going on in Avignon or the surrounding region are proposed every weekend, with a lead-time of around 4 months. It's currently in French only, although there are plans to make it bilingual soon.

Getting Around

ON FOOT   All of Avignon's major sights—as well as its infinitely enchanting back streets—are easily accessible on foot. The helpful tourist office's free maps are marked with four easy walking routes, ideal for getting a feel for the city.

BY BICYCLE & MOTOR SCOOTER   The **Vélopop** bicycle-sharing scheme (www. velopop.fr, from 1€ per day) lets registered riders borrow any of the city's 200 bikes for up to 30 minutes at a time for free. To get out of town and explore the surrounding countryside, **Provence Bike,** 7 av. St-Ruf (www.provence-bike.com; $\mathcal{C}$ **04-90-27-92-61**), rents different models for around 12€ to 40€ per day. It's possible to reserve a bike online.

BY CAR   Traffic and a labyrinthine one-way system means it's best to park once you've arrived in Avignon's town center. Seven fee-paying parking lots and two free ones are dotted around the city. See the Avignon tourist office website for details.

BY TAXI   Taxis Avignon (www.taxis-avignon.fr; $\mathcal{C}$ **04-90-82-20-20**).

BY PUBLIC TRANSPORT   Eco-friendly **Baladine** vehicles (www.tcra.fr; Mon–Sat 10am–12:30pm and 2–6pm; during July and Aug daily 10am–8pm) zip around within the city walls for 0.50€ per ride. Avignon is also currently undergoing extensive roadwork for the construction of a citywide tram system. It's due to begin service around town in 2016.

[FastFACTS] AVIGNON

ATMs/Banks   Avignon's town center is home to banks aplenty, including three along cours Jean-Jaurès.

Doctors & Hospitals Hôpital Général Henri Duffaut, 305 rue Raoul Follereau (www.ch-avignon.fr; $\mathcal{C}$ **04-32-75-33-33**).

Internet Access   The Avignon municipality is in the process of installing free Wi-Fi in public areas around town. It's currently available in **square Perdiguier**, just behind the Tourist Office. However, to get online, you'll need to register a French cell phone number in order to receive an access code by text message. Don't have one to hand? Head a block eastwards to **Milk Shop**, 26 place des Corps Saints (www.milkshop.fr; ☏ **09-82-54-16-82**), a little café that offers its patrons free Wi-Fi.

Where to Stay

La Banasterie ★   This oh-so-pretty B&B is situated in a 16th-century property just opposite the Palais des Papes. It's owned by gregarious chocolate lovers Françoise and Jean-Michel—and their candy-fueled passion permeates throughout. The traditionally decorated bedrooms (exposed stone walls, sumptuous fabrics) are named for varieties of chocolate, and decadent cups of cocoa are offered at bedtime. The indulgent breakfast alone (included in the rate) makes this spot unmissable. Note that there is no elevator.

11 rue de la Banasterie. www.labanasterie.com. ☏ **06-87-72-96-36.** 5 units. 90€–145€ double; 145€–190€ suite. Parking 10€. **Amenities:** Free Wi-Fi.

Le Colbert ★   This cheerful little hotel is Avignon's best budget option. It's well located just north of the town's train station, yet inside the city walls. The hotel manages to be both quiet—due to its position on a side street—and with easy walking distance of Avignon's action. Comfortable guestrooms are painted in warm tones and decorated in traditional Provençal textiles. During sunny weather, breakfast (8€–12€) is served at colorful tables on the patio, under palm and olive trees. Note that the hotel does not have an elevator.

7 rue Agricol Perdiguier. www.avignon-hotel-colbert.com. ☏ **04-90-86-20-20.** 14 units. 78€–140€ double. Parking 20€ in nearby garage. Closed Nov–March. **Amenities:** Free Wi-Fi.

La Mirande ★★★   La Mirande was once a 14th-century cardinal's palace adjoining the Palais des Papes. It now boasts an additional seven centuries of fixtures and features in one gloriously palatial package. The hotel's owners are not from the hotel industry, and it shows. Guestrooms are no-expense-spared collections of locally sourced antique furniture, Carrara marble, authentic Chinoiserie, and Murano chandeliers. The courtyard chairs, for example, used to belong in the Musée d'Orsay in Paris. Six new family-sized suites were added in 2013. La Mirande's gourmet restaurant and Le Marmiton (see p. 49), a classic French cooking school, are headed by chef Jean-Claude Altmayer. Both take an environmentally friendly approach to their creations, using seasonal and organic ingredients sourced from local producers. All-organic afternoon tea—featuring homemade madeleines, thick hot chocolate and Kombucha—is served daily on the patio or terrace.

4 place de l'Amirande. www.la-mirande.fr. ☏ **04-90-14-20-20.** 27 units. 370€–690€ double; 810€–1,715 € suite. Parking 25€. **Amenities:** Restaurant; bar; concierge; room service; free Wi-Fi.

Le Prieuré ★   Those who perceive Provence as breakfast under an arbor, a set of tennis on a leaf-strewn court, a lazy lunch, then a doze by the pool—all topped off by chilled rosé at sunset—have found the right place. What could be calmer than staying in a former 14th-century convent ringed by lavender-scented gardens in the historic suburb of Villeneuve? Individually styled rooms and suites are casually arranged over three ancient buildings. Original floors, hardwood furniture, and locally purchased antiques blend with marble bathrooms, fine linens, and modernist Louis XIV chairs. Lunch (set menu 40€ –50€) and dinner (set menus 78€–140€) in the herb-filled gardens are prepared by young head chef Fabien Fage from Arles. Luxurious locally sourced cuisine includes strawberries from Beaucaire, pigeon from Nimes, and rock-fish from the Mediterranean near Marseille.

7 place du Chapitre. www.leprieure.com. ☎ **04-90-15-90-15.** 38 units. 200€–540€ double; 350€–900 suite. Free parking. Closed Nov–March. **Amenities:** Restaurant; bar; concierge; outdoor pool; room service; tennis; free Wi-Fi.

ALTERNATIVE ACCOMMODATIONS

Thames Résidences ★★ This handful of suites and superbly equipped apart-ments lies a short stroll from both the train station and Avignon's city center. Decor is Provençal-themed, and each one boasts either its own private balcony or panoramic views over the town's medieval ramparts. As well as free satellite television, speedy Wi-Fi, and unlimited free telephone calls abroad, some of the residences also possess kitchenettes and sleek Nespresso Pixie espresso machines. Note that apartments may also be rented (at a discount) by the week.

36 bd. Saint Roch. www.thames-residences.com. ☎ **04-32-70-17-01.** 9 units. 169€–259€ 2-person apartments. Free parking. **Amenities:** Free Wi-Fi.

Where to Eat

La Cuisine du Dimanche ★ PROVENÇAL   For freshly made, seasonal cuisine, look no further than La Cuisine du Dimanche. Chef Marie shops for most of her ingre-dients from the nearby daily market, Les Halles, which in turn are sourced from the immediate region. The menu changes according to market finds, but keep an eye out for fresh gnocchi, made with local *bintje* potatoes, or Sweet William pears steeped in maple syrup. The latter are gratinéed with Pélardon goat's cheese and topped with fresh mint. Dining takes place within the eatery's eclectic dining room—all 15th-century exposed stone walls and colorful furnishings—or on the small outdoor terrace.

31 rue de la Bonneterie. www.lacuisinedudimanche.com. ☎ **04-90-82-99-10.** Reservations recom-mended. Main courses 18€–25€; fixed-price lunch 9€–17€. June–Sept daily noon–1:30pm and 8–9:30pm; Oct–May Tues–Sat noon–1:30pm and 8–9:30pm.

La Fourchette ★★ PROVENÇAL   Set a block back from the bustling place de l'Horloge, this upscale bistro has been a local favorite since it opened its doors in 1982. Philippe Hiély, the sixth generation in his family's long line of chefs, dishes up a cui-sine that's sophisticated yet hearty: Think saffron-infused salt cod *brandade* served with crusty bread, or seared scallops atop fennel puree. Walls are adorned with an eclectic collection of antique cutlery (*la fourchette* translates as "the fork"), making the ambience as alluring as the food.

17 rue Racine. www.la-fourchette.net. ☎ **04-90-85-20-93.** Reservations recommended. Main courses 21€; fixed-price menu 34€. Mon–Fri 12:15–1:45pm and 7:15–9:45pm. Closed 3 weeks in Aug.

La Petite Pêche ★★ SEAFOOD   Hidden away on a back street west of the Palais des Papes, this low-key seafood restaurant is a welcomed surprise. Not only does La Petite Pêche dish up delicious fish and seafood, ranging from grilled calamari to a traditional Provençal fish soup, prices here are also supremely wallet-friendly. The three-course lunch menu—which runs along the lines of sardine-topped salad, fol-lowed by grilled *merlan* (whiting) with homemade ratatouille, and topped off with crème brulée—is a steal at 12€.

13 rue Saint-Etienne. ☎ **04-90-86-02-46.** Main courses 16€–19€; fixed-price lunch 12€. Mon–Sat noon–2:30pm and 7:30–10pm.

AVIGNON pass

If you plan to visit a couple of Avignon's major sights, be sure to pick up an Avignon Pass. This card is a free handout at the Office de Tourisme, as well as most key destinations around town. Pay the full fee to the first site you visit. The Pass then offers a discount of 10–50% off the full entrance price for every additional site you visit. The Avignon Pass is valid for 15 days and can be used for up to five visitors at a time.

Restaurant Christian Etienne ★★★ PROVENÇAL   This Michelin-starred temple of gastronomy is perched atop a 12th-century stone edifice—complete with 15th-century frescoes—just next door to the Palais des Papes. Avignon-born Chef Etienne is wildly innovative, and many of his dishes have a more than a hint of molecular influence. Fixed-price menus are themed around single ingredients such as duck, lobster, truffles, or (summertime only) heavenly heirloom tomatoes.

10 rue de Mons. www.christian-etienne.fr. ℂ **04-90-86-16-50.** Reservations required. Main courses 30€–50€; fixed-price lunch 35€, dinner 80€–150€. Tues–Sat noon–1:15pm and 7:30–9:15pm. Closed 2 weeks in Nov.

Restaurant Fou de Fafa ★★ FRENCH/PROVENÇAL   It may be British-owned, but this cozy little restaurant dishes up authentic local cuisine—often with a contemporary twist—that truly hits its mark. Delicious combinations may include pork filet mignon served with a cider jus and mashed sweet potato, or sea bream in saffron cream paired with Camargue rice. Note that the menu is short and highly seasonal.

17 rue des Trois Faucons. ℂ **04-32-76-35-13.** Reservations recommended. Fixed-price menu 23€–28€. Tues–Sat noon–1:15pm and 7:30–9:15pm. Closed Dec–Jan.

Exploring Avignon

Avignon is one of the prettiest towns in France. From its impressively imposing skyline to the verdant Île de la Barthelasse opposite, it's a delight to simply amble along aimlessly, perhaps stopping at a sidewalk cafe or two en route. Countless hidden gems crop up along the way, including 50 or so trompe-l'œil frescoes that decorate many of Avignon's city center facades. Painted by artists Dominique Durand and Marion Pochy, each one depicts a highlight from past editions of the Avignon Festival. Be sure to keep an eye out for the sun-dappled courtyard of the **Hôtel d'Europe** (www.heurope.com), too. This luxury hotel has been in operation since 1799, welcoming luminaries from Charles Dickens to Jacqueline Kennedy. It's also home to the recently renovated gourmet restaurant, **Vieille Fontaine**, which boasts a single Michelin star.

Poking westward from the grassy banks of the Rhône River, **Pont St-Bénézet ★★** (www.avignon-pont.com; ℂ **04-32-74-32-74**) was constructed between 1177 and 1185. Once spanning the Rhône and connecting Avignon with Villeneuve-lèz-Avignon, it is now a ruin, with only four of its original 22 arches remaining (half of it fell into the river back in 1669). The remains of the bridge have the same opening hours as those of the Palais des Papes (see below). Admission is 4.50€ adults, 3.50€ seniors and students, and free children 7 and under.

Collection Lambert ★★ MUSEUM   This contemporary art space is housed within an 18th-century private home that once belonged to collector and gallery owner Yvon Lambert. It stages three groundbreaking exhibitions each year. Works may range from video and photography to conceptual installations. Major artists such as Anselm Kiefer, Jenny Holzer, and Cy Twombly have all been featured. The popular METropolitan restaurant is located in the museum's peaceful courtyard. After a lengthy expansion project, Collection Lambert is due to reopen in July 2015. In the meantime, the museum organizes exhibitions around town, often in unique venues, such as the ex-Prison Sainte-Anne: see their website for further details.

5 rue Violette. www.collectionlambert.fr. © **04-90-16-56-20.** Admission changes according to exhibition, free for children 5 and under. July–Aug daily 11am–7pm; Sept–June Tues–Sun 11am–6pm.

Jardin du Rocher des Doms ★ GARDENS   Perched at the top of a hill on the banks of the River Rhône, the Jardin des Doms is a petite park, created during the 19th century. These manicured gardens include shady walking trails, a pond populated by koi carp, and **Buvette Café**, which serves cool drinks, wine by the glass, crepes, and other snacks. There's also a small Côtes du Rhône vineyard (entirely appropriate as Avignon is the capital of the Côtes du Rhône appellation), which was entirely replanted in 2014. It's the only vineyard in France located entirely within a city center's limits. The park's location affords superb views over Pont St-Bénézet, Île de la Barthelasse, Villeneuve-lez-Avignon, and Mont Ventoux. From the vineyard, you can descend onto a portion of the old city ramparts, which connect to the eastern side of Pont St-Bénézet.

Access from place des Papes, or via l'Escalier Sainte Anne. Free. June–Aug daily 7:30am–9pm; April–May and Sept daily 7:30am–8pm; Feb and Nov daily 7:30am–6pm; Jan–Feb daily 7:30am–5:30pm.

Musée Angladon ★★ MUSEUM   Haute-couture designer Jacques Doucet (1853–1929) didn't limit himself to the appreciation of finely cut fabrics. His former home is now a showcase for the international artworks that he and his wife collected over their lifetimes—from 16th-century Buddhas and Louis XVI chairs to Degas's famous dancers and canvases by Cézanne, Sisley, and Modigliani. Temporary exhibitions may showcase works by Pierre Bonnard or Henri de Toulouse-Lautrec.

5 rue Laboureur. www.angladon.com. © **04-90-82-29-03.** Admission 6€ adults, 4€ students and children 13–17, 1.50€ children 7–12, free for children 6 and under. Tues–Sun 1–6pm. Closed Tues in winter.

Musée Calvet ★ MUSEUM   Housed in what was formerly an 18th-century private home, the Musée Calvet is Avignon's top fine art museum. Upon his death, native son Esprit Calvet bequeathed to the city a lifetime's worth of acquired art, including works by Vernet, David, Corot, Manet, and Soutine, plus a collection of ancient silverware. Recent additions include a display dedicated to art and artifacts of ancient Egypt, as well as the new Victor Martin Modern Art Room, showcasing paintings by Bonnard, Soutine, Manet, and Sisley.

65 rue Joseph-Vernet. www.musee-calvet-avignon.com. © **04-90-86-33-84.** Admission 6€ adults, 3€ students, free for children 12 and under. Wed–Mon 10am–1pm and 2–6pm.

Musée Louis Vouland ★★ MUSEUM   This superb decorative arts museum houses the private collection of industrialist Louis Vouland. Spilling over a labyrinth of period rooms within one of Avignon's attractive 19th-century mansions, the collection includes tapestries, ornate furnishings, and an entire room dedicated to porcelain. The museum also holds temporary cultural exhibitions periodically throughout the year.

17 rue Victor Hugo. www.vouland.com. © **04-90-86-03-79.** Admission 6€ adults, free for children 12 and under. June–Aug Tues–Sun noon–6pm, Sept–May Tues–Sun 2–6pm.

Musée du Petit-Palais ★ MUSEUM   An ideal complement to the Palais des Papes' architectural austerity, this museum's artworks were originally part of a collection belonging to 19th-century art lover Giampietro Campana. Today the museum exhibits a myriad of paintings from the Italian and Provençal schools of the 13th to 16th centuries. Botticelli's "Madonna with Child" is a particular highlight.

Palais des Archevêques, place du Palais des Papes. www.petit-palais.org. ☏ **04-90-86-44-58.** Admission 6€ adults, 3€ students, free for children 11 and under. Wed–Mon 10am–1pm and 2–6pm.

Palais des Papes ★★★ PALACE   Dominating Avignon from a hilltop is one of the most famous, or notorious, palaces in the Christian world. Headquarters of a schismatic group of cardinals who came close to destroying the authority of the popes in Rome, this fortress is the city's most popular monument. Because of its massive size, you may be tempted to opt for a guided tour, but these can be monotonous. The extremely detailed audio guide, which now includes cutting-edge 3-D animation and is included in the price of admission, will likely suffice.

A highlight is the **Chapelle St-Jean,** known for its frescoes of John the Baptist and John the Evangelist, attributed to the school of Matteo Giovanetti and painted between 1345 and 1348. The **Grand Tinel (Banquet Hall)** is about 41m (134 ft.) long and 9m (30 ft.) wide; the pope's table stood on the south side. The walls of the **Pope's Bedroom,** on the first floor of the Tour des Anges, are painted with foliage, birds, and squirrels. The **Studium (Stag Room)**—the study of Clement VI—was frescoed in 1343 with hunting scenes. The **Grande Audience (Great Receiving Hall)** contains frescoes of the prophets, also attributed to Giovanetti and painted in 1352.

Note that the 12th-century **Cathédrale Notre-Dame des Doms cathedral,** just next door on the main square, contains the elaborate tombs of popes Jean XXII and Benoît XII. Under a full renovation at the time of writing, it is due to reopen to the public in 2015.

Place du Palais des Papes. www.palais-des-papes.com. ☏ **04-32-74-32-74.** Admission (including audio guide) 11€ adults, 9€ seniors and students, free for children 7 and under. Daily Nov–Feb

THE green shores OF ÎLE DE LA BARTHELASSE

Floating in the Rhône midway between Villeneuve-Lez-Avignon and Avignon proper, **Île de la Barthelasse** is arguably the largest river island in Europe. Its 700 verdant hectares are dotted with campsites and a public swimming pool (Club La Palmeraie, 135 allée Antoine Pinay; ☏ **04-90-82-54-25;** admission 4€). It's also crisscrossed by miles of walking and cycling trails. Few foreigners visit the island. Which means come summertime, it makes an idyllic escape from Avignon's town center bustle. For enthusiastic photographers, Île de la Barthelasse also offers some of the most unbeatable panoramas of the city, sweeping over Pont St-Bénézet and Avignon's iconic Palais des Papes-studded skyline. Between mid-February and December, the Avignon municipality offers a free **ferry** service between the city center, north of Pont St-Bénézet, and the island. Frequent boats depart regularly from April to September daily, and on Wednesdays, Saturdays, and Sundays in February, March, and October to December. The ferries also allow free passage for bikes.

Palais des Papes

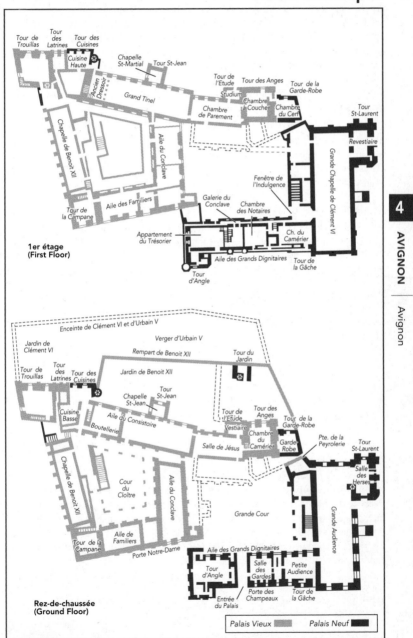

1er étage (First Floor)

- Tour de Trouillas
- Tour des Latrines
- Tour des Cuisines
- Cuisine Haute
- Chapelle St-Martial
- Tour St-Jean
- Ancien Dressoir
- Grand Tinel
- Tour de l'Étude
- Studium
- Tour des Anges
- Tour de la Garde-Robe
- Chambre à Coucher
- Chambre du Cerf
- Tour St-Laurent
- Revestiaire
- Chambre de Parement
- Chapelle de Benoît XII
- Aile du Conclave
- Fenêtre de l'Indulgence
- Grande Chapelle de Clément VI
- Aile des Familiers
- Tour de la Campane
- Galerie du Conclave
- Chambre des Notaires
- Ch. du Camérier
- Appartement du Trésorier
- Aile des Grands Dignitaires
- Tour de la Gâche
- Tour d'Angle

Rez-de-chaussée (Ground Floor)

- Enceinte de Clément VI et d'Urbain V
- Verger d'Urbain V
- Jardin de Clément VI
- Rempart de Benoît XII
- Tour du Jardin
- Tour de Trouillas
- Tour des Latrines
- Tour des Cuisines
- Jardin de Benoît XII
- Cuisine Basse
- Chapelle St-Jean
- Tour St-Jean
- Aile du Consistoire
- Boutellerie
- Tour de l'Étude
- Tour des Anges
- Vestiaire
- Tour de la Garde-Robe
- Salle de Jésus
- Chambre du Camérier
- Garde Robe
- Pte. de la Peyrolerie
- Tour St-Laurent
- Salle des Herses
- Chapelle de Benoît XII
- Cour du Cloître
- Aile du Conclave
- Grande Cour
- Grande Audience
- Tour de la Campane
- Aile de Familiers
- Porte Notre-Dame
- Aile des Grands Dignitaires
- Tour d'Angle
- Salle des Gardes
- Petite Audience
- Entrée du Palais
- Porte des Champeaux
- Tour de la Gâche

Palais Vieux ▓▓▓ Palais Neuf ███

4

AVIGNON | Avignon

45

9:30am–5:45pm; Mar 9am–6:30pm; April–June and Sept–Nov 9am–7pm; July 9am–8pm; Aug 9am–8:30pm

Outlying Attractions

Epicurium ★★ GARDENS & MUSEUM   On Avignon's eastern outskirts, well off the city's tourist track, this "living museum" offers visitors a total immersion into indigenous Provençal fruits and vegetables. The museum itself boasts interactive sensory exhibits, teaching visitors about local agriculture, from seed to plate, as well as sustainability, nutrition, and regional cuisine. Outdoors, the vegetable gardens and orchards are dotted with more than 100 fruit trees. There are plenty of spots to kick back in the shade. Take bus no. 4, which departs from just outside of Avignon's city center train station.

Cité de l'Alimentation, 100 Rue Pierre Bayle, BP 1154. www.epicurium.fr. ☏ **04-32-40-37-71**. Admission 7.50€, 5.50€ students and ages 6–18, free for children 5 and under. April–Oct Mon–Fri 10am–12:30pm and 2–6:30pm, Sat–Sun 2–6:30pm. On-site boutique open daily 9:30am–3:30pm. Open Nov–March for groups and by reservation only.

4 Villeneuve-Lez-Avignon

While the popes lived in exile, cardinals built palaces, or *livrées,* just across the Rhône in sleepy Villenueve-lez-Avignon. Many visitors prefer to stay or dine here—it's quieter and less modernized, while still convenient to Avignon's major attractions. Take bus no. 5, which crosses the larger of the two relatively modern bridges, the **Pont Daladier.**

Avignon's **Office de Tourisme** can provide further information, as can Villeneuve-Lez-Avignon's specific branch in place Charles David (www.tourisme-villeneuveleza-vignon.fr; ☏ **04-90-25-61-33**).

St-André Abbey Gardens ★★ GARDENS   Clustered around the 17th-century Benedictine Abbaye St-André (under new ownership as of 2013), these spectacular gardens include a rose-trellis colonnade, fountains flecked with lily pads, and an olive orchard. They also offer unbeatable views over the Rhône Valley and Avignon's skyline beyond. Fort St-André (separate entrance fee, 5.50€), founded in 1360 by Jean-le-Bon to serve as a symbol of might to the pontifical powers across the river, is adjacent the monastery.

Fort Saint-André, rue Montée du Fort. www.abbayesaintandre.fr. ☏ **04-90-25-55-95**. Admission 5€ adults, 4.50€ students and ages 13–18, free for children 12 and under. Tues–Sun March and Oct 10am–1pm and 2–5pm, April 10am–1pm and 2–6pm, May–Sept 10am–6pm. Closed Nov–Feb.

Val de Bénédiction Chartreuse ★ MONASTERY   France's largest Carthusian monastery, built in 1352, comprises a church, three cloisters, cells that housed the medieval monks, and a 12th-century graveyard where Pope Innocent VI is entombed. Part of the complex houses the Centre National d'Ecritures du Spectacle, a residence for artists and playwrights who live rent-free for up to a year to deepen their crafts. Art exhibitions, concerts, and theater take place throughout the year.

58 rue de la République. www.chartreuse.org. ☏ **04-90-15-24-24**. Admission 8€ adults, 5.50€ students and under 25, free for children 17 and under. Aug daily 9am–7:30pm; July and Sept daily 9am–6:30pm; April–June daily 9:30am–6:30pm; Oct–March Mon–Fri 9:30am–5pm, Sat–Sun 10am–5pm.

Organized Tours

One of the most interactive ways to gain insight into Avignon's rich history is through a guided tour. Avignon's Office de Tourisme organizes a range of themed tours around the city. For non-French speakers, the excellent **"Secret Palace" tour** is an access-all-areas ramble around the Palais de Papes. You'll wind your way through the Palace's private apartments, hidden passageways, and secret gardens (24.50€), areas that few visitors can claim to have seen.

Or be bold and dust off that phrasebook: Many of the Office de Tourisme tours are offered only in French, including **"Once upon a time in the Palace of the Popes"** (15.50€, free for children 7 and under), **"The story of the Palace of the Popes for all ages"** (15.50€, 10.50€ Avignon Pass and children 7 to 18, free for children 7 and under), the quirky **"The Popes and their Pets"** (15.50€, 10.50€ Avignon Pass and children 7 to 18, free for children 7 and under) and—new in 2014—**"Avignon's Legendary Palace and Bridge"** (19.50€, 15.50€ Avignon Pass and children 7 to 18, free for children 7 and under).

Most of the above tours are offered several times a week throughout the months of May, June, September, and October. For further information, contact the **Avignon Office de Tourisme** (www.avignon-tourisme.com).

Alternatively, **Local Avignon Tours** (www.local-avignon-tours.com; ℂ +1-866-663-7017) offers private English-language tours of the city (from 175€ per person) as well as day trips to Orange, Châteauneuf-du-Pape, and rural Provence (from 44€ per person). **Provence Panorama** (www.provencetours-avignon.com; ℂ 04-90-22-02-61; from 50€ per person), **Provence Réservation** (www.provencereservation.com; ℂ 04-90-14-70-00; from 55€ per person), **Avignon Prestige Tour** (www.avignon-prestigetour.com; ℂ 04-90-14-64-83; from 60€ per person), and **Occitania Provence Tours**

WINE TOURS in western provence

Avignon is the capital of the Côtes du Rhône appellation. Locals claim that vines have been cultivated in and around here for more than 2,000 years. Within a region as rich in wine production as this one, it would be a shame not to sip your way through a little of the local tipple.

In Avignon itself, **Le Vin devant Soi,** 4 rue du College du Roure (www.levin-devantsoi.fr; ℂ 04-90-82-04-39), a wine shop located in the city center, organizes regular wine tasting sessions for groups. Prices start from 30€ per person.

To explore further afield, François Marcou at **Avignon Wine Tour** (www.avignon-wine-tour.com; ℂ 06-28-05-33-84) has the tag line: "You drink, I drive…" He offers five different wine-tasting itineraries each week. Each tour visits four local

vineyards, from exploring Châteauneuf-du-Pape (the most famous of the Côtes du Rhônes wine areas) to dropping into *domaines* located in the Luberon, and includes introductory lessons on how to taste wine. Tours are an all-day affair, taking place from 9am to 5pm. Each one costs from 95€ per person.

Alternatively, rent a car and investigate the area on your own. The excellent **Rhône Wines** website (www.rhone-wines.com) maps out 13 different wine trails across Rhône Valley. Each itinerary flags up vineyards, activities, restaurants, and places to stay en-route way. Visitors are truly welcome at every local vineyard, and contribute greatly to the local economy by tasting and touring in this manner.

(www.occitania-provence-tours.com; ℰ **09-71-55-17-58**; from 55€ per person) organize similar bilingual tours, although they tend to concentrate on Avignon's surrounding countryside, rather than the historic town center.

For self-guided bicycle tours of Avignon, Villeneuve-lez-Avignon, and Île de la Barthelasse, contact **Day Tour** (www.daytour.fr; ℰ **04-90-63-50**). Bike rental plus a local itinerary costs around 18€ per person, although the fee decreases according to the number of participants. They're also able to arrange a picnic (from 10€ per person) for you to take along on your ride.

Epicureans may partake in **Avignon Gourmet Tour** (www.avignongourmetours.com; ℰ **06-35-32-08-96**). These 3-hour walking tours discuss local culinary history and visit Provençal shops, where participants will taste traditional products, including Châteauneuf-du-Pape wines. Tours (55€ per person) take place from Tuesday to Saturday, beginning at 9:45am.

And, like many French cities, Avignon's own *petit train* crisscrosses the city center. The circuit starts outside of the Palais des Papes, then cruises up to the Jardin du Rocher des Doms, and past the Pont St Bénézet. It takes around 40 minutes. Tours cost 7€, 4€ for children 5 to 9 years old, and are free for children 4 and under. For further information, see www.petittrainavignon.fr or call ℰ **04-90-86-36-75**.

Especially for Kids

In summer of 2014, **Splashworld** opened in Monteux, northeast of Avignon's city center. This "new generation" water park counts toboggan rides, surf simulators, and a dizzying array of waterslides among its numerous attractions. Opening hours and entrance fees were still to be established at the time of writing; contact the Avignon Tourist Office for further details.

Shopping

The chain boutique **Souleiado**, 19 rue Joseph-Vernet (ℰ **04-90-86-32-05**), sells reproductions of 18th- and 19th-century Provençal fabrics by the meter or made into clothing and linens. There is also a large selection of housewares and gifts.

Hervé Baume, 19 rue Petite Fusterie (ℰ **04-90-86-37-66**), is the place to buy a Provençal table—or something to put on it. A massive inventory includes French folk art and hand-blown hurricane lamps. **Jaffier-Parsi,** 42 rue des Fourbisseurs (ℰ **04-90-86-08-85**), is known for copper saucepans from the Norman town of Villedieu-les-Poêles, which has been making them since the Middle Ages.

For fresh reading material, **Camili Books and Tea**, 155 rue de la Carreterie (www.camili-booksandtea.com, ℰ **04-90-27-38-50**), stocks close to 20,000 books, most of them used. There's also a tea room and free Wi-Fi on site.

In Avignon, foodie souvenirs are delightfully thick on the ground. **Angéla de Beaupréau**, 35 bis rue de la Bonneterie (www.angeladebeaupreau.fr; ℰ **04-90-82-01-95**), is an artisan chocolatier boasting a hugely interactive boutique. She earns top marks in creativity for her colorful high-heeled shoes, made entirely of chocolate. Head over to **Le Comptoir de Mathilde**, 32 rue de la Balance (www.lecomptoirdemathilde.com; ℰ **04-90-85-44-52**), for olive tapenade, local olive oils, *Herbes de Provence* mustard, and flaky Guérande sea salt, as well as plenty of free tastings. **Pâtisserie Mallard**, 32 rue des Marchands (www.patisseriemallard.fr; ℰ **04-90-82-42-38**), makes the hard-to-find local specialty *les papalines d'Avignon*. Dark chocolate is coated in a pink, "thistle"-like pink chocolate, then filled with Origan du Comat liquor, the latter created from 60 local plants and produced by Maison Blachère, Provence's oldest distillery.

AVIGNON'S cooking schools

The Avignonnaise are justly proud of their seasonal, fresh, enthusiastically local cuisine. Learn how to recreate a few of the delectable dishes you've tasted here by signing up for a lesson at one of the city's popular cooking schools.

There's a rotating schedule of superb regional chefs at **Ateliers de Cuisine Le Marmiton**, La Mirande, 4 place de la Mirande (www.la-mirande.fr; ✆ **04-90-14-20-20**). Rare is the visitor who can boast that they have perfected duck breast stuffed with foie gras from Michelin-starred chef Jean-Jacques Prévôt. Or how to make pâtissier Pierre Hermé's quirkily flavored macaroons, with hints of rose and raspberry, or apricot and saffron. Lessons, which start at 80€, are held in the hotel's 19th-century kitchen. Most ingredients used are organic.

During Julien Charvet's **Concept Chef** (www.conceptchef.com; ✆ **06-25-36-12-40**), the cooking team pluck seasonal ingredients from the stands at Les Halles, the city's covered produce market, which are then used in traditional Provençal recipes.

Seeking a class with a little less commitment? **La Petite Cuisine des Halles** also takes place at Les Halles (www.avignon-leshalles.com). Every Saturday morning (except August) at 11am, famous chefs from different local restaurants take turns preparing a favorite dish, answering questions from the general public, and passing out free tastings.

Also decidedly hands-off is La Mirande's **Table d'Hôte**, or Chef's Table, held on the days when the on-site gastronomic restaurant is closed. However, not only are diners privy to a private cooking demonstration from Chef Jean-Claude Altmayer, cooked on the kitchen's ancient wood-fired oven. You'll also indulge in a four-course gourmet meal, paired with regional wines from La Mirande's superbly stocked cellar. Participants are limited to 12, and the one-off experience is priced at 86€.

Further afield, **At Home with Patricia Wells** (www.patriciawells.com) is a Provence-based cooking school taught by Patricia Wells, cookbook author, and famed former restaurant critic for the "International Herald Tribune." The extremely popular 5-day classes take place in Vaison-la-Romaine. They are limited to 10 students and cost $5,500 (accommodation not included).

A covered market with 40 different merchants is **Les Halles**, place Pie, (www.avignon-leshalles.com), open Tuesday through Sunday (6am–1:30pm). The **flower market** is on place des Carmes on Saturday (8am–1pm), and the **flea market** occupies the same place each Sunday morning (6am–1pm).

Nightlife

Start your evening at **Avitus Bar à Vin**, 11 rue du Vieux Sextier (www.avituslacave.com; ✆ **04-84-15-82-71**; closed Sunday and Monday), a cozy wine bar offering a wide range of local wines by the glass. (Note that there's a shop on site, if you're keen to pack away a bottle of the tasty regional tipples from Provence, Bandol, Cassis, and Corsica on offer.)

Avignon's beautiful people head on to **Les Ambassadeurs,** 27 rue Bancasse (www.clublesambassadeurs.fr; ✆ **04-90-86-31-55**), an upscale dance club. The **Red Zone DJ bar,** 25 rue Carnot (www.redzonedjbar.com; ✆ **04-90-27-02-44**), offers a different musical theme every night (salsa, electronic, and more). **83 Vernet,** 83 rue Joseph Vernet (www.83vernet.com; ✆ **04-90-85-99-04**), switches from restaurant into dance

FLOATING DOWN the rhône

The Rhône may be one of France's most popular rivers for cruising. However, Avignon is also home to a selection of boats that simply head out onto the water for shorter sightseeing trips. For full days out, try **Les Croisieres Mireio** (www.mireio.net; ℭ **04-90-85-62-25**). Cruises are priced from 36.50€, or 20€ for children 11 and under. They include stops in Arles or nearby Tarascon, as well as lunch or dinner. Between April and September, Mireio also make brief jaunts onto the river. Their shorter **Promenades en Bateau** take in Avignon's most famous monuments, Île de la Barthelasse, and Villeneuve-lez-Avignon from the water. Tickets cost 8€, 2€ for children 7 and under, free for children 2 and under; the tour lasts around 45 minutes. Alternatively, during July and August **Canoe Avignon**, allée Antoine Pinay, Île de la Barthelasse (www.canoe-avignon.fr; ℭ **06-51-60-13-59**), leads guided tours of Avignon that paddle along the Rhône.

club mode around 10pm, under the high-ceilinged hallways and stone courtyards of a former 1363 Benedictine convent.

Behind the Hôtel d'Europe, disco-bar **L'Esclave,** 12 rue du Limas (www.esclavebar.com; ℭ **04-90-85-14-91**), is a focal point of the city's gay scene.

DAY TRIPS FROM AVIGNON

Orange ★

31km (19 miles) N of Avignon

Antiquities-rich Orange was not named for citrus fruit, but as a dependency of the Dutch House of Orange-Nassau during the Middle Ages. It is home to two UNESCO World Heritage sites: Europe's third-largest **triumphal arch** and its best-preserved **Roman theatre.** Louis XIV, who once considered moving the theatre to Versailles, claimed: "It is the finest wall in my kingdom." The Théâtre Antique is now the site of **Les Chorégies d'Orange** (www.choregies.fr), a summertime opera and classical music festival.

Just 10km (6 miles) south along the D68 is **Châteauneuf-du-Pape,** a prestigious appellation known for its bold red wines. Spend an afternoon visiting the village's numerous tasting rooms, winding your way up to the ruins of a castle that served as a summer residence for Pope John XXII. Wine-lovers may also drop into the **Maison Brotte Wine Museum**, avenue Saint Pierre de Luxembourg (www.brotte.com; ℭ **04-90-83-59-44**). Displays include ancient vineyard tools and a 17th-century wooden wine press. The museum is open mid-April to mid-October from 9am to 1pm and 2pm to 7pm, and mid October to mid April from 9am to noon and 2pm to 6pm. Admission is free.

ESSENTIALS

Frequent **trains** (trip time: 20 min.; 6.20€ one-way) and **buses** (www.sudest-mobilites.fr; ℭ **04-32-76-00-40;** trip time: 1 hr.; 2€ one-way) connect Avignon and Orange. If you're **driving** from Avignon, take A7 north to Orange. The **Office de Tourisme** is at 5 cours Aristide-Briand (www.otorange.fr; ℭ **04-90-34-70-88**).

EXPLORING ORANGE & AROUND

The carefully restored **Théâtre Antique** ★★★, rue Madeleine Roch (www.theatre-antique.com; ✆ **04-90-51-17-60**), dates from the days of Augustus. Built into the side of a hill, it once held 9,000 spectators in tiered seats. Nearly 105m-long (344 ft.) and 37m high (121 ft.), it's open daily November to February 9:30am to 4:30pm; March and October 9:30am to 5:30pm; April, May, and September 9am to 6pm; and June to August 9am to 7pm. Admission (which includes a free audio guide) is 9.50€ adults, 7.50€ students and children 8 to 17, and free children 7 and under. The multimedia show "Ghosts of the Theatre," held regularly year-round, offers visitors the chance to see the monument's showstoppers through the centuries, from pantomime in ancient Rome to Orange 75, nicknamed the "French Woodstock."

The imposing **Arc de Triomphe** ★, avenue de l'Arc-de-Triomphe, comprises a trio of arches held up by Corinthian columns embellished with military and maritime emblems. Also built during the reign of Augustus, it was once part of the original town's fortified walls.

WHERE TO EAT

At **Au Petit Patio,** 58 cours Aristide Briand (✆ **04-90-29-69-27**), contemporary Provençal cuisine is served on a petite outdoor terrace. Sample honey-glazed sea bass or summery strawberry tartare.

Vaison-la-Romaine ★★

50km (31 miles) NE of Avignon

Part medieval village, part Roman ruins, and all crowned by a 13th-century castle, Vaison-la-Romaine sits in the fertile northern reaches of Provence. Well off this region's traditional tourist trail, the combination of history and low-key allure makes for an exquisite escape. To the east of Vaison-la-Romaine towers Mont Ventoux, a monolith of a mountain (1,900m/6,300 ft.) famed for its bogeyman role in the annual Tour de France cycle race.

ESSENTIALS

Frequent **trains** (trip time: 20 min.; 6.20€ one-way) connect Avignon and Orange. From Orange, hop aboard bus nr. 4 (www.vaucluse.fr; trip time: 45 min.; 2€ one-way). If you're **driving** from Avignon, take A7 north, veering northeast onto D977. The **Office de Tourisme** is at place du Chanoine Sautel (www.vaison-ventoux-tourisme. com; ✆ **04- 90-36-02-11**).

EXPLORING VAISON-LA-ROMAINE & AROUND

Ancient capital to the Voconce people, Vaison-la-Romaine is home to two important archeological sites, **Puymin** and **La Vilasse** (www.provenceromaine.com; ✆04-90-36-50-48). Both are peppered with ancient Roman residences, the remains of thermal baths, statues, and mosaics. The sites are open daily November, December, and February 10am to noon and 2pm to 5pm; March and October 10am to 12:30pm and 2pm to 5:30pm; April and May 9:30am to 6pm; and June to September 9:30am to 6:30pm. From January to early February both sites are closed. Admission (which includes a free audio guide and is valid for 24 hours) is 8€ adults, 3€ students and children 12 to 18, and free children 11 and under.

For more detailed information about Vaison-la-Romaine's history, visit the **Musée Archéologique Théo Desplans**, located within Puymin (entrance valid with same ticket, same opening hours), which focuses on local and regional discoveries.

The oldest part of Vaison-la-Romaine itself—the Cité Médiévale—is a medieval wonderland, crisscrossed by winding alleyways and splashed with pretty squares. To the south sits its **Roman bridge,** dating from the first century AD, which spans the Ouvèze River. If possible, time your visit to coincide with the town's superb regional market (Tuesdays, 8am–1pm, held around town).

Every 3 years, Vaison-la-Romaine holds the 10-day **Choralies,** or Choral Festival, in August (www.choralies.fr, next edition 2016). Visitors also descend on the town annually for **Vaison Danses** (www.vaison-danses.com), a prestigious dance festival held every July.

WHERE TO EAT

Head to **Restaurant le Baleteur,** place Théodore Aubanel (www.le-bateleur.com; ✆ **04-90-36-28-04,** closed Mondays) for one of their seasonal lunchtime menus (two courses for 19€, three courses for 23€). Cuisine makes the most of local ingredients, from wild mushrooms and Mediterranean bonito to free-range chicken from nearby Monteux and heirloom tomatoes.

4 L'Isle-sur-la-Sorgue ★★

23km (14 miles) E of Avignon

The picturesque Provençal town of L'Isle-sur-la-Sorgue spills over a cluster of verdant islands. Each one is splashed by the River Sorgue and crisscrossed by its canals. Terraced bars and restaurants overlook the waterways. However, the village is best known for its weekly *brocante* and antiques market, which draws crowds of buyers and browsers from across the entire South of France.

ESSENTIALS

Trains (trip time: 25 min.; 4.90€ one-way) connect Avignon and L'Isle-sur-la-Sorgue. Alternatively, hop aboard **bus nr. 6** (www.vaucluse.fr; trip time: 1 hr.; 2€ one-way) from Avignon's Gare Routière to L'Isle-sur-la-Sorgue. If you're **driving** from Avignon, take D901 east. Try for a parking space in the Parking Portalet or Parking Allée des Muriers (both free). Isle-sur-la-Sorgue's **Office de Tourisme** is located at place de la Liberté (www.oti-delasorgue.fr; ✆ **04-90-38-04-78**).

EXPLORING L'ISLE-SUR-LA-SORGUE

During the 19th-century, L'Isle-sur-la-Sorgue was a thriving hub for textile production. Remnants of this industrious past are still visible in the nine mossy, tumbling water-wheels scattered across the town center. Stop by the Office de Tourisme to pick up a free map, detailed with walking routes and the locations of each the remaining wheels.

But most visitors make their way to this unique town for L'Isle-sur-la-Sorgue's renowned **Déballage Brocante**. It's held on Sundays; the activity starts at 9am and finishes around 6pm. From 8am to 2pm, there's also a Provençal food market, where you can pick up delicious picnic fodder, from crushed olives with garlic to fennel-infused salami.

Antiques are concentrated in the southern part of town, where you'll find warehouses (open all week, regular business hours, as well as Sunday), filled with dealers and treasures. During the weekly market, around 300 small stalls selling both *brocante* and antiques are also dotted throughout the pedestrianized town center.

For out of the ordinary, more contemporary souvenirs, pop into **Carton Noir,** 17 bis rue Théophile Jean (www.carton-noir.com; ✆ **06-21-61-81-56**). Here, Cécile Chappuis purveys her one-of-a-kind cardboard and mirror creations.

If you're keen to explore the area further, head over to avenue Charmasson, where **Club de Canoë Kayak Islois** (canoesurlasorgue.free.fr; ✆ **04-90-38-33-22**), offers 2½ hour canoe trips into the surrounding countryside along the River Sorgue (19€, 13€ children 12 and under). Alternatively, the nearby town of **Fontaine-de-Vaucluse** (www.oti-delasorgue.fr) is equally charming. The source of the River Sorgue gushes up for the earth just east of the pretty village center.

WHERE TO EAT

Tucked within the town's leafy L'Ile aux Brocantes, home to around 40 antiques dealers, **La Marmite Bouillonnante**, 7 ave. des Quatres Otages, Passage du Pont (www.lileauxbrocantes.com; ✆ **04-90-38-51-05**), serves up local, mostly organic lunches on a terrace overlooking the River Sorgue. During the afternoon, the venue is transformed into a tearoom, and purveys superb homemade pastries. Note that La Marmite is only open Saturday to Monday.

Epicureans seeking a spot that tends more toward the gourmet are advised to try **Le Vivier**, 800 cours Fernande Peyre (www.levivier-restaurant.com; ✆ **04-90-38-52-80**). Here chef Ludovic Dziewulski's contemporary spin on classic Provençal cuisine may include red mullet and Mediterranean octopus, served with goji berries and green asparagus, or sautéed Jerusalem artichokes teamed with chestnut mousse, poached egg, truffles, and *lardo di Colonnata*. The daily Menu du Marché is priced at 32€.

Pont du Gard ★★★

26km (16 miles) W of Avignon

The tallest Roman aqueduct in the world (at 49m, or 160ft), Pont du Gard bridges the tumbling Gardon River. It was constructed during the first century AD, and is a world-renowned UNESCO World Heritage Site.

ESSENTIALS

Bus nr. A15 (www.edgard-transport.fr; trip time: 45 min.; 1.50€ one-way, or see combination transport and admission tickets below) connects Avignon's Gare Routière and Pont du Gard (descend at Rond Point Pont du Gard). If you're **driving** from Avignon, take D6100 west. There is on-site parking (see admission information opposite), included in the site's entrance fee. Pont du Gard's **Information Office** is located on the site, at 400 Route du Pont du Gard, Vers-Pont-du-Gard (www.pontdugard.fr; ✆ **04-66-37-50-99**).

EXPLORING PONT DU GARD

The Pont du Gard site spills over both banks of the Gardon River. Like Paris, for orientation these two areas are referred to as the Rive Gauche (Left Bank) and the Rive Droite (Right Bank). The entrance to the site, museum, Ludo Children's Center, cinema, Expo temporary exhibitions space, and various shops sit on the Rive Gauche. Various refreshments, including Café du Pont du Gard, Le Snack, Le Vieux Moulin, Les Croisées Bistrot (open high season only), and La Crêperie are also located on this bank. On the Rive Droite, Les Terrasses restaurant overlooks the Pont du Gard.

Pont du Gard's **Museum** makes for a concise introduction to this ancient Roman site. Multimedia exhibits assist in demonstrating how the aqueduct (originally 50km, or 31 miles long), sourced water from Eure, near Uzés, and transported it to the nearby town of Nîmes. The water was then used for gardens, fountains, and baths, pressurized and gushing out of indoor taps, all utterly futuristic amenities 2,000 years ago! The nearby **Cinema** plays the short fictionalized documentary, "Un Pont Traverse le Temps" (A Bridge Across the Ages).

For kids, the **Ludo Children's Center** offers a range of themed activities for 5 to 12 year-olds, from insight into life as a Gallic-Roman student or market trader to an introduction to archaeology.

The Rive Gauche is connected to the Rive Droite by the Pont du Gard itself. The aqueduct is made up of three levels of limestone arches. Stroll across the lowest one to explore both of the site's banks. Alternatively, loop underneath for sublime photo opportunities, or to splash around in the River Gardon.

If you're looking to explore the site further, the hour-and-a-half walking trail **Mémoires de Garrigue** focuses on the indigenous plants found in the region, including rock roses, honeysuckle, mulberry trees, and juniper. The walk also crosses additional ruins of the ancient aqueduct, as well as demonstrating human impact on this countryside throughout the 19th century.

The Pont du Gard site is open daily May to September 7:30am to midnight, April and October 8am to 8pm, and November to January 8:30am to 7pm. Cultural activities (such as the museum and the Ludo Children's Center, as well as all shops) are open daily July and August 9am to 8pm, June and September 9am to 7pm, March to May and October 9am to 6pm, and November to February 9am to 5pm.

Admission to the site is 18€ for one vehicle, including up to five visitors; 12€ for one motorbike, including up to two visitors; 10€ per person on foot or by bike, or alternatively, 15€ for up to five visitors on foot or by bike; or 10€ for one vehicle, including up to five visitors, during evening hours (when on-site cultural areas are closed). Note that if you arrive from Avignon by bus, **Edgard Transport** (www. edgard-transport.fr; (📞 **08-10-33-42-73**) offers a combination bus day pass and Pont du Gard entry ticket for 10€ per person, or 20€ per family (three to five visitors, of which one must be an adult).

WHERE TO EAT

The Rive Droite's **Les Terrasses** restaurant (📞 **04-66-63-91-37**) occupies a mid-19th-century inn. At lunchtime, the two-course fixed-price menu costs 18€, and may include pork in a mustard marinade with thyme-infused potato gratin, sweet pea velouté, or candied vegetables with Parmesan shavings. As implied by the name, there's a large outdoor seating area with sublime views over Pont du Gard itself.

ARLES & AROUND

ST-RÉMY-DE-PROVENCE ★

710km (440 miles) S of Paris; 24km (15 miles) NE of Arles; 19km (12 miles) S of Avignon; 10km (6¼ miles) N of Les Baux

Though the physician and astrologer Nostradamus was born here in 1503, most associate St-Rémy with Vincent van Gogh, who committed himself to a local asylum in 1889 after cutting off part of his left ear. "Starry Night" was painted during this period, as were many versions of "Olive Trees" and "Cypresses."

Come to sleepy St-Rémy not only for its history and sights, but also for an authentic experience of daily Provençal life. The town springs into action on Wednesday mornings, when stalls bursting with the region's bounty, from wild-boar sausages to olives, and elegant antiques to bolts of French country fabric, huddle between the sidewalk cafes beneath the plane trees.

5

Essentials

ARRIVING A regional bus, the Cartreize, runs four to nine times daily between Avignon's Gare Routière and St-Rémy's place de la République (trip time: 45 min.; 3.60€ one-way). For **bus** information, see www.lepilote.com or call ℃ **08-10-00-13-26.** The St-Rémy tourist office also provides links to up-to-date bus schedules on their website (see below). Drivers can head south from Avignon along D571.

VISITOR INFORMATION The **Office de Tourisme** is on place Jean-Jaurès (www.saintremy-de-provence.com; ℃ **04-90-92-05-22**).

Getting Around

ON FOOT St-Rémy's town center is compact. Much of it is pedestrianized, making it very easy to navigate on foot.

BY BICYCLE If you're interested in exploring the surrounding countryside, or simply having your own wheels, **Sun-e-Bike**, 16 boulevard Marceau (www.location-velo-provence.com; ℃ **04-32-62-08-39**), rents electric bicycles. With a full battery, each bike can scoot around 35km (21 miles) before it needs recharging. Prices start at 35€ per day, with discounts available for longer rentals.

St-Rémy

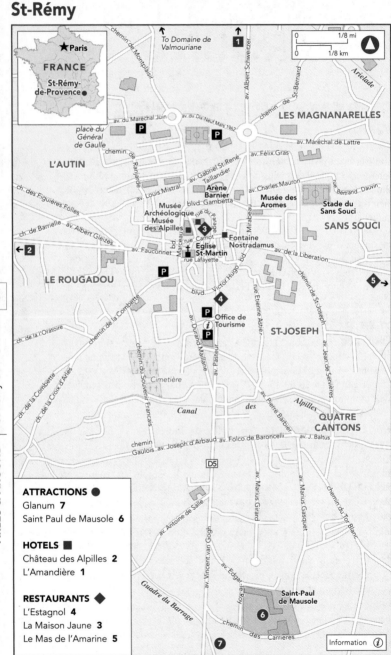

Information ⓘ

5

ARLES & AROUND | St-Rémy-de-Provence

[FastFACTS] ST-RÉMY-DE-PROVENCE

ATMs/Banks   Société Marseillaise de Crédit, 10 bd. Mirabeau (📞 **04-90-92-74-00**).

Mail & Postage   La Poste, 5 rue Roger Salengro (📞 **36-31**).

Pharmacies   Pharmacie Cendres, 4 bd. Mirabeau (📞 **04-32-60-16-43**).

Where to Stay

L'Amandière ★   Tucked into the Provençal countryside around 1.5km (1 mile) north of town, this budget bolt-hole is justly favored by visitors who would rather splurge on the region's gourmet restaurants. L'Amandière's accommodation may be simple, but bedding down here is certainly no hardship. Rooms are spacious, all boast their own balcony or private patio, and there's a large outdoor pool. Breakfast is served under citrus trees in the lavender-trimmed gardens.

Av. Théodore Aubanel. www.hotel-amandiere.com. 📞 **04-90-92-41-00**. 26 units. 76€–95€ double; 95€–105€ triple. Free parking. **Amenities:** Outdoor pool; free Wi-Fi in common areas.

Château des Alpilles ★★★   A former castle situated at the heart of magnolia-studded parkland, Château des Alpilles was constructed by the Pichot family in 1827. Françoise Bon converted the mansion in 1980, creating luxurious double rooms inside the castle itself, with additional private accommodation in the property's former chapel, farmhouse, and washhouse. Decor throughout encompasses a confident mix of antiques (plush upholstery, local artworks) and cool amenities (deep travertine-trimmed bathtubs, iPod docks). It's 2km (1¼ miles) from the center of St-Rémy.

Route de Rougadou. www.chateaudesalpilles.com. 📞 **04-90-92-03-33**. 21 units. 210€–340€ double; 310€–440€ suite; 350€–470€ apartment; 310€–400€ maisonette. Free parking. Closed Jan to mid-March. **Amenities:** Restaurant; bar; outdoor pool; room service; sauna; 2 tennis courts; free Wi-Fi.

Where to Eat

L'Estagnol ★★   MEDITERRANEAN   This popular eatery (which translates as "little pond" in the regional dialect) is owned and operated by the Meynadier family, third-generation restaurateurs. Hearty local cuisine ranges from Camargue bull hamburger topped with goat cheese to Provençal gazpacho with basil sorbet. Dining takes place either in the ancient *orangerie* (private greenhouse) or in the sun-dappled courtyard adjacent.

16 bd. Victor Hugo. www.restaurant-lestagnol.com. 📞 **04-90-92-05-95.** Reservations recommended. Main courses 13€–32€; fixed-price lunch 14€, dinner 27€–34€. May–Sept Tues–Sun noon–2:30pm and 7:15–10pm; Oct–April Tues–Sun noon–2:30pm, Tues–Sat 7:15–10pm.

La Maison Jaune ★   FRENCH/PROVENÇAL   Within an 18th-century village home in St-Rémy's Old Town, handsome tables spill over two chic dining rooms, as well as a terrace overlooking the neighboring Hôtel de Sade's lush gardens. It's here that creative chef François Perraud concocts his Michelin-starred cuisine, relying almost exclusively on local ingredients. Mediterranean anchovies may be doused in a parsley pesto, Provençal lamb seared with smoky eggplant, or the darkest chocolate cake paired with frozen lemon parfait.

15 rue Carnot. www.lamaisonjaune.info. © **04-90-92-56-14.** Reservations required. Main courses 36€–38€; fixed-price lunch 32€; fixed-price dinner 42€–72€. March–Aug Tues–Sat noon–1:30pm, daily 7:30–9pm; Sept–Oct Wed–Sat noon–1:30pm; Tues–Sat 7:30–9pm. Closed Nov–Feb.

Le Mas de l'Amarine ★★ PROVENÇAL Set around 4km (3 miles) southeast of St-Rémy's town center, this 18th-century farmhouse was formerly owned by French artist Roger Bezombes. Today it's home to a perfect pairing of art—including an oversized, colorful mosaic by Bezombes—and Provençal cuisine. Chef Bernard Coloma's menu is short and seasonal, highlighting regional produce such as violet artichokes, plump asparagus, and wild sea bream, while local "Garrigue" herbs (thyme, rosemary, mint) are transformed into sublime sorbets. His wife Alice Monnier's eye for contemporary design has furnished the space in stylish 20th-century *objets d'art*, making this a delightful place to while away a sunny afternoon. Note that the fixed-price lunch menu is not available on Sundays. There are also three guestrooms (190€–270€) and two suites (270€–370€) available on the premises.

Ancienne voie Aurélia. www.mas-amarine.com. © **04-90-94-47-82.** Reservations recommended. Main courses 34€–37€; fixed-price lunch 29€–35€. Mid-June–mid-Sept Thurs–Sun noon–2pm, daily 7:30–10pm; mid-Sept–mid-June Wed–Sun noon–2pm and 7:30–10pm. Closed mid-Jan–Feb and 2 weeks in Nov.

Exploring St-Rémy

St-Rémy's pale stone Old Town is utterly charming. Scattered among its pedestrianized streets are 18th-century private mansions, art galleries, medieval church towers, bubbling fountains, and Nostradamus's birth home. Note that St-Rémy's two major sites (below) lie around 1km (0.6 miles) south of the town center.

Saint Paul de Mausole ★ MONASTERY This former monastery and clinic is where Vincent Van Gogh was confined from 1889 to 1890. It's now a psychiatric hospital for women, which specializes in art therapy. You can't see the artist's actual cell, but there is a reconstruction of his room. The Romanesque chapel and cloisters are worth a visit in their own right, as Van Gogh depicted their circular arches and beautifully carved capitals in some of his paintings. A marked path between the town center and the site (east of ave. Vincent Van Gogh) is dotted with 21 reproductions of Van Gogh's paintings from the period he resided here.

Chemin Saint-Paul. www.saintpauldemausole.fr. © **04-90-92-77-00.** Admission 4.65€ adults, 3.30€ students, free for children 12 and under. April–Sept daily 9:30am–6:30pm; mid-Feb–March, Oct–Dec daily 10:15am–4:45pm. Closed Jan–mid-Feb.

Le Site Archéologique de Glanum ★★ RUINS Kids will love a scramble around this bucolically sited Gallo-Roman settlement, which thrived here during the final days of the Roman Empire. Its monuments include a triumphal arch (across the street, and separated from the main ruins) from the time of Julius Caesar, all garlanded with sculptured fruits and flowers. Another interesting feature is the baths, which had separate chambers for hot, warm, and cold. Visitors can see entire streets and foundations of private residences from the 1st-century town, plus the remains of a Gallo-Greek town of the 2nd century B.C.

Route des Baux-de-Provence. http://glanum.monuments-nationaux.fr. © **04-90-92-23-79.** Admission 7.50€ adults, 4.50€ students, free for European nationals 18–25 and children 17 and under. April–Aug daily 10am–6:30pm; Sept Tues–Sun 10am–6:30pm; Oct–March Tues–Sun 10am–5pm.

Shopping

St-Rémy is a decorator's paradise, with many antiques shops and fabric stores on the narrow streets of the Old Town and surrounding boulevards. **Broc de Saint Ouen,** route d'Avignon (𝄯 **04-90-92-28-90**), is a 6,000-sq.-m (64,583-sq.-ft.) space selling everything from architectural salvage to vintage furniture. The town's famous Provençal market is held Wednesday mornings.

Nightlife

Located in a former Art Deco movie theater, **Le Cocktail Bar,** L'Hôtel de l'Image, 36 bd. Victor Hugo (𝄯 **04-90-92-51-50**), is an unusual destination in this laid-back town. In summertime, it is open Tuesday to Saturday until 1am.

LES BAUX ★★★

720km (446 miles) S of Paris; 18km (11 miles) NE of Arles; 85km (53 miles) N of Marseille

Les Baux de Provence's location and geology are extraordinary. Cardinal Richelieu called the massive, 245m-high (804-ft.) rock rising from a desolate plain "a nesting place for eagles." A real eagle's-eye view of the outcropping would be part moonscape, dotted with archeological ruins and a vast plateau, with boxy stone houses stacked like cards on the rock's east side. The combination is so cinematic that it seems like a living, breathing movie set.

Baux, or *baou* in Provençal, means "rocky spur." The power-thirsty lords who ruled the settlement took this as their surname in the 11th century, and by the Middle Ages had control of 79 other regional fiefdoms. After they were overthrown, Les Baux was annexed to France with the rest of Provence, but Louis XI ordered the fortress demolished. The settlement experienced a rebirth during the Renaissance, when structures where restored and lavish residences built, only to fall again in 1642 when, wary of rebellion, Louis XIII ordered his armies to destroy it once and for all. Today the fortress compound is nothing but ruins, but fascinating ones.

Now the bad news: Because of its dramatic beauty, plus a number of quaint shops and restaurants in the village, Les Baux is often overrun with visitors at peak times, so time your visit wisely.

Essentials

ARRIVING   Les Baux is best reached by car. From St-Rémy, take D27 south; from Arles, D17 east. Alternatively, on weekends in June and September, and every day during July and August, **bus** nr. 59 (35 min.; 2.40€ one-way) runs between Arles and St-Rémy, stopping at Les Baux en route. For bus information, see www.lepilote.com or call 𝄯 **08-10-00-13-26.** You can also book 1-day coach tours through **Autocars Lieutaud** (www.excursionprovence.com; 𝄯 **04-90-86-36-75;** from 55€ per person) in Avignon or the tourist office in Aix-en-Provence (www.aixenprovencetourism.com; 𝄯 **04-42-16-11-61;** from 110€ per person).

VISITOR INFORMATION   The **Office de Tourisme** (www.lesbauxdeprovence. com; 𝄯 **04-90-54-34-39**) is at Maison du Roy, near the northern entrance to the old city.

FAST FACTS   Note that you'll need to head to the nearby town of Maussane-les-Alpilles for access to a bank, pharmacy, or post office.

Where to Stay

Le Mas d'Aigret ★   This charming hotel surrounded by olive trees and shady pines is a 5-minute stroll from Les Baux. Guestrooms are simple yet elegant, and almost all of them have their own private terrace or balcony. Two "cave" rooms are built into Les Baux's rock face itself, a neat contrast with the rooms' modern amenities. An outdoor swimming pool and small *pétanque* run are nestled into the hotel's rustic grounds. There's a recommended restaurant on site too. In winter, meals are served in the cavernous dining room with open fireplace; in summertime, the outdoor terrace overlooks Les Baux's valley and Château.

D27A. www.masdaigret.com. ℂ **04-90-54-20-00.** 16 units. 100€–215€ double; 190€–235€ triple; 180€–250€ family room. Breakfast/half-board available. Free parking. **Amenities:** Outdoor pool; restaurant; free Wi-Fi.

Le Prince Noir ★★   Most of the hotels in this area cluster in Les Baux's foothills. Not so Le Prince Noir. This romantic bed and breakfast is tucked into the hilltop town itself—making not only for unbeatable views over the surrounding countryside, but the chance to discover this remarkable town *sans* tourists come sunset. Each one of the three rooms is utterly unique, from La Suite's exposed stone walls, to top-floor Le Bijou, which possesses a vast private terrace and views over Les Baux's Château. Both of the suites offer additional bedding in a second room, making them ideal for families.

Rue de l'Orme. www.leprincenoir.com. ℂ **04-90-54-39-57.** 3 units. 105€ double; 152€–184€ double suite; 25€ per extra person (suites can sleep 4–5). Breakfast included. Parking 5€ (cars must be left outside of the village). **Amenities:** Free Wi-Fi.

Where to Eat

La Cabro d'Or ★★★ PROVENÇAL   Under Chef Michel Hulin, the Cabro d'Or delivers intelligent, innovative Provençal cuisine with a lightness of touch on the most bucolic restaurant terrace in southern France. Diners savor the unctuousness of Mediterranean langoustines, the crispness of roasted red mullet, the froth of fresh pea velouté, and the crunch of slow-cooked suckling pig. More important, the restaurant is part of a truly fabulous trio of luxury hotels surrounding Les Baux. Together they form the most magical resort in all Provence. These include the **Hotel Cabro d'Or** (www.lacabrodor.com; ℂ **04-90-54-33-21;** doubles 200€–460€), which has enchanting grounds, an organic garden, and a vast swimming pool; the **Le Manoir** annex next door, which looks like a rural French movie set; and **Oustau de Baumanière,** at the foot of the village (www.oustaudebaumaniere.com; ℂ **04-90-54-33-07;** doubles 220€–588€), which has hosted the likes of Queen Elizabeth and Johnny Depp and also purveys an even more acclaimed (and more expensive) restaurant than the Cabro d'Or.

In the Hotel Cabro d'Or, Chemin départemental 27. www.lacabrodor.com. ℂ **04-90-54-33-21.** Reservations recommended. Main courses 48€–60€; fixed-price lunch 58€; fixed-price dinner 80€–130€. Daily midday–2pm and 7:30–10pm. Closed winter.

Le Café des Baux ★★ PROVENÇAL   Hidden just off of one of Les Baux's village roads, mere steps from the entrance to the Château, this petite courtyard café feels pleasantly removed from the town's daytime bustle. Seasonal offerings range from braised lamb paired with market-fresh vegetables, to seared scallops drizzled in Les

Baux's local olive oil. Be sure to save room for dessert: award-winning *pâtissier* Pierre Walter makes a mean lavender *crème brûlée*.

Rue du Trencat. www.cafedesbaux.com. ℂ **04-90-54-52-69.** Main courses 22€–28.50€; fixed-price menu 19.50€–35.50€. July–Aug 11:45am–2:30pm and 7–8:30pm; March–June Sept–Nov 11:45am–2:30pm; closed 1 day each week, however the specific day varies from week to week. Closed mid-Nov–mid-March.

Exploring Les Baux

Les Baux's windswept ruins, **Château des Baux ★★★** (www.chateau-baux-provence.com; ℂ **04-90-54-55-56**), cover an area of 7 hectares (17 acres), much larger than the petite hilltop village itself. Consider visiting them early in the morning before the sun gets too strong.

The medieval compound is accessed via the 15th-century **Hôtel de la Tour du Brau.** Beyond this building are replicas of wooden military equipment that would have been used in the 13th century. Built to scale—that is to say, enormous—are a battering ram and various catapults capable of firing huge boulders. From April to August, these are fired every day at 11am and 1:30pm, 3:30pm, and 5:30pm, with an extra show during July and August at 6:30pm. Medieval jousting demonstrations (noon, 2:30pm, and 4:30pm) are held in summer.

Other stopping points include the **Chapel of St-Blaise** (inside which a film of aerial views of Provence is shown), a windmill, the skeleton of a hospital built in the 16th century, and a cemetery. The **Tour Sarrazin,** so named because it was used to spot Saracen invaders coming from the south, yields a sweeping view. Alongside each of the major points of interest, illustrated panels show what the buildings would have originally looked like and explain how the site has evolved architecturally.

Admission to the Château (including audio guide) is 8€ adults, 6€ children 7 to 17 from September to March. The rest of the year, it costs 10€ adults, 8€ children 7 to 17 (daily April–June and Sept 9am–7:15pm; July–Aug 9am–8:15pm; March and Oct 9:30am–6:30pm; Nov–Feb 10am–5pm).

Carrières de Lumières ★★ MUSEUM   A 10-minute stroll downhill from Les Baux, this temporary exhibition space occupies the site of a former limestone quarry. It's here that images of modern artworks (such as audiovisual exhibitions dedicated to Monet, Renoir, Van Gogh, or Gauguin) are projected against the 7m to 9m (23- to 30-ft.) columns. The museum's Cubist-style entrance featured in Jean Cocteau's final film, "The Testament of Orpheus."

Route de Maillane. www.carrieres-lumieres.com. ℂ **04-90-54-47-37.** Admission 10€ adults, 8€ children 7–17, free children 6 and under. Daily April–Sept 9:30am–7pm; Oct–Jan and mid- to late March 10am–6pm. Closed Feb to mid-March.

Yves Brayer Museum ★ ART MUSEUM   Born in Versailles, figurative painter Yves Brayer (1907–90) was enchanted with the landscapes of Provence. This compact museum, located within Les Baux's 16th-century Hôtel de Porcelet, showcases the artist's oils, watercolors, and drawings of everyday life, created during the first half of the 20th century. Each summer, the museum also hosts a small temporary exhibition, such as 2014's animal-themed "La sculpture animalière, de Barye à César."

Intersection of rue de la Calade and rue de l'Église. www.yvesbrayer.com. ℂ **04-90-54-36-99.** Admission 5€ adults, free children 18 and under. Daily April–Sept 10am–12:30pm and 2–6:30pm; Oct–Dec and March Wed–Mon 11am–12:30pm and 2–5pm. Closed Jan–Feb.

Arles

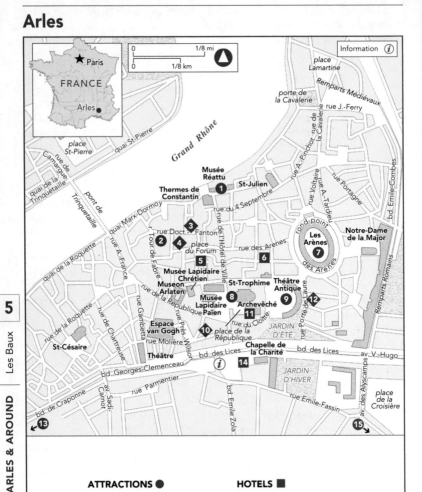

ATTRACTIONS ●

Fondation Vincent
 Van Gogh Arles **2**
Le Cloître et l'Église
 St-Trophime **8**
Les Alyscamps **15**
Les Arènes **7**
Musée Départemental
 Arles Antiques **13**
Musée Réattu **1**
Théâtre Antique **9**

HOTELS ■

Grand Hotel Nord Pinus **5**
Hotel de l'Amphitheatre **6**
Hôtel Jules César **14**
Le Cloitre **11**

RESTAURANTS ◆

Cuisine de Comptoir **4**
L'Atelier de
 Jean-Luc Rabanel **10**
Le Criquet **12**
Le Galoubet **3**

ARLES ★★

744km (461 miles) S of Paris; 36km (22 miles) SW of Avignon; 92km (57 miles) NW of Marseille

On the banks of the Rhône River, Arles (pop. 53,000) attracts art lovers, archaeologists, and historians. To the delight of visitors, many of the vistas van Gogh painted remain luminously present today. Here the artist was even inspired to paint his own bedroom ("Bedroom in Arles," 1888).

Julius Caesar established a Roman colony here in the 1st century. Constantine the Great named Arles the second capital of his empire in A.D. 306, when it was known as "the little Rome of the Gauls." The city was incorporated into France in 1481.

Arles's ancient streets are not as pristinely preserved as, say, Avignon's, but are stunningly raw instead, with excellent restaurants and summer festivals to boot. Its position on the river makes it a gateway to the Camargue, giving the town a healthy dose of Spanish and gypsy influence.

Essentials

ARRIVING   **Trains** run almost every hour between Arles and Avignon (trip time: 20 min.; 7.50€ one-way) and Marseille (trip time: 1 hr.; 15.30€). Be sure to take local trains from city center to city center, not the TGV, which, in this case, takes more time. If **driving,** head south along D570N from Avignon.

VISITOR INFORMATION   The **Office de Tourisme** is on bd. des Lices (www.arlestourisme.com; ✆ 04-90-18-41-20).

SPECIAL EVENTS   **Les Rencontres d'Arles** (www.rencontres-arles.com; ✆ 04-90-96-76-06), held from early July until late September, focuses on contemporary international photography. Tickets range from free to 8€ per exhibition, although passes are also available for 28€ to 48€. The ticket office is located in place de la République for the duration of the festival.

[FastFACTS] ARLES

ATMs/Banks   There are more than a dozen banks in downtown Arles, including three in place de la République.

Internet Access   **CyberSaladelle Informatique Arles,** 17 rue de la République (www.cybersaladelle.fr; ✆ 04-90-93-13-56).

Mail & Postage   **La Poste,** 5 bd. des Lices (✆ 36-31).

Pharmacies   **Pharmacie des Arènes,** 17 rue du 4 Septembre (✆ 04-90-96-02-77).

Where to Stay

Le Cloitre ★★   Perfectly positioned in Arles' Old Town, midway between Les Arènes and place de la République, Le Cloitre is a unique medley of ancient stone features and funky 1950s furnishings. Each room is individually decorated in bright tones, with wooden ceiling beams, mosaic floors, and designer knickknacks. Free bikes are available for guest use. Organic breakfast is served up on the rooftop terrace.

18 rue du Cloître. www.hotel-cloitre.com. ✆ 04-88-09-10-00. 19 units. 90€–180€ double. Parking 10€. **Amenities:** Bar; free Wi-Fi.

Hôtel de l'Amphitheatre ★★   This delightful hotel is a firm favorite with regular visitors to Arles. Tucked into the heart of the Old Town, the building itself was originally constructed in the 17th century and retains its historical atmosphere. Guest rooms feature reproduction Provençal furniture and some—including the plush Belvedere Suite—offer views over the terra-cotta roofs of historic Arles.

5–7 rue Diderot. www.hotelamphitheatre.fr. ☎ **04-90-96-10-30.** 33 units. 69€–119€ double; 109€–129€ triple; 129€–139€ quadruple; 129€–139€ suite. Parking 8€. **Amenities:** Free Wi-Fi.

Hôtel Jules César ★★   The colonnaded Hôtel Jules César has long been one of Arles' landmark hotels, with prestigious guest book that includes Pablo Picasso. Last year the former 17th-century convent was entirely renovated, a project undertaken in collaboration with born and bred local designer Christian Lacroix. Reopening its sleek new doors in June 2014, the hotel's rooms and suites have been thoroughly refreshed, with Lacroix focusing on rustic décor inspired by the nearby Camargue region. The top-notch Lou Marquès restaurant, serving classic Provençal cuisine, is also on site. The hotel's location, opposite the Old Town and next door to the tourist office, is ideal for easy access to Arles' major sights.

9 boulevard des Lices. www.hotel-julescesar.fr. ☎ **04-90-52-52-52.** 53 units. 128€–286€ double; 249€–346€ family room; 249€–434€ suite. Parking 10€. **Amenities:** Outdoor pool; restaurant; free Wi-Fi.

Where to Eat

L'Atelier Jean-Luc Rabanel ★★★ MODERN PROVENÇAL   Put simply, this is the finest restaurant that one of the authors of this book has ever had the pleasure of experiencing. And that's saying something. Double-Michelin-starred chef Jean-Luc Rabanel pairs organic ingredients from his own garden with locally reared bull, pork, and game (and even herbs, mushrooms, and flowers). Delivery combines the deftness of touch of a Japanese samurai (an Asian influence pervades Rabanel's set menus) with the creative vision of a Parisian fashion designer. A wine-accompaniment option offers a unique and passionate oenophile's tour of France. The chef also purveys two adjoining restaurants. The **Bistro Acote** (www.bistro-acote.com; ☎ **04-90-47-61-13**) is softer on the wallet and serves Provençal classics on a 29€ set menu; and **Iode** (www.iode-rabanel.com; ☎ **04-90-91-07-69**) specializes in "hyper-fresh" crustaceans and shellfish. Wow.

In 2014, Rabanel also launched his "Suites Confidentielles," luxury accommodation (designed by the chef) reserved for guests dining at one of his restaurants. Prices range from 250€ to 295€, with special packages comprising breakfast, dinner and/or lunch also available.

7 rue des Carmes. www.rabanel.com ☎ **04-90-91-07-69.** Reservations recommended. Fixed-price lunch 65€–185€; fixed-price dinner 125€–185€. Wed–Sun noon–1:30pm and 8pm–9pm.

Le Criquet ★ PROVENÇAL   Tiny, charming, and worth reserving well in advance, Le Criquet is a classic local restaurant on the back streets of Arles. Friendly service meets unpretentious dishes like *bourride* of salt cod and spices, bowls of local mussels, and stew made from local Camargue bull. Sit outside amid a romantic street setting or in the rather cramped—but undeniably cozy—interior.

21 rue Porte de Laure. ☎ **04-90-96-80-51.** Reservations recommended. Main courses 11€–19€. Tues–Sun noon–1:30pm and 7pm–9pm.

Cuisine de Comptoir ★ FRENCH   This superb little lunch spot is tucked just off place du Forum in an ancient *boulangerie*. Each day, owners Alexandre and Vincent dish up a dozen different *tartines*, or open-faced sandwiches, created using toasted Poilâne bread. Both smoked duck's breast with Cantal cheese and the *brandade* (creamy cod and potato) *tartines* are highly recommended. The laid-back venue hosts a rotating selection of contemporary art.

10 rue de la Liberté. www.cuisinedecomptoir.com ℂ **04-90-96-86-28.** Main courses 11.50€– 13.50€. Mon–Sat 8:30am–2pm and 7pm–9pm.

Le Galoubet ★★ FRENCH/MEDITERRANEAN   Occupying the ground floor of an elegant 18th-century building just off of Arles' place du Forum, this lovely little enclave boasts everything you might be seeking in an ideal Provençal bistro. Friendly owners? Tick. Céline Arribart cooks, while her husband Franck manages the front of house. Atmospheric dining room, leafy outdoor terrace? Tick. Tasty menu? Reasonable prices? Tick and tick. Chef Céline's seasonal three-course set menu (no à la carte here) offers a handful of choices for each course. Depending on the season, it may include octopus, celery, and basil salad; cod atop roasted eggplant, peppers, and black olives; or fat asparagus with poached egg and crispy fried *jambon*. Be sure to reserve far in advance.

18 rue du Docteur Fanton. ℂ **04-90-93-18-11.** Reservations recommended. Fixed-price menu 29€. Tues–Sat 12:30–2pm and 7pm–9:30pm.

Exploring Arles

The **Place du Forum,** shaded by plane trees, stands around the old Roman forum. The Terrasse du Café le Soir, immortalized by Van Gogh, is now the square's Café Van Gogh. Visitors keen to follow in the footsteps of the great artist may pick up a **Van Gogh walking map** (1€, in English), which takes in 10 important sites around the city, from the tourist office. (Alternatively, you can download it for free from the tourist board's website—however this version is only available in French.) On a corner of place du Forum sits the legendary **Grand Hôtel Nord-Pinus** (www.nord-pinus.com): Bullfighters, artists, and A-listers have all stayed here. Three blocks south, the **Place de la République** is dominated by a 15m-tall (49-ft.) red granite obelisk.

Les Taureaux

Bulls are a big part of Arlesien culture. It's not unusual to see bull steak on local menus, and *saucisson de taureau* (bull sausage) is a local specialty. The first bullfight, or *corrida*, took place in the amphitheater in 1853. Appropriately, Arles is home to a bullfighting school (the **Ecole Taurine d'Arles**). Like it or loathe it, *corridas* are still held during the Easter Feria and in September, during the Feria du Riz. The bull is killed only during the Easter *corrida;* expect a few protestors. The Easter event begins at 11:30am or 5:30pm, the September events around 6pm. A seat on the stone benches of the amphitheater costs 18.50€ to 97€. Tickets are usually available a few hours beforehand at the ticket office on **Les Arenes d'Arles** (1 rond-point des Arènes). For information or advance tickets, go to www.arenes-arles.com or contact ℂ **08-91-70-03-70.**

One of the city's great classical monuments is the Roman **Théâtre Antique** ★, rue du Cloître (✆ **04-90-49-59-05**). Augustus began the theater in the 1st century; only two Corinthian columns remain. The "Venus of Arles" (now in the Louvre in Paris) was discovered here in 1651. The theater is open May through September daily 9am to 7pm; March, April, and October daily 9am to 6pm; and November through February daily 10am to 5pm. Admission is 6.50€ adults, 5€ students, and free children 17 and under. The same ticket admits you to the nearby **Amphitheater (Les Arènes)** ★★, rond-pont des Arènes (✆ **04-90-49-59-05;** same opening hours), also built in the 1st century. Sometimes called Le Cirque Romain, it seats almost 25,000. For a good view, climb the three towers that remain from medieval times, when the amphitheater was turned into a fortress.

Les Alyscamps ★ RUINS   Perhaps the most memorable sight in Arles, this once–Roman necropolis became a Christian burial ground in the 4th century. Mentioned in Dante's "Inferno," it has been painted by both Van Gogh and Gauguin. Today it is lined with poplars and studded with ancient sarcophagi. Arlesiens escape here with a cold drink to enjoy a respite from the summer heat.

Avenue des Alyscamps. ✆ 04-90-49-59-05. Admission 3.50€ adults, 2.60€ students, free children 17 and under. May–Sept daily 9am–7pm; March, April, and Oct daily 9am–noon and 2–6pm; Nov–Feb daily 10am–noon and 2–5pm.

Le Cloître et l'Église St-Trophime ★ CHURCH   This church is noted for its 12th-century portal, one of the finest achievements of the southern Romanesque style. Frederick Barbarossa was crowned king of Arles here in 1178. In the pediment, Christ is surrounded by the symbols of the Evangelists. The pretty cloister, in Gothic and Romanesque styles, possesses noteworthy medieval carvings: During July's Les Rencontres d'Arles festival, contemporary photographs are also exhibited here.

East side of place de la République. ✆ 04-90-49-59-05. Free admission to church; cloister 3.50€ adults, 2.60€ students, free for children 17 and under. Church daily 10am–noon and 2–5pm; cloister May–Sept daily 9am–7pm; March, April, and Oct daily 9am–6pm; Nov–Feb daily 10am–5pm.

Fondation Vincent Van Gogh Arles ★★ EXHIBITION SPACE   This much-anticipated permanent home for the Van Gogh Foundation (founded more than three decades ago) opened at long last in April 2014 in the 15th-century private mansion Hôtel Léautaud de Donines. Highlighting the connection between Arles and Van Gogh, it stages a variety of temporary exhibitions, seminars, and interactive debates. The Foundation's inaugural exhibition was entitled "Van Gogh Live!" It was comprised of various contemporary installations created as a tribute to the great artist, as well as a dozen original Van Gogh artworks. Check the website for the current program.

35 ter rue du Docteur Fanton. www.fondation-vincentvangogh-arles.org. ✆ **04-90-93-08-08.** Admission 9€ adults, 7€ seniors, 4€ students and children 12–18, free children 11 and under. Admission may vary depending on temporary exhibition. Daily 11am–7pm, Thurs open until 9pm. Closed 3 weeks in Sept.

Musée Départemental Arles Antiques ★★ MUSEUM   Set within a sleek compound around 1km (½ mile) south of Arles' town center, this archaeological museum hosts finds uncovered throughout the region's rich territories. Vast, airy rooms present Roman sarcophagi, sculptures, mosaics, and inscriptions from ancient times through the 6th century A.D. Temporary exhibitions, such as 2014's show dedicated to the River Rhône, highlight the inspiration the local landscape has had on the city through the ages. In late 2013, the museum opened a brand-new wing to showcase the 31-m (102-ft.) flat-bottomed Roman barge *(chaland)* that was unearthed from the Rhône River in 2010.

Avenue 1ere Division France Libre, presqu'île du Cirque Romain. www.arles-antique.cg13.fr. *C* **04-13-31-51-03.** Admission 8€ adults, 5€, free children 17 and under. Wed–Mon 10am–6pm.

Musée Réattu ★★ ART MUSEUM   Exhibited over the labyrinthine rooms of the 15th-century Grand Priory of the Order of Malta, this museum was opened in 1868 to showcase artworks previously owned by local painter Jacques Réattu. Over the past 150 years, the collection has swollen with donations and annual acquisitions, including dozens of Picasso drawings and close to 4,000 photographs. The building's former archives room is now dedicated to the history of the Order of the Knights Hospitaller. The museum also stages some three temporary exhibitions each year.

10 rue du Grand-Prieuré. www.museereattu.arles.fr. *C* **04-90-49-37-58.** Admission 7€ adults, 5€ students, free children 17 and under. Tues–Sun March–Oct 10am–6pm, Nov–Feb 10am–5pm.

Outlying Attractions

See also Musée de la Camargue, p. 74.

Abbaye de Montmajour ★★ MONASTERY   This medieval monastery, founded in the leafy countryside 6km (3½ miles) northeast of Arles during the 10th century, is now an innovative exhibition venue. Temporary shows, ranging from a recent by Christian Lacroix installation to annual photographic displays as part of Les Rencontres d'Arles, are dotted throughout the atmospheric ruins. A wonderful outdoor restaurant is tucked under the trees at the back of the parking lot opposite.

Route de Fontvieille. http://montmajour.monuments-nationaux.fr. *C* **04-90-54-64-17.** Admission 7.50€ adults, 4.50€ students, free children 17 and under. July–Sept daily 10am–6:30pm; April–June daily 9:30am–6pm; Oct–March Tues–Sun 10am–5pm.

Pont Van Gogh ★ BRIDGE   Officially known as the "Pont de Réginel", for years this 19th-century drawbridge was referred to locally as "Pont de Langlois", taking its name from the operator rose and lowered it daily. The bridge achieved eventual

Mistral, Two Ways

Born just north of Arles, Frédéric Mistral (1830–1914) dedicated his life to defending and preserving the original Provençal language known as Occitan. The poet won the Nobel Prize for his epic work "Mirèio" and his overall contributions to French literature. Mistral joined six other Provençal writers in 1854 to found Félibrige, an association for the promotion of Occitan language and literature. He is the author of "Lo Tresor dóu Félibrige," the most comprehensive dictionary of the Occitan language to this day.

Many think Mistral lent his name to the notorious glacial wind that roars through Provence every year. However, in this case, mistral is the Occitan word for "master"—and those who experience the phenomenon regularly say it's a cruel one. Tearing through the Rhône River Valley toward the Mediterranean, the mistral reaches speeds of 100km (62 miles) per hour and can blow up to 100 days per year. Most of these occur in winter, but it is also common in the spring and, in unlucky years, can persist until early summer.

international fame—and its current moniker—when it was depicted by Van Gogh in four of his oil paintings in 1888. Although the bridge itself is fun to see, it isn't much to write home about. But the 2.7-km (1 and 1/2-mile) walk along sleepy Canal d'Arles à Bouchere, trimmed by weeping willows and houseboats, more than makes up for it. The route is signposted from the center of town; alternatively the tourist office can direct you.

Pont de Langlois.

Nightlife

Because of its relatively small population, Arles doesn't offer as many nightlife options as Aix-en-Provence, Avignon, or Marseille. The town's most appealing spot is the organic wine bar–café **L'Ouvre-Boîte,** 22 rue du Cloître (no phone). Open June to September only, it's set under a majestic canopy of trees in one of the Old Town's loveliest squares. **Le Patio de Camargue,** 49 chemin de Barriol (www.patiodecamargue.com; ✆ **04-90-49-51-76**), is a deservedly popular place south of town, spilling over the banks of the Rhône. The venue stages live folk music most nights. It's owned by Chico Bouchikhi, one of the co-founders of the folk band Gipsy Kings.

DAY TRIP FROM ARLES

Nîmes ★★

33km (21 miles) NW of Arles

Get ready to be swept back in time to Imperial Rome. Two thousand years ago, Nîmes was an important stop on Roman trading road Via Domitia—and it shows. The **Pont du Gard** aqueduct underscored the city's prestige, providing it with fresh water from the Eure springs. Today Nîmes is still an attractive urban center, dotted with parks and ancient Roman architecture. It is particularly vibrant in late spring and summer, when the Arènes (Roman amphitheater) hosts a crowded calendar of festivals and concerts.

ESSENTIALS

Frequent **trains** (trip time: 30 min.; 8.60€ one-way) and **buses** (www.edgard-transport. fr ✆ **04-32-76-00-40;** trip time: 1 hr.; 1.50€ one-way) connect Arles and Nîmes. If you're **driving** from Arles, take E80 northwest to Nîmes. The **Office de Tourisme** is at 6 rue Auguste (www.ot-nimes.fr; ✆ **04-66-58-38-00**).

EXPLORING NÎMES

Nîmes' star attraction is **Les Arènes,** boulevard des Arènes (www.arenes-nimes.com; ✆ **04-66-21-82-56**), an immaculately conserved Roman amphitheater constructed

NÎMES' most famous EXPORT

For many, jeans are the epitome of American fashion. But did you ever wonder where they originally came from? Would you have guessed Nîmes? Nope, us either. But "serge de Nîmes" cloth—aka denim—was created in Nîmes in the 17th century. Stitched up into jeans in Genoa, Italy ("Gênes" in French), these sturdy trousers began being exported to the U.S. in the late 19th century, where denim jeans became an immediate hit.

during the first century A.D. A perfect oval, the complex is composed of two rings of 60 arches, measuring 21 towering meters (69 ft.). A detailed audio guide (included in admission fee) recounts the battles between man and beast (panthers, rhinos, bears) that took place here in ancient times.

After a tour around the amphitheater, pop into the **Quartier des Gladiateurs**. This mock-up of a gladiator's changing room is now a mini-museum showcasing armor and ancient battle gear. Next door, the **Couleurs des Corridas** room is dedicated to *corridas*, with matador costumes, vintage posters, and films of popular bullfights held in the Arènes.

For more detailed information, smartphone and tablet users can download the **Arènes app.** It's chock-full of reconstructions and images showing the amphitheater in all its glory from Roman times until the present day. Alternatively you can hire pre-loaded tablets on site (5€).

Throughout the summertime, big-name international bands play **concerts** in the Arènes. In late spring the annual **Roman Games** and **Feria de Nîmes**' *corridas* draw crowds; and in the fall, the **Harvest Feria** is held here. During these special events, standard visits to the amphitheater are normally suspended. See the Arènes and tourist office websites for details.

The Arènes is open daily July and August 9am to 8pm; June 9am to 7pm; April, May, and September 9am to 6:30pm; March and October 9am to 6pm; and November to February 9:30am to 5pm. Admission (including audioguide) is 9€ for adults, 7€ for children aged 7 to 17, and free for children 6 and under.

A short stroll away sits Nîmes's **Maison Carrée,** place de la Maison Carrée (www. arenes-nimes.com; ✆ **04-66-21-82-56**), a 1st-century A.D. temple and the only one of its kind in the world to be preserved in its entirety. As of 2014, the new film, "Nemausus, the birth of Nîmes" is screened indoors every 30 minutes, portraying the Roman founding of the city.

The Maison Carrée is open daily July and August 9am to 8pm (Thursdays until 9pm); June 10am to 7pm; April, May, and September 10am to 6:30pm; March and October 10am to 6pm (closed from 1pm to 2pm in October); and November to February 10am to 1pm and 2pm to 4:30pm. Admission (including 3-D film) is 5.50€ for adults, 4.50€ for children aged 7 to 17, and free for children 6 and under.

If you're planning to visit both the Arènes and the Maison Carrée, it's worth purchasing a **Nîmes Romaine Pass.** This combination ticket (11.50€ for adults, 9€ for children aged 7 to 17, and free for children 6 and under) allows entrance to both sights, as well as the **Tour Magne,** a 3rd-century B.C. tower that is part of the city's original fortifications.

WHERE TO EAT

Marry history with a heady dose of the contemporary. **Le Ciel de Nîmes,** place de la Maison Carrée (www.lecieldenimes.fr; ✆ **04-66-36-71-70**), is perched atop the sleek cube of contemporary art that is the Norman Foster-designed Musée le Carré d'Art. This Mediterranean restaurant dishes up duck breast with figs and candied orange, or creamy cod *brandade*, along with unbeatable views over the city skyline and the Maison Carrée opposite.

THE CAMARGUE ★★

691km (428 miles) S of Paris; 83km (51 miles) NW of Aix-en-Provence; 98km (61 miles) NW of Marseille

A marshy delta south of Arles, the Camargue is located between the Mediterranean and two arms of the Rhône. The most fragile ecosystem in France, it has been a nature reserve since 1970, with some areas accessible only to the *gardians*, the local cowboys. Their ancestors may have been the first American cowboys, who sailed on French ships to the port of New Orleans, where they rode through the bayous of Louisiana and east Texas, rounding up cattle—in French, no less.

The Camargue is also cattle country. Black bulls are bred here both for their meat and for the regional bullfighting arenas. The whitewashed houses, plaited-straw roofs, plains, sandbars, and pink flamingos in the marshes make this area different, even exotic. There's no more evocative sight than the snow-white horses galloping through the marshlands, with hoofs so tough that they don't need shoes. The breed was brought here by the Arabs long ago, and it is said that their long manes and bushy tails evolved over the centuries to slap the region's omnipresent mosquitoes.

Exotic flora and fauna abound. The birdlife here is among the most luxuriant in Europe, as so many species stop off here on their seasonal migratory routes. Looking much like the Florida Everglades, the area is known for its colonies of pink flamingos *(flamants roses)*, which share living quarters with some 400 other types of birds, including ibises, egrets, kingfishers, owls, wild ducks, swans, and ferocious birds of prey.

Essentials

ARRIVING   Few trains serve the Camargue. You can travel from Arles to Aigues-Mortes (trip time: around 2 hours, 15 min.; 17.20€ one-way), but you'll have to change in Nîmes. For rail information, visit www.voyages-sncf.com or call ✆ **36-35**. Regional **buses** go from Arles to Stes-Maries-de-la-Mer (www.lepilote.com; ✆ **08-10-00-13-26;** trip time: 45 min.; 2.90€ one-way), stopping at Musée de la Camargue and Pont de Gau Parc Ornithologique en route. Buses run from Nîmes to Aigues-Mortes (www.edgard-transport.fr; ✆ **08-10-33-42-73;** trip time: 40 min.; 1.50€ one-way), then on to Le Grau-du-Roi (trip time: 15 min.; 1.50€ one-way. If you're **driving** from Arles, take D570 southwest to Stes-Maries-de-la-Mer. To Aigues-Mortes, take the same route, veering westwards onto D58.

VISITOR INFORMATION   The **Ste-Maries-de-la-Mer Office de Tourisme** is at 5 av. Van Gogh (www.saintesmaries.com; ✆ **04-90-97-82-55**). The **Aigues-Mortes Office de Tourisme** is at place Saint-Louis (www.ot-aiguesmortes.fr; ✆ **04-66-53-73-00**). The **Parc de Camargue Office de Tourisme** is at Mas du Pont de Rousty, just outside of Arles (www.parc-camargue.fr; ✆ **04-90-97-10-82**).

SPECIAL EVENTS   Each year on May 24 and 25, Romany gypsies from around the world descend en mass upon Stes-Maries-de-la-Mer for the **Pélerinage des Gitans,** a celebration of the feast day of Saint Sara. Festivities include parading a statue of Sara from Stes-Maries-de-la-Mer's church crypt to the sea, as well as plenty of singing and wild dancing.

Getting Around

BY BICYCLE & MOTOR SCOOTER   **Le Vélo Saintois**, 19 avenue de la République, Stes-Maries-de-la-Mer (www.levelosaintois.camargue.fr; ✆ **04-90-97-74-56**), rents bicycles from 15€ per day. They can also advise on regional circuits for varying level of difficulty.

BY BOAT   During July and August, a **riverboat** (www.croisieres-camargue.com) connects Aigues-Mortes and Le Grau-du-Roi. The journey takes around half an hour, and costs 4.50€ per adult, 2.50€ per child one-way.

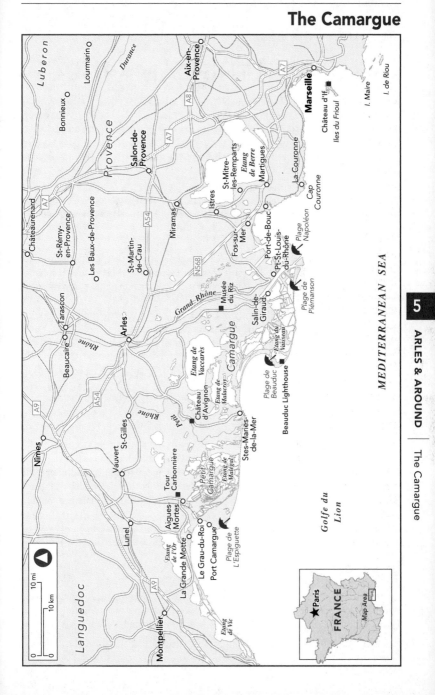

BY CAR   Public transport in this region is patchy at best. If you're keen to get out the Camargue's main towns (and are not up for pedaling), having your own set of wheels will definitely be handy.

[FastFACTS] THE CAMARGUE

ATMs/Banks   Société Marseillaise de Crédit, 3 avenue de la Plage, Stes-Maries-de-la-Mer (*C* **04-90-97-86-09**); **BNP Paribas**, 1 boulevard Diderot, Aigues-Mortes (*C* **08-20-82-00-01**); **Société Générale**, 7 place de la République, Le Grau-du-Roi (*C* **04-66-51-47-06**).

Mail & Postage   La Poste, 2 avenue Léon Gambetta, Stes-Maries-de-la-Mer (*C* **36-31**); **La Poste,** place Viguerie, Aigues-Mortes (*C* **36-31**); **La Poste,** 2 place de la Libération, Le Grau-du-Roi (*C* **36-31**).

Pharmacies   Pharmacie Cambon, 18 rue Victor Hugo, Stes-Maries-de-la-Mer (*C* **04-90-97-83-02**); **Pharmacie du Soleil**, 15 avenue de la Liberté, Aigues-Mortes ([tel] **04-66-53-61-30**); **Pharmaice du Centre**, 7 rue Michel Rédarès, Le Grau-du-Roi (*C* **04-66-51-40-34**).

Where to Stay

Mas de la Fouque ★   This recently renovated *mas*, or Provençal farmhouse, sits on the edge of the Camargue National Nature Reserve. Guestrooms take inspiration from the hotel's unique location, with trendy (faux) mounted animal heads offsetting the décor's natural wood furnishings and white linens. Outdoor spaces almost seem to seep into the surrounding landscape. For a little romance or some serious bird-spotting, there's even a brightly painted gypsy caravan perched on the edge of a pond on the grounds. Mas de la Fouque can also organize guided tours through the Camargue by bicycle or 4x4 Jeep.

Route du Petit Rhone, Stes-Maries-de-la-Mer. www.masdelafouque.com. *C* **04-90-97-81-02.** 26 units. 245€–420€ double; 285€–380€ gypsy caravan; 365€–620€ suite. July–Aug minimum 2-night stay. Half-board rates available. Free parking. **Amenities:** Bar; bicycles; indoor and outdoor pools; restaurant; spa; tennis courts; free Wi-Fi.

Villa Mazarin ★★   Tucked into one of Aigues-Mortes' residential back streets, this medieval hotel was constructed—like many of the town's pale stone edifices—during the 15th century. Tasteful guestrooms are draped with antique-style Provençal textiles, and bathrooms are stocked with luxurious Clarins toiletries. Literally a little oasis, Villa Mazarin's charming courtyard garden is dotted with fountains, and there's an elegant restaurant onsite. A perfect foil to the Camargue's untamed outdoor pleasures.

35 boulevard Gambetta, Aigues-Mortes. www.villamazarin.com. *C* **04-66-73-90-48.** 16 units. 120€–400€ double. Parking 15€. **Amenities:** Bar; outdoor (covered) pool; restaurant; spa; free Wi-Fi.

Where to Eat

Le Particulier ★★ MEDITERRANEAN/FUSION   Wooing local palates since it opened in 2013, Le Particular is tucked into the very heart of Aigues-Mortes' old town. Here accomplished chef Alexandre Fender dishes up a menu that is truly pan-Mediterranean. Try prawn-spiked *taboulet* (couscous) to roasted eggplant salad. Maître d' Mayla, Alexandre's wife, welcomes both local patrons (often stopping in for one of the three different fixed-price lunch menus) and visitors with a smile.

LANGUE D'OC—THE LANGUAGE OF poetry

Occitan, or *Oc*, was spoken all over *Occitania* (an area covering Monaco and southern France as far as the Dordogne, northern Italy and Spain). Having evolved from Vulgar Latin, the language became established through the success of 12th-century poets—the troubadours. Masters in the art of courtly love, these knights wooed virtuous women with songs written in Occitan that spoke of their patient devotion. Famous troubadours in Provence included Folquet de Marseille, Raimbaut d'Orange, Comtesse de Die and Raimbaut de Vaqueiras. After the 1539 Edict of Villers-Cotterêts ruled that Parisian French should be the language of all France, Occitan waned. However, it was kept alive through the centuries by writers and poets such as the Grassoise poet Louis Bellaud, and Frédéric Mistral, who wrote the 19th-century French/Occitan dictionary *Lou Tresor dóu Felibrige*.

Since 2005, interest in this long-forgotten language has been revived through demonstrations against the illegal status of Occitan within France in Carcassonne, Montpellier and Béziers, as well as the annual *Estivada* festival in Rodez, celebrating Occitan language and culture.

You're most likely to see Provençal on restaurant signs: look out for *Lou* (the) before the restaurant name. See if you can spot any of the following on your travels: *Lou Pèbre d'Aï* (savoury), *Lou Fassum* (a cabbage-based recipe), *Lou Pitchoun* ('little one') or *Lou Pistou* (a garlic, basil and tomato-based sauce). You may even come across *Lou Cigalon*—an ironic reference to the 1935 film by Marcel Pagnol about a restaurant owner who is an excellent chef but refuses to serve his customers until his former employee opens another restaurant nearby.

Some Occitan words are very similar to their English counterparts or easily recognizable to Anglophones:

Animal	*Animal*
Apology	*Excusa*
Castle	*Castèl*
Colour	*Color*
Intelligent	*Intelligent*
Gift	*Present*
Question	*Question*
Rare	*Rare*
Village	*Vilatge*
Waterfall	*Cascade*

5 rue Sadi Carnot, Aigues-Mortes. www.leparticulier30.fr. ☎ **04-66-73-37-29.** Reservations recommended. Fixed-price lunch 16€–25€; fixed-price dinner 30€–45€. Thurs–Tues noon–2pm and Mon–Sat 7:30–9pm.

La Siesta ★★ PROVENÇAL   For contemporary Camarguois cuisine, head to this playful brasserie. Regional specialties, such as *tellines à la crème d'ail* (local clams in a creamy garlic sauce) and *gardianne de taureau* (bull's meat stewed in wine), are served against a sleek gray and white backdrop. La Siesta's drinks menu is particularly vast: Particularly tasty are their fruity cocktails and smoothies, available throughout the day, along with a whimsical selection of ice cream creations. In season, there's live music (from flamenco to jazz) every evening from 7pm.

10 avenue Van Gogh, Stes-Maries-de-la-Mer. www.brasserie-lasiesta-13.com. ☎ **04-90-97-83-34.** Main courses 10.95€–21.90€; fixed-price lunch 13€; fixed-price dinner 15.90€–35€. Mon–Sat noon–11pm.

Exploring The Camargue

The 13,000-hectare Camargue National Nature Reserve (www.reserve-camargue.org) sprawls its way across the wetlands to the east of the towns and points of interest listed below. As well as these sights we recommend either joining an organized tour (see p. 75) or—whether by bike, scooter, boat, or car—setting out to explore under your own steam.

AIGUES-MORTES

This fairy-tale town is ringed by perfectly preserved **medieval ramparts** (www.aigues-mortes.monuments-nationaux.fr; © **04-66-53-61-55**), constructed during the 13th and 14th centuries. Stroll along them for gorgeous panoramas over Aigues-Mortes' labyrinth of cobblestoned streets, flower-strewn terraces, sidewalk cafés, and the salt marshes beyond. The ramparts are open between May and August from 10am to 7pm, and between September and April from 10am to 5:30pm (although the ticket office closes from 1pm to 2pm). Admission is 7.50€ for adults, 4.50€ for non-EU visitors between 18 and 25 years old, and free for EU visitors between 18 and 25 years old, as well as children 17 and under.

For a close-up peek at the region's pink-tinged salt marshes, head to **Le Salin d'Aigues-Mortes**, route du Grau-du-Roi (www.visitesalinsdecamargue.com; © **04-66-73-40-24**). *Petit-train* **tours** (90 min.) chug their way around the marshes and salt works, running up to 16 times a day between April and November. The fee is 9€ for adults, 7€ for children between 5 and 13, and free for children 4 and under. Family tickets (two adults and two children) cost 27€. Alternatively, more personalized **4x4 tours** (90 minutes to 3 hours, 30 minutes; maximum 8 participants; fee from 20€ to 38€ for adults, 10€ to 16€ for children aged 5 to 13) are also available. All tours include a visit to Le Salin's **Musée du Sel**.

LE GRAU-DU-ROI

This seaside resort is deservedly popular with French tourists. Light on sights (with the exception of Le Seaquarium, see p. 76), Le Grau-du-Roi is plenty of fun in a kitschy kind of way: Think alfresco restaurants, boisterous bars, and a scattering of shops selling inflatable toys. More importantly, the town is the gateway to miles and miles of sandy dunes. After an ice cream and a stroll around Le Grau-du-Roi's quays, make like the locals and head to the beach. The wild Plage de l'Espiguette, unfurling south of town, is a windswept favorite.

STES-MARIES-DE-LA-MER

Saintes-Maries-de-la-Mer ("Saint Marys of the Sea") takes its unusual name from Sainte Marie-Jacobé and Sainte Marie-Salomé, who reputedly washed up on these Mediterranean shores along with Sainte Sara during the first century AD. The town's central church, **Sanctuaire Notre Dame de la Mer**, 19 place Jean XXIII (© **04-90-97-80-25**), houses a statue and relics of Sainte Sara—patron saint of the Romany population—in its crypt.

Musée de la Camargue ★ MUSEUM   After more than a year of renovations, the regional Musée de la Camargue reopened in late 2013. It makes for a fine introduction to the Camargue, aiming to acquaint visitors with its history, evolution, and topography, as well as the activities typical of those people who reside here. Evocative photographs trace the history of the Camargue over the past two centuries. The museum is also home to the 3.5-km 2-mile) Sentier du Mas du Pont de Rousty, a walking trail through the Rhône delta, past traditional homes, bulls, and wild birds. *Horizons,* artist Tadashi Kawamata's ship-shaped observation deck, was installed in 2013 and now sits at the start of the trail. Although the museum is located a little closer to Arles (10km, or 6.4 miles southwest of the city), as compared to Stes-Maries-de-la-Mer (26km, 16 miles northeast of this seaside town), it's more relevant to visitors exploring the Camargue area.

RD 570, Mas du Pont de Rousty. www.parc-camargue.fr. © **04-90-97-10-82.** Admission 5€ adults, 3€ students and seniors, free children 17 and under. Wed–Mon April–Oct 9am–12:30pm and 1–6pm; Nov–March 10am–12:30pm and 1–5pm.

Parc Ornithologique de Pont de Gau ★★ BIRD RESERVE   This 60-hectare ornithological park—a mix of ponds, salt marshes, and meadows, crisscrossed by 7km (4.6 miles) of paths—is the region's best place to see flamingo colonies. Elevated viewing platforms are ideal for spotting the dozens of other species of birds that make this protected area their home too, including herons, egrets, ibises, and storks. The park is located 4km (3 miles) north of Stes-Maries-de-la-Mer.

Route d'Arles. www.parcornithologique.com. © **04-90-97-82-62.** Admission 7.50€ adults, 5€ children aged 4–12, free children 3 and under. Daily April–Sept 9am–sunset; Oct–March 10am–sunset.

Organized Tours

You can explore the Camargue's rugged terrain by boat, bike, jeep, or **horse.** The latter can take you into the interior, fording waters to places where black bulls graze and wild birds nest. Dozens of stables are located along the highway between Arles to Stes-Maries-de-la-Mer. Virtually all charge the same rate (around 40€ for 2 hr.). The rides are aimed at the neophyte, not the champion equestrian. For details, contact Arles' Office de Tourisme (see above) or Ste-Maries-de-la-Mer's Office de Tourisme (see above). Alternatively, both **Abrivado Ranch,** 1655 route de l'Espiguette (www.abrivado ranch.fr; © 04-66-53-01-00) and **L'Ecurie des Dunes,** route de l'Espiguette (www. ecuriedesdunes.com; © **04-66-53-09-28**) organize horseback riding along the beach outside of Le Grau-du-Roi, as well as pony rides for kids.

One of the prettiest ways to get a feel for the Camargue is by hopping aboard a **boat tour**. Longtime local operator **Croisières en Camargue,** 14 rue Théaulon, Aigues-Mortes (www.croisieres-camargue.com; © 06-03-91-44-63) chugs along the Camargue's canals, passing *gardians* in action, local bulls, nesting flamingos, and salt marshes en route. There are plenty of itineraries too: Prices for adults range from 9€ for a 90-minute tour to 45€ for a full day out. **Le Pescalune,** 12 rue Théaulon, Aigues-Mortes (www.pescalune-aiguesmortes.com; © **04-66-53-79-47**) offers watery tours that span the whole of the Camargue.

Always imagined yourself in the Wild West? French-speakers may try their hand at herding horses or bulls along with local *gardians* at one of the Camargue's *manades*, or traditional ranches. **Manade Clauzel,** Mas du Ménage, Stes-Maries-de-la-Mer (www.manadeclauzel.com; © 06-12-13-77-06) offers both full days out and shorter private visits from 25€ per person.

And for a superb medley of Camargue-flavored tours—from food and wine to horseback-riding and bird-spotting—local boy Sébastien Lopez leads off-the-beaten-track tours of his homeland through **I Am Not a Tourist** (www.iamnotatourist.fr; © **06-25-42-78-22;** tour itineraries and prices on request).

Note that many of the outfits listed here operate between April and October, closing up entirely from November through March. Be sure get in touch before you travel in order to ensure tour times.

Especially for Kids

Le Seaquarium, avenue du Palais de la Mer Rive Gauche, Le Grau-du-Roi (www.seaquarium.fr; ✆ 04-66-51-57-57) is a giant marine world, where kids can peek at 25 different species of shark, plus seals and sea lions, as well as smaller creatures like turtles and sea horses. It's open daily July and August 9:30am to 11:30pm; April to June and September 9:30am to 7:30pm; and October to March from 9:30am to 7:30pm. Admission is 13.50€ for adults, 12€ for students, 10€ for children aged 5 to 15, and free for children 4 and under. Family tickets (two adults and two children) cost 41.50€.

AIX-EN-PROVENCE & THE LUBERON

AIX-EN-PROVENCE ★★

760km (471 miles) S of Paris; 84km (52 miles) SE of Avignon; 34km (21 miles) N of Marseille; 185km (115 miles) W of Nice

One of the most alluring aspects of Aix is its size. Frequently guidebooks proclaim it the very heart of Provence, evoking a sleepy town filled with flowers and fountains, which it is—in certain quarters. But Aix is also a bustling university town of nearly 143,000 inhabitants (the Université d'Aix dates from 1413), which packs manifold museums, sights, and restaurants into a compact city center.

It was founded in 122 B.C. by Roman general Caius Sextius Calvinus who rather modestly named the town Aquae Sextiae, after himself. Aix's most celebrated son, Paul Cézanne, immortalized the Aix countryside in his paintings. Just as he saw it, the **Montagne Sainte-Victoire** still looms over the town today.

Much more recently, local boy turned superstar soccer player Zinedine Zidane recently opened his **Z5** sports complex (www.z5complexe.fr) in Aix. In 2014, rumors were rife that actress Jessica Alba was planning to settle down in the nearby town of Éguilles. But there are still plenty of decades-old, family-run shops on the narrow streets of the Old Town. A lazy summer lunch or early evening aperitif at one of the bourgeois cafes on the **cours Mirabeau** is an experience not to be missed.

Essentials

ARRIVING **Trains** arrive frequently from Marseille (trip time: 45 min.; 7.80€ one-way) and Nice (trip time: 3½ hr.; 34.10€ one-way). High-speed TGV trains—from Paris as well as Marseille and Nice—arrive at the modern station near Vitrolles, 18km (11 miles) west of Aix. Bus transfers to the center of Aix (www.navetteaixtgvaeroport.com) cost 4.10€ one-way. **Airport buses** shuttle between Marseille Provence Airport and Aix's Gare Routiere (trip time: 30 min.; 8.20€ one-way). There are also **buses** from Marseille, Avignon, and Nice. For information about all of these routes, see www.lepilote.com or call ✆ **08-10-00-13-26.** If you're **driving** to Aix from Avignon or other points north, take A7 south to A8 and follow the signs into town. From Marseille or other points south, take A51 north.

VISITOR INFORMATION   The **Office de Tourisme** is at Les Allées Provençales, 300 av. Giuseppe Verdi (www.aixenprovencetourism.com; ✆ **04-42-16-11-61**).

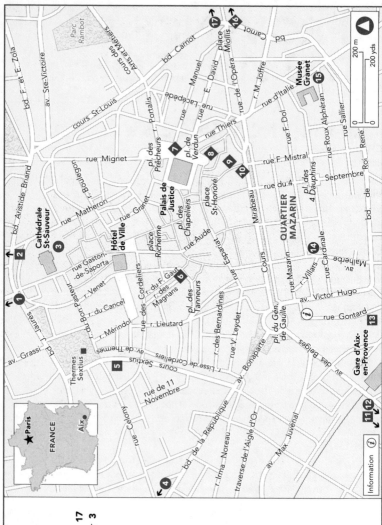

One of the best experiences in Aix is a walk along the well-marked *route de Cézanne*. From the east end of cours Mirabeau, take rue du Maréchal-Joffre across boulevard Carnot to boulevard des Poilus, which becomes avenue des Ecoles-Militaires and D17. The stretch between Aix and the hamlet of Le Tholonet is full of twists and turns where Cézanne used to set up his easel. The route also makes a lovely 5.5km (3½-mile) stroll. Le Tholonet has a cafe or two where you can refresh yourself while waiting for one of the frequent buses back to Aix.

CITY LAYOUT   Aix's **Old Town** is primarily pedestrianized. To the south, it's bordered by the grand **cours Mirabeau,** which is flanked by a canopy of plane trees. The city was built atop thermal springs, and forty fountains still bubble away in picturesque squares around town.

SPECIAL EVENTS   The **Festival d'Aix,** created in 1948 (www.festival-aix.com; ✆ 08-20-92-29-23), mid-June through late July, is undoubtedly Aix's most popular annual event. It features music and opera from all over the world. The **Festival Côté Cour** (www.festival-cotecour.org; ✆ 06-83-60-19-80), runs over the same period, staging concerts from around the world, from jazz and Latin American beats to Provençal baroque and traditional gypsy folk music.

Held for 2 weeks over the Easter holidays, **Festival de Pâques** (www.festival paques.com; ✆ 08-20-13-20-13), is Aix's newest annual festival, celebrating its third edition in 2015. Classical concerts from the likes of Yo-Yo Ma and the Philharmonique de Radio France are performed at Aix's Grand Théâtre de Provence and the Théâtre du Jeu de Paume.

Throughout July and August, **Les Instants d'Eté** is a series of free open-air movies. Films are screened around town in eight of Aix's parks and gardens. Contact the Aix Tourist Office for further details.

On the first Sunday in September, Aix celebrates **La Grande Fête du Calisson**, a festival honoring its traditional local sweet, the *calisson* (see p. 85). Expect live music, Provençal folk dancing, and plenty of *calisson*-tasting. Contact the Aix Tourist Office for further details.

[FastFACTS] AIX-EN-PROVENCE

ATMs/Banks   There are scores of banks in downtown Aix, including three along cours Mirabeau.

Internet Access   **Brasserie Les Deux Garçons,** 53 cours Mirabeau (✆ (0)4-42-26-00-51).

Mail & Postage   **La Poste,** place de l'Hôtel de Ville (✆ 36-31).

Pharmacies   **Pharmacie Victor Hugo,** 16 av. Victor Hugo (✆ 04-42-26-24-93).

Where to Stay

Hôtel Cézanne ★★   This super-chic—and enormously friendly—boutique hotel is best suited to guests seeking a more unusual spot to snooze. Conceived by one of the designers of both Villa Gallici and sophisticated *hotel particulier* **28 à Aix**

(www.28aaix.com), the Cézanne is a mélange of colorful decor and hip designer touches. Baroque furnishings, unique artworks, and an honesty bar all add to the atmosphere. The hotel's location—midway between the train station and Aix's Old Town—makes it ideal for visitors planning day trips farther afield.

40 av. Victor Hugo. http://cezanne.hotelaix.com. ✆ **04-42-91-11-11.** 55 units. 120€–260€ double; 220€–360€ junior suite; 280€–460€ suite. Parking 17€. **Amenities:** Bar; business center; free Wi-Fi.

Hôtel du Globe ★ In a city where expensive is the norm, the Hôtel du Globe is Aix's finest no-frills budget option. Ideally located just west of the Old Town, the hotel's rooms are basic yet bright—although definitely on the small side—and staff is as welcoming as they come. Breakfast is served on the roof terrace in summertime. This is a pleasant spot to bed down.

74 cours Sextius. http://hotelduglobe.com. ✆ **04-42-26-03-58.** 46 units. 88€–93€ double; 105€–123€ triple. Parking 9.80€. **Amenities:** Free Wi-Fi.

Le Pigonnet ★★ Quite literally the best of both worlds: A five-star 'country' hotel set in an 18th-century *bastide*, situated a short hop away from Aix's historic town center. Le Pigonnet's vast gardens, which overlook Mont Sainte-Victoire, are unique. Beset with fountains, one half is Provence-styled with a 16m-long (53ft) heated swimming pool, while the other is an English rose garden stocked with places to breakfast, sip a cocktail, or read a book. Public spaces pair the hotel's 90-year-old family-run tradition with modern touches, like portraits of recent guests Clint Eastwood and Marion Cotillard. The on-site Table du Pigonnet gourmet restaurant snagged Michelin-starred chef Mickaêl Féval in 2014.

5 av du Pigonnet. www.hotelpigonnet.com. ✆ **04-42-59-02-90.** 44 units. 160€–350€ double; 290€–1,135 suite. Free parking. **Amenities:** 2 restaurants; babysitting; bar; concierge; outdoor pool; room service; spa; tennis; free Wi-Fi.

La Villa Gallici ★★★ This 18th-century Provençal house is one of Aix's most luxurious getaways. It also boasts a 7-acre garden and a gastronomic restaurant on-site. It may be just a 5-minute stroll from the town center, yet the countrified ambience makes it feel miles away. Guest rooms are swathed in pastel printed fabrics, while suites have their own private patios. Days may be spent lounging by the terra-cotta-trimmed pool; candlelit dinners are served alfresco under the stars.

Av. de la Violette. www.villagallici.com. ✆ **04-42-23-29-23.** 22 units. 230€–690€ double; 450€–990€ suite. Free parking. Closed Jan. **Amenities:** Restaurant; bar; babysitting; outdoor pool; room service; free Wi-Fi.

Where to Eat

In addition to the restaurants listed below, **Sajna**, 8 rue Lieutaud (www.sajna.fr), is highly recommended. This brand-new Lebanese joint dishes up platters of mezze, from hummus served with homemade pickles to divine falafel. It's perfect for picnics on the go, or alternatively there's just one six-person table for communal dining.

La Fromagerie du Passage ★★ FRENCH Duck through the tiny entrance to Passage Agard by squeezing through the building where Cézanne's father once owned a hat shop. Then follow the (somewhat strange) sounds of bells and farm animals. It's here that the cheery La Fromagerie—part wine and cheese shop, part restaurant—is dedicated to all things cheese-related. Dine on "Le Tour de France" mixed cheese platter paired with local wines (23€) on the rooftop terrace. Or call in at lunchtime, when they whip up delicious sandwiches (6.90€ apiece), such as Le Chevre Chaud, with grilled Sainte Maure goat's cheese.

Passage Agard, 55 cours Mirabeau. www.lafromageriedupassage.fr. ✆ **04-42-22-90-00.** Main courses 15€–25.50€. Daily noon–2:30pm and 7:30–10:30pm.

Lavault ★ FRENCH   This innovative restaurant spills over the charming 15th-century premises. The atmospheric stone vaulted cellar is a favorite dining venue on hot summer evenings. The cuisine is both affordable and creative, and often includes lemongrass-spiked gazpacho with avocado, duck ravioli tossed in a morel mushroom sauce, or the hugely popular foie-gras club sandwich pinched into a sweet brioche. An extensive wine list features a top selection of vintages from the region.

4 rue Felibre Gaut. www.lavault.net. ✆ **04-42-38-57-28.** Reservations recommended. Main courses 15€–23€; fixed-price lunch 17€; fixed-price dinner 29€–36€. Thurs–Sat noon–2:30pm and Tues–Sat 7–11:30pm.

Le Mille Feuille ★★ PROVENÇAL   Nestled into a quiet corner of Aix's Old Town, this excellent eatery stands out against the often-average local dining scene. Little surprise, as the restaurant is the brainchild of chef Nicolas Monribot and sommelier Sylvain Sendra, both former staff at the famous l'Oustau de Baumanière in Les Baux (p. 59). The market-fresh menu changes daily but may include yellow and green zucchini crumble with *cœur de bœuf* tomatoes, Sisteron lamb atop an almond and apricot tajine, or a delectable vanilla bourbon *millefeuille* pastry. You can dine either on the small outdoor terrace or indoors, where the classy decor features crimson walls and chartreuse upholstered furnishings.

8 rue Rifle-Rafle. www.le-millefeuille.fr. ✆ **04-42-96-55-17.** Dinner reservations essential. Main courses 15€; fixed-price lunch 26€–30.50€, dinner 37€–43€. Wed–Sat noon–2pm and 8–9:30pm.

Le Petit Pierre ★★ FRENCH   Little sister to Michelin-starred Restaurant Pierre Reboul, this bistro (opened in 2013) offers a pared-down version of Chef Reboul's creative cuisine. The bistro's seasonal menu is a playful blend of traditional and contemporary, and makes the most of the region's Mediterranean ingredients. Expect rack of lamb with artichoke *barigoule*, cod atop creamy polenta, and lemon crème brûlée. All dishes are cooked in served up with flair against the bistro's modern décor. Note that service can be a little slow, but the price and the quality make the experience well worth it.

11 petite rue St Jean. www.restaurant-pierre-reboul.com. ✆ **04-42-52-30-42.** Dinner reservations recommended. Main courses 16€–21€; fixed-price menus 18€–39€. Tues–Sat noon–2:30pm and 7:30–10:30pm.

Restaurant Le Saint-Estève ★★ FRENCH   Opened in 2013, brand-new Hôtel Les Lodges Sainte-Victoire's gourmet restaurant is headed up by one of the Riviera's super chefs, Mathias Dandine. In 2014 the venue was awarded its first Michelin star. Little wonder: delicious dishes are classically French, yet with an innovative twist—such as line-caught turbot steeped in ginger and coriander, or tender asparagus paired with Corsican *brousse* cheese and black truffles. The restaurant and hotel (double rooms from 225€ to 390€) are set in within Mediterranean gardens at the foot of Mont Sainte-Victoire, around a ten-minute drive east of central Aix.

L'Hôtel Les Lodges Sainte-Victoire, route de Cézanne, Le Tholonet. www.leslodgessaintevictoire.com. ✆ **04-42-27-10-14.** Reservations required. Main courses 42€–75€; fixed-price lunch 45€–55€; fixed-price dinner 85€–135€. Tues–Sun noon–2pm and 7:30–9:30pm.

CÉZANNE passeport

Cézanne aficionados are advised to purchase the **Cézanne Passeport** (12€). The pass allows entry to the Atelier de Cézanne (see p. 82), the artist's family manor Jas de Bouffan (see below), and the inspirational Cubist landscape of the Bibémus Quarries (see below)—garnering an overall saving of 4.50€. The pass can be purchased from Aix Office de Tourisme, Cézanne's Atelier, or the Jas de Bouffan. Note that the shuttle to the Bibémus Quarries (1€ each way) is not included in the pass.

Exploring Aix-en-Provence

Aix's main street, **cours Mirabeau ★**, is one of the most beautiful boulevards in Europe. A double row of plane trees shades it from the Provençal sun and throws dappled daylight onto its rococo fountains. Shops and sidewalk cafes line one side; 17th- and 18th-century sandstone *hôtels particuliers* (private mansions) take up the other. Stop into **Brasserie Les Deux Garçons,** 53 cours Mirabeau, for a coffee or a glass of rosé. The brasserie was founded in 1792 and frequented by the likes of Emile Zola, Cézanne, Picasso, and Sir Winston Churchill. Boulevard Carnot and cours Sextius circle the heart of the old quarter (Vieille Ville), which contains the pedestrian-only zone.

One fun way to check out the lay of the land is aboard an eco-friendly **Diabline** (www.la-diabline.fr; Mon–Sat 8:30am–7:30pm; 0.50€/ride). These vehicles operate three routes along cours Mirabeau and through most of the Old Town.

Atelier de Cézanne ★★★ MUSEUM   A 10-minute (uphill) stroll north of Aix's Old Town, Cézanne's studio offers visitors a unique glimpse into the artist's daily life. Because the building remained untouched for decades after Cézanne's death in 1906, the studio has remained perfectly preserved for close to a century. Note the furnishings, vases, and small figurines on display, all of which feature in the modern master's drawings and canvases

9 av. Paul-Cézanne. www.atelier-cezanne.com. ℂ **04-42-21-06-53.** Admission 5.50€ adults, 2€ children and students 13–25, free for children 12 and under. July–Aug daily 10am–6pm, English tour at 5pm; April–June and Sept daily 10am–noon and 2–6pm, English tour at 5pm; Oct–March daily 10am–noon and 2–5pm, English tour at 4pm. Closed Sun Dec–Feb.

Bastide du Jas de Bouffan ★★ MUSEUM   The Cézanne family home for four decades (1859–1899), it was here that Paul Cézanne laid the foundations for his illustrious painting career. After painting 12 large-scale works directly onto the walls of the ground-floor salon, he used the surrounding landscape as inspiration for 36 oil paintings and 17 watercolors. Note that Jas de Bouffan may be visited by guided tour only (around 45 minutes), which includes a multimedia show.

Route de Galice. www.cezanne-en-provence.com. ℂ **04-42-16-11-61.** Admission 5.50€ adults, 2€ students and children 13–25, free children 12 and under. Guided tours (in French unless otherwise specified): June–Sept daily 10:30, noon, 2pm (in English), 3:30pm; April–May and Oct Tues, Thurs, Sat 10:30am, noon, 2pm (in English), 3:30pm; Nov–March Wed and Sat 10am.

Carrières de Bibémus ★ ATTRACTION   Shacked up in a remote rented cottage in these abandoned ochre sandstone quarries, Cézanne painted what are widely recognized as some of the first Cubist artworks. Among the 11 oil paintings and 16 watercolors (1895-1904) he created here, natural geometric shapes—as well as a scattering of pine trees and Cézanne's beloved Mont Sainte-Victoire—feature heavily. Carrières de Bibémus are now owned by the Aix municipality, and have been lightly landscaped to highlight Cézanne's time here. Note that the area may be visited by guided tour only (around 1 hour). Visitors with limited mobility will find the tour challenging. A shuttle (1€ each way) runs to the Carrières directly from the parking lot 3 Bons Dieux.

3090 chemin de Bibémus. www.cezanne-en-provence.com. ✆ **04-42-16-11-61.** Admission 5.50€ adults, 2€ students and children 13–25, free children 12 and under. Guided tours: June–Sept daily 9:45am; April–May and Oct Mon, Wed, Fri, Sun 10:30am and 3:30pm; Nov–March Wed and Sat 3pm.

Cathédrale St-Sauveur ★ CATHEDRAL The cathedral of Aix is dedicated to Christ under the title St-Sauveur (Holy Savior or Redeemer) and dates from the 4th and 5th centuries. Its pièce de résistance is a 15th-century Nicolas Froment triptych, *The Burning Bush.* One side depicts the Virgin and Child; the other, Good King René and his second wife, Jeanne de Laval.

34 place des Martyrs de la Résistance. www.cathedrale-aixenprovence-monument.fr. ✆ **04-42-23-45-65.** Free admission. Daily 8am–noon and 2–6pm. Mass Sun 10:30am and 7pm.

Hôtel de Gallifet ★★ CULTURAL CENTER This contemporary exhibition space is located within a 18th-century private mansion in Aix's residential Mazarin neighborhood, just a short stroll from cours Mirabeau. Five exhibition rooms display a rotating selection of artworks, from 1960s celebrity photographs to avant-garde sculpture. The shady plane trees, courtyard café, and bookshop on site all contribute to the feeling that you've stumbled across a peaceful corner of Provence. During the summer, evening concerts are held in the gardens.

52 rue Cardinale. http://hoteldegallifet.com. ✆ **0 9-53-84-37-61.** Free admission. Exhibition space: Thurs–Sun noon–6pm; Café, boutique, and gardens: Thurs–Sun noon–8pm.

Musée Granet ★★ MUSEUM One of the South of France's top art venues, this popular museum displays a permanent collection of paintings and sculpture ranging from 15th-century French canvases to 20th-century Giacometti sculptures. However, it's the large-scale temporary exhibitions that truly impress, such as 2014's "Cézanne and Modernity."

Place Saint Jean de Malte. www.museegranet-aixenprovence.fr. ✆ **04-42-52-88-32.** Permanent collection: admission 5€ adults, 4€ students and children 13–25, free children 12 and under. Additional fee for temporary exhibitions. Tues–Sun June–Sept 10am–7pm; Oct–May noon–6pm.

Pavillon Noir ★ PERFORMANCE CENTER Aix's Pavillon Noir is an imposing web of iron, concrete, and glass, created by Rudy Ricciotti (who won France's prestigious Grand Prix National de l'Architecture for its unusual design). The renowned local Ballet Preljocaj is based here, and the edifice contains both a theater and four rehearsal studios. Regular ballet and contemporary dance performances take place throughout the year.

530 Avenue Wolfgang Amadeus Mozart. www.preljocaj.org. ✆ **04-42-93-48-00,** Ticket Office ✆ **04-42-93-48-14.** Ticket prices vary according to performance, see website for details.

Outlying Attractions

Château la Coste ★★ MUSEUM Not to be confused with the Luberon's Château de Lacoste (see p. 95), this Le Puy-Sainte-Réparade vineyard is home to a superb selection of modern sculptures. Opened in 2011, the Château's **Art and Architecture Walk rambles** through the bucolic Provençal countryside, taking in works by Alexander Calder, Tadao Ando, Richard Serra, and Jean Nouvel. Allow around an hour and a half to complete the full walk.

2750 route de la Cride, Le Puy Sainte Réparade. www.chateau-la-coste.com. ✆ **04-42-61-92-92.** Admission 15€ adults, 12€ students and children 10–18, free children 9 and under. Daily 10am– 7pm.

Fondation Vasarely ★ MUSEUM   This dramatic façade of black and white geometric shapes houses 44 monumental artworks created by Hungarian abstract artist Victor Vasarely. Based in France from the age of 24 (in 1930), Vasarely is considered a leader within the early 1960s "op-art" (optical art) movement. It was the artist himself who set up his own Fondation Vasarely in 1966, eventually working together with architects to create this unusual exhibition space. It was inaugurated in 1976 and is assuredly a work of art in its own right. Temporary exhibitions are also staged here.

1 avenue Marcel Pagnol. www.fondationvasarely.fr. ✆ **04-42-20-01-09.** Permanent collection: admission 9€ adults, 6€ students and children 7–26, 4€ children 3–7, free children 2 and under. Additional fee for temporary exhibitions. Tues–Sun 10am–1pm and 2–6pm. Bus: 2.

Organized Tours

Aix's Tourist Office organizes bilingual tours around Aix (✆ **04-42-16-11-61**), including the year-round **tour of the historic city center** (Sat 10am and April–Oct Tues 10am; 2 hours; 8€, 4€ students and over 60s, free for children under 7), and "**In the Steps of Cézanne**" (April–Oct Thurs 10am; 2 hours; 8€, 4€ students and over 60s, free for children under 7).

Especially for Kids

L'Epi Vert, Lieu Dit Grand Pont, La Roque d'Antheron (www.labyrinthe-geant.fr; ✆ **04-42-22-19-15**), is a large outdoor fun park located northwest of Aix's city center. Two giant themed labyrinths are flanked by jungle gyms, trampolines, and, in 2014, new *pétanque* grounds. Entrance (8€, free for children under 1 meter, or 3 ft 4 in) not only includes access to all areas of the park; each visitor is also given a free rosemary or lavender plant. (Perhaps not that practical, but a kind gift all the same!) L'Epi Vert is open from 10am until 9pm, daily during school holidays, and on Wednesday, Saturday, and Sunday the rest of the year.

CHÂTEAU DE vauvenargues

Tucked into the foothills of Mont Sainte-Victoire, **Château de Vauvenargues** was purchased by Pablo Picasso in 1959. At the time, he felt this 17th-century private home and its location so inspiring that he planned to spend the rest of his life here. However, the great artist moved to Mougins just a few years later, although he did return to the Château frequently. Picasso was buried in the grounds upon his death in 1973. Jacqueline Roque, his second wife, was also laid to rest here in 1986. The Château and its grounds are occasionally open to the pubic. Contact the Aix Office de Tourisme for further details.

Aix offers some of the region's best markets. Place Richelme holds a **fruit and vegetable market** every morning from 8:30am to 12:30pm. Come here to buy exquisite products such as garlic-marinated olives and local cheeses. There's a **flower market** every day, with the same hours, at either place de l'Hôtel de Ville or place des Prêcheurs (the former on Tues, Thurs, and Sat; the latter on Mon, Wed, Fri, and Sun). The **fish market** takes place every morning on the south side of place Richelme. Place de Verdun is packed with **crafts and collectibles** every Tuesday and Thursday, with stalls selling clothes and linens joining the others on Saturday. And each week on Tuesday and Thursday, cours Mirabeau is lined with a mix of **regional treats**, from lavender honey to unique handbags.

It's also well worth seeking out the weekly markets that lie further afield. Each one sees scores of local producers gather to sell their seasonal harvest. Imagine sampling spring's first fresh fava beans, summer's sweet Carpentras strawberries, or autumn's violet figs. Every town offers a sidewalk café or two, perfect for an uninterrupted view of locals bartering and catching up on the latest gossip. Monday is market day for Cavaillon; Tuesday for Gordes; Thursday for Roussillon and Ménerbes; Friday for Bonnieux, Lourmarin, and Pertuis; Saturday for Apt; and Ansouis' market takes place on Sunday. Additional farmers' markets are held in Apt on Tuesday morning and Cadenet on Saturday morning, both from May to November, and in Pertuis on Wednesday and Saturday mornings year round.

Shopping

Opened more than a century ago, **Béchard,** 12 cours Mirabeau (✆ **04-42-26-06-78**), is the most famous bakery in town. It specializes in the famous *Calissons d'Aix,* a candy made from ground almonds, preserved melon, and fruit syrup. **Chocolaterie de Puyricard,** 7 rue Rifle-Rafle (www.puyricard.fr; ✆ **04-42-21-13-26**), creates sensational chocolates filled with candied figs, walnuts, or local lavender honey.

Founded in 1934 on a busy boulevard just east of the center of town, **Santons Fouque,** 65 cours Gambetta (www.santons-fouque.com; ✆ **04-42-26-33-38**), stocks close to 2,000 traditional *santons* (crèche figurines).

For a range of truly useful souvenirs, including copper pots and pocket knives by famous French forgers such as Laguiole, try **Quincaillerie Centrale,** 21 rue de Monclar (✆ **04-42-23-33-18**), a hardware/housewares store that's been offering a little bit of everything since 1959.

Nightlife

Au P'tit Quart d'Heure, 21 place Forum de Cardeurs (www.auptitquartdheure.fr) and next-door's **La Curieuse**, 23 place Forum des Cardeurs (✆ **06-06-66-77-01**) are two of the city's liveliest spots to stop for an early evening aperitif. Expect seasonal happy hours, with prices as low as 1€ for beer and 2€ per glass of wine. Open daily from 8am until 2am, **La Rotonde,** 2A place Jeanne d'Arc (www.larotonde-aix.com; ✆ **04-42-91-61-70**)—a bar, cafe, and historic hangout—is also perennially popular.

Under-30s who like thumping beats should head for **Le Mistral,** 3 rue Frédéric Mistral (www.mistralclub.fr; ✆ **04-42-38-16-49**), where techno and house pumps long and loud for a cover charge of around 10€ to 20€.

COOKING CLASSES IN aix & the luberon

In Aix, epicureans will adore **L'Atelier Cuisine de Mathilde**, 58 rue des Cordeliers (www.lateliercuisinedemathilde.com; ✆ **06-72-83-98-28**), which was launched in autumn of 2013. Owner and chef Mathilde studied at the École de Cuisine Alain Ducasse in Paris, and now offers personalized cooking courses (maximum 8 participants) in English. From 65€ per person.

Affable Eric Sapet, chef at Michelin-starred **La Petit Maison de Cucuron**, place de l'Etang, Cucuron (www.lapetite maisondecucuron.com; ✆ **04-90-68-21-99**), teaches food-loving students the

secret to his seasonal cooking every Saturday morning. Courses cost 68€ per person.

Chef Jean-Jacques Prévôt creates fruity menus using the famous Cavaillon melon at his Michelin-starred **Restaurant Prévôt**, 353 avenue du Verdun, Cavaillon (www.restaurant-prevot.com). Itching to recreate his one-of-a-kind Mac Prévôt, a melon, artichoke and foie gras burger, topped with melon seed "ketchup"? Prévôt offers half-day cooking lessons from 110€, one Saturday per month from 4:30pm, followed by dinner. For further information contact ✆ **04-90-71-32-43**.

For jazz produced by a changing roster of visiting musicians, head for the **Scat Club,** 11 rue de la Verrerie (✆ **04-42-23-00-23**), a preferred venue for more mature local patrons.

Last but certainly not least is the **Joïa Glam Club** (www.discotheque-aixen-provence.com; ✆ **06-80-35-32-94**), chemin de l'Enfant, in the hamlet of Les Milles, 8km (5 miles) south of Aix (follow the signs to Marseille). There is also a shuttle bus from La Rotonde in Aix proper—probably a safer bet. On-site are a restaurant, several bars, an outdoor swimming pool, and indoor/outdoor dance floor. Be forewarned that there are long lines on Fridays (when females get in free) and Saturdays. Entrance usually costs around 16€, unless you're a star or self-confident enough to schmooze the doorman.

THE LUBERON ★★★

Gordes (see p. 92) and Roussillon (see p. 94) are part of the Parc Naturel Régional du Luberon (www.parcduluberon.fr), which is made up of three mountain ranges and their common valley. Author Peter Mayle brought attention to the area with his "A Year in Provence" series extolling the virtues of picturesque villages such as Bonnieux, Lourmarin, and Ménerbes. The latter was home to Picasso and his (then) muse Dora Maar, and where Mayle restored his first French residence. Most of the following places to stay, restaurants, and sights are all within 30km (18 miles) of each other, making the Luberon a lovely place to lose yourself for a few days—or longer.

Essentials

ARRIVING   The Luberon is exceptionally difficult to navigate without your own wheels. The most practical train station is Cavaillon, where trains arrive from Avignon's central station (trip time: 35 min.; 7€ one-way) or Marseille (trip time: 75 min.; 15.30€ one-way). For bus travel around the region, seek out specific towns and route on **Trans Vaucluse** (www.vaucluse.fr) and **Lignes Express Régionales** Région PACA (www.info-ler.fr).

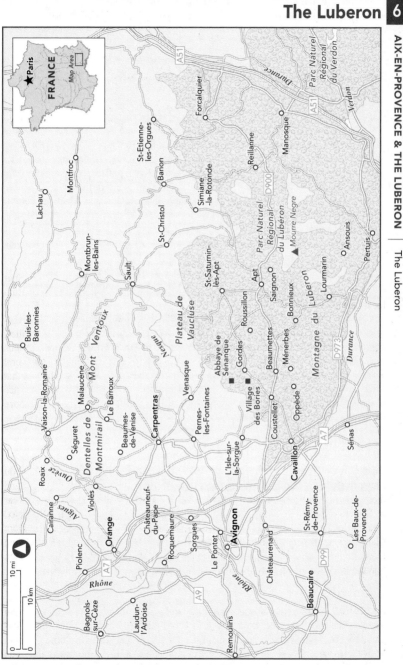

If you're **driving** to the Luberon from Aix or other points south, take A51 north, then D973 west. Most of the Luberon's major points of interest can be reached by following D943 north from here. However do consult a map for detailed driving directions.

VISITOR INFORMATION   The **Office de Tourisme** is at 60 place Jean-Jaurès, Apt (www.parcduluberon.fr; © **04-90-04-42-00**).

Where to Stay

La Coquillade ★★   Set on 42 hectares of sprawling countryside, luxurious La Coquillade is both a working vineyard (www.aureto.fr) and a certified eco-hotel. Solar panels heat the swimming pool, while indoors, the hotel's temperature is regulated via geothermal energy. Fresh from a sympathetic renovation—completed in March 2014—the hotel's guestrooms are a mix of the traditional and the contemporary, with exposed wooden beams, natural stone walls, and sleek, chic furnishings. All-natural bath products come courtesy of favorite local producer, L'Occitane. There are complimentary guided tours of the vineyard (Wednesdays at 10am), and regular wine-tasting sessions (Saturdays 10am, 15€ per person, or 53€ per person including lunch). The gastronomic Le Gourmet restaurant, headed up by chef Christophe Renaud, is highly recommended.

Domaine de la Coquillade, Gargas. www.coquillade.fr. © **04-90-74-71-71.** 28 units. 180€–325€ double; 240€–1,230€ suite. Free parking. Closed Nov–mid-April. **Amenities:** 3 restaurants; bar; outdoor pool; *pétanque* grounds; room service; spa; tennis courts; free Wi-Fi.

Le Domaine de Capelongue ★★   This beautiful *bastide* (country home) makes for an idyllic French getaway. The ambiance is thoroughly Provençal, from the spacious rooms' pale textiles and terracotta floors to the panoramic swimming pool and the organic kitchen garden. The Domaine's newest accommodation is a former *pigeonnier*, or pigeon loft, which has been transformed into three apartments. The double Michelin-starred Restaurant Edouard Loubet, located on site, is one of the Luberon's principal places of foodie pilgrimage.

Les Claparèdes, Chemin des Cabanes, Bonnieux. www.capelongue.com. © **04-90-75-89-78.** 27 units. 140€–480€ double; 795€–1,815€ 2-person apartment per week; 1,095€–2,805€ 2- to 4-person apartment per week; 1,425€–3,245€ 4- to 8-person apartment per week; 1,825€–4,345€ 8- to 12-person apartment per week. Free parking. **Amenities:** Restaurant; additional summer-only restaurant; bar; outdoor pool; room service; free Wi-Fi.

ALTERNATE ACCOMMODATIONS

L'Oustaou d'Olivie ★★   Located on the eastern edge of the Luberon, these two classic Provençal cottages (or *gîtes*) are surrounded by olive trees. Each self-catering cottage possesses its own garden and private terrace, and is well equipped with modern amenities, such as a dishwasher, washing machine, and television. Both sleep four people comfortably, with spare beds available on request. Dutch owners Erik and Joyce Borgmann also organize regular Mediterranean cooking workshops (45€ per person), using ingredients from their own large produce garden on the premises.

Domaine de la Sarette, Oraison. www.oulivie.fr. © **06-73-32-64-29.** 2 units. 950€–1,190€ per week. Free parking. Closed Oct–April. **Amenities:** Free internet access.

Where to Eat

Café des Poulivets ★ PROVENÇAL   An atmospheric family-run eatery, Café des Poulivets is one of the Luberon's five designated *bistrot de pays*. This prestigious

WINE IN the luberon

Oenophiles in the Luberon won't go thirsty. **Provence Wine Tours** (www.provencewinetours.com; ℂ **04-42-16-11-61**), offers a variety of excursions through the countryside around Aix and the Luberon, focusing on Côtes de Provence and Coteaux d'Aix-en-Provence vintages. All tours are led by a wine expert and are limited to eight participants. Tours last around 3 to 4 hours, including visits to two vineyards and tastings of nine different wines, and cost 67€ per person.

For independent explorers, **AOC Vins Luberon** (www.vins-luberon.fr) details local Appellation d'Origine Contrôlée wines, organic producers, vineyard walks, and restaurants along the way.

The Luberon's wine museums include the **Musée du Tire Bouchon** (Corkscrew Museum) in Ménerbes' Domaine de la Citadelle (www.domaine-citadelle.com; ℂ **04-90-72-41-58**); the **La Maison de la Truffe et du Vin du Luberon**, dedicated to wine and truffles, also in Ménerbes (www.vin-truffe-luberon.com; ℂ **04-90-72-38-37**); and Chateau Turcan's **Musée des Arts et des Métiers du Vin** (Museum of the Arts and Professions of Winemaking) in Ansouis (www.chateau-turcan.com; ℂ **04-90-09-83-33**).

And for visitors who fancy dining among the vines? Country restaurant **Le Bistrot des Arts**, Les Bessières, Ansouis (www.lepuydesarts.com; ℂ **06-66-58-81-93**), is set in the heart of a working vineyard. Note that advance reservations are required.

label signifies a convivial atmosphere, encouraging lingering over meals and a dedication to regional produce. The bistro's authentic local dishes are served only at lunchtime, and may include Provençal *petits farcis* (tiny stuffed vegetables) or fried polenta paired with ratatouille. On Fridays, the traditional dish of the day is *aïoli*, salt cod, and vegetables served with a garlicky mayonnaise. Light snacks and drinks are available throughout the day.

400 rue des Poulivets, Oppède. www.cafedespoulivets.com. ℂ **04-90-05-88-31.** Main courses 9€–14€. June–Aug Mon–Sat 8am–10pm, Sun 8am–1pm; Sept–May Mon–Tues and Thurs–Sat 8am–8pm, Wed 8am–3pm.

Le Sanglier Paresseux ★★★ PROVENÇAL   A high-perched village in the Luberon may not be the first place you'd expect to find a top-notch Brazilian chef. Yet Fabricio Delgaudio, a São Paulo-native, dreamed of opening a traditional French restaurant since he was a child. Enter a love story with a local—and Le Sanglier Paresseux was born. The seasonal menu makes the most of the Luberon's bounty, with a hint or two of international inspiration from classic Portuguese and Brazilian cuisine. The fixed-price evening menus allow diners the liberty of selecting an appetizer, main course (or two), and then dessert from the à la carte menu.

St François, Caseneuve. www.sanglierparesseux.com. ℂ **04-90-75-17-70.** Reservations recommended. Main courses 14€–21€; fixed-price lunch 25€; fixed-price dinner 31€–41€. Tues–Sun noon–1:30pm, Mon–Sat 7:30pm–10:30pm. Closed Jan.

La Table de Pablo ★★ PROVENÇAL   This simple restaurant, surrounded by vineyards and cherry orchards, may appear unassuming. Which makes La Table de Pablo's "semi-gastronomic" cuisine is even more of an unexpected delight. Chef Thomas Gallardo's contemporary Provençal dishes range from savory avocado *crème brûlée* to rosemary-infused lamb *mille-feuilles*. Ingredients are sourced almost exclusively from small local producers. The restaurant's ambiance is just as carefully crafted. The dining room is decorated with sculptures and drawings by local artist Mary'o; outdoors the terrace is framed by olive trees.

Les Petits Cléments, Villars. www.latabledepablo.com. ✆ **04-90-75-45-18.** Reservations recommended. Main courses 21€–24€; fixed-price lunch 17€–29€; fixed-price dinner 29€. Sun–Wed and Fri noon–1:30pm, daily 7:30pm–10:30pm. Closed Jan–mid-Feb.

Exploring the Luberon

Abbaye de Valsaintes ★ MONASTERY   Located in the north the Luberon, this Cistercian abbey was an important religious center between the 12th and 18th centuries. Visits take in the restored 17th-century church, as well as the olive groves and dry-stone terraces that surround the abbey, now transformed into a 600-specie *roseraie*, or rose garden. There's also a rose nursery (www.roseraie-abbaye.com) on site. Garden events and concerts are held at the abbey throughout the year—see the website for further details.

Boulinette, Simiane La Rotonde. www.valsaintes.org. ✆ **04-92-75-94-19.** Admission 6.50€ adults, 3.50€ students and children 12–18, free children 11 and under. Daily May–Sept 10:30am–7pm; April and Oct 2–6pm.

Château de Lourmarin ★ ATTRACTION   This 15th-century castle, dotted with spooky gargoyles, was salvaged from the verge of destruction during the 1920s. Its Renaissance wing contains artworks and antiques dating from the 15th to 19th centuries, as well as a superb twisted spiral staircase created from one solid block of stone. Each year, the Château hosts La Fête Renaissance, a Renaissance Festival in late April, and Festival des Musiques d'Eté, a Music and Arts festival that stretches from July to September.

Impasse du Pont du Temple. www.chateau-de-lourmarin.com. ✆ **04-90-68-15-23.** Admission 6.50€ adults, 4€ students and seniors, 3€ children 10–16, free children 9 and under. Daily June–Aug 10am–6:30pm; daily May and Sept 10am–12:30pm and 2:30–6pm; daily March–April and Oct 10:30am–12:30pm and 2:30–5pm; daily Nov–Dec and Feb 10:30am–12:30pm and 2:30–4:30pm; Jan Sat–Sun 2:30–4:30pm.

Enclos des Bories ★ RUINS   Like Gordes' Village des Bories (see p. 94), this cluster of 20 ancient dry-stone dwellings in Bonnieux is other-worldly. Located on a private 4-hectare site within a lush cedar forest (itself crisscrossed by bucolic walking trails), the beehive-shaped buildings were used to house animals and agricultural tools. Some used to host wells, bread ovens, and apiaries as well. The site also looks out over beautiful panoramas of Bonnieux village, Mont Ventoux, and the wider Luberon. Note that Enclos des Bories is accessed via a 500-m (1,650-foot) stroll from the Camping de Bonniex.

Quartier Le Rinardas, Bonnieux. www.enclos-des-bories.fr. ✆ **06-08-46-61-44.** Admission 5€ adults, free children 11 and under. April–Nov daily 10am–7pm.

Jardins du Château Val Joanis ★ GARDENS   These impressive gardens fringe the Château Val Joanis, an important working winery since the 15th century. Created over a 12-year period between 1978 and 1990, the elaborate grounds are composed of three terraces, linked by a long rose-strewn arbor. A vegetable garden sits along the first terrace, including a heady mix of aromatic herbs, lavender, and apple trees. The second terrace mimics the neatly planted layout of the first, scattered with beds of roses and irises. Plane trees, honeysuckle, and fig trees lushly adorn the wild environs of the final terrace.

LAVENDER FIELDS forever

Provence is renowned for its rolling fields of lavender. A brilliant purple, and on occasion almost blue, this crop cloaks the countryside in an ethereal glow each summertime. For six Lavender Routes around the region, as well as places to stay and activities en route, check out **Les Routes de la Lavande** (www.routes-lavande.com).

Or head north to **Sault** and its surrounding valley, considered the "Capital of Lavender." The town's Office de Tourisme (www.saultenprovence.com) provides a downloadable brochure outlining lavender-themed activities in the region, including boutiques, workshops, and a 5-km (3-mile) walking trail. Sault also holds the **Fête de la Lavande** (www.fete delalavande.fr) each year on August 15.

To learn all about lavender, from seed to harvest to fragrant essential oil, visit the **Musée de la Lavande**, 276 route de Gordes, Coustellet (www.museedela lavande.com; © **04-90-76-91-23**). The museum is owned and operated by the Lincelé family, fifth-generation lavender farmers and purveyors of the **Le Château de Bois** (www.lechateaudubois. com) bath and products. It's open daily February to April 9am to noon and 2pm to 6pm, May to September 9am to 7pm, and October to December 9am to 12:15pm and 2pm to 6pm. Admission—which includes a free audio guide—is 6.80€ for adults, 5.80€ for students, and free for children 14 and under.

And remember, if you're looking to shoot perfectly purple pictures, be sure to time your visit right: Lavender blooms between mid-June and mid-August.

2404 route de Villelaure, Pertuis. www.val-joanis.com. © **04-90-79-20-77.** Admission 4.50€ adults, free children 17 and under. Daily July–Aug 10am–7pm; April–June and Sept–Oct 10am–1pm and 2–7pm.

Organized Tours

One-day coach tours to the Luberon depart from both Avignon and Aix-en-Provence. **Autocars Lieutaud** (www.excursionprovence.com; © **04-90-86-36-75;** from 55€ per person) offers this service from Avignon, visiting Gordes, as well as St-Rémy de Provence and Les Baux. The Aix-en-Provence Tourist Office (www.aixenprovence tourism.com; © **04-42-16-11-61;** from 60€ per person) organizes a variety of tours throughout the Luberon.

Rendez-vous Provence's (www.rendez-vous-provence.com; © **04-42-96-30-72**) guided tours through the Luberon take in Bonnieux, Lacoste, and Roussillon en route. The tour lasts around 5 hours and costs 68€ per person. There's a full-day (9-hour) tour too, including these villages but heading up to Gordes and the Abbaye de Senaque as well, that costs 122€. Rendez-vous Provence also offers special lavender tours through the Luberon in early to mid-summer (5 hours, 68€).

Tours in Provence (www.tours-in-provence.com; © **06-24-19-29-91**) leads guided excursions through the Luberon, usually stopping in Lourmarin, Gordes, Roussillon, and the Abbaye de Séanque along the way. Tours—which last around 7 hours, from 9:15am to 4pm—are priced from 80€ per person, depending on the number of participants (up to 7 max).

CYCLING THROUGH THE luberon

For avid cyclists, **Vélo Loisir en Luberon** (eng.veloloisirluberon.com) has marked hundreds of kilometers of bike routes throughout the region's vineyards and lavender fields. See the website for maps and bicycle rental agencies, as well as a bunch of bucolic dining spots en route. **La Provence à Vélo** (www.provence-cycling.co.uk) is also a superb website for similar information about cycling throughout the Vaucluse region, the Luberon included. Both organizations highlight the Luberon's "Le Calavon" *voie verte*, or green road—28km (18 miles) of smooth, car-free cycling paths, particularly well suited to families—that

ripples through the heart of the countryside.

Find the mere mention of all that pedaling far foo challenging? **Sun-E-Bike,** 1 avenue Clovis Hugues, Bonnieux (www.location-velo-provence.com; ☏ **04-90-74-09-96**), stocks more than 200 electric bicycles that can be used to whizz around the countryside. Partners throughout the region mean you can recharge your bike's battery as needed. The outfit's website offers eight down-loadable cycling circuits that ramble their way around the Luberon. Electric bikes are priced from 35€ per day, with dis-counts for longer-term rentals.

GORDES ★★★

720km (446 miles) S of Paris; 75km (48 miles) N of Aix-en-Provence; 92km (57 miles) N of Marseille

Hilltop Gordes is a supremely chic rocky outcrop deep in Provence. From afar, this gorgeous *village perché* (perched village) is a pastiche of beiges, grays, and terra cotta that blushes golden at sunrise and sunset. The place also served as a backdrop for the love affair between Marion Cotillard and Russell Crowe in the hit movie *A Good Year*.

Essentials

ARRIVING   Gordes is difficult to reach via public transportation. From Cavaillon, bus nr. 15.3 departs three times daily for place du Château in Gordes (www.sudest-mobilites.fr; trip time: 35 min.; 2€ one-way). By car, Gordes is a 75km (48-mile) drive north of Aix-en-Provence via the A7.

VISITOR INFORMATION   The **Office de Tourisme** is at Le Château (www.gordes-village.com; ☏ **04-90-72-02-75**).

[Fast FACTS] GORDES

Mail & Postage   **La Poste,** place du Jeu de Boules (☏ **36-31**). Note that the post office also offers an ATM.

Pharmacies   **Pharmacie de Gordes,** 2 rue de l'Eglise (☏ **04-90-72-02-10**).

Where to Stay

La Ferme de la Huppe ★★   This combination bed-and-breakfast, and its superb Provençal restaurant (also open to nonguests), spills over a pristinely renovated 18th-century farmhouse. Country-style guest rooms are named after their former functions, such as Hay Loft or Wine Cellar, and all boast cute modern bathrooms. An abundant buffet breakfast (croissants, fresh juices, local cheeses) is served on the poolside terrace. La Ferme's location, just down the road from Gordes itself, makes it perfectly positioned for exploring the wider Luberon region, including the gorgeous villages of Bonnieux and Roussillon.

R.D. 156, Les Pourquiers. www.lafermedelahuppe.com. ℭ 04-90-72-12-25. 10 units. 145€–225€ double, breakfast included. Half-board available. Free parking. **Amenities:** Restaurant, outdoor pool; free Wi-Fi. Closed Nov to Feb.

Where to Eat

L'Artegal PROVENÇAL A standout venue among Gordes' handful of eateries, this family-run restaurant prides itself on its creative local cuisine. Well-conceived dishes include lentil and salmon tartare, rich lamb *navarin* stew, and the restaurant's own generous adaptation of duck-heavy *salade Landaise.* Tucked into the shadow of the Château de Gordes, L'Artegal is a romantic spot to dine, particularly in the evening when the town's daytrippers have disappeared.

Place du Château. ℭ 04-90-72-02-54. Main courses 16€–26€; fixed-price lunch 22€; fixed-price dinner 36€. Thurs–Tues noon–1:45pm; Thurs–Mon 7:15–8:45pm. Closed mid-Jan–mid-March.

Exploring Gordes

Gordes is best explored on foot. Its primarily pedestrianized streets unwind downhill from the Château de Gordes, the Renaissance rehabilitation of a 12th-century fortress. Its windows still bear grooves from bows and arrows used to protect Gordes during Gallo-Roman times, when it was a border town. Today Gordes is more likely to be invaded by easels. Its austere beauty has drawn many artists, including Marc Chagall and Hungarian painter Victor Vasarely, who spent summers here gathering inspiration for his geometric abstract art.

Caves du Palais St. Firmin ★ RUINS Steep Gordes lacks an abundance of surface area, so early settlers burrowed into the rock itself, creating an underground network of crude rooms and stairways over seven levels. Over the centuries, these rooms have housed the village's production of olive oil and grain. Though the tunnels are adequately lit, children are provided with a small headlamp to let them feel like true explorers.

Rue du Belvédère. www.caves-saint-firmin.com. ℭ 04-90-72-02-75. Admission 6€ adults, 4.50€ students. Free audio guide. May–Sept Wed–Mon 10am–6pm. Oct–April by reservation only.

Château de Gordes ★ HISTORIC HOME/ART MUSEUM Access to the ancient château is reserved for visitors of its small museum, previously dedicated to contemporary Flemish painter Pol Mara (1920–98), a former resident of Gordes. In 2014, the museum was given over exclusively to short-term temporary shows, such as a recent exhibition by National Geographic photographer, Reza.

Place Genty Pantaly. ℭ 04-90-72-98-64. Admission 4€ adults, 3€ children 10–17, free for children 9 and under. Daily 10am–1pm and 2–6:30pm.

Outlying Attractions

Abbaye Nôtre Dame de Sénanque ★★★ MONASTERY One of the prettiest sights in the Luberon—indeed, in all of Provence—is the Abbaye Nôtre Dame de Sénanque, even more so when the lavender is in bloom. Five kilometers (3 miles) down the road from Gordes, it was built by Cistercian monks in 1148. Just a handful of monks continue to live on the premises today. The structure is noted for its simple architecture and unadorned stone—though standing in a sea of lavender purple, from

THE LAST HOME OF albert camus

Author of "The Stranger," among many other works, Algerian-born Albert Camus (1913–60) moved to France at the age of 25. A member of the French Resistance, political journalist, and philosopher, he was awarded the Nobel Prize for Literature in 1958 "for his important literary production, which with clear-sighted earnestness illuminates the problems of the human conscience in our times."

That same year, drawn by its "solemn and austere landscape despite its bewildering beauty," Camus and his wife moved to Lourmarin, 30km (18 miles) southeast of Gordes along D36. Just 2 years later, Camus was killed in a car accident near Paris. According to his wishes, he was buried in Lourmarin's cemetery.

In 1999, former French president Nicolas Sarkozy—with whom Camus would have had little in common philosophically or politically—proposed moving the writer's ashes to the Pantheon in Paris, to rest aside such literary giants as Alexander Dumas, Victor Hugo, and Emile Zola. His descendants politely declined.

June to late July, it's dramatic indeed. The abbey is open daily to visitors. A gift shop sells items made by the resident monks, as well as lavender honey.

D177. www.senanque.fr. 📞 **04-90-72-05-86.** Admission 7€ adults, 5€ students and ages 19–25, 3€ children 6–18, 20€ families, free children 5 and under. Hours vary; call or see website.

Village des Bories ★ RUINS Bories are beehive-shaped dwellings made of intricately stacked stone—and not an ounce of mortar. They date back as far as the Bronze Age and as recently as the 18th century in Provence. An architectural curiosity, their thick walls and cantilevered roofs beg the question: How did they do that? The Village des Bories is the largest group of these structures in the region, comprising 30 huts grouped according to function (houses, stables, bakeries, silkworm farms, and more). Traditional tools are on display, along with an exhibit on the history of dry-stone architecture in France and around the world.

1.5km (1 mile) west of Gordes on the D15. 📞 **04-90-72-03-48.** Admission 6€ adults, 4€ children 12–17, free children 11 and under. Daily 9am–sunset.

ROUSSILLON ★★

65km (40 miles) N of Aix-en-Provence; 100km (62 miles) N of Marseille; 10km (6 miles) E of Gordes

The remarkable town of Roussillon is perched atop an undulating terrain, stained by the region's unique ochre earth. Vineyards and forests cleave the countryside, revealing stunning stripes of this natural pigment, each one ranging from amber gold to a deep scarlet. A hundred years ago, dozens of quarries mined the much-coveted Provençal ochre from the surrounding area, and used it to add color to paints and textiles.

Essentials

ARRIVING Like much of the Luberon, Roussillon is difficult to reach via public transportation. Infrequent daily **buses** (www.vaucluse.fr) connect Roussillon with Gordes (trip time: 30 min.; 1.50€ one-way), Apt (trip time: 35 min.; 1.50€ one-way) and Cavaillon (trip time: 50 min.; 2€ one-way). By **car**, Roussillon is a 65km (40-mile) drive north of Aix through the countryside, via N296, A51, D561, and D943. If you're driving from nearby Gordes, take D2 east to Roussillon.

A VILLAGE OF one's own

Home to the infamous Marquis de Sade during the 18th century, the town of Lacoste has been associated with a different famous face over the last 15 years. In 2001, fashion designer Pierre Cardin purchased **Château de Lacoste**, quickly followed by many of the town's residential properties, with a view to creating a dedicated cultural center within the Luberon. With stunning views over nearby Bonnieux, it's easy to see the attraction. Yet locals are wary: Cardin has purchased so many village homes that Lacoste's property prices have skyrocketed. Some say his actions have effectively squeezed locals out of the market—killing daily village life in the process.

Each July the town hosts the popular **Festival de Lacoste** (www.festivaldelacoste.com), with 2 weeks of concerts, theater, and ballet performances.

VISITOR INFORMATION The **Office de Tourisme** is at place de la Poste (www.roussillon-provence.com; ✆ 04- 90-05-60-25).

[FastFACTS] ROUSSILLON

Mail & Postage **La Poste,** place de la Poste (✆ 36-31). Note that the post office also offers an ATM.

Pharmacies **Pharmacie Chauvet**, place du Pasquier (✆ 04-90-05-66-15).

Where to Stay

Le Clos de le Glycine ★★This charming hotel is ideally located at the heart of Roussillon's ochre-toned town center. Provençal-themed guestrooms—a handful with their own private terrace, which are well worth the splurge—peek out over the surrounding countryside. Some take in views of Mont Ventoux on the horizon. Also on site is Restaurant David (fixed-price menus 33€-53€), a local favorite for gourmet regional cuisine.

Place de la Poste. www.luberon-hotel.fr. ✆ 04-90-05-60-13. 9 units. 115€–190€ double, 165€–270€ suite. Half-board available. Free parking. **Amenities:** Restaurant, free Wi-Fi.

Where to Eat

Le Piquebaure ★ PROVENÇAL   Head to this popular eatery for a modern take on Provençal classics, such as grilled beef *entrecôte*, followed by lavender *crème brûlée*. Both the wine list and the seasonal ingredients are locally sourced. Note that service can be a little slow, particularly when crowded.

Les Estrayas. www.lepiquebaure.com. ✆ 04-90-05-79-65. Main courses 16€–26€; fixed-price lunch 23€; fixed-price dinner 23€–28€. Tues–Sun noon–2:30pm and 7:30–11pm. Closed 2 weeks in Jan.

Exploring Roussillon

Begin with an amble through Roussillon itself. The town's compact center is trimmed by multicolored homes, each façade tinted in warm ochre hues. Every Thursday morning, **place du Pasquier** is given over to a large Provençal market. Then it's time to explore the otherworldly landscape that surrounds the town. Follow the signposts from Roussillon center about a 5 minute walk out of town to the **Sentier des Ocres de**

Roussillon (Ochre Footpath), where the neon orange countryside is exposed by the remains of century-old quarries. The footpath is open daily July to August 9am–7:30pm, June 9am–6:30pm, May and September 9:30am–6:30pm, April 9:30am–5:30pm, March 10am–5pm, October 10am–5:30pm, first 2 weeks of November 10am–4:30pm, mid-November to December and last 2 weeks of February 11am–3:30pm; 2.50€, free children 9 and under. The short walk takes around 35 minutes, and the longer walk around 50 minutes.

The *sentier* isn't difficult. But for visitors with limited mobility, little ones in tow, or those seeking a more comfortable way to explore the countryside, there's also another option that's just as enjoyable. In 2013, **Provence Hippo Services** (www.provencehippo services.com; © **07-81-18-98-78**) began offering tours of Roussillon and its ochre quarries by *calèche*, or horse-drawn carriage. Standard tours depart from the Mines de Bruoux, then loop around to include the Conservatoire des Ocres et des Couleurs (www.okhra.com) and the Sentier des Ocres de Roussillon. Fees for a 1-hour tour start at 12€ per adult, and 8€ for children 9 and under.

> ## Author Peter Mayle on the Luberon:
>
> *"The accent is as thick and soupy as ever, the bizarre notion of punctuality is frequently ignored, and a minimum of 2 hours is still required for a proper Sunday lunch. Wonderful. Long may it last."*

HAUTE PROVENCE

Bordered by plateaus and limestone ravines, Provence's sparsely populated Alpine hinterland rises up to 3,000m (9,850 ft.). You can wander through car-free, cobblestoned villages, fly in a hot-air balloon over lavender fields, and marvel at the impregnable citadels that stand above every mountain pass and river crossing. Scale the hilltop fortresses of Entrevaux or Sisteron. Paddle around deep-blue mountain lakes on pedalos. Or plunge giddily down deep limestone ravines in the Parc Naturel Régional du Verdon. Accessible via the fertile valley of the Durance or aboard the Train des Pignes à Vapeur, Provence's least-discovered region will put a smile on the face of the most adventurous travellers.

ALONG THE TRAIN DES PIGNES★★

If you think that Provence's most challenging train route is just for tourists, then think again. The **Train des Pignes'** (www.trainprovence.com) single gauge railway rattles through tunnels, bridges, and viaducts to connect the region's most isolated communities. The scenery is immense. The topography shunts from the palm trees of Nice to the rugged Gorges de Vésubie, before hitting the Alpine woodland of Puget-Théniers and the (almost) year-round snows before Digne-les-Bains.

The coal burners aboard the first steam trains were lit with *pignes* (pine-cones), hence the train's current name. The original steam engine still plies the route every Sunday morning in summer. It's run by volunteers who are particularly receptive to rail enthusiasts. More modern trains make the same journey three to four times daily.

Essentials

ARRIVING The **Train des Pignes** (www.trainprovence.com; ℂ Nice: **04-97-03-80-80**; Puget-Théniers: **04-93-05-00-46**; Entrevaux **04-93-05-41-38**; Digne-les-Bains: **04-92-31-01-58**) operates at least three times daily from Nice to Digne-les-Bains, stopping at Entrevaux and Puget-Théniers en route. SNCF (www.voyages-sncf.com; ℂ **36-35**) offers **bus services** (bookable on its website) from Sisteron and Aix-en-Provence to many towns and villages in Haute Provence. If you're **driving** from Aix-en-Provence, take A51 northeast; from St-Tropez D955 due north; and from Nice M6202 north, then N202 northwest.

Haught Provence

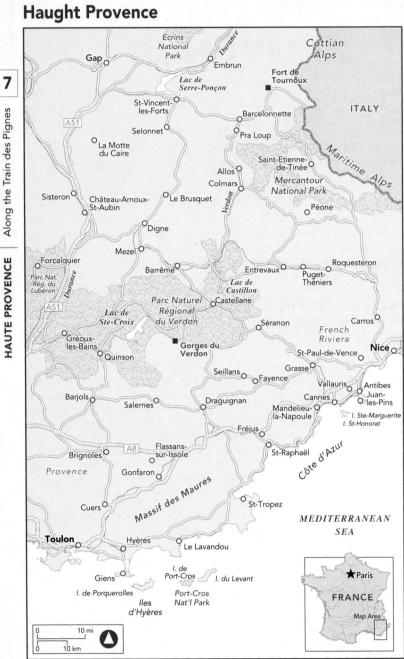

Ecrins National Park

Gap

Durance

Embrun

Cottian Alps

Fort de Tournoux

Lac de Serre-Ponçon

ITALY

St-Vincent-les-Forts

Barcelonnette

A51

Selonnet

Pra Loup

La Motte du Caire

Allos

Saint-Etienne-de-Tinée

Colmars

Mercantour National Park

Maritime Alps

Sisteron

Château-Arnoux-St-Aubin

Le Brusquet

Verdon

Péone

Digne

Mezel

Forcalquier

Barrême

Entrevaux

Puget-Théniers

Roquesteron

Parc Nat. Rég. du Lubéron

Durance

Lac de Castillon

A51

Parc Naturel Régional du Verdon

Castellane

Lac de Ste-Croix

Séranon

Carros

French Riviera

Gréoux-les-Bains

Gorges du Verdon

St-Paul-de-Vence

Nice

Quinson

Seillans

Fayence

Grasse

Vallauris

Antibes

Barjols

Salernes

Draguignan

Cannes

Juan-les-Pins

Mandelieu-la-Napoule

I. Ste-Marguerite

I. St-Honorat

Fréjus

Brignoles

A8

Flassans-sur-Issole

St-Raphaël

Côte d'Azur

Provence

Gonfaron

Cuers

Massif des Maures

St-Tropez

MEDITERRANEAN SEA

Toulon

Hyères

Le Lavandou

Giens

I. de Port-Cros

I. du Levant

I. de Porquerolles

Port-Cros Nat'l Park

Iles d'Hyères

0   10 mi

0   10 km

★ Paris

FRANCE

Map Area

VISITOR INFORMATION   Digne-les-Bains' **Office de Tourisme** is at place du Tampinet (www.ot-dignelesbains.fr; ✆ **04-92-36-62-62**). Entrevaux's **Office de Tourisme** is at Porte Royale du Pont-Levis (www.entrevaux.info; ✆ **04-93-05-46-73**). Puget Théniers' **Office de Tourisme** is at route Nationale 202, (www.provence-val-dazur.com; ✆ **04-93-05-05-05**).

SPECIAL EVENTS   For 5 days in early August, Digne-les-Bains is purple as far as the eye can see for the town's annual **Corso de la Lavande** (Lavender Festival, www.cdf-dignelesbains.fr). Action climaxes on the final day, with fireworks, flower-covered floats and costumed dancers parading down the town's main street, while the whole town sprayed with lavender-scented water.

Getting Around

BY CAR   Other than the Train des Pignes, public transport is thin on the ground throughout the whole of this region. However, for visitors with their own wheels, winding, scenic *routes départementales* link the area's main roads with more remote villages.

BY PUBLIC TRANSPORT   Bus nr. 790 (www.cg06.fr; ✆ **04-97-18-60-00**) connects Puget-Théniers and Entrevaux once daily (trip time: 15 min.; 1.50€ one-way). Buses (www.info-ler.fr; ✆ **08-21-20-22-03**) also connect Dignes-les-Bains with Aix-en-Provence, Nice, Avignon, and Marseille. See website for details.

[FastFACTS] ALONG THE TRAIN DES PIGNES

ATMs/Banks   BNP Paribas, 5 boulevard Gassendi, Dignes-les-Bains (✆ **08-20-82-00-01**); there is an ATM at **La Poste,** place Louis Moreau, Entrevaux (✆ **36-31**); **Crédit Agricole Provence Côte d'Azur**, 11 place Adolphe Conil, Puget-Théniers (✆ **04-93-05-07-15**).

Doctors & Hospitals Centre Hospitalier de Digne, Montée St Charles, Dignes-les-Bains (✆ **04-92-36-18-22**).

Mail & Postage   La Poste, 4 rue André Honnorat, Dignes-les-Bains (✆ **36-31**); **La Poste,** place Louis Moreau, Entrevaux (✆ **36-31**); **La Poste,** place

Général de Gaulle, Puget-Théniers (✆ **36-31**).

Pharmacies   Pharmacie Principale Pietri, 22 boulevard Gassendi, Dignes-les-Bains (✆ **04-92-31-34-22**); **Pharmacie d'Entrevaux**, place Louis Moreau, Entrevaux (✆ **04-93-05-40-06**); **Pharmacie J.M et E. Dupuy**, 9 avenue Alexandre Baréty (✆ **04-93-05-00-07**).

Where to Stay

There are few great hotels in this region. However, any of our recommended places to stay in the Parc Naturel Régional du Verdon (p. 101) also make a solid base for exploring this adjacent area.

La Maison de Julie ★★   This cute 18th-century B&B boasts just two country-style rooms and a petite *gîte* cottage. Each one is as cozy as it is traditional, with Provençal quilts and antique furnishings. Christian and Carole are welcoming hosts, full of ideas and advice on regional activities, from off-the-beaten-track bike rides to hearty local restaurants. Breakfast is an abundant affair, with croissants, yogurts, local honey, homemade jams, and seasonal fruit salads. La Maison de Julie's location—2km (1.5 miles) outside of Entrevaux proper—means that guestrooms afford stunning views over the medieval town. Walking trails run from the hotel's front door into the wilderness beyond.

Place Ste Marguerite, Le Plan, Entrevaux. www.maisonjulie.com. ✆ **04-93-02-46-42.** 3 units. 56€–63€ double; 70€–80€ 4-person *gîte*. Breakfast included. Free parking. No credit cards. Closed Nov–March. **Amenities:** Free Wi-Fi.

Where to Eat

Auberge des Acacias ★ PROVENÇAL   A true find. Step off the Train des Pignes into this bona fide country eatery. Mountain delights include giant slabs of Côte de Boeuf and Alpine-fresh Sisteron lamb. Local herbs spice fresh fish dishes like sea bream, which arrive via the mountain roads from Nice. English is spoken fluently (a rarity on these back roads of Provence) and portions will feed the hungriest of hikers.

Route de Digne, 06260 Puget Theniers. ✆ **04-93-05-05-25.** Main courses 9€–16€; fixed-price menu 22€ –30€. Thurs–Tues noon–2.30pm and 7–11pm.

Restaurant du Pont Levis ★★ PROVENÇAL   A refined rural restaurant overlooking the drawbridge at Entrevaux. Although far from the cheapest restaurant in this picturesque walled town, it offers country cuisine at its best. Try trout *meunière* or duck *confit* with rosemary. It's also the place to sample *secca d'Entrevaux*, a local dried salt-beef dish. The view from the capacious sun terrace stretches all the way down to the Mediterranean.

Place Moreau, 04320 Entrevaux. ✆ **04-93-05-40-12.** Main courses 12€–16€; fixed-price menu 26€–35€. Sat–Tues noon–10pm.

Exploring Along the Train des Pignes

The Train des Pignes shudders out of Nice's Gare du Sud station three to four times each day. This tiny *gare* is a 10-minute walk north of the main Nice-Ville train station. The scenery gets interesting after the first few stops, as the River Var forms a gorgelike tunnel around the tracks.

Travelers may alight anywhere, but we recommend **Puget-Théniers** for a first stop. Its pretty old town is studded with shops and ringed by hiking trails that run into the forests beyond. **Entrevaux**, some 20 minutes further on, is even more enchanting. With its fortified town walls, it looks like a Disney castle, protected from intruders with a drawbridge over a rushing river. The highlight is the **17th-century battlements** above town. A 3€ entrance ticket grants you access to the 156m (512 ft.) of steps up to the top. The Mediterranean and the Alpes-Maritimes mountains can be glimpsed in every direction.

Tunnels, loops, bridges, and switchbacks mark the route's next 30 minutes. **Le Fugeret** and **Méailles** are just two of the effortlessly cute towns en-route. Take note of the River Verdon at **Saint André-les-Alpes** station; it flows on from here into the Gorges du Verdon (see p. 104). The village of **Barrème**—a center for hiking, biking, and kayaking—is up next.

Digne-les-Bains finally appears as the Train des Pignes leaps along a mountain plateau. In winter expect snow; in summer wild flowers carpet the countryside around the tracks. Digne's hearty restaurants serve up local game and mountain lamb all year round.

L'OCCITANE EN provence

Bath and beauty product specialist **L'Occitane** (www.loccitane.com) began humbly in 1976 in the Haute-Provence village of Volx. Although the company has expanded worldwide to become a familiar name, its signature fragrances have remained true to Provençal roots, relying heavily on local ingredients like olive, lavender, honey, rose, and almond. The travel range is particularly handy, such as the shea butter moisturizer and the biodegradable mosquito repellent towelettes with insect-repelling essential oils. You can visit the factory on the outskirts of Manosque (Z.I. Saint Maurice; (✆ **04-92-70-19-00**) from Monday to Friday. Book via the tourist office in Manosque ((✆ **04-92-72-16-00**); tours are free. There's a factory shop on site, too, although discounts on the products are fairly modest.

Jardin des Papillons ★★ BUTTERFLY PARK   A stroll through the Jardin des Papillons is a good way to put names to the many butterflies you'll see in the wild around Haute-Provence. This 1-hectare butterfly park straddles both the region's typical Mediterranean and Alpine climates. Of the 250 or so kinds of butterfly in France, more than half have been spotted here. The particular flowers and shrubs cultivated in the park have been specially selected to attract butterflies from around the region.

BP44, Digne-les-Bains. www.proserpine.org. (✆ **04-92-36-70-70**. Admission 5€ adults, 3€ children 7–14, free for children 6 and under. Daily June–Aug 9:30am–12:30pm and 2–5pm, April–May and Sept Mon–Fri 9:30am–12:30pm and 2–5pm.

PARC NATUREL RÉGIONAL DU VERDON ★★

Created in 1997 and thus one of France's newer nature reserves, the **Parc Naturel Régional du Verdon** (www.parcduverdon.fr) possesses more than 700km (450 miles) of walking trails and bridle paths, yours to explore on foot, on horseback, or by mountain bike. In fact, this region is one of the top adventure-sports destinations in the whole of France, offering everything from white-water kayaking and canyoning to parascending, abseiling, and free-climbing. It's also home to the magnificent **Gorges du Verdon,** nicknamed Europe's "Grand Canyon." In the wilder reaches of the park, above the tree line, the limestone peaks are home to chamois, wild goats, marmots, and some spectacular birds, including golden eagles and Lammergeier (bearded) vultures. You'll find gentler country with tidy patchworks of green and purple lavender fields on the sunny Valensole plateau.

Essentials

ARRIVING   There are no passenger **rail** services to the Parc Naturel Régional du Verdon. Regional buses run from Marseille and Aix-en-Provence (30 min. later) to Castellane (www.info-ler.fr; (✆ **08-21-20-22-03;** trip time: 3.5 hr.; 25.80€ one-way), stopping at Moustiers-Sainte-Marie (trip time: 2 hr. 20 min.; 18.30€ one-way) en route. Buses from Nice (www.phoceens-cars.com; (✆ **08-10-00-40-08**) also serve Castellane (trip time: 2 hr. 10 min.; 14.60€ one-way). But if you want to explore the region, you'll really need a car. If you opt to **drive** from Marseille, take A51 northeast to exit 20, then N85 and D4085 southeast to Castellane. If you're driving from Nice, take E80 southwest to Le Cannet, then D6185 northwest to Grasse, followed by D6085 and D4085 north to Castellane. From Cannes, follow the A8 west towards Fréjus. Take exit 36 for Le Muy, and continue on D54 and then D955 for Montferrat. From there, continue on D955 past Comps-sur-Artuby north to Castellane. Or keep an eye out for D71: Heading west here will take you directly to the canyon.

VISITOR INFORMATION The Parc Naturel Régional du Verdon's **Maison du Parc** is Domaine de Valx, Moustiers-Sainte-Marie (www.parcduverdon.fr; ✆ **04-92-74-68-00**). Castellane's **Office de Tourisme** (www.castellane.org; ✆ **04-92-83-61-14**) can also provide a wealth of information about the region.

[Fast FACTS] PARC NATUREL RÉGIONAL DU VERDON

ATMs/Banks **Crédit Agricole**, place Marcel Sauvaine, Castellane (✆ **32-35**); **Crédit Agricole Provence Côte d'Azur**, avenue Lérins, Moustiers-Sainte-Marie (✆ **08-26-27-06-73**).

Doctors & Hospitals **Hôpital Local**, quartier Notre Dame, Castellane (✆ **04-92-83-98-00**).

Mail & Postage **La Poste,** place Marcel Sauvaire, Castellane (✆ **36-31**); **La Poste,** rue Seigneur de la Clue, Moustiers-Sainte-Marie (✆ **36-31**).

Pharmacies **Pharmacie Léocard**, 18 rue Nationale, Castellane (✆ **04-92-83-61-01**); **Pharmacie du Verdon**, avenue Lérins, Moustiers-Sainte-Marie (✆ **04-92-74-60-61**).

Where to Stay

Note that La Maison de Julie (p. 99) also makes a good base for exploring the Parc Naturel Régional du Verdon.

Hôtel au Naturel Moulin du Château ★ Proprietors Edith and Nicolas preside over this lovely guesthouse. As it's the sole hotel within the Parc Naturel Régional de Verdon, hikes into the park start from the front door. The two garden rooms are particularly family-friendly (although kids will love every aspect of the establishment), as birds and butterflies flutter throughout. There're no swimming pool, but guests may paddle in a small lake 1½ km (around 1 mile) away. Tennis and riding facilities are sited 2km (1½ miles) away. The Moulin's real pull is its homestyle restaurant (closed Mondays and Thursdays). Expect six courses of regionally sourced organic fare, paired with local wines. Half-board deals are also available.

Saint Laurent du Verdon. www.moulin-du-chateau.com. ✆ **04-92-74-02-47.** 10 units. Doubles 122€–147€. Rates include breakfast. Extra bed 16€. **Amenities:** Restaurant; games; riding; tennis; free Wi-Fi.

Moulin de la Camandoule ★★ A charming former olive mill converted into an equally adorable country hotel, each one of La Camadoule's flower-covered guestrooms, suites, and apartments is unique. Yet all feature period furniture and oh-so-pretty Provençal fabrics. Passers-by should make a pit stop at the hotel's fabulous l'Escourtin restaurant. Try Provençal *bourride* seafood stew or slow-braised spring lamb on the restaurant's 21.50€ lunch menu, or higher-end fare at dinner. The best insider's tip is the hotel's massive poolside dining option, open to non-guests during June, July, and August. It's guaranteed to relax tired bodies en-route to the Gorges du Verdon.

159 chemin de Notre Dame des Cyprès, Fayence. www.camandoule.com. ☏ **04-94-76-00-84.** 11 units. 88€–138€ double. **Amenities:** Restaurant; bar; babysitting; concierge; outdoor pool; free Wi-Fi

Terre Blanche ★★ One of Provence's most famous resorts sits 45 minutes from Nice, 30 minutes from Cannes, and 1 hour from the Gorges du Verdon. Yet there is no distinct reason to leave the confines of your private bungalow or suite. Take a contemporary art tour around the hotel's sculpture park, or wander the endless grounds, which are punctuated by a championship golf course. A member of the Leading Hotels of the World union, Terre Blanche is equally proud of its relationship with Grasse perfumer Fragonard, whose products are found in every room. The spa is akin to a Greek temple: think flowing fountains, giant columns, and a dozen plunge pools. The gastronomic restaurant Faventia is faultless.

Route de Bagnols en Foret, Tourrettes. www.terre-blanche.com. ☏ **04-94-39-90-00.** 115 units. 295€–890€ double; from 380€ suite. Free parking. **Amenities:** Bar; golf course; indoor pool; outdoor pool; 3 restaurants; sauna; free Wi-Fi.

Alternative Accommodations

Camping Les Collines de Castellane ★ It's hard to source bargain accommodation in the middle of the Parc Naturel Régional du Verdon. So this well-regarded 'camp village' a few miles from the Gorges and Lac du Castillon is a steal. You don't have to pitch your own tent; chalets and mobile homes for four to six people come with adequate kitchens. They spread out over mountain pasture surrounded by snow-capped peaks. The big draw here is the vast camp swimming pool, complete with waterslides. There's a new adventure park, too, plus volleyball and football tournaments. Older guests are catered to with themed evenings, hiking maps, and free electric bike rental.

Castellane. www.rcn-campings.fr. ☏ **04-92-83-68-96.** 160 tent pitches; 30 chalets/mobile homes. Tent pitches from 16€, chalets/mobile homes 41€–145€. Free parking. **Amenities:** Restaurant; games (football, volleyball, boules); pool and paddling pool; tennis. Closed mid-Sept–mid-April.

Where to Eat

Auberge Point-Sublime ★ PROVENÇAL The view from Le Point Sublime's tree-shaded terrace simply shouts Gorges du Verdon. Spectacular valley views are backed up by honest 'Pays Gourmand' cuisine: goats' cheese ravioli, grilled local trout, and truffle omelet. The homemade tarts (blueberry, hazelnut, strawberry, and honey) render it a fine stop for snacks while you're driving through. This classic *auberge* also boasts 13 simple guestrooms. We're not talking The Ritz (after all, doubles range from 67€ to 75€, quads from 97€ to 105€) but all are comfy and clean. Half-board options are also available.

RD952, Rougon. www.auberge-pointsublime.com. ☏ **04-90-85-69-15.** Reservations recommended. Main courses 11€–16€; fixed-price lunch 17€; fixed-price menu 26€–35€. Mon–Sat noon–2pm and 7–10pm. Closed Oct–March.

Bastide de Moustiers ★★ In the two decades since Michelin-starred super-chef Alain Ducasse opened the Bastide, cuisine has morphed from country inn to

EUROPE'S grand canyon

No visit to Haute Provence would be complete without a trip to see the **Gorges du Verdon** (www.lesgorges duverdon.fr). This spectacular limestone ravine measures up to 700m (2,300 ft.) deep in some parts. Nicknamed the "God of the Green Waters," the River Verdon that runs through the canyon is known for its emerald hue, which it gets from its high fluorine content. Three main tributaries (the Jabron, Artuby, and Colostre) join to form the canyon's rapid waters, although five dams forming five retention lakes have tamed its tempestuousness over the years.

The Gorges du Verdon form the largest canyon in Europe and the second largest in the world, after America's Grand Canyon. Straddling the border between the Var and the Alpes de Haute-Provence, these hollowed-out limestone gorges meander for 21km

(13 miles) from Pont de Soleils to Pont du Galetas. From Pont de Galetas, you'll see pedalos and canoes floating from the watersports haven of Lac de Sainte-Croix towards the gorges' mouth. Vertiginous roads wind along both rims of the canyon; among the best viewpoints to stretch your legs and take a drink are at Balcons de la Mescla on the southern rim or Point Sublime on the northern rim. Between Rougon and Castellane, the road dips down to the gorges—ideal for stopping to dip your toes into the ice-cold rapids. The canyon enjoys an Alpine climate, so you'll need a sweater for cooler summer nights.

Information about how best to take advantage of the region's natural beauty and sporting options, as well as information on events, is available from the tourist offices in Castellane and Moustiers Sainte-Marie (see p. 104).

refined rustic fare, without losing its Provençal heart. The mostly organic ingredients are sourced, in part, from the establishment's vast vegetable garden. Try grilled pigeon on a bed of *cep* mushrooms, crushed vegetables with the establishment's own olive oil, or chilled soup with garden peas. Dine alfresco from local faïence ceramics, or in one of several tiny, elegant restaurant rooms.

Even if you're not dining here, the Bastide is a surefire bet for charming accommodation a short drive from the Gorges du Verdon. The dozen guestrooms are suites ranging from 215€ to 720€, and are surrounded by 4 hectares (10 acres) of leafy grounds.

Chemin de Quinson, Moustiers-Sainte-Marie. www.bastide-moustiers.com. (*) **04-92-70-47-47.** Reservations required. Main courses 22€–37€; fixed-price lunch 38€; fixed-price menu 48€–79€. Daily noon–1:30pm and 7:30–9pm (closed Tues and Wed in March, Nov & Dec). Closed Jan–Feb.

Les Santons ★ PROVENÇAL   Arguably one of the finest restaurants in what is classified as one of the Most Beautiful Villages of France. The alfresco terrace of this gourmet establishment overlooks the village church. Inside, the stone-sided dining room oozes sophistication and charm. Recommended by Guide Michelin as a culinary bargain, the restaurant's seasonal dishes include a summery iced tomato soup, an autumn truffle menu, and *confit* of lamb in winter.

Place Pomey, Moustiers-Ste-Marie. (*) **04-92-74-66-48.** www.lessantons.com. Reservations required. Main courses 21€–31€; fixed-price menu 31€–36€. Wed–Sun noon–2pm and 7:30–9:30pm. Closed mid-Nov–mid-Feb.

EXPLORING PARC NATUREL RÉGIONAL DU VERDON

Castellane

High up in the Verdon valley, Castellane is the region's top spot for active visitors. The town is also a great base for gathering information and tips about the wider Parc Naturel Régional de Verdon. Unsurprisingly, Castellane's streets are crammed with shops selling outdoor clothing and equipment, from kayaks to inflatable rafts, including **L'Échoppe** (see p. 106). It's a cheerful, cosmopolitan place in summer, and there are lots of pleasant campsites nearby, including **Camping Les Collines de Castellane** (p. 103), many of them with lakeside or riverside locations.

Lac de Sainte Croix

The turquoise expanse of Lac de Sainte Croix is an inland sea that was created by damming the River Verdon in 1974. Today it's France's third-largest lake, its petite beaches splashed by emerald waves. On a hot summer's day, Lac de Sainte Croix is best explored by water. **Le Petit Port**, Plage de la Fontaine, Sainte Croix du Verdon (www.lepetitport04.com; **© 04-92-73-08-77**), rents **pedalos** (from 14€/hr.) and small **boats** (from 20€/hr.).

Moustiers Sainte Marie

High above the Lac de Sainte Croix, Moustiers is one of the prettiest villages in Haute Provence, with a babbling brook running through its center and views from the cliff-top church of Notre Dame. Unfortunately—partly due to the popularity of super-chef Alain Ducasse's Bastide de Moustiers (p. 103)—it's far from a secret. In summer its cafés and restaurants can be packed, although the village is still lovely enough to make a well-timed visit worthwhile. For unique souvenirs, be sure to peruse the dozen or so ateliers that create Moustiers' exquisite ceramics.

Musée de Préhistoire des Gorges du Verdon ★★ MUSEUM   Beneath its sweeping contemporary shell—the edifice was designed by Sir Norman Foster—this museum examines 1 million years of the Gorges du Verdon's history. Check out the permanent Stone Age dioramas, including Neanderthals, Cro-Magnons, bison and an impressive wooly mammoth. Or explore the museum's temporary shows, like 2014's *Premiers Nomades de Haute-Asie*, detailing the nomadic peoples of Mongolia and Siberia. Then head outdoors for a peek at history in situ. Guided tours (additional fee 4.50€ adults, 4€ children 7–17) make their way along the hiking trail that connects the museum to the Baume Bonne cave, discovered in 1946 and the site where many of the museum's ancient exhibits were unearthed. Separate tours visit the museum's "archae-ological village" (additional fee 4.50€ adults, 4€ children 7–17). Visitors may get a feel for Stone Age life in Haute Provence, trying their hand at shooting a bow and arrow, or lighting a fire by rubbing two sticks together. Note that most of the museum's infor-mation is only available in French, although audio guides are available.

Route de Montmeyan, Quinson. www.museeprehistoire.com. **© 04-92-74-09-59**. Admission 7€ adults, 5€ students and children 6–17, free for children 5 and under, family ticket (two adults and two children) 20€. Audio guide included in entrance fee. July–Aug daily 10am–8pm; May–June and Sept Wed–Mon 10am–7pm; Oct–Dec and Feb–April Wed–Mon 10am–6pm. Closed Jan–mid-Feb.

HOT-AIR balloning

Hot-air ballooning is big in France (no surprise—it was invented here). It's also one of the best ways to see Haute Provence. Lavender fields and olive groves spread out below you as you drift over the Durance valley, with the high country of the Verdon and Valensole stretching off into the distance. **France Montgolfières Balloon Flights** (www.france-balloons.com; ℭ **03-80-97-38-61**) operates regular flights between June and August, lifting off from Forcalquier. You get to watch the balloon being inflated, then scramble into the basket and float effortlessly into the air. The trip lasts around 3 hours, with just over an hour in the air. If it's your first-ever flight, there's a traditional ceremony on landing involving fizzy drinks and having a lock of your hair scorched off to prove you're a real *aéronaut*. Minimum age is 6 years old. Note that flights take off either at sunrise or just before sunset between April and October, and last around an hour. Fees range from 189€ to 249€ for adults, with flights for children aged 6–12 priced at 155€.

Organized Tours

You can explore the Gorges du Verdon and its surrounding landscape with guided hikes from the **Maison des Guides du Verdon**, La-Palud-sur-Verdon (www.escalade-verdon.fr; ℭ **04-92-77-30-50**). Canoeing and kayaking are available through the **Aqua Viva Est** in Castellane (www.aquavivaest.com; ℭ **04-92-83-75-74**), and the **Club Nautique,** Esparron de Verdon (www.cnev.online.fr; ℭ **04-92-77-15-25**). Rafting trips, canyoning, and aqua-rando (water rambling) are conducted by **Aboard Rafting** (www.aboard-rafting.com; ℭ **04-92-83-76-11**) in Castellane. All three of these outfits are in full swing between April and September, with peak season (and the widest range of activities) in July and August. Infrequent activities are also organized in March, October, and November. If you haven't booked in advance, you can head to Lac de Sainte-Croix (see p. 105), where you'll find plenty of pedalos for rent.

Note that there are plenty of local **bicycling** firms throughout the Parc Naturel Régional du Verdon, but unless you're seriously in top shape, the steep ascents and descents are likely to be a real challenge. Local tourist offices can give you specific details of outfits leading cycling tours throughout the region.

Especially for Kids

Rafting down the Verdon River is the not-to-be-missed Haute-Provence experience for those with older children. Lots of companies in and around Castellane run a huge variety of trips, some of which are frankly terrifying and only for adrenaline-crazed teens and grown-ups. Our favorite trip, run by **Aboard Rafting** (see above) for ages 8 and up, lasts 2 hours and ends up at the company's private riverside beach at La Pinede, an excellent picnic spot. Basic training, fully qualified guides and safety equipment are provided including lifejacket, helmet, and wetsuit. This trip is run between April and September, and costs 35€ per person.

Shopping

Located on Castellane's main street, **L'Echoppe**, 36 rue Nationale, Castellane (www.lechoppe-castellane.fr; ℭ **04-92-83-60-06**), can service pretty much every adventure sport need, from providing river equipment such as helmets and lifejackets, to advising on tents, sleeping bags, and camp stoves. It can also assist with obtaining local fishing permits and repairing bicycles.

DAY TRIP FROM PARC NATUREL RÉGIONAL DU VERDON

Sisteron ★

80km (49 miles) NW of Castellane

Sitting on the west bank of the Durance, Sisteron is one of the gateways to Haute Provence. Its red-roofed houses look like mini-skyscrapers as they rise from the banks of the jade-green river. Above the town, the intimidating medieval citadelle is perched upon on a limestone crag and affords far-reaching views from its ramparts.

ESSENTIALS

One **bus** (www.phoceens-cars.com; ✆ **08-10-00-40-08;** trip time: 1 hr. 50 min.; 6€ one-way) per day runs back and forth between Castellane and Sisteron, stopping at Digne-les-Bains en route. If you're **driving** from Castellane, take N85 northwest to Sisteron. The **Office de Tourisme** is Hôtel de Ville, 1 place de la République (www. sisteron-tourisme.fr; ✆ **04-92-61-36-50**).

EXPLORING SISTERON

Situated high above the roofs of Sisteron, the formidable **Citadelle de Sisteron** (www. citadelledesisteron.fr; ✆ **04-92-61-27-57**), has guarded the river crossing since the 13th century. It last saw action during World War II, when it was garrisoned by the Germans and shelled by the Allies, but its turrets and bastions are still in pretty good shape, as is the 15th-century stained glass in its chapel. It also houses a small museum dedicated to Napoleon, who passed through here after escaping exile on Elba, on the way to reclaiming the imperial throne in 1815, as well as a collection of horse-drawn carriages. It's open daily July and August 9am to 7:30pm, June and September 9am to 7pm, May 9am to 6:30pm, April 9am to 6pm, October 9am to 5:30pm, and the first 2 weeks of November 10am to 5pm. Admission is 6.20€ for adults, 2.70€ for children ages 6 to 14, and free for children 5 and under.

Note that the **Théâtre de la Citadelle** is also one of the venues (along with the Cathédrale Notre-Dame des Pommiers and Le Cloître Saint-Dominique) used for performances during Sisteron's annual **Nuits de la Citadelle** (www.nuitsdelacitadelle. fr; late July through mid-August), a classical music and dance festival that's been held most years since its inception in 1928.

WHERE TO EAT

For a quick bite to eat or an afternoon pick-me-up, newly renovated **L'Akène**, 67 rue de la Saunerie (www.creperielakene.fr; ✆ **04-92-61-20-39**) dishes up tasty buckwheat *galettes* and sweet crêpes—be sure to try the delectable salted caramel *galette* with fresh goat's cheese. Three-course fixed-price menus start at 10.50€.

MARSEILLE & AROUND

MARSEILLE ★★

776km (481 miles) S of Paris; 203km (126 miles) SW of Nice; 32km (20 miles) S of Aix-en-Provence

Marseille is France's oldest metropolis. It was founded as a port by the Greeks in the 6th century B.C. Today it's the second-largest city in France, as well as one of its most ethnically diverse, with nearly 1.5 million inhabitants.

Author Alexandre Dumas called teeming Marseille "the meeting place of the entire world." Never was this statement truer than in 2013, when Marseille proudly held the prestigious role of **European Capital of Culture**. More than 11 million visitors funneled into the city. They took in a flurry of new cultural venues and landmark museums, as well as the completion of long-term architectural projects, in particular the old docklands neighborhood west of the Vieux Port. **XL Airways** (www.xl.com) even launched the first direct flight from New York to Marseille, making this vibrant city all the more accessible.

On a day-to-day basis, Marseille is utterly real, in a way that other gentrified, tourist-targeted villages in the region are decidedly not. A view from high up reveals the colorful Vieux Port, with its elegant old buildings, boat-filled harbor, and the Mediterranean beyond. Yet it's a working city with many faces, both figuratively and literally.

Marseille is sprawling and can be down at heel in parts. But it's also a cosmopolitan nexus of vibrant sounds, smells, and sights. The city's age-old problems may include unemployment, the Mafia, and racial tension (around a quarter of the population is of North African descent, with significant Armenian, Jewish, and Asian communities), but civic pride is strong, and the city is firmly focused on the future, evidenced by the ongoing **Euroméditerranée urban regeneration project** (www.euromediterranee.fr).

The Capital of Culture crowds have now departed. But 2013's legacy remains and a handful of Marseille's newest projects came to fruition in early 2014. Therefore there's never been a better time to visit the city than right now. From the vintage shops that pepper Le Panier's backstreets to the boutique bolt-holes that are flinging open their doors, it's evident that France's second city has finally come of age.

Essentials

ARRIVING   **Marseille-Provence Airport** (www.marseille-airport.com; ✆ **04-42-14-14-14**), 27km (17 miles) northwest of the city center, receives international flights from all over Europe. From the airport, shuttle buses (*navettes;* www.navettemarseilleaeroport.com; ✆ **08-92-70-08-40**) make the trip to Marseille's St-Charles rail station, near the Vieux-Port, for 8.20€,

Marseille

ATTRACTIONS ●
Basilique Notre-Dame de la Garde **20**
Cathédrale de la Major **4**
Centre de la Vieille Charité **5**
Château Borély **16**
FRAC PACA **6**
La Friche la Belle de Mai **10**
MuCEM **1**
Musée Cantini **19**
Musée d'Histoire de Marseille **11**
Musée des Beaux-Arts **10**
Musée Regards de Provence **3**
Stade Vélodrome **23**

HOTELS ■
Au Vieux Panier **8**
C2 Hotel **21**
Casa Honoré **17**
Hotel Dieu **9**
Hotel Le Corbusier **22**
Mama Shelter **24**

RESTAURANTS ◆
Grain du Sel **18**
L'Epuisette **15**
La Kahena **13**
La Miramar **12**
La Table du Mole **2**
Le Glacier du Roi **7**
MinaKouk **25**
Toinou **14**
Viaghji di Fonfon **15**

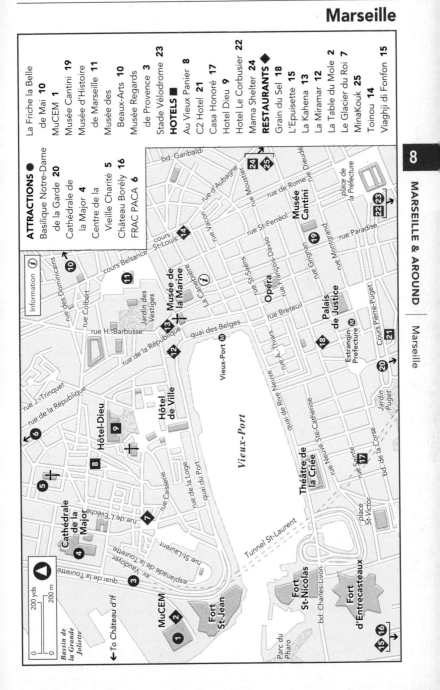

5.80€ passengers 12 to 26, and 4.10€ children under 12. The shuttle buses run daily every 20 minutes from 5am until midnight; the trip takes 25 minutes.

Marseille has **train** connections from all over Europe, particularly to and from Nice, and on to Italy. It's also linked to Paris via the TGV bullet train, which departs almost every hour from the Gare de Lyon (trip time: 3 hr., 20 min.; 30€–113€ one-way). **Buses** serve the **Gare Routière,** rue Honnorat (✆ **04-91-08-16-40**), adjacent to the St-Charles railway station. Several buses run daily between Aix-en-Provence and Marseille (www.navetteaixmarseille.com; trip time: 40 min.; 5.70€ one-way). If you're **driving** from Paris, follow A6 south to Lyon, and then continue south along A7 to Marseille. The drive takes about 8 hours. From Provence, take A7 south to Marseille.

VISITOR INFORMATION The **Office de Tourisme** is at 11 la Canebière (www.marseille-tourisme.com; ✆ **08-26-50-05-00;** Métro: Vieux-Port).

CITY LAYOUT Marseille is a large, sprawling metropolis. Unlike any of the other towns mentioned in this chapter, if you're keen to explore different parts of the city, you'll probably need to take advantage of its comprehensive public transport.

NEIGHBORHOODS IN BRIEF The major arteries divide Marseille into 16 *arrondissements.* Like Paris, the last two digits of a postal code tell you within which *arrondissement* an address is located. Visitors tend to spend most of their time in four main neighborhoods. The first is the **Vieux Port,** the atmospheric natural harbor that's a focal point for the city center. From here, the wide La Canebière boulevard runs eastwards, bisected by Marseille's most popular shopping avenues. To the north lies **Le Panier,** the original Old Town, crisscrossed by a pastel network of undulating alleyways. This neighborhood's western edge is trimmed by former docklands, which have been completed redeveloped over the past few years. Southeast of the Vieux Port, the alternative neighborhood around **cours Julien** is home to convivial restaurants and one-off boutiques aplenty. And come summertime, action shifts to the **Plages du Prado,** a strip of beaches due south of the city center.

SPECIAL EVENTS Le Défi de Monte-Cristo (www.defimonte-cristo.com)—also known as the Monte-Cristo Challenge—is inspired by Alexandre Dumas' 19th-century novel, *The Count of Monte Cristo*. In the story, main character Edmond Dantès escapes from Château d'If by swimming to the French mainland. In late June, hundreds of participants battle it out to replicate Dantès' 5-km (3-mile) swim, each one hoping to win the race's 3,000€ prize.

The city's **Festival de Marseille** (www.festivaldemarseille.com), a citywide celebration of music, dance, and arts, is held from mid-June to mid-July.

As summer winds down, **Septembre en Mer** (September at Sea, www.office delamer.com) celebrates any and everything sea-related, from boating and paddle-boarding to Mediterranean cuisine and an environmentally sound coastline. Festivities take place from late August until early October and culminate with the Vieux Port's Marine Parade.

For runners, Marseille holds an annual **Marathon** (www.runinmarseille.com), half-marathon and 10km-run each year in September. Too lightweight? The first edition of Marseille's much anticipated **5150 Triathlon** (www.ironman.com) took place in 2013. Centered around the city's Plages du Prado, the event is now takes place each year in late July.

The city's most popular music festival since its inception in 1992 is **Fiesta des Suds** (www.dock-des-suds.org). It's held annually in late October. Live acts include prominent South American and African bands, as well as big international names such as Patti Smith.

MARSEILLE city pass

If you plan to visit more than a few of Marseille's sites and museums, purchase a 1-day (24€), 2-day (31€), or 3-day (39€) **City Pass** from the Marseille Tourist Office. The pass covers all public transport, including the round-trip ferry trip to **Château d'If** (p. 118), as well as entrance to more than a dozen of the city's museums and a ride on the *petit-train*

(p. 119) up to the **Basilique Notre-Dame de la Garde** (p. 116). Free tastings at various artisanal shops and discounts at a selection of citywide boutiques are also included. Kids' passes, valid for children aged 7 to 15 years old, are available for 17€ (1 day), 20€ (2 days), and 23€ (3 days).

Getting Around

ON FOOT   Each of Marseille's neighborhoods is easily navigable on foot. However, unless you're an avid walker, you may want to rely on either the Métro or the tramway (see below) to zip around town.

BY CAR   Parking and car safety are so problematic that your best bet is to park in a garage and rely on public transport. The website **www.parking-public.fr** lists Marseille's public parking lots and hourly fees.

BY TAXI   Contact **Taxis Radio Marseille** (www.taximarseille.com; ✆ **04-91-02-20-20**).

BY PUBLIC TRANSPORT   **Métro** lines 1 and 2 both stop at the main train station, Gare St-Charles, place Victor Hugo. Line 1 makes a U-shaped circuit from the suburbs into the city and back again; Line 2 runs north and south in the downtown area. Also with two lines, the tramway services the Canabière and the refurbished Joliette Docks district, as well as continuing out to the suburbs. Individual tickets are 1.50€; they're valid on Métro, tram, and bus lines for up to 60 minutes after purchase. If you plan to take public transport several times during your stay, buy a **pass journée,** valid for 1 day for 5€ or 3 days for 10.50€. Public transit maps are downloadable from the Régie des Transport de Marseille (www.rtm.fr; ✆ **04-91-91-92-10**).

To take a load off of weary toes, Marseille's municipality also offers a **free ferry service** across the Vieux Port. Regular departures, which take around 5 minutes to cross the width of the port, set off from quai du Port outside Town Hall between 8am and 5pm.

[Fast FACTS] MARSEILLE

ATMs/Banks   Marseille's banks are plentiful, including three along La Canebière.

Doctors & Hospitals Hopital Saint Joseph, 26 bd. de Louvain (www.hopital-saint-joseph.fr; ✆ **04-91-80-65-00**).

Embassies & Consulates   **British Consulate**

Marseille, 24 av. du Prado (www.gov.uk; ✆ **04-91-15-72-10**); **Consulate General of the United States Marseille,** place Varian Fry (http://marseille.usconsulate. gov; ✆ **04-91-54-92-00**).

Internet Access   In 2013, Marseille's municipality installed 50 free Wi-Fi hotspots around the city.

Central locations (including Jardin du Pharo, the square outside the Hôtel de Ville, and La Vieille Charité) are indicated on the free maps distributed by the tourist office.

Mail & Postage   **La Poste,** 1 cours Jean Ballard (✆ **36-31**).

local interviews and recent openings.

Pharmacies **Leader Santé,** 37 la Canebière (✆ **04-91-91-32-06**).

Safety As in any big city, it's wise to keep to keep a close eye on your belongings and avoid poorly lit areas at night.

Where to Stay

Although slightly removed from the city center, the iconic **Hôtel le Corbusier** (www. gerardin-corbusier.com) is a must for architecture aficionados. In 2013, local French designers transformed the hotel's rooftop gym into a hip contemporary art space, **MAMO** (www.mamo.fr).

Au Vieux Panier ★★ This funky little bed-and-breakfast is not only one of Marseille's great bargains, it's also utterly unique. Tucked within an atmospheric 17th-century edifice, all five rooms are redesigned annually by different local and international artists, which means you're bedding down within a one-of-a-kind work of art. Recent collaborations included Pascale Robert's 3-D line drawings and Thomas Canto's urban-inspired installations. Temporary exhibitions are also dotted throughout the hotel's corridors; all of the artwork on the walls is for sale. The rooftop terrace peeks out over the surrounding Le Panier neighborhood, Marseille's original Old Town. Views sweep from the Cathédrale de la Major to the city's new Zaha Hadid contemporary skyscraper. Note that the hotel does not have an elevator.

13 rue du Panier. www.auvieuxpanier.com. ✆ **04-91-91-23-72.** 5 units. 100€–140€ double; 175€ apartment. Métro: Vieux-Port. Tram: Sadi Carnot. **Amenities:** Communal living room; free Wi-Fi.

C2 Hotel ★★★ Marseille's newest hotel, the five-star C2 was launched in spring 2014. Twenty luxurious, light-filled rooms spill over a 19th-century merchant family mansion, each one decked out in exposed brick walls and designer furnishings. Some have a private hammam steam bath. There's a superb Filorga Spa onsite with indoor pool and Jacuzzi, as well as a cocktail bar. But the hotel's *pièce de résistance*? That would have to be C2's beach, located on the private Mediterranean island of Île Degaby. Pack a picnic and castaway.

48 rue Roux de Brignoles. www.c2-hotel.com. ✆ **04-95-05-13-13.** 20 units. 169€–429€ double; breakfast included if rooms are booked via the website. Free valet parking. Métro: Estrangin-Préfecture. **Amenities:** Bar; private beach; concierge; spa; free Wi-Fi.

Casa Honoré ★ Interior designer Annick Lestrohan, creator of the Honoré brand of homewares, has transformed this former print shop into an ultra-stylish bed-and-breakfast. Unsurprisingly, guest rooms are decorated with Lestrohan's exquisite creations, from sleek designer furnishings to quality linens (and all are for sale too). An oasis of tranquility just south of Marseille's Vieux Port, the B&B's four rooms all center around a courtyard splashed with tropical foliage and a small swimming pool. Book as far in advance as you dare.

123 rue Sainte. www.casahonore.com. ✆ **04-96-11-01-62.** 4 units. 150€–200€ double. Minimum 2-night stay. No credit cards. Métro: Vieux-Port. **Amenities:** Breakfast room; outdoor pool; free Wi-Fi.

Hôtel-Dieu ★★ Opened in 2013, the luxurious Hotel Dieu is perched just behind Marseille's Hôtel de Ville, overlooking the Vieux Port from Le Panier. This five-star hotel occupies what was once an 18th-century hospital. It's now managed by the

InterContinental Group with aplomb. As well as modern, minimalist guest rooms with superb views, guest may enjoy the indoor pool, the Clarins Spa, brasserie **Les Fenêtres,** and gastronomic restaurant **Alcyone** onsite.

1 place Daviel. www.ihg.com. ℂ **04-13-42-42-42.** 194 units. 220€–440€ double; 500€–1,500€ suite. Parking 25€. Métro: Vieux-Port. **Amenities:** Restaurant; bar; business center; fitness center; indoor pool, room service; spa; free Wi-Fi.

Mama Shelter ★★   Tucked into the hipster cours Julien district, this unique hotel is the brainchild of designer Philippe Starck. Rooms are bright and cool, from the modular furnishings to the wall-mounted iMacs offering dozens of free on-demand movies. Downstairs, Egyptian graffiti artist Tarek has tagged the industrial-chic restaurant's ceiling. And outdoors, Mama Shelter's yellow-striped courtyard hosts a pastis bar where guests can sip their way through more than four dozen variants of the city's beloved anise-flavored tipple. This is an excellent bet for a contemporary taste of France's second city.

64 rue de la Loubière. www.mamashelter.com. ℂ **04-84-35-20-00.** 127 units. 69€–109€ double; 129€ family room; 199€ suite. Parking 19€. Métro: Notre Dame du Mont. **Amenities:** Restaurant; bar; free Wi-Fi.

Where to Eat

For diners interested in recreating Marseille's famous *bouillabaisse* fish stew at home, **Miramar Restaurant** (www.lemiramar.fr) offers cooking classes (120€/5-hr. lesson including lunch). Contact the tourist office for details.

As well as the restaurants listed below, **Le Glacier du Roi,** 4 place de Lenche (ℂ **04-91-91-01-16**) is well worth a detour. Locals claim that ice cream here—homemade by owner Florence Bianchi on the premises—is the best in town. *Glace à la navette* (flavored with orange flower water, like Marseille's distinctive cookie, see p. 121) is the house specialty.

L'Epuisette ★★ SEAFOOD/MEDITERRANEAN   This Michelin-starred option is undoubtedly the premier place in Marseille to sample **bouillabaisse** stew. Pack your appetite: Fresh fish is poached in saffron-infused soup; the final product is served as two separate courses, accompanied by *rouille,* a mayonnaise-like sauce flavored with garlic, cayenne pepper, and saffron. L'Epuisette's setting is as sublime as the cuisine: The seaside dining room overlooks Château d'If from the picturesque fishing port of Vallon des Auffes, 2.5km (1½ miles) south of Marseille's Vieux Port.

Vallon des Auffes. www.l-epuisette.fr. ℂ **04-91-52-17-82.** Reservations required. Main courses 18€–65€; fixed-price dinner 70€–125€. Tues–Sat noon–1:30pm and 7:30–9:30pm. Closed Aug. Bus: 83.

Le Grain du Sel ★★ MODERN MEDITERRANEAN   Marseille-born chef Pierre Giannetti concocts what many locals consider to be the city's most creative bistro cuisine. Dishes are infinitely innovative, often taking inspiration from Giannetti's years of cooking in Barcelona. Following morning market finds, the daily menu may include Sardinian gnocchi with clams, mussel *escabèche,* or Spanish rice with shellfish harvested from the Camargue seaside town of Saintes-Maries-de-la-Mer. The wine list is carefully considered, and you can dine outside on sunny days in the petite courtyard.

39 rue de la Paix Marcel Paul. ℂ **04-91-54-47-30.** Reservations recommended. Main courses 16€–35€; fixed-price lunch 16€–19€. Tues–Sat noon–2pm, Fri–Sat 8–10pm. Closed Aug. Métro: Vieux-Port.

La Kahena ★ TUNISIAN   Among Marseille's many Tunisian restaurants, this 35-year-old eatery stands out from the crowd. Named for a 6th-century-B.C. Tunisian princess, La Kahena's specialty is couscous: Among the 10 varieties are versions with lamb, *merguez* spicy sausages, and cod. Other Tunisian classics such as *mechoua* salad (spicy grilled vegetables), tajines, and crispy *brick* pastry stuffed with shrimp are also served up in the ornate blue-tiled dining room. A solid budget choice.

2 rue de la République. ℰ **04-91-90-61-93.** Reservations recommended. Main courses 10€–18€. Daily noon–2pm and 7–10:30pm. Métro: Vieux-Port.

MinaKouk ★ ALGERIAN   This contemporary Algerian eatery and tea shop sits on a narrow backstreet in Marseille's cours Julien district. All bright colors and modern furnishings, Mina is ideal for wallet-friendly *chorba* soup, savory *beurek* pastries, *tajine* bakes, and couscous come lunchtime. Mid-afternoon, attention is given over to steaming pots of mint tea and towering trays of traditional North African sweets. A neighborhood favorite.

21 rue Fontange. www.minakouk.com. ℰ **04-91-53-54-55.** Main courses 10.50€–23€; fixed-price menu 10.50€–12€. Tues–Sat 8am–7pm, open late Fri and Sat evenings. Métro: Notre-Dame du Mont-Cours Julien.

La Table du Môle ★★★ MODERN MEDITERRANEAN   Triple Michelin-starred-chef Gérard Passédat's newest restaurant, this "chic bistro" opened atop the MuCEM (p. 117) in 2013. Much like the MuCEM itself, stellar dishes herald from across the Mediterranean, including seafood tart served with a creamy ginger jus, crab paired with spicy harissa, or grilled turbot with truffled potatoes. All are served against a sweeping backdrop of Marseille's port and the Mediterranean Sea. Note that it's also possible to dine at La Table's lower-key (and cheaper) sister restaurant, **La Cuisine ★★★** (lunch only), located the adjacent dining room—no sea views however. The fabulous two-course buffet lunch here is a steal at just 21.50€. Almost all the produce used in both restaurants is sourced from the organic Les Olivades d'Ollioules farm. And finally—if you're keen to recreate some of this delectable cuisine at home— Passédat launched his brand-new cooking school **L'école de cuisine de Gérald Passédat** (www.passedat.fr, from around 75€ per person) in spring 2014.

MuCEM, 1 esplanade du J4. www.passedat.fr. Reservations required, available via internet only. Main courses 18€–65€; fixed-price lunch 43€; fixed-price dinner 73€. Wed–Mon 12:30–2:30pm; Wed-Sat and Mon 7:30–10:30pm. Métro: Vieux-Port. Bus: 49, 60, or 82.

Toinou ★★ SEAFOOD   For the veritable seafood aficionado, there is no better place to dine in Marseille than this landmark restaurant. Platters are piled high with dozens of varieties of mussels, oysters, clams, and this region's famous sea urchins, as well as sea snails of all shapes and sizes. Doing a bustling local business for close to 50 years, Toinou's format changed from table service to a slightly more chaotic variation on self-service in late 2013. No matter: the seafood dished up here is just as sublime. Want your fish with a sea view? Choose your own selection of shellfish from the restaurant's kiosk out front, then head down to the coast for a beachside picnic.

3 cours St-Louis. www.toinou.com. ℰ **08-11-45-45-45.** Reservations recommended. Shellfish by the half dozen 2.10€–9€; fixed-price platters 15.70€–88.90€. Daily 11:30am–11:30pm. Métro: Vieux-Port or Noailles.

Viaghji di Fonfon ★★ TAPAS   Yep, this brand-new bistro and wine bar is known for their tapas. But no, they're not like any Iberian bites that you've tasted before. Mother restaurant Chez Fonfon (www.chez-fonfon.com) serves one the best bouillabaisses in Marseille. Modern little Viaghji dishes up nibbles from all across the Mediterranean instead, ranging from Corsican cured *figatellu* salami and Italian *osso buco*

LA FRICHE LA belle de mai

Occupying a former tobacco factory, **La Friche la Bette de Mai** (www.lafriche. org; ℰ **04-95-04-95-95**) has been the city's favorite cultural center since 1992. It includes eclectic artist's residences and television studios (where Marseille's ultra-popular soap opera, "*Plus belle la vie*" is shot), as well as performance spaces for all artistic disciplines. There's also the "Street Park" skate park, a restaurant, gardens, weekly produce market (Monday evenings), and a library on site. Music festivals and club nights are now held on the center's brand-new terraced roof space. In 2013, the vast **Tour-Panorama** contemporary exhibition space opened here too. There are two entrances to the complex, at 41 rue Jobin and 12 rue François Simon. It's a short walk to the Friche from the Musée des Beaux-Arts (see p. 117). Alternatively, hop aboard bus 49 or 52.

to local grilled sardines. Evenings are playful, with a rotating schedule of live music and the odd backgammon tournament.

138 vallon des Auffes. www.viaghjidifonfon.com. ℰ **04-91-52-78-28.** Reservations recommended. Tapas 5€–15€; fixed-price menu 15€. Daily 9am–11pm. Closed 2:30–6pm Oct–March. Bus: 83.

Exploring Marseille

Immerse yourself in local life with a wander through Marseille's busy streets, including along the famous **La Canebière.** Lined with hotels, shops, and restaurants, it used to be a very seedy street indeed, saturated with sailors from every nation. With Marseille's ongoing urban regeneration, however, it is rapidly becoming the heart and soul of the city.

La Canebière joins the **Vieux Port ★★**, dominated at its western end by the massive neoclassical forts of St-Jean and St-Nicolas. The harbor is filled with fishing craft and yachts and ringed by seafood restaurants. For a panoramic view, head to the **Jardin du Pharo,** a promontory facing the entrance to the Vieux-Port. From the terrace of the Château du Pharo, built by Napoleon III, you can clearly see the city's old and new cathedrals, as well as the recently redeveloped docklands, now the **Cité de la Méditerranée,** which includes **Fort Saint-Jean** and the architectural wonder that is **MuCEM** (Museum of European and Mediterranean Civilizations).

North of the old port is **Le Panier,** Marseille's Old Town. Small boutiques and designer ateliers now populate these once-sketchy streets. To the south, the **corniche Président-J.-F.-Kennedy** is a 4km (2½-mile) promenade. You'll pass villas and gardens facing the Mediterranean, before reaching the popular **Plages du Prado.** Patrolled by lifeguards in the summer, these spacious, sandy beaches have children's playgrounds, sun loungers, and waterside cafes. Serious hikers can continue south of here into the **Parc National des Calanques** (www.calanques-parcnational.fr), France's newest national park (see box p. 124). This series of stunning limestone cliffs, fjords, and rocky promontories stretches along the coast for 20km (12 miles) southeast of Marseille.

To get a feel for the city's most popular sights, the Tourist Office distributes a handy map detailing a **Walking Tour of Marseille Museums.** The itinerary makes a good starting point for first-time visitors, circling the Vieux Port and lingering along atmospheric boulevards. Alternatively, the Tourist Office's free map of the city has three easy walking tours of Marseille marked on it.

Basilique Notre-Dame-de-la-Garde ★ CHURCH This landmark church crowns a limestone rock overlooking the southern side of the Vieux-Port. It was built in the Romanesque-Byzantine style popular in the 19th century and topped by a 9.7m (32-ft.) gilded statue of the Virgin. Visitors come for the views (best at sunset) from its terrace. Spread out before you are the city, the islands, and the shimmering sea.

Rue Fort-du-Sanctuaire. www.notredamedelagarde.com. ✆ **04-91-13-40-80.** Free admission. Daily April–Sept 7am–7:15pm, Oct–March 7am–6:15pm. Métro: Estrangin-Préfecture. Bus: 60.

Cathédrale de la Major CATHEDRAL One of the largest cathedrals (some 135m/443 ft. long) built in Europe during the 19th century, this massive structure has almost swallowed its 12th-century predecessor, built on the ruins of a temple of Diana. Its striped exterior is a bastardized Romanesque-Byzantine style with domes and cupolas; the intricate interiors include mosaic floors and red-and-white marble banners. The cathedral's architecture is particularly arresting now that it overlooks Marseille's redeveloped port and dockland areas. It also provides shady respite from sightseeing on a summer's day.

Esplanade de la Major. ✆ **04-91-90-53-57.** Free admission. Hours vary. Head west of Le Panier district. Métro: Vieux-Port. Bus: 49, 60, or 82.

Centre de la Vieille Charité ★ MUSEUM Designed by Pierre Puget during the 17th century, this quadrant of arcades—surrounding a picturesque central chapel—originally served as a poorhouse. The imposing structure was nearly destroyed following a condemnation order during the mid 20th century. It was architect Le Corbusier who successfully launched a campaign for its preservation. Today the center houses the **Musée d'Archéologie Méditerranéenne** (Museum of Mediterranean Archaeology), the **Musée Africain, Océanien et Amérindien** (Museum of Africa, Oceania, and Amerindian Culture), a temporary exhibition space, and Le Miroir, an art house cinema. Among recent popular shows staged here is 2014's *Visages: Picasso, Magritte, Warhol*....

2 rue de la Charité. www.vieille-charite-marseille.com. ✆ **04-91-14-58-80.** Admission 5€ adults, 3€ students and seniors, free for children 17 and under. Admission varies for temporary exhibitions. Tues–Sun 10am–6pm. Bus: 35, 49, or 55.

Château Borély ★★ ATTRACTION An impressive 18th-century private mansion surrounded by manicured gardens (now the Parc Borély and botanical gardens), Château Borély has been entirely renovated, reopening in 2013. It now holds the **Musée des Arts Décoratifs, de la Faïence et de la Mode** (Museum of Decorative Arts, Earthenware and Fashion), exhibiting a mix of ceramics, furnishings, and fashion. The Château also contains the popular **Café Borély**, Pavillon Est (www.cafe borely.fr; ✆ **04-91-22-46-87**), a courtyard café that sources exclusively local ingredients for its seasonal menu and weekend brunch.

134 avenue Clot-Bey. www.musee-des-beaux-arts.marseille.fr. ✆ **04-91-55-33-60.** Admission 5€ adults, 3€ students and seniors, free for children 17 and under. Tues–Sun 10am–6pm. Métro: Rond-Point du Prado. Bus: 19, 44, or 83.

FRAC PACA (Fonds Régional d'Art Contemporain Provence-Alpes-Côte d'Azur) ★★ MUSEUM Formerly located in Le Panier, the brand-new premises for FRAC PACA, Marseille's regional contemporary art museum, are now situated squarely in the up-and-coming Joliette Docks district. The museum's mosaic-like recycled glass structure was designed by Japanese architect Kengo Kuma. It's a fitting tribute to the FRAC's thousand-strong collection of artworks. It was inaugurated—like so many cultural spaces in this city—in 2013. Within the museum itself, exhibitions are displayed over two galleries. There's also a restaurant, two terraces, artists' residences, a performance hall, and a bookstore.

20 boulevard de Dunkerque. www.fracpaca.org. © **04-91-91-27-55.** Admission 5€ adults, 2.50€ 18–25 years old, students, and seniors 60 and older, free for children 17 and under. Wed–Sat 10am–6pm, Sun 2–6pm. Open one Fri per month until 9pm. Métro: Joliette. Tram: Joliette. Bus: 35, 49, 55, or 82.

MuCEM (Museum of European and Mediterranean Civilizations) ★★

MUSEUM   Opened in 2013, the long-anticipated MuCEM is the first national gallery in France to be located outside of Paris. More than 250,000 ancient and modern items have been collected from throughout the region and are exhibited here, along with local prints and historical postcards. The permanent collection is superbly displayed, mixing objects and artworks with video diaries, commissioned cartoons, and enchanting photographs from around the Mediterranean. Architect Rudy Ricciotti designed the museum's contemporary form, which is encased in unique concrete lace. The premises are linked to the 17th-century **Fort Saint-Jean** and its suspended gardens via a panoramic elevated walkway; Michelin-starred-chef Gérard Passédat's two **Le Môle** restaurants (p. 114) are also on site.

1 esplanade du J4. www.mucem.org. © **04-84-35-13-13.** Admission 5€ adults, 3€ seniors and students, 9€ family ticket, free children 17 and under. Additional fee for temporary exhibitions. May–Oct Wed–Thurs and Sat–Mon 11am–7pm, Fri 11am–10pm; Nov–April Wed–Thurs and Sat–Mon 11am–6pm, Fri 11am–10pm. Métro: Vieux-Port. Bus: 49 or 82.

Musée des Beaux-Arts ★ MUSEUM   The 150-year-old Museum of Fine Arts

is Marseille's oldest exhibition venue. Following 2013's blockbuster show "Le Grand Atelier du Midi: Van Gogh a Bonnard," held in tandem with the **Musée Granet** in Aix (p. 83), the museum reopened its permanent collection to the public in 2014, after an incredible 9 years of renovations. Exhibits range from 16th-century Italian works to 19th-century French masterpieces, including Rodin's sculpture "La Voix Intérieure" ("The Inner Voice").

Palais Longchamp. www.musee-des-beaux-arts.marseille.fr. © **04-91-14-59-30.** Admission 5€ adults, 3€ students and seniors, free for children 17 and under. Additional fee for temporary exhibitions. Tues–Sun 10am–6pm. Métro: Longchamp. Tram: Longchamp. Bus: 81.

Musée Cantini ★ ART MUSEUM   Fully renovated for Marseille's European

Capital of Culture 2013 festivities, this 17th-century *hôtel particulier* (private mansion) organizes outstanding modern art exhibitions. Recent shows have been dedicated to Chilean surrealist Roberto Matta and native Marseillaise sculptor César. The museum also houses a permanent collection, particularly strong on masterpieces (by Picasso, Dufy, de Staël, Ernst, and others) created during the first half of the 20th century.

19 rue Grignan. www.musee-cantini.marseille.fr © **04-91-54-77-75.** Admission 5€ adults, 3€ students and seniors, free for children 17 and under. Tues–Sun 10am–6pm. Métro: Estrangin/Préfecture. Bus: 18, 21, 41S, 54, or 221.

Musée d'Histoire de Marseille ★★ MUSEUM   Thirty years after its creation,

Marseille's Musée d'Histoire was entirely renovated and reopened at the end of 2013. Today, the light-filled exhibition halls are flanked by large picture windows. Each one overlooks the ruins of the city's Port Antique in the garden outside. Displays include the remains of vast Roman ships, constructed in oak between the sixth and the second centuries BC, as well as a scale model of the *pont à transbordeur*, an impressive bridge over the Vieux Port that was destroyed in World War II. Note that almost all of the exhibits' explanations are in French only.

Centre Bourse, 2 rue Henri-Barbusse. www.musee-histoire-de-marseille.marseille.fr. ℂ **04-91-55-36-00**. Admission 5€ adults, 3€ students and seniors, free for children 17 and under. Additional fee for temporary exhibitions. Tues–Sun 10am–6pm. Métro: Vieux Port. Tram: Belsunce/Alcazar. Bus: 31, 32, 41S, 55, 57.81. 82, 82S, 89, 97, or 221.

Musée Regards de Provence ★★ MUSEUM   Located within what used to be the city's *station sanitaire* (quarantine station), this museum forms part of the cluster of brand-new exhibition spaces lining Marseille's polished J4 esplanade. It showcases the permanent "Memory of the Quarantine Station," a sound and light show. Popular temporary exhibitions have included *Marseille éternelle*, a collection of artworks inspired by the city, and *L'école de Nice*, focusing on the group of innovative 1960s Niçois artists that included Yves Klein and Arman. The museum's terraced **Régards Café** offers superb views over the Mediterranean. There's also an **L'Occitane en Provence** shop, stocking Provençal lotions, potions, and bath products, located on the premises.

Allée Regards de Provence, avenue Vaudoyer. www.museeregardsdeprovence.com. ℂ **04-96-17-40-40**. Admission 7.50€ adults, 6.50€ seniors, 5.50€ students and children 13–18 years old, free for children 12 and under. Daily 10am–6pm. Bus: 82 or 82S.

Stade Vélodrome ★★ ATTRACTION   Soccer fans should make a beeline for Marseille's newly-reopened (June 2014) Olympique de Marseille (OM) football stadium, home to one of France's most popular soccer teams. After more than 3 years of renovations, the modern Stade is now one of the largest soccer grounds in France, and boasts 67,000 seats. Which means it's more than perfectly placed to host matches throughout the upcoming **2016 UEFA European Championship** ("Euro2016"). Behind-the-scenes tours of the grounds and the stadium are also offered three times each week. See the Stade Vélodrome website for details.

Rue Raymond Teisseire, boulevard Michelet. www.arema-velodrome.com. ℂ **08-26-10-40-44**. Stadium tours 10€ adults, 8.50€ students. Métro: Rond-point du Prado.

Outlying Attractions

You can take a 25-minute ferry ride to the **Château d'If** (if.monuments-nationaux.fr), a national monument built by François I as a fortress to defend Marseille. Alexandre Dumas used it as a setting for the fictional adventures of *The Count of Monte Cristo*. The château is open daily May 16 to September 16 9:30am to 6:10pm; September 17

La Marseillaise

Few know that France's national anthem was actually composed in Strasbourg. Originally titled "War Song of the Army of the Rhine," it was written in one night by army captain Claude-Joseph Rouget de Lisle in 1792. That same year, revolutionaries from Marseille (who had been given printed copies) marched into Paris singing it. In their honor, the song became known as "La Marseillaise" and was quickly adopted as the rallying cry of the French Revolution. It was officially declared the national anthem of France in 1795, only to be banned by Napoleon during the Empire, Louis XVIII in 1815, and Napoleon III in 1830. The anthem was reinstated for good in 1879.

to March 31 Tuesday to Sunday 9:30am to 4:45pm; and April 1 to May 15 daily 9:30am to 4:45pm. Entrance to the island is 5.50€ adults, free children 17 and under. Boats leave approximately every 45 to 60 minutes, depending on the season; the round-trip transfer is 10.10€. For information, contact the **Frioul If Express** (www. frioul-if-express.com; ℂ **04-96-11-03-50**; Métro: Vieux-Port).

North of Marseille proper, **L'Estaque** was once a picturesque seaside village (although it now looks out over the city's more urban skyline). It was painted by Provence's artistic greats—including Cézanne, Renoir, and Braque—between the 1860s and 1920s. Today, visitors can tread these legendary footsteps and easel sites, following the "Painters' Path" signposted around town (strolling time around 2 hours). Popular local snacks are purveyed from L'Estaque's seafront stalls, including *chichi frégi* (sugar-topped fritters flavored with orange blossom water) and *panisses* (savory chickpea flour fritters). You can reach L'Estaque via bus no. 35 from Marseille's place de la Joliette (journey time around 30 minutes). Between April and September, there's also a *navette* ferry service from the Vieux Port to L'Estaque for 3€ (journey time 40 min.).

Organized Tours

One of the easiest ways to see Marseille's centrally located monuments is aboard the fleet of open-top **Le Grand Tour Buses** (www.marseillelegrandtour.com; Métro: Vieux-Port). You can hop off at any of 13 different stops en route and back on to the next bus in the day's sequence, usually arriving between 1 and 2 hours later, depending on the season. The buses run four to eight times a day during each month except January. A 1-day pass costs 18€ adults and 16€ seniors and students with ID; the fare for children ages 4 to 11 is 8€. Two-day passes are also available for just a few euros more.

The motorized **Trains Touristiques de Marseille** (www.petit-train-marseille.com; ℂ **04-91-25-24-69**; Métro: Vieux-Port), or *petit-trains*, make circuits around town too. Year-round, train no. 1 drives a 75-minute round-trip to Basilique Notre-Dame-de-la-Garde and Basilique St-Victor. From April to mid-November, train no. 2 makes a 65-minute round-trip of old Marseille by way of the cathedral, Vieille Charité, and the Quartier du Panier. Both trains make a 30-minute stop for sightseeing en route. The trains depart from the quay just west of the Hôtel de Ville. The fare for train no. 1 is 8€ adults and 4€ children; train no. 2 is 1€ less for both.

Marseille's Office de Tourisme offers two bilingual tours of the city center. The first explores the **Vieux Port and Le Panier** (Saturdays at 10:30am, included free with purchase of a City Pass, p. 111). The second meanders its way around **cours Julien's contemporary art galleries and street art** (one Saturday per month at 3:30pm, 10€). In 2014, the Office de Tourisme also began leading bilingual guided tours of Le Corbusier's **Cité Radieuse**, site of Hôtel le Corbusier (p. 112). Taking place from Tuesday to Saturday at 2:30pm and 4:30pm, tours cost 10€ per person and can be reserved through the tourist office.

Another dozen or so other Office de Tourisme tours are offered in French only. These range from as exploration of MuCEM's architecture to a nighttime tour of the Vieux Port. Contact the tourist office for further details.

Rendez-vous Provence's (www.rendez-vous-provence.com; ℂ **04-42-96-30-72**) "Marseille Panorama" tour navigates its way around the city, taking in Le Panier, Notre Dame de la Garde, and Vallon des Auffes en route. The tour lasts around 4 hours, and costs 62€ per person. The same outfit also offers a combination drive and boat trip to explore Marseille's nearby coastline, stopping in Cassis' picturesque port and atop the sea-facing Cap Canaille, Europe's tallest cliff. This tour is priced as 79€ and takes around 4 hours.

Alternatively, boat tours to the **Parc National des Calanques** also depart directly from Marseille's Vieux Port. Many tour operators with different prices and formulas (for example, three Calanques in 2 hr./22€, or eight in 3 hr./28€) can be found on the quai des Belges. For more information about visiting the Calanques from nearby Cassis, see p. 123.

For an unusual way to see Marseille and its coastline, try one of the catamaran cruises offered by **Levantin** (www.levantin.fr; ✆ **04-91-24-40-40**). Levantin organizes a variety of tours, from sailing around Château d'If followed by a swim in Baie des Quarantaines (35€ per person), to sunset cruises with dinner and live music onboard (70€ per person). Tours depart from the Vieux Port's quai d'Honneur, just outside of the Town Hall (Mairie). The staffed catamarans are also available for private hire. **Goélette Alliance** (www.goelette-alliance.com; ✆ **06-11-63-47-44**) offers more exclusive personalized tours at sea aboard a 27-meter (88-ft.) sailing yacht, departing from the same quay. The vessel can accommodate up to 27 passengers, and is priced from 1,500€ per half-day.

Shopping

Only Paris and the French Riviera can compete with Marseille for its breadth and diversity of merchandise. Your best bet is a trip to the streets just southeast of the **Vieux-Port,** crowded with stores of all kinds.

Rue Paradis and **rue Saint Ferréol** have many of the same upscale fashion boutiques found in Paris, as well as a Galeries Lafayette, France's largest chain department store. For more bohemian wear, try **cours Julien** and **rue de la Tour** for richly brocaded and beaded items on offer in North African boutiques.

Le Panier is now home to a vibrant range of unique boutiques. Try **5.7.2,** 23 rue du Panier (www.5-7-2.com; ✆ **06-07-14-62-92**) for 1930s to 1970s homewares, or **Les Baigneuses,** 3 rue de l'Eveche (www.lesbaigneuses.com; ✆ **09-52-68-67-64**), which sells a gorgeous range of retro-styled swimwear. **La Boutique Éphémère**, 20 rue du Panier (✆ **06-09-83-86-51**), is also well worth seeking out. Designer apparel, as well as homewares and vintage treasures, are regularly overhauled and themed according to owner Laure Tinel's whims—one month everything may be inspired by Alice in Wonderland; another month it's all black. At **Coucoukoulou,** 42 rue du Panier (www.coucoukoulou.fr; ✆ **06-59-24-44-56**), Koulthoumi Ali creates colorful clothes, cushions, and dolls in traditional fabrics from the Comoro Islands.

For unique souvenirs, head to **Ateliers Marcel Carbonel,** 49 rue Neuve-Ste-Catherine (www.santonsmarcelcarbonel.com; ✆ **04-91-13-61-36**). This 80-year-old business specializes in *santons,* clay figurines meant for Christmas nativities. In addition to personalities you may already know, the carefully crafted pieces depict Provençal common folk such as bakers, blacksmiths, and milkmaids. The figurines sell for around 12.60€ and up.

Alternatively, **Marseille in the Box,** 13 rue Reine Elisabeth (www.marseilleinthebox.com; ✆ **04-91-91-32-39**) is packed to the rafters with offbeat Marseille-themed goodies, including books, beer, and vintage-style tins. **Le Comptoir du Panier,** 1 montée des Accoules (www.lecomptoirdupanier.fr; ✆ **04-91-91-29-65**), is stocked with clothing, jewelry, hats, and handbags crafted by regional designers. South of the port, the petite gallery **L'Image en Provence,** 28 quai de Rive Neuve (www.

martin-raget.com; ✆ **04-91-33-01-20**), also sells gorgeous photos of Marseille, the Calanques, and Provence (from 15€), with particularly arresting shots of the coastline and the sea.

Navettes, small cookies that resemble boats, are a Marseillaise specialty. Flavored with secret ingredients that include orange zest and orange flower water, they were invented in 1791 and are still sold at **Le Four des Navettes,** 136 rue Sainte (www. fourdesnavettes.com; ✆ **04-91-33-32-12**), for around 9.60€ per dozen. On the opposite side of the port in Le Panier, José Orsoni also purveys top-notch *navettes* (5€ for around ten), as well as other traditional baked goods such as Corsican *canistrelli* and *cucciole,* at **Navettes des Accoules,** 68 rue Caisserie (www.les-navettes-des-accoules. fr; ✆ 04-91-90-99-42).

Microcosmos Chai Urbain, 42 rue de l'Evêché (www.microcosmoschaiurbain. com; ✆ **06-87-15-60-98**) is a one-of-a-kind find. France's first city-center winery is located in Le Panier and headed up by Fabienne Vollmy. Pop in to pick up a bottle or two of their organic, Provençal wine, sold exclusively on the premises.

One of the region's most authentic fish markets at **Quai des Belges** (daily 8am–1pm), on the old port, is partially sheltered under the new Norman Foster–designed Ombrière mirrored canopy. On **cours Julien,** you'll find a market with fruits, vegetables, and other foods (Tues, Thurs, and Sat 8am–1pm); exclusively organic produce (Wed 8am–1pm); stamps (Sun 8am–1pm); and secondhand goods (3rd Sun of the month 8am–1pm).

Nightlife

For an amusing and relatively harmless exposure to the town's saltiness, walk around the **Vieux-Port,** where cafes and restaurants angle their sightlines for the best views of the harbor.

L'Escale Borély, avenue Pierre Mendès France, is 20 minutes south of the town center (take bus no. 83). With a dozen animated bars and cafés, plus restaurants of every possible ethnicity, you'll be spoiled for choice.

Kick off the evening at **Barberousse Shooter Bar,** 7 rue Glandeves (www. barberousse.wix.com/barberoussemarseille; ✆ **04-91-33-78-13**), a popular local spot for—you guessed it—shots. The pirate-themed bar stages a rocking happy hour from 9pm to 10pm daily, and all night on Tuesdays.

Marseille's dance clubs are habitually packed out, especially **Trolley Bus,** 24 quai de Rive-Neuve (www.letrolley.com; ✆ **04-91-54-30-45;** Métro: Vieux-Port), known for techno, house, hip-hop, jazz, and salsa. Equally buzzing is **l'Exit,** 12 quai de Rive-Neuve (✆ **06-42-59-96-24;** Métro: Vieux-Port), a bar/disco with a terrace that profits from Marseille's sultry nights and two floors of seething nocturnal energy (happy hour starts at 5pm, and runs all night on Thursdays). The **New Can Can,** 3–7 rue Sénac (www.newcancan.com; ✆ **04-91-48-59-76;** Métro: Noailles), is a lively, sprawling bar and disco that identifies itself as a gay venue but attracts many straight folks too. It's open Friday through Sunday midnight until 7am. Brand-new sister bar **Le Petit Can-can,** 10 rue Beauvau (www.lepetitcancan.com; ✆ **06-52-26-90-75;** Métro: Vieux-Port) is open daily from 6pm for cocktails and tapas.

For jazz right on the port, head to **La Caravelle,** 34 quai du Port (www.lacaravelle-marseille.com; ✆ **04-91-90-36-64;** Métro: Vieux-Port), an aperitif bar and dinner club that serves a different flavor almost every night, including *manouche,* the French gypsy style most associated with guitarist Django Reinhardt.

CASSIS ★★

806km (501 miles) S of Paris; 128km (80 miles) SE of Avignon; 50km (31 miles) S of Aix-en-Provence; 32km (20 miles) E of Marseille

Cassis is unarguably the prettiest coastal town in Provence. The settlement dates from Ancient Greek times—that's as far back as both Marseille and Nice—but its fame rose in the early 20th century, when famous personalities like Virginia Woolf and Sir Winston Churchill guzzled its crisp white wines. The resort recently found a new outdoor-orientated audience as the capital of France's first mainland National Park since 1979.

Essentials

ARRIVING   Cassis Station is a cinch to reach by rail. Half-hourly **trains** arrive from Marseille (trip time: 25 min.; 6€ one-way). Sound easy? It's not, as Cassis Station is then a 3km (1¾ miles) downhill walk to the Cassis town center. Walk down, grab one of the waiting taxis (10€), or catch the Marcouline city bus (.80€) every 30 minutes. If you're **driving** from Marseille, take A50 east.

VISITOR INFORMATION   The helpful **Office de Tourisme** is on the beachfront quai des Moulins (www.ot-cassis.com; ✆ **08-92-39-01-03**).

[FastFACTS] CASSIS

Mail & Postage   **La Poste,** 3 rue Arène (✆ **36-31**). Note that the post office also offers an ATM.

Pharmacies   **Pharmacie Trossero,** 11 av Victor Hugo (✆ **04-42-01-70-03**).

Where to Stay

L'Alvila ★★   This impossibly romantic B&B sits a ten-minute hike from the seafront promenade on the way to Cassis train station. It is managed by amiable French-Cuban couple Corinne and Humberto. Five modernist guestrooms (with interior touches from the likes of Starck and Kartell) are set across a 1920s villa. The top rooms boast a panoramic sea view. From Easter onwards, designer sun loungers are positioned in the fragrant gardens beside the outdoor pool.

15 avenue Joseph Liautaud. www.lavila-cassis.com. ✆ **04-42-03-35-37.** 5 units. 140€–200€ double including breakfast. Free parking. Closed Nov–mid-March. **Amenities:** Outdoor pool; free Wi-Fi.

Hotel La Rade ★   The pick of Cassis's mid-range hotels, La Rade gazes out over the ocean, a 3-minute walk from the pedestrian only quays. Its enviably tranquil position is also convenient for strolls west to plage du Bestouan and into the Calanques National Park beyond. In summer, the hotel's locally sourced breakfast—think Cassis jams and Provençal *saucisson*—is served by the swimming pool, the only sea view *piscine* in town. The hotel terrace is justly popular with artists. Indeed, Sir Winston Churchill honed his painting skills at the Camargo Foundation (www.camargo foundation.org) artist residency just across the street.

1 avenue des Dardanelles. www.bestwestern-cassis.com. ✆ **04-42-01-02-97.** 28 units. 90€–215€ double. Breakfast 16€ per person. **Amenities:** Restaurant, outdoor pool; free Wi-Fi.

Where to Eat

Bar de la Marine ★ BISTRO   This harborside eatery won't feature in the Michelin guide or any other French foodie bible. And thank heavens for that. This no-nonsense bar and bistro has been dishing up *steak-frites*, *salade Niçoise*, and seafood salad to tired fisherman since time began. In season, its proximity to Cassis's working port makes it a prime spot to try sea urchins, the local delicacy. Simply order a platter from the septuagenarian street vendor to be delivered to your table. Like almost every other restaurant in Cassis, Bar de la Marine boasts rustic service and age-old tableware.

5 quai des Baux. © **04-42-01-76-09.** Main courses 10€–17€. Daily noon–2:30pm and 7–10:30pm.

La Poissonnerie ★★SEAFOOD   The Giannettini family have been serving harbor-fresh seafood at this portside emplacement since 1940. They've had 75 years to perfect their simple recipes. My goodness they're good. Grilled sardines, octopus salad, and the special house spicy aïoli share the menu with local urchins (in season) and oysters from near Marseille. Bouillabaisse, the famed seafood stew from the latter city, may be ordered in advance.

5 quai Barthélémy. © **04-42-01-71-56.** Main courses 11€–24€. Tues–Sun noon–1:30pm; (June–Sept Tues–Sat 7:30–10pm). Closed Jan.

Exploring Cassis

The deliciously beautiful center of Cassis is best explored on foot. The coastal path winds from the wide expanse of Grande Plage beach past restaurant terraces and boutiques all the way to Plage du Bestouan and the start of the Parc Nationale des Calanques. Each August the entire town comes alive for a series of literary festivals, fireworks shows, and sea jousting tournaments (yes, involving lances and motor boats).

Cassis Snorkeling Tour TOUR   As you might expect from a town that borders a massive marine and land National Park, Cassis is awash with diving schools. These include **Cassis-Plongée** (www.cassis-calanques-plongee.com) and **Narval Plongée** (www.narval-plongee.com). Novice divers may also scuba or snorkel along the **Sentier Sous-Marin de Cassis**, or underwater trail. This self-guided 30-minute swim route begins on the Promenade des Lombards. Four buoys mark marine life discovery spots along the way. Be aware that a mineral water source (as in thousands of bottles of chilled Evian) seeps from the limestone cliffs into Cassis harbor, so sea temperatures are often chilly!

Cassis Wine Tour ★ WALKING TOUR   White wines from Cassis (www.vinsde cassis.fr) are so superb that they were protected as an AOC region in 1936 (along with Chateauneuf-du-Pape see p. 50 outside of Avignon). Most vintages are infused with flowery Marsanne from the Rhone Valley, and herby Clairette from Provence. Just a dozen small, mostly organic producers tend their ocean-facing vineyards that are planted from the port up to the Cassis train station. All can be toured (with free tasting sessions to those who wish to purchase a bottle or three) by foot or by bicycle using the free Vineyard Tour map from the Cassis Tourist Office. Cheers.

Cassis environs. www.vinsdecassis.com.

Outlying Attractions

In 2012, Cassis was declared the capital of the new **Parc Nationale des Calanques** (see box p. 124). The calanques are towering cliffs created 120 million years ago. They were then split apart by rising sea levels and bleached white by the Provençal sun. Each calanque crashes into the azure sea from heights of up to 565m (nearly 2000ft). Like Norway's fjords, they surround a series of boat-only bays that stretch for 32km (20 miles) from Cassis to Marseille. So sturdy is the snow-white stone from Calanque

FRANCE'S LATEST national park

In 2012 the Parc Nationale des Calanques (www.calanques-parcnational.fr) was designated as the 7th National Park in mainland France—and the first since 1979. Some 50,000 hectares (193 square miles) of land, coastline and sea are now protected forever more, including the wildlife, flora and 60 species of fish that reside therein. Cars, scooters, jet skis, and speedboats are prohibited in the National Park, so tranquility is assured.

Southern French travelers hoping to hike further off the beaten track are spoiled for choice. On their doorstep is the Port-Cros National Park (see p. 126, www.portcrosparcnational.fr), which covers a series of sub-tropical islands. The Mercantour National Park (www.mercantour.eu), a haven for wolves, deer, and butterflies, sits just north of Nice.

Port-Miou, a creek within walking distance of Cassis, that it was used to build the base of the Statue of Liberty in New York.

The main public pathway through the park is the GR51, a long distance hiking trail known as the 'Balconies of the Mediterranean.' This *grande randonnée* route links Marseille with Monaco. Those visitors without Ironman thighs (or without a spare 3 weeks of vacation) may hike along a score of shorter marked paths instead, passing lonely islands, rocky passes, secret beaches, and gaping creeks. Park maps are available from Cassis's ever-helpful Tourist Office.

A more relaxed way to tour the park is by sea. From Cassis harbor regular **boat trips** take in three calanques (45m, adults 16€, children under 10 9.50€), five calanques (65m, adults 19€, children 13€,) or nine calanques (2 hours, adults 27€, children 16€). A particular favorite is Calanque de Sugiton, which crumbles into an island-strewn bay. The postcard-perfect **Calanque d'En Vau** is also well worth seeking out. As non-official motorboats are banned from the National Park, try paddling under into the calanques by kayak or SUP instead. For equipment hire contact **Cassis Sport Loisirs Nautiques** (www.cassis-kayak.com).

ÎLES D'HYÈRES ★★

39km (24 miles) SE of Toulon; 119km (74 miles) SW of Cannes

Bobbing off the French Riviera in the Mediterranean Sea, a small group of islands encloses the eastern boundary of Provence. During the Renaissance, they were coined the Îles d'Or (Golden Islands), named for the glow the rocks give off in sunlight. As might be expected, their location only half an hour from the French coast means the islands are often packed with tourists in summer—but there is still space on its breathtaking beaches for everyone.

If you have time for only one island, choose the beautiful, lively **Île de Porquerolles.** The **Île de Port-Cros** is quieter—and perhaps better for an overnight stay in order to take advantage of the great hiking, exploring, and snorkeling that would be too rushed for a 6-hour day trip. As for the **Île du Levant,** 80% belongs to the French army and is used for missile testing; the remainder is a nudist colony.

Essentials

GETTING TO ÎLE DE PORQUEROLLES   Ferries leave from several points along the Côte d'Azur. The most frequent, cheapest, and shortest trip is from the harbor of La Tour Fondue on the peninsula of Giens, a 32km (20-mile) drive east of Toulon. Depending on the season, there are 5 to 19 departures per day. The round-trip fare for the 15-minute crossing is 19.50€ adults and 17.30€ children 4 to 10. For information, contact **TLV-TVM,** La Tour Fondue, Giens 83400 (www.tlv-tvm.com; ℂ 04-94-58-21-81). **Bateliers de la Côte d'Azur** (www.bateliersdelacotedazur.com; ℂ 04-94-05-21-14) and **Les Vedettes Île d'Or & Le Corsaire** (www.vedettesilesdor.fr; ℂ 04-94-71-01-02) also offer services from La Londe-les-Maures and Le Lavandou respectively.

GETTING TO ÎLE DE PORT-CROS   The most popular ferry route to the island is the 35-minute crossing that departs from Le Lavandou 3 to 7 times daily, depending on the season (28.10€ adults, 24.90€ children 4–12 round-trip). For information, contact **Les Vedettes Île d'Or & Le Corsaire** (see above). The **TLV-TVM** and **Bateliers de la Côte d'Azur** (see above) also service Île de Port-Cros. Some of the former's services travel onwards to Île de Levant.

VISITOR INFORMATION   Other than temporary, summer-only kiosks that distribute brochures and advice near the ferry docks in Porquerolles and Port-Cros, there are no tourist bureaus on the islands. For further information, contact the **Office de Tourisme de Hyères, Bureau de Porquerolles,** Rotonde du Park Hôtel, av. de Belgique, Hyères (www.hyeres-tourisme.com; ℂ 04-94-01-84-50). Information can also be found at www.porquerolles.com and www.portcrosparcnational.fr.

MAIL/POSTAGE & MONEY   The post office, **La Poste,** place d'Armes, Porquerolles (ℂ 36-31), also has an ATM, but it's best to bring petty cash. Most establishments accept credit cards.

Exploring Île de Porquerolles ★★

Île de Porquerolles is the largest and westernmost of the Îles d'Hyères. It has a rugged southern coast, but the northern strand, facing the mainland, boasts a handful of pristine white-sand beaches. The island is about 8km (5 miles) long and 2km (1¼ miles) wide, and is 4.8km (3 miles) from the mainland. The permanent population is only 400.

The island is said to receive 275 days of sunshine annually. The landscape is one of rocky capes, pine forests twisted by the mistral, sun-drenched vineyards, and pale ochre houses. It's best explored on foot or by bike (look for plenty of bike-rental agencies just behind the harbor). The **place d'Armes,** former site of the garrison, is home to several quaint cafes—your best bet for lunch if you're here for a day trip.

The island has a history of raids, attacks, and occupation by everyone from the Dutch and the English to the Turks and the Spaniards. Ten forts, some in ruins, testify to its fierce past. The most ancient is **Fort Ste-Agathe,** built in 1531 by François I. In time, it was a penal colony and a retirement center for soldiers of the colonial wars.

In 1971, the French government purchased a large part of the island and turned it into a national park. Indigenous trees such as fig, mulberry, and olive are protected, as well as plants that attract butterflies.

WHERE TO EAT & STAY

Hotel et Residence Les Medes (www.hotel-les-medes.fr) also offers good-value guest rooms and apartments.

Mas du Langoustier ★★　This Provençal-style hotel is far and away Porquerolles' most luxurious accommodation. Located on the island's western tip, it's set in a 40-hectare park shaded by eucalyptus and Aleppo pines, and overlooks a lovely pine-ringed bay. Elegant rooms are decorated with classic local textiles; many have their own private patio. And come evening time, there's no need to leave paradise. The onsite **Restaurant L'Olivier** (open to nonguests) is Michelin-starred: Prepare for unique pairings like steamed crayfish and fig ravioli or foie gras with hibiscus jelly.

83400 Ile de Porquerolles. www.langoustier.com. ℭ **04-94-58-30-09.** 50 units. 300€–660€ double; 690€–760€ suite; 920€–1,200€ family room. Rates include half-board. Closed Oct to late April. **Amenities:** 2 restaurants; bar; babysitting; outdoor pool; tennis court; free Wi-Fi.

Exploring Île de Port-Cros ★★

The most mountainous island of the archipelago, Port-Cros has been France's smallest national park since 1963. It's just 5km (3 miles) long and 2km (1¼ miles) wide. It's blanketed with beautiful beaches, pine forests, and subtropical vegetation (birders flock here to observe nearly 100 different species). A hiker's paradise, it also has a number of well-marked trails. The most popular and scenic is the easy, 1-hour *sentier des plantes*. The more adventurous and athletic take the 10km (6¼-mile) *circuit de Port-Man* (and pack their lunch). There is even a 274m (899-ft.) "underwater trail" along the coast, where you can snorkel past laminated signs identifying the plants and fish you'll see.

WHERE TO EAT & STAY

Le Manoir de Port-Cros　Port-Cros's only hotel sits within an 18th-century whitewashed building. Accommodation may be simple—crisp white sheets, oversized copper vases, terra-cotta tiled floors—but guests stay here to truly switch off. Paddle in the pool, head out for a hike, or simply amble the surrounding palm- and eucalyptus-studded gardens. Rates are half-board, although plenty of day-trippers visit for the restaurant's hearty three-course lunch (58€).

83400 Hyeres, Ile Port Cros. www.hotel-lemanoirportcros.com. ℭ **04-94-05-90-52.** 21 units. 165€–265€ double; 210€–240€ family room; 230€–265€ bungalows for 4. Closed Nov–March. **Amenities:** Restaurant; bar; outdoor pool; room service; free Wi-Fi in common areas.

ST-TROPEZ & AROUND

ST-TROPEZ ★★★

874km (542 miles) S of Paris; 76km (47 miles) SW of Cannes

While this sun-kissed town has a well-known air of hedonism, Tropezian style is blissfully understated—it's not in-your-face. St-Tropez attracts artists, musicians, models, writers, and an A-lister movie colony each summer, with a flamboyant parade of humanity trailing behind. In winter it morphs back into a boho fishing village, albeit one with modern art galleries and some of the best restaurants along the coast.

The 1956 Brigitte Bardot movie "And God Created Woman" put St-Tropez on the tourist map. Droves of decadent tourists baring all on the peninsula's white-sand beaches followed in her wake. Two decades ago, Bardot pronounced St-Tropez dead, "squatted by a lot of no-goods, drugheads, and villains." But even she returned, followed in recent years by celebrities like David Beckham, Paris Hilton, Jay-Z, and Beyoncé.

Essentials

ARRIVING   The nearest rail station is in St-Raphaël, a neighboring coastal resort (see p. 135). **Boats** depart (www.bateauxsaintraphael.com; ✆ 04-94-95-17-46) from its Vieux Port for St-Tropez (trip time: 1 hr.) five times a day in high summer, reducing to once- or twice-daily sailings in winter. The one-way fare is 15€. Year-round, 10 to 15 Varlib **buses** per day leave from the Gare Routière in St-Raphaël (www.varlib.fr; ✆ 04-94-24-60-00) for St-Tropez. The trip takes 1½ to 2 hours, depending on the bus and the traffic, which during midsummer is usually horrendous. A one-way ticket is 3€. Buses also run from Toulon train station, 56km (35 miles) away.

If you **drive,** note that parking in St-Tropez is tricky, especially in summer. For parking, follow the signs for **Parking des Lices** (✆ 04-94-97-34-46), beneath place des Lices, or **Parking du Nouveau Port,** on waterfront avenue Charles de Gaulle (✆ 04-94-97-74-99). To get here from **Cannes,** drive southwest along the coastal highway (D559), turning east when you see signs to St-Tropez.

VISITOR INFORMATION   The **Office de Tourisme** is on quai Jean-Jaurès (www.ot-saint-tropez.com; ✆ 08-92-68-48-28). Note that they charge 2€ for a town map. Meanies.

[FastFACTS] ST-TROPEZ

ATMs/Banks   **Crédit Agricole,** 17 place des Lices (✆ 32-25).

Internet Access   There's free Wi-Fi—as well as a handy table and stools—at the **Casino Supermarket,** av. Genéral Leclerc.

St-Tropez

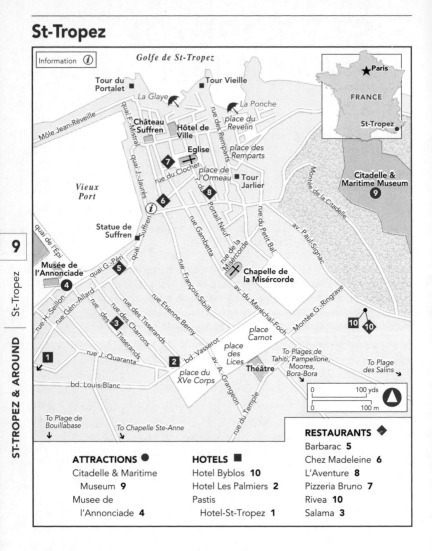

Golfe de St-Tropez

Information ⓘ

Tour du Portalet
La Glaye
Tour Vieille
La Ponche
place du Revelin
Château Suffren
Hôtel de Ville
Eglise ✚ **7**
place des Remparts
place de l'Ormeau
Tour Jarlier
8
Vieux Port
ⓘ **6**
Statue de Suffren
Musée de l'Annonciade
4
5
Chapelle de la Misércorde ✚
3
1
2
place Carnot
place des Lices
Théâtre
place du XVe Corps
Citadelle & Maritime Museum **9**

To Plages de Tahiti, Pampellone, Moorea, Bora-Bora
To Plage des Salins
10 **10**
To Plage de Bouillabase
To Chapelle Ste-Anne

FRANCE ★Paris · St-Tropez

0 —— 100 yds
0 —— 100 m

ATTRACTIONS ●
Citadelle & Maritime
    Museum **9**
Musee de
    l'Annonciade **4**

HOTELS ■
Hotel Byblos **10**
Hotel Les Palmiers **2**
Pastis
    Hotel-St-Tropez **1**

RESTAURANTS ◆
Barbarac **5**
Chez Madeleine **6**
L'Aventure **8**
Pizzeria Bruno **7**
Rivea **10**
Salama **3**

9

ST-TROPEZ & AROUND | St-Tropez

Mail & Postage   **La Poste,** rue de la Poste (ℂ **36-31**).

Pharmacies   **Pharmacie du Port,** 9 quai Suffren (ℂ **04-94-97-00-06**).

Where to Stay

Hôtel Byblos ★★★   Opened in 1967 on a hill above the harbor, this hamlet of pastel-hued, Provençal-style houses is opulence personified. Inspired by the legendary Phoenician city of the same name, Byblos is favored by visiting celebrities, rock stars, aristocrats, and the über-rich. Its patios and private spaces are splashed with antiques, rare objects, bubbling fountains, and ancient olive trees. Rooms range in size from medium to mega; some units have such special features as four-posters with furry spreads or sunken whirlpool tubs. The breakfast is to die for. Served around the deep swimming pool, we're talking chocolate fountains, hand-baked pastries, their own organic granola, and unique teas from across the globe.

20 av. Paul Signac. www.byblos.com. ☎ **04-94-56-68-00.** 96 units. 420€–1,180€ double; 840€– 2,960€ suite. Parking 35€. Closed Nov–mid-April. **Amenities:** 2 restaurants; 1 bar; nightclub; baby-sitting; concierge; exercise room; massage; outdoor pool; room service; sauna; spa; free Wi-Fi.

Hôtel Les Palmiers ★
In a town packed with pricey accommodation options, this friendly, family-run hotel is a real find. Apart from its fantastic location—directly astride place des Lices in the center of St-Tropez—Les Palmiers boasts compact Provençal-style rooms and a sun-dappled courtyard garden. Part of the hotel dates from the late 18th century and gives the place a cozy, vintage feel.

24–26 bd. Vasserot (place des Lices). www.hotel-les-palmiers.com. ☎ **04-94-97-01-61.** 25 units. 85€–275€ double. **Amenities:** Bar; free Wi-Fi.

Pastis Hôtel-St-Tropez ★★
This portside Provençal house feels more like a sophisticated, eclectic home than a hotel—albeit one decorated with a phenomenal eye for design. British owners John and Pauline Larkin have arranged their private collection of Matisse prints, vintage photographs, 1970s framed album artwork, and Provençal antiques in and around the guest-only lounge and inspired guestrooms surrounding the courtyard swimming pool. Each unique unit is spacious yet intimate and possesses its own balcony or breakfast terrace. Highly recommended.

75 av. du Général Leclerc. www.pastis-st-tropez.com. ☎ **04-98-12-56-50.** 10 units. 225€–750€ double. Free parking. Closed Nov–Jan. **Amenities:** Bar; outdoor pool; free Wi-Fi.

Le Refuge ★
Granted, Le Refuge is not everyone's cup of tea (or indeed glass of chilled rosé). But if you want to kick back in beachy solitude on St-Tropez's lush peninsula, this long-time author favorite is the place for you. This bare bones establishment sits just seconds from the golden sands of family-friendly Plage Gigaro. It offers a handful of mini cottages and studios with shared terraces, all surrounded by fragrant Mediterranean shrubbery. Coastal paths and secret beaches pan out from the establishment's front door.

Plage de Gigaro, La Croix Valmer. www.lerefuge-cotedazur.fr. ☎ **04-94-79-67-38.** 16 units. 68€– 160€ double. Free parking. Closed Oct –March. **Amenities:** None.

Where to Eat

St-Tropez's dining scene is both expensive and exclusive, particularly during the summer season. Reserve well in advance or be prepared to dine very early or very late. In addition to the suggestions below, the long-established Moroccan restaurant **Salama,** 1 rue Tisserands (☎ **04-94-97-59-62**), cooks up a fine selection of couscous, pastilla, and tajines; **Chez Madeleine,** 4 place aux Herbes (☎ **04-94-96-59-81**), behind the fish market, serves stellar seafood platters; and **Barbarac,** 2 rue Allard (www.barbarac.fr; ☎ **04-94-97-67-83**), scoops up the finest ice cream in town.

L'Aventure ★ MODERN PROVENÇAL
A backstreet St-Tropez eatery beloved of locals and visitors alike, L'Aventure serves globally inspired market-fresh cuisine: think snails, Provençal lamb, and harbor-fresh fish alternately laced with pesto, honey, and ginger. Blessedly unpretentious, right down to the authentically battered tables on the petite terrace.

4 rue du Portail-Neuf. ☎ **04-94-97-44-01.** Reservations recommended. Main courses 21€–34€. Tues–Sun 7:30–10pm.

ST-TROPEZ on the cheap

You could drop 1,000€ on a round of drinks a Les Caves du Roy. Or spend 1,000,000€ a week on a super-yacht charter. But it's far healthier (and occasionally more satisfying) to watch other people waste money instead. In St-Tropez, grab a set of *pétanque* boules in **place des Lices**, or browse its Tuesday or Saturday street market instead. Picnics taste best when purchased from a *maître epicier* like **Tarte Tropezienne** (on place des Lices, with four branches around town) and eaten alfresco on plage des Graniers beach. A bottle of chilled supermarket champagne will set you back 15€, as opposed to several hundred in any eatery in town. And there are no laws against popping open a bottle in public in happy-go-lucky France.

Cheap sleeps in St-Tropez are hard to find. But B&Bs around the less crowded peninsula from Ramatuelle to Plage Gigaro are easier to come by. See the tourist office website for a full list. One serious find is **Tikki Hutte** (www.tiki-hutte.com; (☎ **04-94-55-96-96**) on Plage Pampelonne, a chic Caribbean-style beach hut operation. Book in advance for sea view bungalows from around 600€ per week per cabin.

Or you could do what hundreds of local workers do every day, and commute in by boat. **Bateaux Vertes** (www.bateauxverts.com; (☎ **04-94-49-29-39**) shuttle the 15-minute hop across the Bay of St-Tropez from Ste-Maxime every hour. Tickets cost 7.50€, or 3.90€ for children aged 12 or under.

Pizzeria Bruno ★ ITALIAN   Proving that not all good meals in St-Tropez have to break the bank, this casual joint has been turning out thin, crispy, wood-fired pizzas since 1959. Even Bardot was a regular. The menu includes a handful of creative salads, pasta dishes, and grilled meats. Note that the restaurant's copious wood-paneled and overly snug seating isn't the comfiest, but the atmosphere is among the liveliest in town.

2 rue de l'Eglise. ☎ **04-94-97-05-18.** Main courses 12€–20€. Daily noon–2pm and 7–11pm. Closed Oct–April.

Rivea ★★ MODERN PROVENÇAL   In 2013, French restaurateur Alain Ducasse's latest offering opened downstairs from the Hotel Byblos. Set across a palm-shaded posing terrace, it has wow-factor in spades. Head chef Vincent Maillard uses ingredients sourced exclusively from the French and Italian Rivieras to create tapas-style sharing dishes, including *vitello tonnato,* marinated tuna, sardines *confit*, and perfect mini portions of *spaghetti alle vongole*. Rivea is also the best places to sample Brad and Angelina's exclusive Château Miraval wine—named the world's finest rosé in late 2013—which is produced a few miles inland.

27 avenue Maréchal Foch 56 68 20. ☎ **04-94-56-68-20.** Main courses 25€–44€. Daily 7pm–12.30am. Closed Oct–mid-April.

Exploring St-Tropez

During summertime, St-Tropez's pleasure port is trimmed with super-yachts, each one berthing stern-to after a day of hedonistic excess at nearby Plage de Pampelonne. Yacht owners, their lucky guests, spectators, and celebrity-seekers all intermingle along the town's chic quays.

In the Old Town, one of the most interesting streets is **rue de la Miséricorde.** It's lined with stone houses that hold boutiques and evokes medieval St-Tropez better than any other in town. At the corner of rue Gambetta is **Chapelle de la Miséricorde,** with a blue, green, and gold tile roof. Locals come to swim on **Plage de la Ponche**, an old fishing boat launching beach beyond the old town, or at **Plage des Graniers**, a longer beach 5 minutes further east underneath the Citadelle.

Port Grimaud makes for a rather wacky outing. From St-Tropez, drive 4km (2¾ miles) west on A98 to route 98, and then 1.5km (1 mile) north to the Port Grimaud exit. If you approach the village at sunset it looks like a 16th-century version of Venice. However, that vision is a mirage: Port Grimaud is the Venetian dream of far-out architect François Spoerry. Flanking Spoerry's man-made canals, fingers of land extend from the village center to the sea. Boat owners can anchor at their doorsteps. One newspaper called the port "the most magnificent fake since Disneyland." Visitors can join in the fun by hiring an electric boat from **Barques Electriques de Port Grimaud**, place de l'Eglise (✆ **06-73-87-76-84**; no license needed) for a cruise through the canals.

Citadelle de St-Tropez & Maritime Museum ★★ MUSEUM & CASTLE

Towering above town is the Citadelle, a fortified castle complete with drawbridges and stunning views across the Bay of St-Tropez. It's also the best place in town for escaping the crowds, soaking up the sun, and exhausting tiny travelers bored by too many cafés. In 2013, a brand-new Maritime Museum opened within the Citadelle. It charts local historical figures and their travels around the world including Admiral Suffren, who whupped the British several times during the War of American Independence.

Above St-Tropez. ✆ **04-94-54-84-14.** Admission 3€ adults, free for children 8 and under. April–Sept daily 10am–6.30pm. Oct–March daily 10am–12:30pm and 1:30-5:30pm. Closed Nov.

Musée de l'Annonciade (Musée St-Tropez) ★★★ MUSEUM

If you leave town without seeing this spellbinding museum, you've missed a colorful part of St-Tropez's past. Set inside a 16th-century chapel just off the harbor, it showcases a collection of superb post-Impressionist paintings (1890–1950). Many of the artists, including St-Tropez's adopted son, Paul Signac, painted the port of St-Tropez, a backdrop that lies right outside the building. The museum includes such masterpieces as Bonnard's "Nu devant la Cheminée" as well as artworks by Matisse, Braque, Dufy, Marquet, and Derain. Temporary shows are held on the ground floor.

Place Grammont. ✆ **04-94-17-84-10.** Admission 6€ adults, 4€ children 11 and under. Wed–Mon 10am–1pm and 2–6pm. Closed Nov.

Organized Tours

This is St-Tropez, darling. Guests keen to be guided around town are handed a **pre-programmed iPod Touch** (3€ per day) and told discreetly to get on with it. The interactive tour takes around 60 minutes. Alternatively, official English-language guided tours of St-Tropez take place every Wednesday at 10am from April to October, departing from in front of the tourist office. Tickets cost 6€, or free for children aged 12 and under.

Outdoor Activities

BEACHES The hottest Riviera beaches are at St-Tropez. The best for families are closest to the center, including **Plage de la Bouillabaisse** and **Plage des Salins.** More daring and infinitely more famous is the 5km (3-mile) crescent of **Plage de Pampelonne,** about 10km (6¼ miles) from town. Here, around 35 hedonistic beach clubs dot the sand. Overtly decadent is **Club 55** (www.club55.fr; ✆ **04-94-55-55-55**), a former Bardot hangout, while the American-run **Nikki Beach** (www.nikkibeach.com; ✆ **04-94-79-82-04**) is younger and more understated, if painfully chic. Gay-friendly **Aqua Club** (✆ **04-94-79-84-35**) and bare-all **Plage de Tahiti** (www.tahiti-beach.com; ✆ **04-94-97-18-02**) are extremely welcoming.

You'll need a car, bike, or scooter to get from town to Plage de Pampelonne. Parking is around 10€ for the day. More than anywhere else on the Riviera, topless bathing is the norm.

BOATING   In St-Tropez port, **Octopussy** (www.octopussy.fr; ✆ **04-94-56-53-10**) rents boats 5 to 16m (16–52 ft.) long. Larger ones come with a captain at the helm. Prices begin at 320€ per day.

DIVING   Multilingual scuba training and equipment rental is available from the European Diving School (www.europeandiving.com; ✆ 04-94-79-90-37), on Plage de Pampelonne. Regular dives, including all equipment, cost 38€.

WINE-TASTING   The St-Tropez peninsula is justly famed for its white and rosé vintages. Wine Tours Provence (www.winetoursprovence.com; ✆ 06-17-14-43-41) organize half- and full-day expeditions starting in place des Lices and visiting up to 3 local wineries for tastings in the company of an experienced oënologue. Tours of the "Côte de Provence" and "Coteaux d'Aix" appellations are also offered. Call for pricing.

The wider Provence area produces 8% of the world's rosé. **Route des Vins'** (www.routedesvins-svp.com; ✆ **06-52-97-84-04**) half-day tour concentrates on 3 or 4 assuredly local vineyards, with tasting sessions in each. Tours cost 90€ per person for a minimum of two guests. Alternatively, rent a car and strike out on your own. The peninsula is littered with friendly vineyards of all descriptions. Particularly welcoming is **Chateau Minuty,** 2491 route de la Berle (www.chateauminuty.com; ✆ **04-94-56-12-09**). They offer complimentary wine tasting sessions to guests who plan to buy at least a bottle or two.

Shopping

St-Tropez is awash with stylish shops. The merchandise is Mediterranean, breezy, and sophisticated. Dotted throughout the town's *triangle d'or,* the rough triangle formed by place de la Garonne, rue François Sibilli and place des Lices, chic labels include

---

FRENCH boules

A game of *pétanque,* or French boules, is seriously cool for kids. Hop to **Le Café** (www.lecafe.fr; ✆ **04-94-97-44-69**), one of many alfresco bars in place des Lices, and request a handful of *pétanque* boules to toss around the tree-dappled square. The game was created down the coast and is about as Provençal as it gets. Pick up some tips by watching the locals. Games begin with a toss of the jack, or *bouchon.* Teams then take turns to throw. Whoever is farthest away keeps trying to get closest to the *bouchon,* with any remaining balls tossed in at the end. A point is awarded for each steel ball that's closer to the jack than any balls from the opposing team.

Hermès, Sonia Rykiel, and Louis Vuitton. For the past 5 years, a summer pop-up shop has occupied the old Hotel la Mistralée at 1 av. du Général Leclerc, while nearby, Michelin-starred chef Yannick Alléno dishes up delights at **Dior des Lices,** 13 rue François Sibilli, the fashion house's own summertime pop-up eatery. There are also scores of unique boutiques around the Vieille Ville (Old Town), including **Chichou 88,** 27 rue Georges Clémenceau (© **04-94-96-48-93**), which stocks Indian-inspired homewares and neon handbags; **Truffaux Chapelier,** 44 rue de la Citadelle (© **04-94-45-33-14**), packed with Panama hats; and **K. Jacques,** 25 rue Allard (www.lestropeziennes. com; © **04-94-97-41-50**), with its iconic *tropéziennes* sandals. Place des Lices hosts an excellent **outdoor market,** Marché Provençal, with food, clothes, and *brocante,* on Tuesday and Saturday mornings.

Nightlife

On a lower level of the Hôtel Byblos' grounds, **Les Caves du Roy,** 20 avenue Paul-Signac (www.lescavesduroy.com; © **04-94-56-68-00**), is the most self-consciously chic nightclub in St-Tropez. Entrance is free, but drink prices are eye-wateringly high. It's open nightly from Easter to early October from 11:30pm until dawn. Brand-new for 2013 was **White 1921,** place des Lices (www.white1921.com; © **04-94-45-50-50**), a champagne and cocktail bar set within a jasmine-cloaked courtyard garden. **Le Papagayo,** port de St-Tropez (www.papagayo-st-tropez.com; © **04-94-97-95-95**), is one of the largest nightclubs in town. The decor is inspired by the psychedelic 1960s. Entrance is around 20€ and includes one drink, although those dining at the attached restaurant can routinely sneak in for free. Adjacent to Le Papagayo is **Le VIP Room,** in the Résidence du Nouveau-Port (www.st-tropez.viproom.fr; © **06-38-83-83-83**), a younger yet similarly chic version of Les Caves du Roy. Paris Hilton and Snoop Dogg have been known to drop by. Cocktails hover around the 20€ mark.

Le Pigeonnier, 19 rue de la Ponche (© **06-33-58-92-45**), rocks, rolls, and welcomes a mostly gay and lesbian crowd between 20 and 50. **L'Esquinade,** 2 rue de Four (© **04-94-56-26-31**), equally gay-friendly, is the habitual sweaty follow-up club.

Below the Hôtel Sube in the port, **Café de Paris** (www.cafedeparis.fr; © **04-94-97-00-56**), is one of the most popular—and friendly—hangouts in town. It has 1900s-style globe lights, masses of artificial flowers, and a long zinc bar. **Café Sénéquier,** quai Jean Jaurès (www.senequier.com; © **04-94-97-20-20**), is historic, venerable, snobbish by day, and off-puttingly stylish by night.

DAY TRIPS FROM ST-TROPEZ

Ramatuelle ★

11km (7 miles) S of St-Tropez

Ramatuelle has the village feel of St Tropez in the 1950s. Retired actors, bona fide locals, and discreet A-listers wander this *village perché*'s medieval streets. In truth, cosmopolitanism runs through the village's veins. Saracen marauders, Ligurian tribesmen, and visiting film crews have long been entranced by its roving sea views. Plage Pampelonne—where American troops disembarked in 1944 and where American celebrities still pop champagne seven decades later—shimmers in the distance.

ESSENTIALS

Irregular **buses** (www.varlib.fr; © **04-94-24-60-00**); trip time: 30 minutes; 2€ one-way) putter south from St-Tropez's Gare Routière to Ramatuelle, passing Gassin en-route.

HEAD TO THE hills

Unfurling along the shores between St-Tropez and Cannes is a scarlet stretch of coastline known as the **Esterel** (see p. 141). It's a regional nature reserve and a cluster of mountains (the Massif de l'Esterel), the latter renowned for their ethereal crimson hue. The area is criss-crossed with hiking trails and splashed by tiny turquoise beaches, perfect for private picnics. Best of all, the Esterel receives just a fraction of the tourists that congregate along the Riviera's more popular seaside resorts. Regular trains run from Cannes to Théoule-sur-Mer, a village in the center of the park. One-way tickets cost 2.50€, and journey time is around 10 minutes. The **Théoule-sur-Mer Tourist Office,** 2 bd. de la Corniche d'Or (www.theoule-sur-mer.org; ℂ **04-93-49-28-28**) distributes walking and cycling maps of the region.

If you're **driving** take D93 all the way there. It's far quieter than the coast road. The **Office de Tourisme** is at place de l'Ormeau (www.otorange.fr; ℂ **04-98-12-64-00**).

EXPLORING RAMATUELLE & AROUND

Entrance to the village is via an imposing **Saracen-era gate**. Step into the pedestrian-only lanes to **place de l'Ormeau**. A colorful **street market** takes place here every Thursday and Sunday, when local cafés and restaurant terraces become more animated than usual. Visitors may also shop alongside Ramatuelle's 2,500 residents everyday for local handicrafts, boho-chic fashions, and contemporary art. A wander through the pastel-shuttered, jasmine-strewn streets is an attraction in itself. Follow the signposted village walking route. Or snap your smartphone on the tourist office's new **QR code tour** around town, which describes the **Napoleonic prisons** and **Chapelle Ste-Anne** church in greater detail.

If you have a car, it's worth driving deeper into the St-Tropez peninsula. Five minutes from Ramatuelle, in a forest of wild olives, is the wonderfully restored **Moulin de Paillas** windmill. When in operation, it grinds wheat on an ancient millstone. Further inland is **Gassin**. Another perfectly kept medieval village, it's a far cry from the temptations of St-Tropez, although legendary hell-raiser Mick Jagger did his best to disturb the peace here in 1971, when he married Bianca Bianca Pérez-Mora Macias in the local village church. An orgy of drinking and partying carried on back on place des Lices after the ceremony.

WHERE TO STAY & EAT

If you choose to sleep in Ramatuelle, **Villa Marie** ★★ (www.villamarie.fr ℂ **04-94-97-40-22**) is the model of blissfully unreconstructed luxury. An unseemly array of fragrant grounds, Provençal patios, and a delicately manicured pool make this elegant retreat an oasis of decadence. The alfresco gastronomic restaurant peeks over the peninsula towards Plage Pampelonne. Their signature tiramisu (served in a glass hemisphere) is blowout bliss. Guests may work off the calories in the Pure Altitude indoor-outdoor spa the following morning. Doubles from 330€; suites from 620€.

The restaurants around place de l'Ormeau are your best bet for local bites. **Le Jardin des Mets**, 31 rue Georges Clemenceau (ℂ **04-94-79-18-68**), serves Provençal classics like fish soup and grilled Sisteron lamb in a charming interior garden. **La Reserve** (www.lareserve-ramatuelle.com; ℂ **04-94-44-94-44**) is an A-list escape with a world-renowned spa. Doubles start from 500€ per night.

Rayol-Canadel ★

29km (18 miles) W of St-Tropez

The southern French coastline becomes beach-laden from Rayol-Canadel to La Lava-dou. No less than **12 blissful beaches** run underneath the coastal road. The two finest, Plage du Cap Nègre and Plage de Pramousquier, are found on either side of Carla Bruni's seaside mansion. Former French president Nicholas Sarkozy is a regular on these sun-kissed shores.

No site better sums up this area's sub-tropical sunbaked shores than the **Domaine Rayol** botanical gardens. Imagine a Jurassic park laden with black bamboo, sultry ferns, and giant palms, and choked with bougainvillea. This family-friendly must-see also boasts a snorkeling trail on the private beach below.

ESSENTIALS

The 7801 and 8814 **buses** (trip time: 35 min.; 3€ one-way) from St-Tropez loops through Rayol-Canadel every hour. The prettiest (but by no means the shortest) **driving** route from St-Tropez takes the D559 out of town, then continues west on the D93. The **Office de Tourisme** is at place Michel Goy (www.lerayolcanadel.fr; ☎ **04- 94-05-65-69**). The friendly team has maps detailing several fragrant walks along the coast.

For those interested in staying in Rayol-Canadel, **Villa du Plageron ★★★** (www.plageron.com. ☎ **04-94-05-61-15**) is a short walk or drive from the Domaine-Rayol botanical gardens. With its tiny private beach, pool, garden hammocks, and palm-shaded grounds, choose one of these 10 rooms, priced from 160€, as the perfect place to recover after excessive sightseeing. Bi-lingual owners Virginie and Bruno cater to every whim (a glass of rosé? a local restaurant reservation?) and preside over the never-ending Provençal breakfast.

Domaine Rayol ★★ BOTANICAL GARDENS & PRIVATE BEACH   Classed as a *Jardin Remarquable* by France's Ministry of Culture, the remarkable Domaine Rayol tumbles down to the sea over 20 flower-filled hectares. Several thousand plant species fight for space over 11 climatic areas. Find giant succulents in the South African section, bamboo thickets in the Chinese zone, and fragrant eucalyptus and mimosa from Australasia. Permanent features in the park include hidden totems and Indiana Jones-like bridges. Snorkeling the *sentier marin* (undersea trail) costs 23€, or 15€ for children aged 17 or under, inclusive of your entrance ticket. This 3-hour experience glides over sea cucumbers, Poseidon grass, and friendly octopi. Picnicking in the park is banned, which is just as well. **Le Café des Jardiniers** (open mid-April to mid-October, Wednesday to Sunday) conjures up garden-inspired Mediterranean delights on a vast sea view-dining terrace.

Boulevard du Rayol. www.domaineodurayol.org. ☎ **04-98-04-44-02.** Admission 10.50€, 7.50€ for children ages 7–17, free for children 6 and under. July–Aug daily 9.30am–7.30pm; Sept–June daily 9:30am–6:30pm (until 5:30pm Nov–March).

ST-RAPHAËL ★★

40km (25 miles) E of St Tropez; 43km (27 miles) SW of Cannes

St-Raphaël sits between the red lava peaks of the Massif de l'Estérel and the densely forested hills of the Massif des Maures. It became popular during Roman times, when rich families came to vacation here, bequeathing the rambling ruins at the neighboring town of Fréjus today. Barring a brief barbaric interlude of 1,500 years, it's still a place of rest and recreation. That's right, the Saracen invaders that terrorized the coast during the Middle Ages didn't come here to sip rosé. Not until 1799, when a proud Napoleon landed at the small harbor beach on his return from Egypt, did the city once again draw attention of a positive kind.

In 1864, Alphonse Karr, journalist and ex-editor of *Le Figaro,* helped to reintroduce St-Raphaël as a resort. Dumas, Maupassant, and Berlioz came here from Paris on his recommendation. Gounod also arrived; he composed *Romeo et Juliet* here in 1866. Belle Époque–era villas and grand hotels were built for holidaying English gentlemen decades later. Most were requisitioned by American soldiers during World War II when St-Raphaël served as a key invasion point for Allied forces. The city still offers the wide beaches and coastal ambience of other Côte d'Azur resorts—at a fraction of the price.

Essentials

ARRIVING   St-Raphaël is ideally located, making it a great place from which to explore the area. It sits directly on the **rail** lines running parallel to the coast between Marseille to the west and the Italian border town of Ventimiglia to the east, en route to Cannes, Antibes, and Nice. You can ride a fast **TGV train** all the way to Paris in around 4 hours. For train information and schedules, call ☏ **36-35** or visit www.voyages-sncf.com. Trains leave Marseille for St-Raphaël every hour during the day, costing about 30€ one-way (trip time: 1 hr. 30 min.). Trains from Cannes head east to St-Raphaël every 30 minutes during the day (trip time: 25 min.); one-way fares cost 7.20€.

The **bus** station behind the train station provides local and regional services alike. There's a bus service from St-Raphaël to Fréjus every 30 minutes or so (one-way tickets cost 1.10€). The Varlib (www.varlib.fr; ☏ **04-94-24-60-00**), bus to St-Tropez takes 1½ hours and costs 3€ one-way. For more information, contact the St-Raphaël bus station at ☏ **04-94-44-52-70.**

You can also arrive in St-Raphaël by **boat.** Vessels (www.bateauxsaintraphael.com; ☏ **04-94-95-17-46**), depart for St-Tropez's Vieux Port (trip time: 1 hr.) five times a day during high summer, reducing to once- or twice-daily sailings in winter. The one-way fare is 15€.

By **car** from St-Tropez in the west, take D98A northwest to N98, at which point you drive east toward St-Raphaël. To reach St-Raphaël from Nice or Cannes, head west along the A8 before cutting south at exit 38 on the D37 to Fréjus and then east on the D100 to St-Raphaël.

VISITOR INFORMATION   The gleaming new **Office de Tourisme** is on the seafront at 99 Quai Albert 1er (www.saint-raphael.com; ☏ **04-94-19-52-52**).

[FastFACTS] ST-RAPHAËL

ATMs/Banks   **LCL,** 78 boulevard Felix Martin (☏ **94-40-26-47**).

Mail & Postage   **La Poste,** avenue Victor Hugo (☏ **36-31**).

Pharmacies   **Pharmacie Borel Louis,** place Pierre Coullet (☏ **04-94-95-04-05**).

Where to Stay

Best Western Hôtel La Marina ★   You don't stay in La Marina to soak up the Provençal charm. The attraction here is undoubtedly the hotel's seafront location, with easy access to St-Tropez and Cannes—for a fraction of the price charged in both of those resorts. Rooms range from modern doubles to capacious family-sized affairs. It's best to skip the 15€ buffet breakfast and dine out in the sunshine in front of the bobbing boats below.

Nouveau Port Santa Lucia. www.bestwestern-lamarina.com. *(C)* **04-94-95-31-31**. 100 units. 109€–160€ double. **Amenities:** Restaurant; bar; babysitting; concierge; fitness room; pool; free Wi-Fi.

La Villa Mauresque ★★   It's not hard to understand why La Mauresque is St-Raphaël's most sought-after hotel. Expect complimentary fruit bowls on arrival, free mineral water, and a pillow menu, all at prices that won't break the bank. Chichi guest rooms are each named after a different artist; many overlook the shimmering sea in front of the hotel. Kayaks can be launched from the nearby beach (a 5-minute stroll away). Or ask for a sea shuttle into St-Tropez on the hotel's private boat. The on-site **Bougainvillier gastronomic restaurant** (open Wed–Sun lunch and dinner; lunchtime menu 45€) run by head chef Philippe Nogier dishes up meals to write home about. In an atmosphere that's less stuffy than other top restaurants, diners may sample a symphony of local flavors, including Camargue bull ribs, and crunchy veal sweetbreads with spinach shoots.

1792 rte. de la Corniche, Boulouris. www.villa-mauresque.com. *(C)* **04-94-83-02-42**. 15 units. 225€–480€ double; from 530€ suite. Free parking. Closed Nov–Jan. **Amenities:** Bar; indoor pool; outdoor pool; restaurant sauna; free Wi-Fi.

Where to Eat

Elly's ★★ MODERN PROVENÇAL   What is hands-down the best restaurant in town is overseen by head chef Franck Chabod, a veteran of countless Michelin-starred kitchens. This young restaurant (open since 2011) has an enthusiastic clientele who aren't afraid to experiment. Try dishes like slow-cooked *pata negra* pork ribs, or crayfish and smoked fish maki by going à la carte. Or sample ray wings with lemon, or roast duckling fillet with pear, on the 35€ fixed-price lunch and dinner menus. The seven-course dinner menu promises to be a holiday highlight.

54 rue de la Liberté. www.elly-s.com. *(C)* **04-94-83-63-39**. Reservations recommended. Main courses all 32€; fixed-price lunch menu 24€; fixed-price dinner 35€ –70€. Tues–Sat noon–1:30pm and 7:30–9:30pm. Closed Jan.

Exploring St-Raphaël

St-Raphaël is sliced into two halves by its railway line. The historical **Vieille Ville (Old Town)** lies inland from the tracks. Here you'll find St-Raphaël's only intact ancient structure, the **Église San Rafèu** (also known as Eglise des Templiers), rue des Templiers (*(C)* **04-94-19-25-75**). The 12th-century church is the third to stand on this site; two Carolingian churches underneath the current structure have been revealed during digs. A watchtower sits atop one of the chapels, and at one time, watchers were posted to look out over the sea for ships that might pose a threat. The church would then serve as a fortress and refuge in case of pirate attack. Climb up the 129 steps yourself for a 360-degree panoramic view over town. In the courtyard are fragments of a Roman aqueduct that once brought water from Fréjus. You can visit the church from Tuesday to Saturday from 9am to noon and 2 to 6:30pm; entrance costs 2€ for adults, and is free for children under 18 years. Ironically, no Masses are conducted in this church on Sunday—it's a consecrated church, but one that's been relegated to something akin to an archaeological rather than religious monument.

The Vieux Port area has changed beyond recognition in recent years. Pleasure boats, diving schools, and island excursion vessels line the quays. The new 20,000 square meter **Jardin Bonaparte** gardens tumble out to sea under a high-tech arbor. As well as a hosting a children's playground, the gardens serve a venue for outdoor summer concerts and shows.

Near the Église des Templiers, the **Musée d'Archéologie Sous-Marine (Museum of Underwater Archaeology)**, rue des Templiers (www.musee-saintraphael.com; ✆ **04-94-19-25-75**), displays amphorae, ships' anchors, ancient diving equipment, and other interesting items recovered from the ocean's depths. At one time, rumors circulated about a "lost city" off the coast of St-Raphaël. Jacques Cousteau came to investigate; instead of a sunken city, he discovered a Roman ship that had sunk while carrying a full load of building supplies. The museum is open Tuesday to Saturday from 9am to noon and 2 to 6pm. Admission is free.

You'll find **flower and fruit markets** in the Old Town. Every morning, there's a **fish market** that takes place in the Vieux Port. Foodies are also advised to check out the **Marché Alimentaire de St-Raphaël**, where carloads of produce, fish, meat, wines, and cheeses are sold Tuesday to Sunday from 8am to 1pm in place Victor-Hugo and place de la République. (Note that the two squares are a 5-minute walk apart.) On Tuesdays from 9am to 6pm in place Coullet, there's also a *marché de brocante* (flea market).

Organized Tours

Every Thursday at 10am, a **culinary walking tour** of St-Raphaël's markets and shops starts from the tourist office. Tours last 2 hours and cost 3€ per person. Explanations are nominally in French, although guides do their best to accommodate English-speaking guests. Tastings of delicious tapenades, jams, and chutneys defy language barriers anyway. The tourist office also encourages visitors to download the **Cultural Treasure Hunts app** for iPhone and Android. Users can pick up historical clues around town. The trail then leads along the coast to the beaches of Dramont and Agay.

Outdoor Activities

BEACHES   Of course, most visitors come to St-Raphaël for its beaches. The best ones (some rock, some sand) are located between the Vieux Port and Santa Lucia. Here you'll find plenty of stands that rent watersports equipment on each beach. The closest beach to the town center is the **Plage du Veillat,** a long stretch of sand that's crowded and family friendly. Further east in Agay, you'll find the sandy beaches of **Plage d'Agay** and **Plage de la Baumette**; these are partly private beaches where you can rent recliners and umbrellas for a fee. Within a 5-minute walk east of the town center is **Plage Beau Rivage,** whose name is misleading because it's covered with a smooth and even coating of light-gray pebbles that might be uncomfortable to lie on without a towel. History buffs will enjoy a 7km (4½-mile) excursion east of town to the **Plage du Dramont,** a public pebble stretch with watersports and a restaurant that was hurled into world headlines on August 15, 1944, as one of the main sites of the Allied Forces' Provence Landings. Today expect relatively uncrowded conditions, except during the midsummer crush.

BIKES   You can rent bikes and scooters from **Patrick Moto,** 260 avenue du Général-Leclerc (✆ **04-94-53-65-99**). Bikes are priced at 9€ per day; mountain bikes 13€; and scooters 30€. Two **mountain bike trails** loop inland from the tourist office. Ask for a map inside, then try the 32km **Balcons d'Azur** ride for panoramic views, or the gentler 12km **Lac de l'Écureuil** lakeside route.

the mysterious ILE D'OR

Opposite Dramont beach is the private island of Ile d'Or. Its history is as enigmatic as its ominous look, as the island glows gold then blood red against the setting sun. After being sold for a song by the French government, it was allegedly won in a game of cards by physician Augustus Lutaud a century ago. Lutaud organized wild parties then declared himself king of the island in 1913, purportedly issuing his own currency in the process. The story is said to have inspired the Tintin story, The Black Island, in which Hergé's hero chases a mad doctor. The surrounding snorkeling and diving is among the best in coastal Provence.

BOAT TRIPS   **Bateaux St-Raphaël** (www.bateauxsaintraphael.com; ✆ 04-94-95-17-46) run 90-minute tours of the Esterel Coves daily in July and August. Prices are 16€ for adults, or 10€ for children aged 9 and under. Midnight return trips from St-Tropez, and shuttles to the Porquerolles and Lérins Islands, are also offered in summer. Serious fishermen should contact **Verdon Pêche** (www.verdonpeche.free.fr; ✆ 06-07-16-20-96). Take their speedboat out for giant bass and bream, or join Christophe and team for river and lake fishing inland. Expect to pay around 250€ for three or more guests for the entire day.

DIVING   The local coastline is spectacular. Dives with both **Agathonis Diving** (www.agathonisplongee.com; ✆ 06-16-16-20-96) and **Aventure Sous Marine** (www. aventuresousmarine.com; ✆ 06-09-79-90-37) can be booked at the St-Raphaël tourist office. The latter operates a dive boat docked in the Vieux Port. Regular dives with both agencies, including all equipment, cost around 40€.

DAY TRIPS FROM ST-RAPHAËL

Fréjus ★

3km (2 miles) S of St-Raphaël

Gaul's oldest roman city, Fréjus is chock-full of impressive ancient remains. It was founded by Julius Caesar in 49 B.C. as Forum Julii; later, under Augustus's rule, it became a key naval base. The warships with which Augustus defeated Antony and Cleopatra at the battle at Actium were built here in 31 B.C. Remnants from Roman times still stand in the Vieille Ville, including Roman gateways and ramparts, as well as parts of an aqueduct, an amphitheater, and a theatre. You can spot a double-headed Hermes (now the emblem of Fréjus) at the Musée Archéologique and visit some of France's oldest ecclesiastical buildings in the spellbinding Cité Episcopale.

The picturesque old town is also home to various well-priced art galleries, following a successful local government makeover that replaced dodgy bars with subsidized artists' studios. Today it's a thriving art community.

ESSENTIALS

AggloBus (www.agglo-var-esterel-mediterranee.fr; ✆ 04-94-53-78-46), runs a **bus service** into Fréjus from St-Raphaël every 30 minutes or so. One-way tickets cost 1.10€. If you're driving from St-Raphaël, take the D1098 west to Fréjus. The **Office de Tourisme** is at Le Florus II, 249 rue Jean-Jaurès (www.frejus.fr; ✆ 04-94-51-83-83).

EXPLORING FRÉJUS

If you plan to visit several sites in the area, you can purchase a **Fréjus Pass** for 4.60€ for adults or 3.10€ for children ages 12 to 18. The pass is free for children 11 and under.

The best preserved of the Roman ruins is the **Amphithéâtre (Les Arènes)** ★, rue Henri-Vadon (℘ **04-94-51-34-31**). In Roman times, it could accommodate up to 10,000 spectators. The upper levels of the galleries have been reconstructed with the same greenish stone that was used to create the original building. Bullfights were held here until recently, although today it's a venue for outdoor concerts.

A half kilometer (⅓ mile) north of town on avenue du Théâtre-Romain, the **Théâtre Romain Philippe Léotard** (℘ **04-94-53-58-75**)—not to be confused with the amphitheater—is largely in ruins. However, one wall and a few of the lower sections remain and are used as a backdrop for a summertime theater festival. The theater is open Tuesday to Sunday 9:30am to 12:30pm and 2 to 6pm (until 4:30pm October through March). Northwest of the theater, you can see a few soaring arches as they follow the coastal road leading to Cannes. These pieces are the remains of the 40km (25-mile) aqueduct that once brought fresh water to Fréjus' water tower.

The grand neoclassical **Villa Aurélienne,** avenue du Général-d'Armée Calliès (℘ **04-94-52-90-49**), was originally a holiday home for an English industrialist in the 1880s. Updates a century ago lend a Great Gatsby feel. It's a popular venue for photographic exhibitions and classical concerts. Admission prices and opening hours vary according to the event, so call for information. The park surrounding is bucolic and a great place for kids to run around.

Spread over 260 hectares (642 acres), **Etangs de Villepey** (www.frejus.fr), off the D1098 west of Fréjus, is a nature reserve that is often known as the "Petite Camargue" of the Var, due to the marshlands here. You'll also find dry zones and sand dunes, as well as walking and cycling paths. The reserve is particularly busy during migration season in spring and autumn, when you can spot over 250 species of birds. There are no specific opening hours and entry is free.

Aqualand, Quartier Le Capou along D1098 (www.aqualand.fr; ℘ **04-94-51-82-51**), is a theme park with 19 water-based rides for kids of all ages, as well as snack bars and a shop. It's open every day from mid-June to mid-September from 10am to 6pm (until 7pm from early July to late Aug). Entry costs 26€ for adults and kids 13 years and over, 18.50€ for kids from 3 to 12 years, and 10€ for kids under 1.10m tall (3 ft.).

Cité Episcopale ★★ CATHEDRAL   No visit to Fréjus is complete without a visit to the age-old cathedral in the even more ancient town center. The **Cathédrale St-Léonce** took six centuries to complete, and it shows. The four main buildings—the baptistery, the cathedral, the canonical building, and cloister—have visible vestiges of the 12th and 13th centuries. The Renaissance era effects, including carved walnut doors showing scenes from the Virgin's life, are awe-inspiring.

The 1,500-year-old **baptistery** ★★ is one of the country's oldest. Jet-black granite columns rise to the ceiling. The central pool was used by bishops to bless the faithful. Most stunning of all the structures is the **cloister** ★★. Imagine a 14th-century ceiling covered with 300 painting panels illustrating typical Provençal life. Wild beasts and hunting scenes are thrown into the mix. Columns rise to the ceiling, and there's a giant bell tower too.

58 rue de Fleury. www.frejus.fr. ℘ **04-94-51-26-30.** Admission 5.50€, 4€ for children aged 16 and under. Admission includes entrance to all sites, the museum, and (optional) guided tour of cloister and baptistery. June–Sept daily 9am–6:30pm; Oct–May Tues–Sun 9am–noon and 2–5pm.

WHERE TO EAT

In the heart of historical Fréjus, **L'Amandier**, 9 rue Desaugiers (✆ **04-94-53-48-77**), is a local favorite. Dine on a classic 22€ lunchtime set menu (or 28€ evening menu) featuring roast duck with fig chutney, or game ravioli with a mushroom jus.

ESTEREL NATURAL PARK ★★

51km (32 miles) E of St-Tropez; 11km (7 miles) W of Cannes

It's a wonder that the Massif de l'Esterel exists at all. This 150 square km protected parkland stretches for 30km (19 miles) along some of the South of France's most attractive (and most sought-after) coastline. Big hotels and bling are out; wild olive trees and Peregrine falcons are in.

This pristine coastline has a history of adventure. And we're not talking about the 100km (62 miles) of mountain bike trails or 40km (24 miles) of walking trails that wind through the red volcanic rocks along the shore. On Plage de Débarquement, one of the quietest beaches in the South of France, all hell let loose in August 1944 as 20,000 soldiers of the 36th Texas Division stormed ashore. Nearby the peaks of Pic de l'Ours or Cap Roux make for glorious—and well sign-posted—hikes.

At the eastern end of the Massif de l'Esterel are the sandy beaches of Golfe de la Napoule. In 1919, the fishing village of La Napoule was a paradise for the sculptor Henry Clews and his wife, Marie, an architect. Fleeing America's "charlatans," whom he believed had profited from World War I, the New York banker's son built a fairy-tale castle by the sea, now the **Musée Henry Clews** (see p. 142).

Essentials

ARRIVING   A car is useful for **driving** to isolated beaches in the Massif de l'Esterel. Otherwise regular **trains** connect the Esterel towns of La Trayas, Théole-sur-Mer, and Agay on the St-Raphaël-Cannes line every 30 minutes or so. For information and schedules, call ✆ **36-35** or visit www.voyages-sncf.com.

VISITOR INFORMATION   Théole-sur-Mer's **Office de Tourisme** on 2 corniche d'Or (www.theoule-sur-mer.org; ✆ **04-93-49-28-28**), serves as a gateway for the Esterel, as does the **Office de Tourisme** in Agay on Place Giannetti (www.agay.fr; ✆ **04-94-82-01-85**), at the western edge of the park. Both offer downloadable maps of the park and its nature trails.

Where to Stay & Eat

Oasis ★★ FRENCH   What is arguably the finest restaurant in the Esterel is not one gourmet experience, but two. The Raimbault family manages a Michelin-starred sea-front extravaganza on La Napoule's port. The menu may include sea bass and clam *bourride* or herby squid with kumquats. Such dishes can also be recreated in the on-site **Cooking School** (2 hours, 50€ per person), which includes a wine testing session by sommelier Pascal Paulze. The elegant upstairs bistrot has an acclaimed 31€ fixed-price lunch and dinner menu. Expect light elegant bites like Japanese tuna tartare and Niçois jellied beef cheeks.

6 rue Jean Honoré Carle, La Napoule. www.oasis-raimbault.com. ✆ **04-93-49-95-52**. Reservations required. Main courses 18€–43€; fixed-price lunch menu 76€; fixed-price dinner 98€. Wed–Sun noon–2pm and 7:30–9:30pm (Bistrot open Tues).

Tiara Miramar Beach Hotel ★★   La Tiara opened in the middle of the Esterel's red cliffs in spring 2014. A short walk from Théole-sur-Mer center, it's a luxury beachfront oasis with a seawater therapy spa. The private beach and sea sports club is truly special. Day visitors may join the party for lunch of dinner, or hit the nearby beach of L'Aiguille, a long, soft, stretch of sand. Just watch out for naturists on the tiny coves just past the cliffs.

47 av. de Miramar, Théoule-sur-Mer. www.tiara-hotels.com. ✆ **04-93-75-05-05.** 60 units. 210€–480€ double. Amenities: Restaurants; bar; beach club; outdoor pool; room service; spa; tennis; free Wi-Fi.

Exploring the Esterel

Hiking, biking, kayaking, and swimming up sum up the Esterel's simple pleasures. In Théole-sur-Mer, **Bat-Ski** (www.batski.fr, ✆ **04-93-75-02-39**), rents kayaks and paddleboards from 12€ per hour on the beach. In Théole's port, **Centre de Plongée** (www.centre-plongee-rague.com, ✆ **04-93-49-74-33**) explores the local sea life from 45€ per dive.

Agay has even more to offer. Scuba trips to the mysterious Ile d'Or, a private island teaming with fish, are operated by **Diving Centre Ile d'Or** (www.dive.fr, ✆ **04-94-82-73-67**) for 30€ per dive. Visitors may bob around the bay on their own rented boat (no license required) with **Bateau Loc** (ww.bateauloc.com; ✆ **06-69-07-86-51**) for 200€ per day. Kayaks weigh in at an altogether cheaper 15€ per hour. **Esterel Adventure** (www.esterel-aventure.com; ✆ **04-94-40-83-83**) offers mountain bike hire from 20€ per day, as well as organizing guided hikes.

Musée Henry Clews ★ HISTORIC HOME/MUSEUM   The only official 'sight' in the Esterel park has a pretty wacky history. Bon viveurs Henry and Mary Clews decamped from decadent New York to this intoxicatingly pretty corner of France in 1919. They snapped up a seaside castle for a song, then held wild parties for local aristocrats. Henry fancied himself as a modern Don Quixote and insisted on calling himself "Mancha." The couple covered their 4-acre (1.6 hectare) gardens with a grotesque menagerie—scorpions, pelicans, monkeys, and lizards. Sculptures from visiting artists now cover these vast grounds. There's a treasure hunt for kids too.

Boulevard Henry-Clews. www.chateau-lanapoule.com. ✆ **04-93-49-95-05.** Admission 6€, 4€ for children ages 16 and under. Feb 7–Nov 7 daily 10am–6pm; Nov 8–Feb 6 Mon–Fri 2–5pm, Sat–Sun 10am–5pm.

CANNES & AROUND

CANNES ★★★

905km (561 miles) S of Paris; 163km (101 miles) E of Marseille; 26km (16 miles) SW of Nice

When Coco Chanel came here and got a suntan, returning to Paris bronzed, she shocked the milk-white society ladies—who quickly began to copy her. Today the bronzed bodies, clad in nearly nonexistent swimsuits, line the beaches of this chic resort and continue the late fashion designer's example. A block back from the famed promenade de la Croisette are the boutiques, bars, and bistros that make Cannes the Riviera's capital of cool.

Essentials

ARRIVING By **train,** Cannes is 10 minutes from Antibes, 30 minutes from Nice, and 45 minutes from Monaco. The TGV from Paris reaches Cannes in an incredibly scenic 5 hours. The one-way fare from Paris is 45€ to 129€, although advance purchase bargains can be has for as low as 26€. For rail information and schedules, visit www.voyages-sncf.com or call ✆ **36-35. Lignes d'Azur** (www.lignesdazur.com; ✆ **08-10-06-10-06**) provides bus service from Cannes' Gare Routière (place Bernard Cornut Gentille) to Antibes every 20 minutes during the day (trip time: 25 min.). The one-way fare is 1.50€.

The **Nice international airport** (www.nice.aeroport.fr; ✆ **08-20-42-33-33**) is a 30-minute drive east. **Bus no. 210** picks up passengers at the airport every 30 minutes during the day (hourly at other times) and drops them at Cannes' Gare Routière. The one-way fare is 20€, round-trip is 30€.

By **car** from Marseille, take A51 north to Aix-en-Provence, continuing along A8 east to Cannes. From Nice, follow A8 or the coastal D6007 southwest to Cannes.

VISITOR INFORMATION The **Office de Tourisme** is at 1 bd. de la Croisette (www.cannes-destination.fr; ✆ **04-92-99-84-22**).

SPECIAL EVENTS Cannes is at its most frenzied in mid-May during the **International Film Festival** (www.festival-cannes.com) at the Palais des Festivals, on promenade de la Croisette. It attracts not only film stars (you can palm the cement molds of their handprints outside the Palais des Festivals), but also seemingly every photographer in the world. You have a better chance of being named prime minister of France than you do attending one of the major screenings, although if you're lucky, you may be able to swing tickets to screenings of one of the lesser films. (Hotel rooms and tables at restaurants are equally scarce during the festival.) But the people-watching is absolutely fabulous!

Cannes

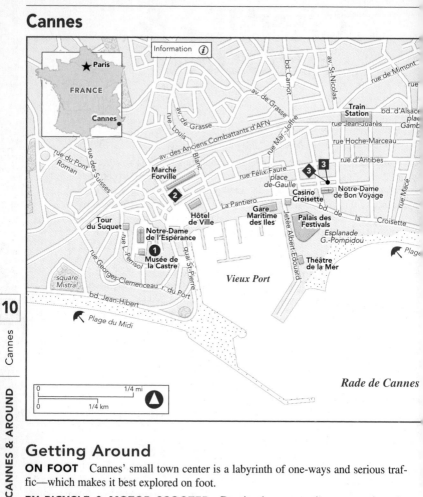

Information ⓘ

FRANCE
★ Paris
● Cannes

bd. Carnot
av. St-Nicolas
rue de Mimont
rue
av. de Grasse
Train Station
bd. d'Alsace
rue Jean-Juarès
plac
Gamb
rue Hoche-Marceau
rue de Grasse
rue Louis
rue Mar. Joffre
av. des Anciens Combattants d'AFN
rue d'Antibes
rue du Pont Roman
rue des Suisses
rue Blanc
Marché Forville
rue Félix-Faure
place de-Gaulle
3 **3**
Casino Croisette
Notre-Dame de Bon Voyage
av. Mace
La Pantiero
bd. de la Croisette
2
Hôtel de Ville
Gare Maritime des Iles
Palais des Festivals
Tour du Suquet
Notre-Dame de l'Espérance
jetée Albert-Edouard
Esplanade G.-Pompidou
Plage
rue L.-Perissol
1
Musée de la Castre
quai St-Pierre
square Mistral
rue Georges-Clemenceau r. du Port
Théâtre de la Mer
bd. Jean-Hibert
Vieux Port
Plage du Midi
Rade de Cannes

0   1/4 mi
0   1/4 km

Getting Around

ON FOOT Cannes' small town center is a labyrinth of one-ways and serious traffic—which makes it best explored on foot.

BY BICYCLE & MOTOR SCOOTER Despite the summertime commotion, the flat landscapes between Cannes and satellite resorts such as La Napoule and Juan-les-Pins are well suited for bikes and motor scooters. At **Daniel Location,** 7 rue de Suffren (www.daniel-location-2roues.com; ✆ **04-93-99-90-30**), *vélos tout terrain,* or VTT (mountain bikes) cost 16€ a day. Motorized bikes and scooters cost from 30€ per day. For larger motorbikes, you must present a valid driver's license. Another bike shop is **Mistral Location,** 4 rue Georges Clémenceau (www.mistral-location.com; ✆ **04-93-39-33-60**), which also charges 16€ per day for bike rentals.

BY CAR The Cannes Tourist Office website offers a downloadable document (under "Cannes Practical," then "Useful Information") listing all of the town's **public parking lots** and their hourly fees.

BY TAXI **Allô Taxi Cannes** (www.allo-taxis-cannes.com; ✆ **08-90-71-22-27**).

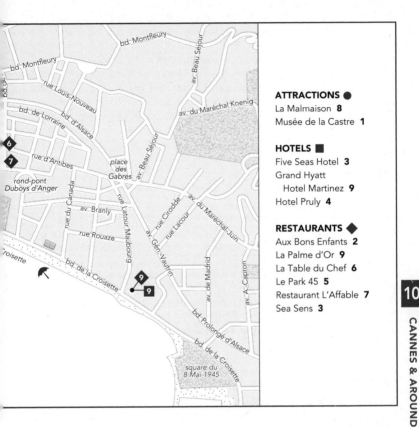

ATTRACTIONS ●
La Malmaison **8**
Musée de la Castre **1**

HOTELS ■
Five Seas Hotel **3**
Grand Hyatt
   Hotel Martinez **9**
Hotel Pruly **4**

RESTAURANTS ◆
Aux Bons Enfants **2**
La Palme d'Or **9**
La Table du Chef **6**
Le Park 45 **5**
Restaurant L'Affable **7**
Sea Sens **3**

BY PUBLIC TRANSPORT   **Bus Azur** (www.busazur.info; © **08-25-82-55-99**) operates all public transport in and around Cannes. There's little need for public transport in the city center—although the open-top nr. 8, which runs along the seafront from the port in the west to the Palm Beach peninsula in the east, makes for a fun and scenic ride. Tickets cost 1.50€ and can be purchased directly aboard any bus.

[FastFACTS] CANNES

ATMs/Banks   Banks are dotted throughout the city, including more than a dozen along the central rue d'Antibes.

Dentists   For emergency dental services, contact **SOS Dentaire** (© **04-93-68-28-00**).

Doctors & Hospitals **Hopital de Cannes,** 15 av. Broussailles (www.ch-cannes. fr; © **04-93-69-70-00**).

Internet Access   Cannes is in the process of blanketing the city with free Wi-Fi. The first area with coverage is the Jardins de l'Hotel de

Ville, just behind the port; the network is "Cannes sans fil."

Mail & Postage   **La Poste,** 22 rue Bivouac Napoléon (© **36-31**).

Pharmacies   **Pharmacie du Casino,** 9 bis square Mérimée (© **04-93-39-25-48**).

145

Where to Stay

Five Seas Hôtel ★★ The newest, coolest hotel in Cannes harks back to a Gatsby era of Art Deco furnishings and no-limits lavishness. The style is Louis Vuitton meets vintage ocean liner. The furniture design is based on classic traveling cases, albeit with Apple computers and Nespresso machines thrown into the mix. Popular with both guests and non-residents is the hotel's **Cinq Mondes & Carita Spa.** The top-floor terrace features a small infinity pool, a cocktail bar, and linen-shaded sun loungers. It's also the location of the acclaimed **Sea Sens** modern Mediterranean restaurant (fixed-price dinner 39€–95€ Tues–Sat) under the direction of head chef Arnaud Tabarec. And boy, what a view it has. Desserts come courtesy of 29-year-old World Pastry Champion Jérôme de Oliveira, who also maintains **Intuitions by J** (see p. 150), a tea and pastry shop on the ground floor.

1 rue Notre Dame. www.five-seas-hotel-cannes.com. ℂ **04-63-36-05-05.** 45 units. 295€–805€ double; from 595€ suite. **Amenities:** Restaurant; bar; concierge; outdoor pool; room service; spa; free Wi-Fi.

Grand Hyatt Hotel Martinez ★★★ The Martinez has been the socialite hub of the South of France for a century. The great and good have marched through its revolving doors including recent guests Eva Longoria, Nicole Kidman, and Steven Spielberg. This Art Deco masterpiece is more than just an ultra-luxe hotel. Nonguests can mingle with celebrities in the **l'Amiral** cocktail bar, bathe next to A-listers in the **ZPlage** beach club, or dine alongside minor royalty in one of the finest restaurants in the South of France, **La Palme d'Or** (p. 146). Hotel management was taken over by Hyatt in 2013, which ushered in a sleek refurbishment and a popular bicycle-sharing scheme—and what deliciously cool bikes they are.

73 bd. de la Croisette. http://cannesmartinez.grand.hyatt.com. ℂ **04-93-90-12-34.** 409 units. 750€–990€ double; from 3,300€ suite. Parking 40€. **Amenities:** 3 summer restaurants, 2 winter restaurants; bar; babysitting; private beach; free bikes; children's center; concierge; exercise room; outdoor pool; room service; sauna; spa; free Wi-Fi.

Hôtel Pruly ★★ Relatively new on the local scene, this delightful hotel spills from a renovated century-old townhouse. Charming rooms are decorated in bright colors and Provençal textiles; some boast traditional terra-cotta *tomette* floors or private balconies. An afternoon nap on a sun lounger in the hotel's palm-splashed private garden is a welcome respite from Cannes' summertime crowds. It's located just behind the train station.

32 bd. d'Alsace. www.hotel-pruly.com. ℂ **04-93-38-41-28.** 12 units. 65€–270€ double; 110€–320€ triple. **Amenities:** Garden; free Wi-Fi.

Where to Eat

Cannes' dining scene is all-encompassing: expect to stumble across everything from Michelin-starred gastronomy to traditional Provençal peasant cuisine. Restaurants are scattered across the city center, with a particularly heavy concentration around Le Suquet, Cannes' Old Town.

EXPENSIVE

La Palme d'Or ★★★ MODERN FRENCH Double-Michelin-starred chef Christian Sinicropi has presided over this theater of fine dining for more than a decade. His level of innovation knows no bounds. Think algae lollipops, flavored smoke, herb perfume. Guests are greeted at the table by the man himself, and then taken on an intensely seasonal 5- to 10-course gastronomic journey in a dining room so rococo that even Liberace would feel at home. Sinicropi also serves the Cannes Film Festival jury a special set dinner each spring. Spellbinding dishes created for recent festival presidents, like Tim Burton and Woody Allen, can be sampled from the menu. Unforgettable.

In the Grand Hyatt Hotel Martinez, 73 bd. de la Croisette. http://cannesmartinez.grand.hyatt.com. ✆ **04-92-98-74-14.** Reservations required. Jacket and tie recommended. Main courses 68€–84€; fixed-price menu 90€–205€. Wed–Sat 12:30–2pm and 8–10pm. Closed Jan–Feb.

Le Park 45 ★★★ MEDITERRANEAN   One of the most inventive—and least expensive—Michelin-starred restaurants on the Riviera is run by one of the coast's youngest chefs, baby-faced Sébastien Broda. Nicknamed the "Petit Prince de la Croisette," Broda scooped up his first Michelin star before the age of 30, after a career at La Palme d'Or in Cannes and L'Amandier in Mougins, two dens of fine Riviera dining. Locally grown vegetables and Atlantic seafood sparkle with additions of yuzu condiment, ponzu cream, Parmesan bouillon, and zingy Granny Smith apple *jus*. Surrounding Le Park 45 is the modernist splendor of **Le Grand Hotel** (www.grand-hotel-cannes. com; ✆ **04-93-38-15-15**). Originally the first hotel on the Croisette, this current 1960s incarnation boasts the best sea views in Cannes and perfectly preserved period features—from funky plastic telephones to Art Decl lampshades. Prices run 140€ to 500€ for a double and from 450€ for a suite, including free Wi-Fi.

In Le Grand Hotel, 45 bd. de la Croisette. www.grand-hotel-cannes.com. ✆ **04-93-38-15-15.** Reservations recommended. Main courses 32€–44€; fixed-price lunch 55€, dinner 55€–120€. Daily mid-day–2pm and 7:30–10pm.

MODERATE

Restaurant L'Affable ★★ MEDITERRANEAN   Chef Jean-Paul Battaglia's menu may be petite. But his creations are as innovative and as contemporary as can be. The frequently changing selection of dishes may include pumpkin soup with foie gras foam, ceviche 'Grenoble-style' drizzled with capers and lime, or tartare of scallops and oysters served with lemon Chantilly cream. Be sure to save space for Battaglia's signature *soufflé au Grand-Marnier*. Note the ambiance is decidedly formal and the service is superb—making L'Affable a good choice for a special occasion.

5 rue Lafontaine. www.restaurant-laffable.fr. ✆ **04-93-68-02-09.** Reservations recommended. Main courses 36€–40€; fixed-price lunch 24€–28€; fixed-price dinner 43€. Mon–Fri 12:30–2pm, Mon–Sat 7–10pm. Closed Aug.

La Table du Chef ★ FRENCH/PROVENÇAL   Just off Cannes' premier shopping street, rue d'Antibes, this unassuming little bistro serves up some of the city's tastiest cuisine. Chef Bruno Gensdarme (who spent almost 20 years working alongside superchef Guy Savoy in Paris) puts his own spin on traditional French dishes, such as Muscadet-infused rabbit terrine, or eggplant *millefeuilles* drizzled in goat's cheese cream and olives. Picky eaters beware: Menus are either fixed or offer very limited choice.

5 rue Jean Daumas. ✆ **04-93-68-27-40.** Reservations recommended. Fixed-price menu 24€–41€. Tues–Sat noon–2pm; Thurs–Sat 7–10pm.

INEXPENSIVE

Aux Bons Enfants ★ PROVENÇAL   You could easily miss this old-fashioned eatery, tucked among a crowd of mediocre tourist-targeted restaurants. But what an oversight that would be. Family-run for three generations, the authentic Aux Bons

Enfants today is headed up by Chef Luc Giorsetti. Dishes are traditional: *daube de canard,* slow-cooked *duck à la niçoise;* zucchini flower fritters; or house-cured salmon gravlax. Seasonal ingredients are sourced each morning from Marché Forville. Note that the restaurant has no telephone and does not accept reservations or credit cards.

80 rue Meynadier. www.aux-bons-enfants.com. No telephone; no reservations. Main courses 16€–23€; fixed-price menus 27€–34€. No credit cards. Tues–Sat noon–2pm and 7–10pm.

Exploring Cannes

Far and away, Cannes' most famous street is the **promenade de la Croisette**—or simply La Croisette—which curves along the coast. It's lined by grand hotels (some dating from the 19th c.), boutiques, and exclusive beach clubs. It's also home to temporary exhibition space **La Malmaison,** 47 La Croisette (✆ **04-97-06-44-90**), which holds three major modern art shows each year. It's open daily July to August 11am to 8pm (Friday until 9pm), September 10am to 7pm, and October to April Tuesday to Sunday 10am to 1pm and 2 to 6pm. Admission is 3.50€, 2.50€ for ages 18–25, and free for children under 17. Above the harbor, the Old Town of Cannes sits on Suquet Hill, where visitors can climb the 14th-century **Tour de Suquet.**

Musée Bonnard ★★ ART MUSEUM   The only museum in the world dedicated to the Impressionist painter Pierre Bonnard is located 3km (1¼ miles) north of Cannes, in the suburb of Le Cannet. Portraits, sculptures, and sketches on display in this petite museum were created primarily between 1922 and 1947, the period during which the artist was a local resident. The museum's audio guide comes courtesy of an iPod Touch.

16 bd. Sadi Carnot, Le Cannet. www.museebonnard.fr. ✆ **04-93-94-06-06.** Admission 5€–7€ adults, 3.50€–5€ children 12–18, free for children 11 and under. June–Sept Tues–Sun 10am–8pm (Thurs until 9pm); Oct–May Tues–Sun 10am–6pm (Thurs until 8pm). Closed 3 weeks in Jan. Bus nos. 1 and 4 from Cannes city center.

Musée de la Castre ★ MUSEUM   Perched above Cannes' Old Town within the medieval Château de la Castre, this museum focuses primarily on ethnographic finds from around the world. Spears from the South Seas and Tibetan masks are interspersed with Sumerian cuneiform tablets and 19th-century paintings of the Riviera. Many visitors, however, will be most impressed by the astounding views from the museum's viewing tower—accessed via 109 steeps steps. The shady Mediterranean gardens, just outside the museum's entrance, are a welcome respite for tired sightseers.

Le Suquet. ✆ **04-93-38-55-26.** Admission 6€ adults, 3€ ages 18–25, free for children 17 and under. July–Aug daily 10am–7pm (Wed until 9pm); Sept and April–June Tues–Sun 10am–1pm and 2–6pm (June and Sept Wed until 9pm); Oct–March Tues–Sun 10am–1pm and 2–5pm.

Organized Tours

One of the best ways to get your bearings in Cannes is to climb aboard the **Petit Train touristique de Cannes** (www.cannes-petit-train.com; ✆ **06-22-61-25-76**). The vehicles operate every day from 9 or 10am to between 7 and 11pm, depending on the season. Three itineraries are offered: Modern Cannes, with a ride along La Croisette and its side streets (35 min.); Historical Cannes, which weaves through the narrow streets of Le Suquet (35 min.); or the Big Tour, a combination of the two (1 hr.). All trains depart from outside the Palais des Festivals every 30 to 60 minutes. Shorter tours cost 7€ for adults and 3€ for children aged 3 to 10; the Big Tour costs 10€ for adults and 5€ for children aged 3 to 10.

Outdoor Activities

BEACHES   Beachgoing in Cannes has more to do with exhibitionism than actual swimming. **Plage de la Croisette** extends between the Vieux Port and the Port Canto. The beaches along this billion-dollar stretch of sand are *payante,* meaning entrance costs between 15€ to 30€. You don't need to be a guest of the Martinez, say, to use the beaches associated with a high-end hotel (see "Where to Stay," above), and Cannes has heaps of buzzing beach clubs dotted around, including sassy **3.14 Beach** (www.314cannes.com; ℂ **04-93-94-25-43**). Why should you pay an entry fee at all? Well, the fee includes a full day's use of a mattress, a chaise lounge (the seafront is more pebbly than sandy), and a parasol, as well as easy access to freshwater showers. There are also outdoor restaurants and bars (some with organic menus, others with gourmet burgers and sushi) where no one minds if you dine in your swimsuit. Every beach allows topless bathing. Looking for a free public beach without chaises or parasols? Head for **Plage du Midi,** just west of the Vieux Port, or **Plage Gazagnaire,** just east of the Port Canto. Here you'll find families with children and lots of RV-type vehicles parked nearby.

BOATING   Several companies around Cannes's Vieux Port rent boats of any size, with or without a crew, for a day, a week, or even longer. An outfit known for short-term rentals of small motorcraft is **Boat Evasion**, 110 boulevard du Midi (www.boatevasion.com; ℂ **06-26-59-10-77**). For kayak rental and guided tours of the coastline by canoe, try **SeaFirst,** place Franklin Roosevelt (www.seafirst.fr).

GOLF   Cannes is ringed by 10 golf courses, almost all within a 20-minute drive of the city. The **Old Course,** 265 route de Golf, Mandelieu (www.golfoldcourse.com; ℂ **04-92-97-32-00**), is a leafy gem dating from 1891. Greens fees start at 90€, with big reductions for lunch deals and afternoon tee-offs. The prestigious **Royal Mougins Golf Club,** 424 av. du Roi, Mougins (www.royalmougins.fr; ℂ **04-92-92-49-69**), also boasts a gourmet restaurant and spa. Greens fees start at 180€, including cart hire; it's half-price for 9 holes.

PADDLEBOARDING   Cannes is nothing if not cutting edge. And like the rest of the world, this city has fallen in love with stand-up paddleboarding (SUP). Rent your own from **Cannes Standup Paddle Location,** Plage du Mouré Rouge, bd. Gazagnaire, Palm Beach (www.cannesstanduppaddle.fr; ℂ **06-82-17-08-77**). Fees start at 12€ per hour.

TENNIS   Some resorts have their own courts. The city of Cannes also maintains 16 synthetic courts and 6 clay-topped ones at the **Garden Tennis Club,** 99 av. Maurice Chevalier (ℂ **04-93-47-29-33**). You'll pay from 13€ to 17€ per hour, plus 3.70€ per hour for floodlights.

Shopping

Cannes achieves a blend of resort-style leisure, glamour, and media glitz more successfully than many of its neighbors. You'll see every big-name designer you can think of, plus a legion of one-off designer boutiques and shoe stores. There are also real-people shops; resale shops for star-studded castoffs; flea markets for funky junk; and a fruit, flower, and vegetable market.

BOOKS   **Ciné-Folie,** 14 rue des Frères-Pradignac (ℂ **04-93-39-22-99**), is devoted entirely to film. Called "La Boutique du Cinema," it is the finest film bookstore in the south of France; vintage film stills and movie posters are also for sale. **Cannes English**

Bookshop, 11 rue Bivouac Napoleon (www.cannesenglishbookshop.com; ℭ **04-93-99-40-08**), stocks locally based classics from Peter Mayle and Carol Drinkwater, plus bestselling novels, travel guides, and maps.

DESIGNER SHOPS   Most of the big names in fashion line promenade de la Croisette, the main drag running along the sea. Among the most prestigious are **Dior,** 38 La Croisette (ℭ **04-92-98-98-00**), and **Hermès,** 17 La Croisette (ℭ **04-93-39-08-90**). The stores stretch from the Hôtel Carlton almost to the Palais des Festivals, with the top names closest to the **Gray-d'Albion,** 38 rue des Serbes (www.lucienbarriere.com; ℭ **04-92-99-79-79**), both a mall and a hotel (how convenient). Near the train station, department store **Galeries Lafayette** has all the big-name labels crammed into one smallish space at 6 rue du Maréchal-Foch (www.galerieslafayette.com, ℭ **04-97-06-25-00**).

Young hipsters should try **Bathroom Graffiti,** 52 rue d'Antibes (ℭ **04-93-39-02-32**), for sexy luggage, bikinis, and designer homeware. The rue d'Antibes is also brilliant for big-brand bargains (Zara and MaxMara), as well as one-off boutiques.

FOOD   The Marché Forville (see below) and the surrounding streets are unsurprisingly the best places to search for picnic supplies. For bottles of Côtes de Provence, try **Cave du Marché,** 5 place Marché Forville (ℭ **04-93-99-60-98**). It also serves up glasses of local rosé and olive crostini at tables outside. **La Compagnie des Saumons,** 12 place Marché Forville (ℭ **04-93-68-33-20**), brims with caviar, bottles of fish soup, and slabs of smoked salmon. Local cheese shop **Le Fromage Gourmet,** 8 rue des Halles (ℭ **04-93-99-96-41**), is a favorite of celebrated chef Alain Ducasse. Closer to the seafront, World Pastry Champion Jérôme Oliveira creates fairy-tale desserts in bite sizes—from flower-topped tarts to a pastel rainbow of *macarons*—at **Intuitions by J,** 22 rue Bivouac Napoléon (www.patisserie-intuitions.com; ℭ **04-63-36-05-07**).

MARKETS   The **Marché Forville,** in place Marché Forville just north of the Vieux Port, is a covered stucco structure with a few arches but no walls. From Tuesday to Sunday, 7am to 1pm, it's the fruit, vegetable, and flower market that supplies the dozens of restaurants in the area. Monday (8am–6pm) is *brocante* day, when the market fills with dealers selling everything from Grandmère's dishes and bone-handled carving knives to castaways from estate sales. Tuesdays to Sundays, 8am to 12:30pm, the small **Marché aux Fleurs** (Flower Market) takes place outdoors along the edges of the allée de la Liberté, across from the Palais des Festivals.

Nightlife

BARS & CLUBS   A strip of sundowner bars stretches along rue Félix Faure. Most are chic, some have happy hour cocktails, and several have DJs after dinner. Tapas bar **Le Bivi,** 7 rue des Gabres (www.lebivi-cannes.com; ℭ **04-93-39-97-90**), is a convivial spot to sample more unusual South of France wines. For an aperitif with history, the **Bar l'Amiral,** in the Hôtel Martinez, 73 La Croisette (ℭ **04-93-90-12-34**), is where deals have always gone down during the film festival. The bar comes complete with the nameplates of stars that once propped it up, Humphrey Bogart among them. Alternatively, head to **Le 360,** Radisson Blu 1835 Hotel & Thalasso, 2 bd. Jean Hibert (www.radissonblu.com; ℭ **04-92-99-73-20**), a panoramic rooftop terrace overlooking the port that's idyllic for a cocktail as the sun sets. Continue the party at **B.Pub,** 22 rue Macé (ℭ **04-93-38-17-30**), with live pop, international DJs, and the resident bartenders' favorite trick, a flaming ring of alcohol-fueled fire round the bar. At **Le Bâoli,** Port Pierre Canto, La Croisette (www.lebaoli.com; ℭ **04-93-43-03-43**), Europe's partying elite, from Prince Albert of Monaco to Jude Law, dance until dawn. Dress to the nines to slip past the über-tight security and into this Asian-inspired wonderland.

CASINOS   Cannes is invariably associated with easygoing permissiveness, film-making glitterati, and gambling. If the latter is your thing, Cannes has world-class casinos loaded with high rollers, voyeurs, and everyone in between. The better established is the **Casino Croisette,** in the Palais des Festivals, 1 espace Lucien Barrière (www.lucienbarriere.com; ✆ 04-92-98-78-00). A well-respected fixture in town since the 1950s, a collection of noisy slot machines it is most certainly not. Its main competitor is the newer **Palm Beach Casino,** place F-D-Roosevelt, Pointe Croisette (www.casinolepalmbeach.com; ✆ 04-97-06-36-90), on the southeast edge of La Croisette. It attracts a younger crowd with a summer-only beachside poker room, a beach club with pool, a restaurant, and a disco that runs until dawn. Both casinos maintain slots that operate daily from lunchtime to around 4am. Smarter dress is expected for the *salles des grands jeux* (blackjack, roulette, craps, poker, and chemin de fer), which open nightly 8pm to 4am. The casino also pulls in daytime visitors with tasty inexpensive lunches and Sunday brunches, both of which come with free gaming chips.

DAY TRIPS FROM CANNES
Îles de Lérins ★★
Short boat ride from Cannes

Floating in the Mediterranean just south of Cannes' southern horizon, the Lérins Islands are an idyllic place to escape the Riviera's summertime commotion. Head for Cannes port's western quai Laubeuf, where ferryboats operated by **Trans-Côte d'Azur** (www.trans-cote-azur.com; ✆ 04-92-98-71-30) offer access to Île Ste-Marguerite. To visit Île St-Honorat, head for the same quay, to the **Transports Planaria** (www.cannes-ilesdelerins.com; ✆ 04-92-98-71-38) ferryboats. Both companies offer frequent service to the islands at intervals of between 30 and 90 minutes, depending on the season, and operate daily and year-round. Round-trip transport to Île Ste-Marguerite costs 13€ per adult and 8€ for children 5 to 10; round-trip transport to Île St-Honorat costs 15.50€ per adult and 7.50€ for children 5 to 10 (although discount tickets 1€ to 1.50€ cheaper are often available if you book in advance online). Travel to both islands is free for children 4 and under. As dining options on the islands are limited, pack up a picnic lunch from Cannes' Marché Forville before you set off.

EXPLORING ÎLE STE-MARGUERITE
Île Ste-Marguerite is one big botanical garden—cars, cigarettes, and all other pollutants are banned—ringed by crystal-clear sea. From the dock, you can stroll along the island to Fort Royal, built by Spanish troops in 1637 and used as a military barracks and parade ground until World War II. The infamous "Man in the Iron Mask" was allegedly imprisoned here, and you can follow the legend back to his horribly spooky cell.

  Musée de la Mer, Fort Royal (✆ 04-93-38-55-26), traces the history of the island, displaying artifacts of Ligurian, Roman, and Arab civilizations, plus the remains discovered by excavations, including paintings, mosaics, and ancient pottery. The museum is open June to September daily from 10am to 5:45pm, and Tuesday to Sunday October to May 10:30am to 1:15pm and 2:15 to 4:45pm (closing at 5:45pm April–May). Admission is 6€, 3€ for visitors 25 and under, and free for children 17 and under.

EXPLORING ÎLE ST-HONORAT ★★

Only 1.6km (1 mile) long, the Île St-Honorat is much quieter than neighboring Ste-Marguerite. But in historical terms, it's much richer than its island sibling and is the site of a monastery whose origins date from the 5th century. The **Abbaye de St-Honorat** ★ (www.abbayedelerins.com; ✆ 04-92-99-54-00) is a combination of medieval ruins and early-20th-century ecclesiastical buildings, and is home to a community of about 25 Cistercian monks. Most visitors content themselves with a wander through the pine forests on the island's western side, a clamber around the ruined monastery on the island's southern edge, and a bathe on its seaweed-strewn beaches.

The monks also transform the island's herbs, vines, and honey into a wealth of organic products, including lavender oil and wine. All can be purchased in the monastery shop. There is also an excellent lunch-only seafood restaurant, **La Tonnelle** (www.tonnelle-abbayedelerins.com; ✆ 04-92-99-54-08). It's closed from November to mid-December. And no, it's not the monks who cook, but they can organize a wine-tasting or small island tour if arranged in advance.

Vallauris ★

7km (4½ miles) NE of Cannes

Once simply a stopover along the Riviera, Vallauris's ceramics industry was in terminal decline until it was "discovered" by Picasso just after World War II. The artist's legacy lives on both in snapshots of the master in local galleries and in his awesome "La Paix et La Guerre" fresco.

ESSENTIALS

Envibus **bus** (www.envibus.fr; ✆ 04-89-87-72-00) connects Cannes' train station with Vallauris every 30 minutes (journey time 20 min.). Tickets cost 1€ each way. There's an **Office de Tourisme** (www.vallauris-golfe-juan.fr) on square du 8 Mai 1945 (✆ 04-93-63-82-58).

EXPLORING VALLAURIS

In Vallauris, Picasso's **"l'Homme au Mouton"** ("Man and Sheep") is the outdoor statue at place Paul Isnard in front of which Prince Aly Kahn and screen goddess Rita Hayworth were married. The local council had intended to enclose this statue in a museum, but Picasso insisted that it remain on the square, "where the children could climb over it and dogs piss against it."

Musée Magnelli, Musée de la Céramique & Musée National Picasso La Guerre et La Paix ★★ ART MUSEUM   Three museums in one, this petite cultural center developed from a 12th-century chapel where Picasso painted "La Paix" ("Peace") and "La Guerre" ("War") in 1952. Visitors can physically immerse themselves in this tribute to pacifism. Images of love and peace adorn one wall; scenes of violence and conflict the other. Also on site is a permanent exposition of works by Florentine-born abstract artist Alberto Magnelli, as well as a floor dedicated to traditional and innovative ceramics from potters throughout the region.

Place de la Libération. www.musees-nationaux-alpesmaritimes.fr. ✆ **04-93-64-71-83.** Admission 4€ adults, 2€ for visitors 25 and under, free for children 15 and under. July–Aug daily 10am–7pm; June 16–30 and Sept 1–15 Wed–Mon 10am–12:15pm and 2–6pm; Sept 16–June 15 Wed–Mon 10am–12:15pm and 2–5pm.

WHERE TO EAT & SHOP

Join the locals for lunch at **Le Cafe du Coin,** 16 place Jules Lisnard (www.cafe-du-coin.com; ✆ 04-92-90-27-79), where a small selection of market-fresh specials are scribbled on the chalkboard daily. For souvenirs, head around the corner to avenue Georges-Clemenceau, lined with small shops selling brightly glazed, locally made ceramics. In early 2014, Vallauris's Tourist Office began offering free tours of the newly renovated **Galerie Madoura,** rue Georges et Suzanne Ramié, Picasso's former ceramics studio. Tours take place Monday to Friday at 10:30am in French-only; be sure to book in advance.

MOUGINS ★★

906km (562 miles) S of Paris; 179km (111 miles) E of Marseille; 31km (19 miles) SW of Nice; 7km (4½ miles) N of Cannes

A fortified hill town, Mougins preserves the quiet life in a postcard-perfect manner. The town's artsy legacy—Picasso, Jean Cocteau, Paul Eluard, Fernand Léger, Isadora Duncan, and Christian Dior were all previous residents—has blessed the town with must-see galleries. Real estate prices are among the highest on the Riviera, and the wealthy residents support a dining scene that also punches well above its weight.

Essentials

ARRIVING   The best way to get to Mougins is to **drive**. From Nice, follow E80/A8 west and then cut north on route 85 into Mougins. From Cannes, head north of the city along D6285.

In 2005, the French railway, **SNCF,** reactivated an antique rail line stretching between Grasse and Cannes, linking the hamlet of Mouans-Sartoux en route. Mouans-Sartoux lies only 457m (1,499 ft.) from the center of Mougins. Rail service costs 3.10€ one-way from Cannes to Mouans-Sartoux (journey time 25 minutes), and 2.10€ from Grasse to Mouans-Sartoux (journey time 6 minutes). From Nice, the journey costs 9€ and takes around an hour. **Trains** zip between all of these stations every hour. For further train information, visit www.voyages-sncf.com or call ✆ **36-35.**

By bus, **Société Tam** (www.cg06.fr; ✆ **08-00-06-01-06**) runs bus no. 600 from Cannes to Val-de-Mougins, a 10-minute walk from the center of Mougins. One-way fares cost 1.50€.

VISITOR INFORMATION   The **Office de Tourisme** is at 18 bd. Courteline (www.mougins.fr; ✆ **04-93-75-87-67**).

SPECIAL EVENTS   The **Etoile des Mougins food festival** (www.lesetoilesdemougins.com), held each September, is a highbrow gastronomic love-in featuring Michelin-starred chefs from across the globe.

[FastFACTS] MOUGINS

ATMs/Banks   There are a handful of banks and ATMs just outside of Mougins' Old Town, along avenue de Tournamy, including **LCL Banque** at nr. 78 (✆ **04-97-97-31-31**) and **Caisse d'Epargne Côte d'Azur** at nr. 308 (✆ **08-26-08-36-74**).

Mail & Postage   **La Poste,** Impasse Commdandt Lamy (✆ **36-31**).

Pharmacies   **Pharmacie de Mougins,** 71 avenue de Tournamy (✆ **04-93-90-00-46**).

Where to Stay

For golfers, the **Royal Mougins Hotel** (www.royalmougins.fr), with its private club and Robert von Hagge-designed 18-hole course (see p. 149) is highly recommended. **Le Moulin de Mougins** (see below) also rents elegant guestrooms.

Le Mas de Mougins ★★ Owners Sonia and Joel have lovingly renovated this former farmhouse, transforming it into a five-room bed and breakfast. Guestrooms are decked out in Provençal linens, with bathrooms of cool marble, and each one possesses its own private terrace. In summertime, an abundant breakfast is served at a communal table alongside the gardens. The grounds are lush with olive trees and shady oaks, and contain a swimming pool. Note that Le Mas is located around 2km (1.4 miles) northeast of Mougins' medieval town center.

91 avenue du Général de Gaulle. www.lemasdemougins.com. © **04-92-92-28-92.** 5 units. 130€–145€ double; 200€–250€ suite. Free parking. **Amenities:** Outdoor pool, free Wi-Fi.

Where to Eat

Le Moulin de Mougins ★★ FRENCH/PROVENÇAL   Inside an enchanting 16th-century mill, talented chef Erwan Louaisil follows in the footsteps of founder Roger Vergé and previous head chef Alain Llorca with modern twists on culinary traditions from both Provence and his native Brittany. Exquisite offerings (courtesy of menus with names like "Elizabeth Taylor" and "César") include Brittany lobster fricassée with a Sauternes and pink peppercorn sauce, or sea bass slow-roasted in aniseed butter and served alongside a braised fennel mousse. Le Moulin also rents six double rooms (200€–250€) and three suites (250€–300€) on site. An established place of epicurean pilgrimage.

Notre Dame de Vie. www.moulindemougins.com. © **04-93-75-78-24.** Reservations required. Main courses 37€–70€; fixed-price menu 65€–120€. Wed–Sun noon–2pm and 7:30–10pm.

Le Resto des Arts ★★ FRENCH   On a budget? Try this traditional bistro in the heart of Mougins' medieval village. Here head chef Denise proffers authentic French dishes while affable maître d' Greg welcomes visiting foodies and regular patrons alike. Hearty specials may include basil-spiked *soupe au pistou,* red mullet doused in tomato sauce, or seared steak with morel mushrooms. The wine list is both extensive and reasonably priced.

2 rue Maréchal Foch. www.le-resto-des-arts.pagesperso-orange.fr © **04-93-75-60-03.** Main courses 13€–24€; fixed-price lunch 22€; fixed-price dinner 25€. Tues–Sat noon–2:30pm and 7:30–9:30pm.

Exploring Mougins

Picasso discovered Mougins' tranquil maze of flower-filled lanes in the company of his muse, Dora Marr, and photographer Man Ray, in 1935. The Vieux Village's pedestrianized cobblestone streets—each corner prettier than the last—have changed little over the decades since. The setting is so romantic that, according to locals, French President François Hollande wined and dined his former first lady, Valérie Trierweiler, in one of the restaurants listed below. He then proceeded to indulge his mistress, Julie Gayet, in the same establishment. Classy guy.

Chapelle Notre-Dame de Vie ★ RELIGIOUS SITE   The most romantic site in Mougins—unless you are the President of France—is surely this medieval chapel. It lies 1.5km (1 mile) southeast of Mougins. It was built in the 12th century and reconstructed in 1646. Its tree-dappled grounds were once painted by Sir Winston Churchill. More importantly, the priory next door was once Picasso's studio and private residence for the last 12 years of his life. It's still a private home occupied intermittently by the Picasso heirs.

Chemin de la Chapelle. Admission free.

Musée d'Art Classique de Mougins ★★ MUSEUM   The newest addition to Mougins' art scene is wonderfully quirky: Egyptian, Greek, and Roman artifacts are juxtaposed alongside similarly themed modern artworks, including sculptures, drawings, and canvases from Matisse, Dufy, Cézanne, Dali, and Damien Hirst. A personal favorite pairing matches an ancient statue of Venus with Yves Klein's neon-blue "Venus" sculpture.

32 rue Commandeur. www.mouginsmusee.com. ✆ **04-93-75-18-65.** Admission 12€ adults, 7€ students and seniors, 5€ children 10–17, free for children 9 and under. Daily 10am–6pm.

Musée de la Photographie André Villers ★ ART MUSEUM   Picasso's close friend, photographer André Villers, chronicled the artist's Mougins years in black-and-white photos. Images line the walls of an ancient medieval home: Some are hilarious, such as the photo showing Picasso sitting down for breakfast in his trademark Breton shirt, pretending he has croissants for fingers. Additional portraits by Villars—including snaps of Dali, Catherine Deneuve, and Edith Piaf—are frequently on display, along with three major temporary exhibitions each year.

Porte Sarrazine. ✆ **04-93-75-85-67.** Free admission. Daily 10am–12:30pm and 2–6pm (until 7pm from June–Sept). Closed Jan.

GRASSE ★

918km (570 miles) S of Paris; 191km (118 miles) E of Marseille; 37km (22 miles) W of Nice; 18km (11 miles) N of Cannes

Grasse, a 20-minute drive from Cannes, has been renowned as the capital of the world's perfume industry since the Renaissance. It was once a famous resort, attracting such royals as Queen Victoria and Princess Pauline Borghese, Napoleon's lascivious sister. Edith Piaf too fell under the town's spell, vacationing and then living out her final years in the village of Plascassier, just east of the town center.

Today some three-quarters of the world's essences are produced here from thousands of tons of petals, including violets, daffodils, wild lavender, and jasmine. (It takes some 10,000 flowers to produce just over 1 kilogram of jasmine petals, and almost a ton of petals is needed to distill 1 liter of essence.)

The quaint medieval town, which formed the backdrop for the 2006 movie "Perfume," has several free perfume museums where visitors can enroll in workshops to create their own scent.

Essentials

ARRIVING   **Trains** run to Grasse from Nice, Cannes, and all stations in between, depositing passengers a 10-minute walk south of town. From here, a walking trail or shuttle bus leads visitors into the center. One-way train tickets cost 4.30€ from Cannes, and journey time is around 30 minutes; from Nice 9.10€, with a journey time of around just over an hour. For further train information, visit www.voyages-sncf.com or call ✆ **36-35. Buses** pull into town every 10 to 60 minutes daily from Cannes (trip time: 50 min.), arriving at the Gare Routière, place de la Buanderie (✆ **04-93-36-37-37**), a 5-minute walk north of the town center. The one-way fare is 1.50€. Visitors arriving by **car** may follow RN85 from Cannes. Alternatively, A8 funnels in traffic from Monaco, Aix-en-Provence, and Marseille.

VISITOR INFORMATION   The **Office de Tourisme** is at place du cours Honoré Cresp (www.grasse.fr; ✆ **04-93-36-66-66**).

SPECIAL EVENTS   In early May, **Exporose** celebrates the most romantic of flowers with a 4-day festival. More than 50,000 blossoms decorate the town's museums, churches, and public squares; highly competitive horticultural shows also take place. Admission is 5€ for adults, and 3€ children 12 and under.

At the beginning of August, Grasse's 3-day **Fête du Jasmin** (Jasmine Festival) has been a landmark annual festival since its inception 1948. Expect parades of jasmine-decked floats, complete with Miss Grasse tossing handfuls of the fragrant flowers into the crowds.

Contact the Grasse Tourist Office for further information about both of these events.

[FastFACTS] GRASSE

ATMs/Banks   **Banque Populaire Côte d'Azur**, 7 boulevard du Jeu de Ballon (✆ **04-83-59-88-05**).

Mail & Postage   **La Poste,** 9 boulevard Fragonard (✆ **36-31**).

Pharmacies   **Pharmacie de la Fontaine,** 28 place aux Aires (✆ **04-93-36-05-36**).

Where to Stay

Les Palmiers ★   Located just outside of Grasse's historic center, this welcoming bed and breakfast is truly a home away from home. The three guestrooms are simple, with modern furnishings and the period accents. All face southwards over the town and the Mediterranean Sea beyond, although just two of the rooms possess their own panoramic balcony. There's also a communal kitchen (including a washing machine) which guests are welcome to use.

17 avenue Yves Emmanuel Baudoin. www.les-palmiers-grasse.fr. ✆ **04-93-36-07-24.** 3 units. 75€–85€ double; 90€–115€ triple; 110€–140€ suite. Breakfast included. Minimum 2-night stay. Discounts for weeklong stays. **Amenities:** Communal kitchen, free Wi-Fi.

Where to Eat

Lou Candeloun ★★ FRENCH   Talented chef Alexis Mayroux has trained in France's finest kitchens (including Juan-les-Pins' Belles Rives, see p. 159). Along with Monegasque wife and maître d' Sophie, he's now heading up his own restaurant—and his gastro training shows. Seared scallops are paired with cardamom-spiced sweet potatoes, tender chicken breast is served with fromage frais, baby spinach, lemon confit, and cashews. The wallet-friendly lunch menu (priced at 20€) includes the *plat du jour*, a glass of wine and coffee. Note that the highly seasonal menu is changed every 3 weeks.

5 rue des Fabreries. www.loucandeloun.eresto.net. ☏ **04-93-60-04-49.** Main courses 25€; fixed-price lunch 20€–40€; fixed-price dinner 32€–57€. Mon–Sat 12:30–2:30pm; Tues–Sat 7:30–10pm.

Le Péché Gourmand ★★ PROVENÇAL   For light lunch or an afternoon snack, pop into this combination mini-restaurant, tearoom and ice cream parlor. Sample the goat's cheese and candied tomato crumble, or the seasonal artichoke quiche. Le Péché's dessert menu is particularly abundant: Order a scoop of fragrant rose sorbet, or plump for the pistachio-filled chocolate fondant.

8 rue de l'Oratoire. ☏ **06-62-69-61-57.** Fixed-price menu 12€–28€. Tues–Sun 10am–7pm. No credit cards. Takeout also available.

Exploring Grasse

Musée Fragonard ★ HISTORIC HOME/ART MUSEUM   This tranquil artsy gem occupies a large 18th-century private home surrounded by terraced gardens. It displays paintings by Jean-Honoré Fragonard, born in Grasse in 1732, his descendents and two of his contemporaries—his sister-in-law Marguerite Gérard and fellow Grassois Jean-Baptiste Mallet. The museum was fully renovated in 2014, and reopens to the public in early 2015.

Hôtel de Villeneuve, 14 rue Jean Ossola. www.fragonard.com. ☏ **04-93-36-02-07.** Free admission. June–Aug daily 10am–7pm; Sept–May 10am–6pm. Closed Sun Dec–early Feb.

Musée International de la Parfumerie ★ MUSEUM   This comprehensive museum chronicles both Grasse's fragrant history, as well as worldwide perfume development over the past 4,000 years. Wander among raw materials, ancient flasks (including Marie Antoinette's 18th-century toiletry set) and scented soaps, all set against a backdrop of temporary exhibitions and contemporary artworks. Kids age 7 and older have their own dedicated pathway, lined with interactive exhibits to touch—and, of course, smell.

2 bd. du Jeu-de-Ballon. www.museesdegrasse.com. ☏ **04-97-05-58-00.** Admission (depending on exhibition) 4€–6€ adults, 2€–3€ students, free for children 17 and under. April–Sept daily 10am–7pm; Oct–March Wed–Mon 10:30am–5:30pm. Closed Nov.

Organized Tours

Both **Parfumerie Molinard,** 60 bd. Victor Hugo (www.molinard.com; ☏ **04-93-36-01-62**), and **Parfumerie Fragonard,** 20 bd. Fragonard (www.fragonard.com; ☏ **04-93-36-44-65**), offer factory tours, where you'll get a firsthand peek into scent extraction and perfume and essential oil production. You can also purchase their products on-site.

ANTIBES & JUAN-LES-PINS

JUAN-LES-PINS ★★

913km (566 miles) S of Paris; 9.5km (6 miles) S of Cannes

Just west of the Cap d'Antibes, this Art Deco resort burst onto the South of France scene during the 1920s, under the auspices of American property developer Frank Jay Gould. A decade later, Juan-les-Pins was already drawing a chic summer crowd, as the Riviera "season" flipped from winter respites to the hedonistic pursuit of summer sun, sea, and sensuality. It has been attracting the young and the young-at-heart from across Europe and the U.S. ever since. F. Scott Fitzgerald decried Juan-les-Pins as a "constant carnival," no doubt after a sojourn in his seaside villa, which is now the Hôtel Belles-Rives. His words ring true each and every summer's day.

Juan-les-Pins is famed throughout France for its International Jazz Festival. In 2014, the festival's alfresco seaside stage hosted George Benson and Stacey Kent. Picasso also adored this most liberal of summer resorts, renting seven different local villas here during his yearly painting vacations during the 1920s and 1930s. He was no doubt spellbound by the Iles de Lérins that bob just offshore: Local ferries zip over to them all summer long.

Essentials

ARRIVING   Juan-les-Pins is connected by **rail** to most nearby coastal resorts, including Nice (trip time: 30 min.; 3.90€ one-way), Antibes, and Cannes. For further train information, visit www.voyages-sncf.com or call ✆ **36-35**. A **bus** (www.envibus.fr; ✆ **04-89-87-72-00**) leaves for Juan-les-Pins from Antibes' Gare Routière (bus station) daily every 20 minutes and costs 1€ one-way (trip time: 10 min.). To **drive** to Juan-les-Pins from Nice, travel along coastal D6007 south; from Cannes, follow the D6007 north.

VISITOR INFORMATION   In 2014, the Juan-les-Pins **Office de Tourisme** moved to the brand new convention centre at 60 chemin des Sables (www.antibesjuanlespins.com; ✆ **04-22-10-60-01**).

SPECIAL EVENTS   The town offers some of the best nightlife on the Riviera. The action reaches its peak during the annual 10-day **Festival International de Jazz** (www.jazzajuan.com) in mid-July. It attracts jazz, blues, reggae, and world music artists who play nightly on the beachfront Parc de la Pinède. Recent performers have included Maceo Parker, Norah Jones, and B. B. King. Tickets cost 25€ to 75€ and can be purchased at the Office de Tourisme in both Antibes and Juan-les-Pins, as well as online.

[FastFACTS] JUANS-LES-PINS

ATMs/Banks　**BNP Paribas,** 14 av. Maréchal Joffre ((C) **08-20-82-00-01**).

Internet Access　**Mediterr@net-phone.com,** av. du Dr Fabre ((C) **04-93-61-04-03**).

Mail & Postage　**La Poste,** 1 av. Maréchal Joffre ((C) **36-31**).

Pharmacies　**Pharmacie Provençale,** 144 bd. Président Wilson ((C) **04-93-61-09-23**).

Where to Stay

The opening of the new Juan-les-Pins convention center in 2014 ushered in the renovation of several inexpensive local hotels. Near the train station, **Eden Hôtel,** 16 avenue Louis Gallet (www.edenhoteljuan.com, (C) **04-93-61-05-20**; 77€–120€ double), is a great bet for short stays in the sun.

Le Grand Pavois ★　Nestled in an unbeatable location between the base of the Cap d'Antibes and Juan-les-Pins' center, this Art Deco edifice is literally a 2-minute walk to the beach. The elegant period lobby has been perfectly restored, and a live pianist often graces the ground-floor **La Rotonde** bar with jazzy tunes. Guestrooms are simply decorated with Provençal furnishings; many possess private balconies and sea views. Breakfast is served in the palm-fringed garden outside. An absolute bargain outside of the busy summer season.

5 av. Saramartel. www.bestwestern-legrandpavois.com. (C) **04-92-93-54-54.** 60 units. 78€–195€ double; 117€–278€ suite. Parking 8€. **Amenities:** Bar; restaurant; room service; free Wi-Fi.

Hôtel Belles-Rives ★★★　This luxurious hotel is one of the Riviera's most fabled addresses. It started life in 1925 as a holiday villa rented by Zelda and F. Scott Fitzgerald (as depicted in Fitzgerald's semi-autobiographical novel *Tender Is the Night*). Today, 85 years after her grandparents first opened the Belles-Rives' doors, the elegant Madame Estène-Chauvin owns and oversees this waterside gem. Guestrooms are sumptuous yet eclectic—each one its own unique size and shape. The lower terraces hold garden dining rooms, an elegant bar and lounge, as well as a private jetty. Also on site is the superb **La Passagère** restaurant and a private beach. If you're daring, you can even try waterskiing at the waterside aquatic club where, almost a century ago, the sport was invented.

33 bd. Edouard Baudoin. www.bellesrives.com. (C) **04-93-61-02-79.** 43 units. 180€–960€ double; 750€–2,000€ suite. Parking 30€. Closed Jan–Feb. **Amenities:** 2 summer restaurants; 1 winter restaurant; 2 bars; private beach; room service; free Wi-Fi.

Hôtel Mademoiselle ★★★　Juan-les-Pins' newest, coolest hotel offers 14 individually styled rooms in the absolute center of town. Décor is seriously funky. We're talking velvet headboards, golden robot statuettes, floral cushions, rocking horses, and a figurine of Her Majesty The Queen. Breakfast, drinks, and afternoon tea are served in the oasis-like rear garden. Homemade cakes and biscuits come under the tuteledge of the hotel's young pastry chef, Alexandra. Alas, the Mademoiselle may not be for everyone, as guests step out onto the main boulevard of one of Europe's most liberal resorts. The sandy beach is a 60 second stroll away.

12 avenue Docteur Dautheville. www.hotelmademoisellejuan.com. (C) **04-93-61-31-34.** 14 units. 100€–185€ double; 140€–225 € suite. **Amenities:** Room service; free Wi-Fi.

Hôtel La Marjolaine ★　One of Juan-les-Pins' oldest hotels is also one of its least expensive. Just 2 minutes on foot from both the beach and train station, La Marjolaine serves as a cozy base from which to explore the region. Guestrooms mirror the cutesy lobby: elegantly dated and *trés* Provençal. Of course, the experience is lo-fi. Reservations may only be made by telephone or on Booking.com. Parking is free. And simple breakfasts are served on the flower-filled terrace. A simple delight.

15 avenue du Docteur Fabre. ✆ **04-93-61-06-60.** 17 units. 60€–90€ double. Free parking. Closed Nov–Dec. **Amenities:** Room service, free Wi-Fi.

Where to Eat

Cap Riviera ★★ FRENCH   One of Juan-les-Pins' most appealing attributes is its endless ripple of beachside restaurants, all peering out over the picturesque Iles de Lérins. And Cap Riviera is undoubtedly one of this resort's finest. Cuisine is classically French. Think shrimp flambéed in pastis, lemon-infused sardine *rillettes*, or *sole meunière*; staff are charming and attentive. It's well worth popping by in advance to select your own special sea-facing table. Each evening the 39€ three-course set menu makes a great bet for a trustworthy splurge. Items may include half-lobster or shellfish cassolette to start, beef fillet with *morilles* mushrooms or flambéed kidneys for a main course, and rum baba or iced nougat to finish.

13 bd. Édouard Baudoin. www.cap-riviera.fr. ✆ **04-93-61-22-30.** Reservations recommended. Main courses 23€, fixed-price menu 39€. Daily noon–3pm, Mon–Sat 8–10pm. Closed Nov–mid-Dec and Jan.

Le Capitole ★ CLASSIC FRENCH   This restaurant's décor, menu, and service has hardly changed since its inception in the 1950s. And that's no bad thing. Expect impeccable service—with limited English—in a mirrored dining room filled with more lamps, boxes, and *objets d'art* than Gatsby's mansion. Classic French fare is a delight. Menu items may include smoked herrings with potatoes, *steak-frites*, snails in garlic, and créme caramel. Best value of all is the 16€ early dining menu. Arrive for dinner before 8pm for three bargain courses, with coffee and wine included in the deal.

22 av. Amiral Courbet. ✆ **04-93-61-22-44.** Reservations recommended. Main courses 9€–17€; fixed-price lunch 16€; fixed-price dinner 22€–39€. Wed–Sun noon–2pm and 7–10pm.

Le Perroquet ★★ PROVENÇAL   One of the finest restaurants in Juan-les-Pins, Le Perroquet attracts both casual visitors and longtime locals. The *assortiment de poissons grillés*—grilled sea bream, John Dory, giant prawns, and red mullet—is an excellent introduction to the best of the Mediterranean. The pretty sidewalk seating looks out over La Pinède's Aleppo pines, and a good-value fixed-price lunch menu changes daily.

Av. Georges-Gallice. www.restaurantleperroquet.fr. ✆ **04-93-61-02-20.** Reservations recommended. Main courses 16€–32€; fixed-price lunch 18€; fixed-price dinner 30€–39€. Daily noon–2pm and 7–10pm. Closed Nov–Dec.

Les Pirates ★ ITALIAN/MEDITERRANEAN   For casual toes-in-the-sand dining, head to this family-friendly seaside restaurant. Within its palm-trimmed oasis, Les Pirates' summery menu is perfect for punctuating lazy afternoons on the beach. There's a very good range of salads, including La Jazz (local baby-leafed mesclun, violet artichokes, Parma ham, and avocado), as well as more extravagant offerings, such as seared scallops or *fritto misto* (Italian-style fried fish). *Tiramisu della Mamma* is whipped up in the kitchen by true Italian mamma Anna.

23 bd. Édouard Baudoin. www.plage-les-pirates.fr. ✆ **04-93-61-00-41.** Main courses 17€–45€. Daily noon–3pm and 8–10pm. Closed Nov–Jan.

Star Plage ★★ MEDITERRANEAN   'Star Beach' represents dining in the sand at its most fabulous—and least expensive. Juan-les-Pins' great and good drop by for 19€ bottles of rosé, a weekend brunch, or a lazy afternoon on a sun lounger. Cuisine is Mediterranean modern. Read gourmet cheeseburgers, octopus salad, and giant seafood sharing platters. For toes-in-the-water dining, nobody in beachy Juan-les-Pins does it better.

Bl. Charles Guillaumont. ℂ **04-93-61-55-63**. Main courses 13€–32€; fixed-price dinner 29€–45€. Daily 10am–11pm (closed Wed & Thu in May, Oct). Closed Nov–April.

Exploring Juan-les-Pins

Spilling over from Antibes' more residential quarter, Juan-les-Pins is petite—which makes the resort town best navigated on foot. Be sure to swing by the shady square known as **La Pinède** (square Frank Jay Gould) to check out the legions of local *pétanque* players. Nearby, the town's long-awaited **Palais des Congrès**, or Convention Center (www.antibesjuanlespins-congres.com) opened to much fanfare in 2014. With the perennial success of year-round conferences in nearby Cannes, Juan-les-Pins' local municipality is hoping to shift some of the business action here.

Most of us, however, would rather stroll the long, beachside promenade to Golfe-Juan. It's here where Napoleon kicked off his march to Paris and famous Hundred Days in power in 1815. Alternatively, pick a beach bar, order a glass of rosé, and watch the sun drop over the Îles de Lérins (see p. 151). For a closer look, boat trips to Ile Sainte-Marguerite, the larger of the two islands, run several times daily from mid-April to mid-October with **Riviera Lines** (www.riviera-lines.com; ℂ **04-93-63-86-76**). Return tickets costs 18€ for adults, 12€ children aged 4–10, and free for children under 4.

Cycles (16€ per day) and **electric bikes** (30€ per day) can be hired from **Egorent**, 136 boulevard Wilson (www.egorent.fr; ℂ **08-11-69-02-10**).

Outdoor Activities

BEACHES   Part of the reason people flock to Juan-les-Pins is for the town's wealth of sandy beaches, all lapped by calm waters. The town also basks in a unique micro-climate, making it one of the warmest places on the Riviera to soak up the sun, even in winter. **Plage de Juan-les-Pins** is the most central beach, although quieter stretches of sand wrap around the Cap d'Antibes and include family-friendly **Plage de la Salis** and chic **Plage de la Garoupe.** If you do want to stretch out on a sun lounger, go to any of the beach-bar concessions that line the bay, where you can rent a mattress for around 12€ to 20€. Topless sunbathing and overt shows of cosmetic surgery are the norm.

WATERSPORTS   If you're interested in scuba diving, try **Easy Dive,** bd. Edouard Baudouin (www.easydive.fr; ℂ **04-93-61-26-07**). A one-tank dive costs 30€ to 55€, including all equipment. **Sea kayaking, pedalos, parasailing,** and **donuts** are available at virtually every beach in Juan-les-Pins. **Waterskiing** was invented at the Hôtel des Belles-Rives in the 1920s, and it's still a great place to try out the sport.

Nightlife

For a faux-tropical-island experience, head to **Le Pam Pam,** 137 bd. Wilson (www.pampam.fr; ℂ **04-93-61-11-05**), a time-honored "rhumerie" where guests sip rum and people-watch while reggae beats drift around the bar. More modern is **La Réserve,** av. Georges Gallice (ℂ **04-93-61-20-06**), where a younger crowd sips rosé on leopard-print seats under.

FRENCH RIVIERA pass

The new **French Riviera Pass** lets visitors explore the coast for 26€ for 24 hours, 38€ for 48 hours, or 56€ for 72 hours. Over 60 choice sights are completely free including the **Villa Kerylos** on Cap Ferrat, the **Musée Chagall** in Nice, and the **Oceanographic Museum** in Monaco. City tours like **Nice–Le** Grand open-top bus route, the **Mobilboard Segway** tour, and the **Train Touristique de Nice** are also free. Holders of the 72-hour pass are granted free entry into the normally wallet-busting **Marineland** in Antibes. Passes are available to purchase on the Nice Tourism website (www.nicetourisme.com).

If you prefer high-energy partying, you're in the right place. The entire Riviera descends upon Juan-les-Pins' discos every night in summer, and it's best to follow the crowds to the latest hotspot. **Le Village,** 1 bd. de la Pinède (✆ **04-92-93-90-00**), is one of the more established clubs and boasts an action-packed dance floor with DJs spinning summer sounds from salsa to soul. The cover charge is usually 16€ including one drink; more for themed evenings. For top jazz, head to **Le New Orleans,** 9 av. Georges Gallice (✆ **04-93-67-41-71**), a relatively new addition to the local live music scene.

ANTIBES ★★

913km (566 miles) S of Paris; 21km (13 miles) SW of Nice; 11km (6¾ miles) NE of Cannes

Antibes has a quiet charm unique to the Côte d'Azur. Its harbor is filled with fishing boats and pleasure yachts. The likes of Picasso and Monet painted its oh-so-pretty streets, today thronged with promenading locals and well-dressed visitors. A pedestrianized old town center, the Vieux Ville, makes it a family-friendly destination as well, and a perfect place for an evening stroll. An excellent covered market is also located near the harbor, open every morning except Mondays.

Spiritually, Antibes has long possessed a liberal edge. The Vieille Ville's western quarters are made up of the Commune Libre de Safranier—the Free Commune of Safranier. Residents in this artsy enclave have adopted the motto: "*Je ne crains rien, je n'espère rien, je suis libre*", which translates as "I fear nothing, I hope for nothing, I'm free." Safranier's warren of lanes is filled with flower boxes and alfresco art. The town's latest open-minded outpouring is the giant meditating statue by Catalan artist Jaume Plensa, which looks out endlessly to sea from underneath the Musée Picasso.

Essentials

ARRIVING   **Trains** from Cannes arrive at the rail station, place Pierre-Semard, every 20 minutes (trip time: 15 min.); the one-way fare is 2.90€. Around 25 trains arrive from Nice daily (trip time: 20 min.); the one-way fare is 3.60€. For further train information, visit www.voyages-sncf.com or call ✆ **36-35.** The **bus** station, or Gare Routière, place Guynemer (www.cg06.fr or www.envibus.fr; ✆ **04-89-87-72-00**), offers bus service throughout Provence. Bus fares to Nice, Cannes, or anywhere en route cost 1.50€ one-way.

To **drive** to Antibes from Nice, travel along coastal D6007 south; from Cannes, follow the D6007 north. The Cap d'Antibes is clearly visible from most parts of the Riviera. To drive here from Antibes, follow the coastal road south—you can't miss it.

The **Office de Tourisme** is at 11 place du Général de Gaulle (www.antibesjuanlespins.com; ℰ **04-97-23-11-11**).

[FastFACTS] ANTIBES

ATMs/Banks Among others, there are half a dozen banks dotted along av. Robert Soleau.

Internet Access **Wilson.net,** 74 bd. Wilson (ℰ **04-92-90-25-34**).

Mail & Postage **La Poste,** 2 av. Paul Doumer (ℰ **36-31**).

Pharmacies **Grande Pharmacie d'Antibes,** 2 place Guynemer (ℰ **04-93-34-16-12**).

Where to Stay

Le Relais du Postillon ★★ Like Antibes itself, Le Relais is charmingly individualistic with bags of character. It's sited on the town's principal square, with a café and terrace right on the action. The interior bar—with cozy fireplace in winter—has toasted a century of local color. Guestrooms aren't exactly the Ritz, but they are tidy, Frenchy, and spotlessly clean. Moreover, they cost well under 100€ per night even in high summer. Le Relais also rents a 40-square-metre holiday apartment next door to the hotel from 600€ per week.

8 rue Championnet. www.relaisdupostillon.com. ℰ **04-93-34-20-77**. 16 units. 69€–129€ double. Parking 20€. **Amenities:** Café; bar; room service; spa; tennis; free Wi-Fi.

Royal Antibes Hotel ★★ This award-winning hotel overlooks the sandy beach of Plage de la Salis near Antibes' Archaeological Museum. It's airy, light, and delightfully modern. Tropical trees and an indoor/outdoor lobby welcome guests to the reception desk. From here, it's a hop across the street to Royal Plage. Open from April to September, it offers jet-ski hire and seaside sofas, plus sun loungers for 20€ per day. All guests are granted complimentary access to the luxurious new Royal Spa, a haven that includes Cinq Mondes products, hammam, sauna, yoga classes, Jacuzzi, and fitness studio.

16 bl Maréchal Leclerc. www.royal-antibes.com. ℰ **04-83-61-91-91**. 39 units. 200€–450€ double; from 400€ suite. Closed Nov–Dec. **Amenities:** Restaurant; bar; babysitting; exercise room; room service; spa; free Wi-Fi.

Rue Sade B&B ★ A hip B&B that promises "the luxury of a hotel with the ambiance of a B&B." This Swedish-run establishment achieves its goal in spades. The breakfast is among the finest in Antibes' Vieille Ville. Think local pastries, market-fresh fruit, pickles, and preserves. Rooms are small and simple, as befits a colorful neighborhood where locals live cheek by jowl. Instead of TVs, each room has an iPod dock and access to speedy Wi-Fi. The proprietor will also reserve guests a restaurant table from his notebook of fabulous recommendations.

19 rue Sade. www.ruesade.se. ℰ **06-77-64-43-86**. 6 units. 90€–155€ double. **Amenities:** Free Wi-Fi.

Where to Eat

Antibes' Marché Provençal street market is a top spot for picnic items. Purchase olives, cheese, or a whole-roast chicken and simply dine on the beach. For light bites and unusual local wines, stop into **Entre 2 Vins,** 2 rue James Close (ℰ **04-93-34-46-93**).

L'Armoise ★★ PROVENÇAL Talented chef Laurent Parrinello, who honed his skills at Eze's Chèvre d'Or à Eze and the nearby Hôtel du Cap–Eden-Roc, crafts modern adaptations of traditional dishes, such as pesto-drizzled asparagus, fennel, and goat-cheese salad, or sea bream served with curry-infused red cabbage. Fresh ingredients come from Antibes' daily market; cheeses and wines are sourced from local producers. Note that advance reservations at this tiny restaurant are strongly recommended.

2 rue de la Tourraque. ℂ **04-92-94-96-13.** Reservations recommended. Main courses 22€–24€; fixed-price menu 48€–80€. Tues–Sun 7:30–9:30pm, Sat–Sun 12:30–2pm. Closed 2 weeks in July & 2 weeks in Dec.

Bistro Le Rustic ★ FRENCH/PIZZA For hearty local dishes on a budget, it's hard to beat family-run Le Rustic. The menu here focuses on wood-fired pizzas and rich pots of fondue, with plenty of Riviera classics (fish soup, a fresh shrimp platter, slow-roasted duck) thrown in too. The restaurant is located at the heart of Antibes' Old Town, with spacious (and kid-friendly) outdoor seating in the square.

33 place Nationale. ℂ **04-93-34-10-81.** Main courses 10€–18€; fixed-price menu 14€–19€. Daily noon–3pm and 7–11pm.

Chez Helen ★ VEGETARIAN Whether you're a vegetarian on the road or simply seeking a little bit of lighter fare—despite the fact that Southern French food tends to eschew butter, cream, and heavier meats—this petite restaurant is a delight. All ingredients are organic and locally sourced. Expect subtle dishes like roasted tomato salad with basil *pistou* and mustard leaves, or spinach and feta stuffed Tunisian-style *brik*. Lunch only, or try Chez Helen for afternoon tea and a homemade pastry (8.50€). **Le Café Jardin** across the street at 23 rue des Bains, offers more vegetarian delights.

35 rue des Revennes. www.chezhelen.fr. ℂ **04-92-93-88-52.** Main courses 12€; fixed-price menu 12€–15€. Mon–Sat 11am–5pm.

Exploring Antibes

Antibes' largely pedestrianized Old Town—all pale stone homes, weaving lanes, and window boxes of colorful flowers—is easily explored on foot. A dip into Picasso's former home, now a museum, and a stroll along the bling-tastic pleasure port, are undoubtedly its highlights.

Antibes' Tourist Office offers a number of different tours. English language tours around the historic old town take place every Wednesday at 10am. Prices are 7€ for adults, 3.50€ for children under 16, and free for children ages 8 and under. French-only tours around Antibes' artist hotspots take place each Friday at 10am for the same prices.

A touristy **Petit Train** (www.capdantibestour.com; ℂ **06-15-77-67-47**), also does a circuit around Antibes highlights, including the Musée Picasso and the Port Vauban pleasure harbor. Tickets cost 8€ for adults, 4€ for children under the age of 10. Cooler cats may rent a five-person speedboat (no license required) from **Antibes Bateau Service** (www.antibes-bateaux.com; ℂ **06-15-75-44-36**), in Port Vauban. Prices are 100€ per half day, 150€ per full day.

Musée d'Archéologie ★ ARCHAEOLOGICAL MUSEUM In the 5th century BC, the protected port of Antibes was a thriving Greek colony. Olive oil and natural dyes were transported to and from here from as far afield as Lebanon and Morocco. Some 500 years later, the Romans brought roads, aqueducts, glassware, and amphoras, all of which were scattered along the local coastline and, occasionally, on the seabed.

This petite museum may be housed in a 17th-century defensive bastion, but it charts early Antibes history by way of coins, ceramics, and two very ancient toilets. Maps prove that ancient trading vessels docked in the very spot where the world's largest superyachts are now tied up. Perhaps archaeologists will ponder over their discarded Louis Vuitton sunglasses and empty Veuve Clicquot bottles two thousand years from now.

Bastion Saint André. ✆ **04-92-90-53-36.** Admission 3€ adults, free for children 18 and under. Mid-June–mid-Sept Tues–Sun 10am–noon and 2–6pm (July–Aug Wed and Fri until 8pm); mid-Sept–mid-June Tues–Sun 10am–noon and 1–5pm.

Musée Picasso ★★ ART MUSEUM   Perched on the Old Town's ramparts, the 14th-century Château Grimaldi was home to Picasso in 1946, when the Spanish artist lived and worked here at the invitation of the municipality. Upon his departure, he gifted all the work he'd completed to the chateau museum: 44 drawings and 23 paintings, including the famous "La Joie de Vivre." In addition to this permanent collection, contemporary artworks by Nicolas de Staël, Arman and Modigliani, among many others, are also on display.

Château Grimaldi, Place Mariejol. ✆ **04-92-90-54-28.** Admission 6€ adults, 3€ students and seniors, free for children 17 and under. Mid-June–mid-Sept Tues–Sun 10am–6pm (July–Aug Wed and Fri until 8pm); mid-Sept–mid-June Tues–Sun 10am–noon and 2–6pm.

DAY TRIPS FROM ANTIBES

Biot ★

6.5km (4 miles) NW of Antibes

Biot has been famous for its pottery since merchants began to ship earthenware jars to Phoenicia and throughout the Mediterranean. It's also where Fernand Léger painted until the day he died, leaving a magnificent collection of his work on display just outside town.

ESSENTIALS

Bus lines no. 10 from Antibes's Gare Routière, place Guynemer (www.envibus.fr; ✆ **04-89-87-72-00**), runs to Biot's town center. Tickets cost 1€. To **drive** to Biot from Antibes, follow D6007 east, then head west on the D4. Biot's **Office de Tourisme** is at 46 rue St-Sébastien (www.biot-tourisme.com; ✆ **04-93-65-78-00**).

EXPLORING BIOT

Exploration of Biot's small historic center begins at **place des Arcades,** where you can see the 16th-century gates and the remains of the town's ramparts. The **Musée d'Histoire et Céramique Biotoise,** 8 rue St-Sebastien (www.musee-de-biot.fr; ✆ **04-93-65-54-54**), has assembled the best works from local artists, potters, ceramists, painters, and silver- and goldsmiths. Hours are mid-June to mid-September Tuesday to Sunday 10am to 6pm, and mid-September to mid-June Wednesday to Sunday 2 to 6pm. Admission is 4€, 2€ for seniors and students, and free for children 16 and under.

Outside of town, the excellent **Musée National Fernand Léger,** 316 chemin du Val de Pôme (www.musees-nationaux-alpesmaritimes.fr/fleger; ✆ **04-92-91-50-20**), displays a comprehensive collection of the artist's colorful creations, from 1930s Cubist ladies to circus scenes of the 1950s. Hours are Wednesday to Monday May to October 10am to 6pm, November to April 10am to 5pm. Admission is 5.50€, 4€ for students and seniors, and free for ages 25 and under. There are temporary exhibitions and a café garden on site.

The very Zen **Musee du Bonsaï**, 299 chemin du Val de Pôme (www.museedubonsai-biot.fr, ✆ **04-93-65-63-99**), is located just around the corner. Cultivated by father and son team Jean and Karol Okonek, more than $1,000m^2$ ($1,076$ ft^2) of Japanese-style gardens are dedicated to bonsai trees collected from as far afield as Australia and China. It's open Wednesday to Monday from 10am to noon and from 2pm to 6pm. Admission is 4€, 2€ for students and seniors. Note that the museum is closed from early January until the third week of February.

WHERE TO EAT & SHOP

For a Provençal take on crêpes—such as summery tomato, olive tapenade with basil or the house specialty, crêpe-pizza—stop in to **Crêperie Auberge du Village,** 29 rue Saint Sébastien (www.creperie-aubergeduvieuxvillage.com; ✆ **04-93-65-72-73**). This low-key lunch spot sits at the northern end of Biot's main shopping street. In the late 1940s, local glassmakers created a bubble-flecked glass known as *verre rustique.* In brilliant cobalts and emeralds, it's purveyed in the many store windows here.

ESPECIALLY FOR KIDS

Just south of Biot sits a kid-tastic complex of theme parks. **Marineland** (www.marineland.fr) offers the chance to get personal with penguins, polar bears, and sharks. **Aqualand** (www.aqualand.fr) boasts more than 2km (1¼ miles) of waterslides, including toboggan-style Le Draguéro and the Rainbow Cannon. **Adventure Golf** is criss-crossed by two dinosaur-dotted miniature golf courses. And, new for 2014, **Kid's Island** caters to animal-loving little ones, with pony rides and a petting zoo, plus plenty of jungle gyms and a Magic River. Admission is as follows: Marineland 39€, 31€ children between 3 and 12; Aquasplash 27€, 21€ children between 3 and 12; Adventure Golf 11€, 9€ children between 3 and 12; and Kid's Island 13.50€, 10.50€ children between 3 and 12. All are free for children 2 and under; combination entrance tickets are also available. Marineland is open daily July and August 10am to 11pm, mid-April to June and September 10am to 7pm, and mid-March to mid-April 10am to 6pm. Aquasplash, Adventure Golf, and Kid's Island all have varying opening hours. See the Marineland website for more details.

CAP D'ANTIBES ★

914km (567 miles) S of Paris; 23km (14 miles) SW of Nice; 12km (7½ miles) NE of Cannes

The Cap d'Antibes has been the preserve of the rich and famous since Ernest Hemingway and F. Scott Fitzgerald partied upon its pine-backed beaches in the roaring 1920s. Anyone who was anyone in South of France folklore—Pablo Picasso, Man Ray, Jean Cocteau—called by to join in the fun. Alas, where impoverished artists discover, the ultra-rich soon follow. From the 1960s, Le Cap became the summer playground of Brits and Americans, and more recently Russians and Arabs, who built French chateaux, Moorish palaces, and English castles upon this paradisiacal peninsula.

This being socialist France, paradise is assuredly public, not private. A lovely 6km (3¾ miles) coastal path rings the headland, passing picnic and diving spots en route. It even loops underneath the home of many a multi-billionaire. All too tiring? Then download the movie instead. The 2014 Woody Allen release, *Magic in the Moonlight,* was filmed on this fabled stretch of land.

Essentials

ARRIVING   Take a **train** to Antibes and Juan-les-Pins then simply start wandering along the Cap d'Antibes. Alternatively, take the no. 2 bus from Antibes Gare Routière, or bus station, which runs around the Cap every hour. The one-way fare is 1€.

The Cap d'Antibes sticks out from the coast and is clearly visible from most parts of the Riviera. To **drive** here from Antibes, follow the coastal road south—you can't miss it.

[FastFACTS] CAP D'ANTIBES

Mail & Postage   **La Poste,** 85 boulevard Francis Meilland (✆ **36-31**).

Pharmacies   **Pharmacie Kuleyan Laurent,** 85 boulevard Francis Meilland (✆ **04-93-61-24-53**).

Where to Stay

Hôtel du Cap-Eden-Roc ★★★   This legendary hotel was first launched in 1887, serving as a Mediterranean getaway for visitors seeking winter sunshine. Over the intervening years, it's played host to the world's most famous clientele, from the Duke and Duchess of Windsor (who escaped here after the former king's abdication) to the Hollywood superstars who cavort at the "Vanity Fair" Cannes Film Festival party. Surrounded by a maze of manicured gardens, accommodation is among the most sumptuous on the Riviera. Guest rooms benefitted from a 2013 renovation that outfitted every one with sleek modern fittings, iPod docks, and LED screens. Guests lounge by the seawater swimming pool, carved from natural basalt rock, while evenings are spent at the panoramic **Restaurant Eden-Roc** or the **Bellini Bar.** Looking to splurge? Pick up an exclusive Eden-Roc-label beach sarong. Alternatively, signature treatments at the onsite spa come courtesy of luxury Swiss brand La Prairie.

Bd. J.F. Kennedy. www.hotel-du-cap-eden-roc.com. ✆ **04-93-61-39-01.** 118 units. 830€–1,400€ double; 1,700€–2,250€ suite; villa rates available upon request. Closed mid-Oct–mid-April. **Amenities:** 2 restaurants; 2 bars; babysitting; exercise room; massage; outdoor pool; room service; spa; tennis, free Wi-Fi.

La Jabotte ★   Just a 5-minute stroll from one of Antibes' sandy beaches, this cozy little bed-and-breakfast is a favorite with regular visitors. Eight rooms, each with its own small terrace, cluster around a jasmine-splashed courtyard garden, and a suite and another double are upstairs. Guestrooms may be petite, but rooms are brightly decorated and beds are all brand-new. Owners Nathalie and Pierre make warm and welcoming hosts.

13 av. Max Maurey, Cap d'Antibes. www.jabotte.com. ✆ **04-93-61-45-89.** 10 units. 80€–209€ double; 139€–239€ triple; 129€–249€ suite (sleeps up to 4). Parking 10€. **Amenities:** Garden; bar; free Wi-Fi.

La Villa ★★   A luxurious embodiment of Asian colonial chic on the foot of the Cap d'Antibes. Leather club chairs blend with Buddhist statues and tropical plants in this quiet corner of the coast. The public spaces are truly special. Lounge in the orchid-strewn bar, in the palm-shaded gardens, or on a hammock by the glimmering swimming pool. Guestrooms are a mix of modernity and Zen: read cool cotton linen, bamboo vases, and hardwood floors. Each accommodation option boasts a private balcony, plus a sea or pool view. In 2013, La Villa opened its family-friendly pavilion rooms, which have large private terraces. The town centers of both Juan-les-Pins and Antibes are a 15-minute walk away, or a 5-minute ride on one of the hotel's rented bicycles.

Avenue Saramartel. www.hotel-villa-antibes.com. © **04-92-93-48-00.** 26 units. 139€–530€ double; from 318€ suite. Free parking. **Amenities:** Restaurant; bar; outdoor pool; room service; spa; free Wi-Fi.

Where to Eat

Bring your gold card. Or better still, ask your bodyguard/minder/nanny to settle the check on your behalf. The Zelda and Scott Fitzgeralds of today head for the **Restaurant Eden-Roc** at the Hôtel du Cap-Eden-Roc for grand service or the excellent **Restaurant de Bacon** for an elegant seafood blowout. For light bites on a relative budget (and we mean *relatively*), diners may pick at buffalo mozzarella and sea urchins at Plage Keller on La Garoupe beach.

Restaurant de Bacon ★★★ SEAFOOD   It's hard to believe that one of the French Riviera's most famous fish restaurants started life as a humble beach shack. Back in 1948, the Cap d'Antibes was a haul out for fishing nets—and Bacon dished up tuna sandwiches and beer from two trestle tables. How times change. It took 20 years to perfect their bouillabaisse fish stew recipe, and another ten to secure a Michelin star. The family-run restaurant menu now extends to simple crayfish salad, sea bass with truffles, and local red mullet in basil butter. Items are best sampled on the 55€ four-course lunch menu, a bargain for such a venerable establishment.

Bd. de Bacon. www.restaurantdebacon.com. © **04-93-61-50-02.** Reservations required. Main courses 49€–140€; fixed-price lunch 55€–85€, dinner 85€. Wed–Sun noon–2pm; Tues–Sun 7:30–10pm. Closed Nov–Feb.

Restaurant Eden-Roc ★★★ CLASSIC FRENCH   A tour de force of precision, perfection, luxury, and location. The world's A-list descend upon the Hotel du Cap's signature restaurant during the Cannes Film Festival, and don't depart until the Riviera's classiest hotel closes in October. Menu items under the stewardship of head chef Arnaud Poëtte are as good looking as their film star diners. A rosette of roasted John Dory is adorned with Japanese tapioca pearls and Tosazu seaweed. Even the crab salad is interwoven with crushed coriander, green apple, and wasabi sorbet. Desserts from pâtissier-chocolatier Lilian Bonnefoi lend a new definition to the word profligate. A shade less formal—but still awash with glitterati and glamour—is the **Eden-Roc Grill**. It overlooks the Lérins Islands from an unbeatable position on the very pinnacle of the Cap d'Antibes.

Bd. J.F. Kennedy. www.hotel-du-cap-eden-roc.com. © **04-93-61-39-01.** Reservations required. Main courses 48€–98€; fixed-price menu 143€. Daily noon–3pm and 7–11pm.

Exploring the Cap d'Antibes

Like all of the prominent peninsulas on the French Riviera, the Cap d'Antibes boasts a scenic hiking trail around its perimeter. Highlights include the rustic coastal path south of Plage de la Garoupe, as well as a stop—if you can time it correctly—at the **Villa Eilenroc Gardens**, 460 av. L.D. Beaumont (© **04-93-67-74-33**). It's open July to September Wednesday, Saturday, and Sunday 3pm to 7pm; April to June Wednesday and Saturday 10am to 5pm; and October to March Wednesday and Saturday 1pm to 4pm. Admission is 2€, free for children 11 and under. There's a rose garden, sun-dappled olive groves, and a small eco-museum on site.

Passengers may peek into the gardens of resident A-listers aboard the **Cap d'Antibes Open Top Bus** (www.capdantibestour.com; ✆ **06-15-77-67-47**). The same company also runs a far less cool **Petit Train** around the peninsula. Prices for both are 8€ for adults, 4€ for children under the age of 10; departures are from Port Vauban in Antibes. Those with a better balance may paddle past paradise instead on an SUP. **Cap Kayak** (www.capkayak.fr; ✆ **06-62-28-09-54**) rents both stand-up paddleboards and sea kayaks from Port Gallice at the foot of the Cap d'Antibes. Prices start at 15€ per hour.

Espace du Littoral et du Milieu Marin ★★ MARITIME CENTER   Located within this stone-sided fort and tower on the Cap d'Antibes, built in stages in the 17th and 18th centuries, is a child-friendly space showcasing a permanent Jacques Cousteau exhibition. Prominent displays range from models of Costeau's research vessel, the Calypso, as well as the explorer's intimidating shark cage. Visitors keen to escape the crowds will revel in the center's seaside park (which overlooks the grounds of the ultra-exclusive Hôtel du Cap–Eden-Roc!). The view of the coastline here is worth the admission price alone.

Boulevard J.F. Kennedy. ✆ **04-93-61-45-32.** Admission 3€ adults, free for children 18 and under. Tues–Sat 10am–4:40pm.

ST-PAUL-DE-VENCE ★★

926km (574 miles) S of Paris; 23km (14 miles) E of Grasse; 28km (17 miles) E of Cannes; 31km (19 miles) N of Nice

Of all the hilltop villages of the Riviera, St-Paul-de-Vence is by far the most famous. It gained popularity in the 1940s and '50s, when artists including Picasso, Chagall, and Matisse frequented the town, trading their paintings for hospitality at the Colombe d'Or inn. Art is now the town's principal attraction, and the winding streets are studded with contemporary galleries and museums. Circling the town are magnificent old ramparts (allow about 30 min. to walk the full loop) that overlook flowers and olive and orange trees.

Essentials

ARRIVING   The nearest **rail** station is in Cagnes-sur-Mer. Some 20 **buses** per day (no. 400) leave from central Nice, dropping passengers off in St-Paul-de-Vence (1.50€ one-way, journey time 1 hr.), then in Vence 10 minutes later. For information, contact **Lignes d'Azur** (www.lignesdazur.com; ✆ **08-10-06-10-06**). If you're **driving** from Nice, take either the A8 highway or the coastal route du Bord du Mer west, turn inland at Cagnes-sur-Mer, and follow signs north to St-Paul-de-Vence.

VISITOR INFORMATION   The **Office de Tourisme** is at 2 rue Grande (www.saint-pauldevence.com; ✆ **04-93-32-86-95**).

Getting Around

St-Paul's Old Town is entirely pedestrianized, and most of the narrow streets are paved in cobblestones. Note that driving a car here is prohibited, except to drop off luggage at an Old Town hotel, and by prior arrangement only. The Fondation Maeght is around half a mile out of town.

ATMs/Banks **BNP Paribas,** rd-pt Sainte Claire (📞 **08-20-82-00-01**).

Mail & Postage **La Poste,** rd-pt Sainte Claire (📞 **36-31**).

Pharmacies **Pharmacie Saint Paul,** rd-pt Sainte Claire (📞 **04-93-32-80-78**).

Where to Stay

La Colombe d'Or rents deluxe rooms (see "Where to Eat," below). Note that Vence's hotels make an accessible base for exploring St-Paul-de-Vence too.

La Vague de Saint-Paul ★★★   La Vague opened in 2013 to fill a glaring gap in the St-Paul accommodations market: an affordable hotel for art lovers seeking country tranquillity and wow-factor design. It delivers with aplomb. The wavelike main hotel building was originally conceived by far-out architect André Minangoy in the 1960s. Color-coded guestrooms now look out onto a vast garden complete with *pétanque* run, tennis court, bar, and pool. The attached (almost 100% organic) restaurant delivers five daily starters and mains on 22€ and 29€ set menus. The complex sits a short walk from the Fondation Maeght contemporary art museum—and a longer stroll through the forest to St-Paul-de-Vence village via a secret trail. Highly recommended.

Chemin des Salettes. www.vaguesaintpaul.com. 📞 **04-920-11-20-00.** 37 units. 96€–240€ double; from 253€ suite. Free parking. **Amenities:** Restaurant; bar; concierge; outdoor pool; room service; spa; tennis; free Wi-Fi.

Where to Eat

St-Paul's petite size means that dining options are limited and may also be pricey. That said, the views and the ambience of pretty much any local eatery often make up for these shortcomings.

La Colombe d'Or ★★ PROVENÇAL   This celebrated restaurant opened its doors in 1920. At the time it was little more than a scattering of tables overlooking an overgrown artichoke patch. It was Paul Roux, the restaurant's art-adoring owner, who encouraged the era's struggling artists, such as Raoul Dufy, Paul Signac, and Chaime Soutine, to swap a canvas or two for generous room and board. Picasso, Braque, and Miró followed—and today La Colombe d'Or's art collection is one of the finest in the world. For a peek at these masterpieces, you'll need to dine here, either indoors beneath works by the likes of Signac, Matisse, and Braque or outdoors on the fig-trimmed terrace. The house specials include a selection of fresh hors-d'oeuvres (such as *crudités* and *anchoïade,* a traditional anchovy dip), and crispy roast chicken. It also offers 25 luxurious doubles and suites sprawling over the original 16th-century stone house and the two 1950s wings. Prices are 250€ for a double, 430€ for a suite.

1 place du Général-de-Gaulle. www.la-colombe-dor.com. 📞 **04-93-32-80-02.** Reservations required. Main courses 17€–35€. Daily noon–2pm and 7:30–10pm. Closed late Oct–3rd week of Dec and 10 days in Jan.

Les Terrasses ★ PROVENÇAL   A few minutes' stroll downhill from the Fondation Maeght, this laidback eatery offers classic regional cuisine and superb views over St-Paul's Old Town. Opt for *aïoli,* steamed vegetables and cod served with a garlic-spiked mayonnaise dip; *secca d' Entrevaux,* a locally cured beef dished up with grilled goat cheese; or one of a dozen different pizzas. Prices are the best in the area, and the atmosphere is convivial—do note, however, that the restaurant is a favorite with large groups.

20 chemin des Trious. www.laterrassesursaintpaul.com. ϕ **04-93-32-85-60.** Main courses 11€–29.50€; fixed-price menu 29€. Thurs–Tues 9am–10pm. Closed 2 weeks in Nov.

Exploring St-Paul

Perched at the top of the village, the **Collégiale de la Conversion de St-Paul** ★ was constructed in the 12th and 13th centuries and has been much altered over the years. The Romanesque choir is the oldest part, containing some remarkable stalls carved in walnut in the 17th century. Look to the left as you enter: You'll see the painting "Ste-Cathérine d'Alexandrie," which has been attributed to Tintoretto. The **Trésor de l'Eglise** is one of the most beautiful in the Alpes-Maritimes, with a spectacular ciborium. Look also for a low relief of the "Martyrdom of St-Clément" on the last altar on the right. It's open daily 9am to 6pm (to 7pm July–Aug). Admission is free.

Just around the corner is the light-flooded **Chapelle des Pénitents Blanc** (ϕ **04-93-32-41-13**). The artist Jean-Michel Folon, who worked on this unmissable masterpiece until his death in 2005, decorated the church with stained-glass windows, shimmering mosaics, and rainbow-hued frescos. It's open April to September daily 11am to 1pm and 3 to 6pm, and October to March daily from 2 to 5pm. Admission is 3€ adults, 2€ students and children 6 to 18, and free for children 5 and under.

Foundation Maeght ★★★ ART MUSEUM   Established by Parisian art dealers Aimé and Marguerite Maeght in 1964, this avant-garde building houses one of the most impressive modern art collections in Europe. It was Spanish architect José Luis Sert who designed the pagoda-like exhibition space, ensuring the artwork it displays sits in perfect harmony with the surrounding pine-studded woods. In the gardens, colorful Alexander Calder installations are clustered with skinny bronze sculptures by Alberto Giacometti. A rotating selection of artworks is displayed over the various levels inside, showcasing key pieces by artists like Matisse, Chagall, Bonnard, and Léger. Each summer the museum stages a large seasonal show. There's also a library, a cinema, a cafeteria, and a magnificent museum store onsite.

623 chemin des Gardettes, outside the town walls. www.fondation-maeght.com. ϕ **04-93-32-81-63.** Admission 15€ adults, 10€ students and ages 10–18, free for children 9 and under, 5€ fee for photographs. July–Sept daily 10am–7pm; Oct–June daily 10am–6pm.

Organized Tours

With advance booking, the local tourist office offers 10 different walking tours of the town's historic core and outskirts. **Themed tours** (5€, free for children under 12) last around an hour and a half. They include following in the footsteps of former resident Marc Chagall, trying your hand at the beloved Provençal pastime of *pétanque* (also known as *boules*) under the instruction of accomplished locals, or guided tours of the Fondation Maeght. Almost all tours are given in both English and French.

In nearby La Colle sur Loup, culinary legends Alain and Jean-Michel Llorca offer cooking workshops for adults and children at their **Ecole de Cuisine** (www.alainllorca.com; 60€–170€ per person). Lessons are in French and English and are often followed by an informal dinner.

Shopping

The pedestrian-only **rue Grande** is St-Paul's most evocative street, running the length of the town. Most of the stone houses along it are from the 16th and 17th centuries, and several still bear the coats of arms placed there by the original builders. Today many of the houses are antiques shops, arts-and-crafts galleries, and souvenir and gift shops; some are still artists' studios.

Galerie du Vieux Saint-Paul, 16–18 rue Grande (www.galeries-bartoux.com; ✆ 04-93-32-74-50), is the place to pick up serious art, from sculptures by local artist Arman to bronze works by Salvador Dali. Just down the road, **Galerie Capricorne,** 64 rue Grande (www.galeriecapricorne.com; ✆ 04-93-58-34-42), offers a colorful array of prints, including a selection by Marc Chagall. **Galerie Paul Rafferty,** 67 rue Grande (www.raffertyart.com; ✆ 04-93-58-78-31), purveys paintings inspired by the local village life. Stock up on olive oils, fruit vinegars, and olive-wood chopping boards at **Premier Pression Provence,** 68 rue Grande (www.ppp-olive.com; ✆ 04-93-58-07-69). It's worth plunging into the town's winding streets, too: **Saint Georges Editions,** 5 montée de l'Eglise (✆ 09-71-57-68-21), stocks superb, unique handbags, each one created from lengths of unusual antique textiles. Nearby **Atelier Silvia B**, 11 place de la Mairie (www.silviabertini.com; ✆ 04-93-32-18-13) is packed with bright collages of St-Paul.

VENCE ★

926km (574 miles) S of Paris; 31km (19 miles) N of Cannes; 24km (15 miles) NW of Nice

Often bypassed in favor of nearby St-Paul-de-Vence, the pretty village of Vence is well worth a detour. Its pale stone Old Town is atmospheric yet untouristy, splashed with shady squares and pavement cafés. The highlight is undoubtedly Matisse's Chapelle du Rosaire, set among a countryside studded with cypresses, olive trees, and oleanders.

Essentials

ARRIVING   Frequent **buses** (no. 94 or 400) originating in Nice take 65–80 minutes to reach Vence, passing the nearest **rail** station in Cagnes-sur-Mer, about 10km (6¼ miles) southwest from Vence, en route. The one-way fare is 1.50€. For bus information, contact **Lignes d'Azur** (www.lignesdazur.com; ✆ 08-10-06-10-06). For train information, visit www.voyages-sncf.com or call ✆ **36-35.** To **drive** to Vence from Nice, take D6007 west to Cagnes-sur-Mer, and then D36 north to Vence.

VISITOR INFORMATION   The **Office de Tourisme** is on place due Grand-Jardin (www.ville-vence.fr; ✆ 04-93-58-06-38).

[Fast FACTS] VENCE

ATMs/Banks   Many banks are dotted around Vence, including **BNP Paribas,** 28 place du Grand-Jardin (✆ 08-20-82-00-01).

Internet Access   SIMS, 165 av. des Poilus (www.secretariat-services-vence.weebly.com; ✆ 04-93-58-23-27), offers high-speed Internet access, but no Wi-Fi.

Mail & Postage   La Poste, place Clemenceau (✆ 36-31).

Pharmacies   Pharmacie du Grand-Jardin, 30 place du Grand-Jardin (✆ 04-93-24-04-07).

Where to Stay

Note that St-Paul-de-Vence's hotels also make an excellent base for exploring Vence.

Cantermerle Hotel ★   Just south of Vence's Old Town, this hotel, restaurant, and spa is set within 3 acres of lush gardens. Spacious guestrooms feature terra-cotta tile floors and Provençal fabrics; many also boast their own private terrace. At the gourmet restaurant **La Table du Cantemerle,** chef Jérôme Héraud dishes up grilled Aveyron lamb in a parsley crust and lobster ravioli in the elegant dining room or outdoors alongside the pool. Use of the spa's heated indoor pool, mosaic Turkish baths, and fitness area is complimentary for guests.

258 chemin Cantemerle. www.cantemerle-hotel-vence.com. ✆ **04-93-58-08-18.** 27 units. 180€–298€ double; 537€–587€ suite. Closed Nov–March. **Amenities:** Restaurant; 2 bars; outdoor pool; spa; free Wi-Fi.

Château Saint-Martin & Spa ★★★   Just 20 minutes from the Nice airport, amid 14 hectares (35 acres) of enchanting gardens, lies one of the most sumptuous hotels in the world. Take, for example, the Château Saint-Martin's spa. In addition to massages, it offers La Prairie and Bamford signature treatments, yoga lessons, color chromotherapy, and a wellness shower than can emulate the misting breeze of a tropical rainstorm. Moreover, the hotel complex is shared by a mere handful of guests, who revel in the vast infinity pool, the outdoor **Oliveraie** grill restaurant set in an ancient olive grove, and mammoth chateau suites that overlook the shimmering sea below. Six independent villas are larger and more luxurious still. The Michelin-starred restaurant is under the accomplished command of Franck Ferigutti, new head chef in 2014. The cuisine switches from modern French fare to infused foam creations and desserts chilled with nitrogen steam. And it sits atop a wine cellar worth far more than the average Riviera mansion.

2490 av. des Templiers. www.chateau-st-martin.com. ✆ **04-93-58-02-02.** 39 units, 6 villas. 250€–640€ double; 660€–1,500€ suite; 1,470€–3,800€ villa. Rates include breakfast. Closed Oct–mid-April. **Amenities:** 3 restaurants; bar; babysitting; outdoor pool; room service; sauna; spa; tennis; free Wi-Fi.

The Frogs' House ★★   This gem of a B&B is a 10-minute drive from Vence, in the cutesy village of St Jeannet. Renoir used to paint in the charming village and surrounds, which also forms its own AOC wine appellation, one of France's smallest. Bilingual hosts Benoît and Corinne welcome guests to The Frog's shared outdoor terrace. Here is where breakfasts and—to those visitors who desire them—communal dinners are served. Group hikes are also led into the surrounding countryside. Several of the seven simple bedrooms overlook the sea.

35, rue du Saumalier, St Jeannet. www.thefrogshouse.fr. ✆ **06-28-06-80-28.** 7 units, 79€–104€ double. Rates include breakfast. Closed Jan–Feb. **Amenities:** Free Wi-Fi.

Where to Eat

Vence's unpretentious attitude is also evident in the local cuisine. It tends to be traditional and tasty, occasionally Michelin-starred, and often dished up in a sublime setting. For homemade hot chocolate or artisanal sweets, **Entre Mes Chocolats,** 12 av. Marcellin Maurel (www.entre-mes-chocolats.com; ✆ **09-81-82-34-59**), is highly recommended.

The **Le Château du Domaine St-Martin** (see review in "Vence's Hotels," below) also offers award-winning dining.

Les Bacchanales ★★ PROVENÇAL   A short stroll from the Chapelle du Rosaire, Les Bacchanales is located inside a century-old villa, overlooking Chef Christophe Dufau's enchanting kitchen garden. The creative menu uses almost exclusively local ingredients, transforming them into strikingly innovative versions of traditional Provençal cuisine. Mediterranean bream may be paired with apricots and Italian Taggiasche olives; sweet cantaloupe melon is grilled and served with fresh almonds and Corsican *brousse* cheese. Note that the market-fresh weekly menu is limited: Diners may simply select their preferred number of courses (two to five at lunch, four to seven at dinner). The restaurant holds one Michelin star.

247 av. de Provence. www.lesbacchanales.com. ℂ **04-93-24-19-19.** Reservations recommended. Fixed-price menus 28€–85€. July–Aug Wed–Fri & Mon 7:30–9:30pm, Sat–Sun 12:30–2pm & 7:30–9:30pm; Sept–June Thurs–Mon 12:30–2pm and 7:30–9:30pm. Closed last 2 weeks of Dec, 3 weeks in Jan.

Le Pigeonnier ★ PROVENÇAL   One of the Old Town's most welcoming eateries, Le Pigeonnier spills across the dining rooms of a 14th-century building and a sunny square, the latter perfect for people-watching. The restaurant menu is traditional. Linger over slow-cooked *daube* (a classic Niçois beef stew), a generous steak, or fish soup served with garlic croutons and *rouille,* saffron mayonnaise.

5-7 place du Peyra. ℂ **04-93-58-03-00.** Main courses 11€–19€; fixed-price menu 23€. July–Aug daily noon–2:30pm and 7:30–10pm; Sept–June Tues–Sat noon–2:30pm and 7:30–10pm, Sun noon–2:30pm.

Exploring Vence

Vence's medieval **Vieille Ville (Old Town)** is compact, making it easy to explore on foot. A poke around its picturesque squares reveals place du Peyra's bubbling **Vieille Fontaine (Old Fountain),** while nearby the **Chateau de Villeneuve/Fondation Émile Hugues,** 2 place du Frêne (www.museedevence.com; ℂ **04-93-58-15-78**), is a temporary exhibition space dedicated to 20th-century art. Recent exhibits have showcased works by Matisse, Cézanne, and Jean-Michel Basquiat. Hours are Tuesday to Sunday 10am to 12:30pm and 2 to 6pm. Admission is 7€, 5€ for students, and free for children under 12. Also in the Old Town is **place Godeau,** where the **mosaic** "Moses saved from the Nile" by Marc Chagall adorns the 11th-century **cathedral**'s baptistery (free).

Vence's main draw, however, lies just outside the fortified main town. The Chapelle du Rosaire represents one of Matisse's most remarkable achievements.

Chapelle du Rosaire ★★ RELIGIOUS SITE   From the age of 47, Henri Matisse made Nice his home. But Vence held a special place in the artist's heart: It was his place of residence during World War II, as well as home to Dominican nun Sister Jacques-Marie, Matisse's former nurse and muse. So in 1947, when Matisse discovered that the sisters were planning the construction of a new chapel, he offered not only to design it, but fund the project as well. Matisse was 77 at the time.

The Chapelle du Rosaire was completed in 1951. A beautifully bright space, it offers the exceptional possibility of stepping into a three-dimensional artwork. Matisse described his creation: "What I have done in the chapel is to create a religious space . . . in an enclosed area of very reduced proportions and to give it, solely by the play of colors and lines, the dimensions of infinity."

From the front of the chapel, you may find the structure unremarkable and pass it by—until you spot a 12m (39-ft.) crescent-adorned cross rising from a blue-tile roof. Within, dozens of stained-glass windows shimmer cobalt blue (symbolizing the sea), sapphire green (the landscape), and golden yellow (the sun). Most remarkable are the

14 black-and-white-tile Stations of the Cross, featuring Matisse's self-styled "tormented and passionate" figures.

The bishop of Nice came to bless the chapel in the late spring of 1951; Matisse died 3 years later.

466 av. Henri-Matisse. (*C* **04-93-58-03-26.** Admission 6€ adults; contributions to maintain the chapel are welcome. Mon, Wed, and Sat 2–5:30pm; Tues and Thurs 10–11:30am and 2–5:30pm. Closed mid-Nov–mid-Dec.

CAGNES-SUR-MER ★

918km (569 miles) S of Paris; 7km (5 miles) SW of Nice; 21km (13 miles) NE of Cannes

Cagnes-sur-Mer has two visitor-friendly centers. Perched on a hill overlooking the Riviera, **Haut-de-Cagnes** is one of the most stunning hill villages on the Riviera. It's quieter than Eze (see p. 209), another *village perché* near Monaco, and is alive with flower-filled lanes and alfresco eateries. At the foot of the hill is the working fishing port and beach resort of **Cros-de-Cagnes,** which lies midway between Nice and Antibes.

For years Haut-de-Cagnes attracted the French literati, including Simone de Beauvoir. A colony of painters also settled here, most famously Pierre Auguste Renoir. He claimed the village was "the place where I want to paint until the last day of my life." His museum is the highlight of any visit to the area.

Essentials

ARRIVING   Cagnes-sur-Mer **train** station lies in Cagnes-Ville (the nondescript commercial part of town) at avenue de la Gare. It serves trains that run along the Mediterranean coast, with arrivals every 30 minutes from both Nice (trip time: 10 min.; 2.90€ one-way) and Cannes (trip time: 25 min.; 4.50€ one-way). For rail information, call (*C* **36-35** or visit www.voyages-sncf.com.

Frequent no. 200 **buses,** costing 1.50€ from Nice and Antibes zip along the coast every 30 minutes. For information, contact **Lignes d'Azur** (www.lignesdazur.com; (*C* **08-10-06-10-06**). Stops include Square Bordet, which is within walking distance of both Cros-de-Cagnes and the Renoir Museum.

To **drive** from any of the coastal towns, follow the A8 coastal highway, exiting at Cagnes-Sur-Mer/Cros-de-Cagnes.

VISITOR INFORMATION   The main **Office de Tourisme** is at 6 bd. Maréchal Juin, Cagnes-sur-Mer (www.cagnes-tourisme.com; (*C* **04-93-20-61-64**). Another branch exists in the medieval village of Haut-de-Cagnes on place du Docteur Maurel ((*C* **04-92-02-85-05**).

[FastFACTS] CAGNES-SUR-MER

ATMs/Banks   Countless ATMs are strewn around Cagnes-sur-Mer, including **BNP Paribas,** 11 place de Gaulle ((*C* **08-20-82-00-01**), but there are none in the medieval village above town.

Internet Access   For free Wi-Fi, hit the main Cagnes-sur-Mer Office de Tourisme, 6 bd. Maréchal Juin.

Mail & Postage   **La Poste,** 5 av. Hôtel des Postes ((*C* **36-31**).

Pharmacies   **Pharmacie du Sagrandi,** 29 av. Auguste Renoir ((*C* **04-93-20-64-58**).

Where to Stay

Cagnes-sur-Mer's accommodation options are often less expensive than nearby Nice and Antibes. Several cute B&Bs dot the medieval town of Haut-de-Cagnes. These include **Villa Estelle**, 5 montee de la Bourgade (www.villa-estelle.com; ✆ **04-92-02-89-83**; doubles from 115€ to 140€), and **Les Terrasses du Soleil**, place notre Dame de Protection (www.terrassesdusoleil.com; ✆ **04-93-73-26-56**; doubles from 115€ to 140€).

Chateau Le Cagnard ★★   One of the French Riviera's most secret retreats is back on the menu. This Haut-de-Cagnes hideaway once hosted low-key celebrities from Jacques Chirac to Marcel Pagnol. It reopened in 2013 after a painstaking renovation by its new Swedish owners. The family's hotelier daughter, Frida Ivarsson, now presides over 26 individually-designed rooms. Each one is stocked with one-off antiques and *trompe l'oeil* paintings. The restaurant is something to write home about, serving up pan-fried scallops with diced lime, and mussel soup spritzed with Champagne. Set lunches cost 29€, set dinners 45€.

54 rue Sous Barri. www.lecagnard.com. ✆ **04-93-20-73-22.** 26 units. 120€–180€ double. **Amenities:** restaurant; bar; babysitting; massage; room service; spa; free Wi-Fi.

Where to Eat

Josyjo ★★ PROVENÇAL   Teetering on the edge of Haut-de-Cagnes, the ever-popular Josy-Jo was the home and studio of painters Modigliani and Soutine during their hungriest years. Started by chef Josy Bandecchi and her now-retired husband Jo in 1970, it dishes up Provençal and Niçoise delights on a leafy terrace or inside the elegant dining room. Local flavors are dreamlike. Expect zucchini flowers stuffed with aubergine and breadcrumbs, wild *cep* mushrooms pan-fried with garlic, or local squid tossed in olive oil. Josyjo is best known for its charcoal grill. Choice cuts of Charolais beef, Alpine lamb, and duck breast are loaded on to order.

2 rue du Planas. www.restaurant-josyjo.com. ✆ **04-93-20-68-76.** Reservations recommended. Main courses 14€–26€; fixed-price lunch 29€. Wed–Sat noon–2pm and 7:30–10pm. Closed Dec.

Exploring Cagnes-sur-Mer

The orange groves of the upper village of Haut-de-Cagnes provide a beautiful setting for the narrow flower-filled streets and 17th- and 18th-century homes. The climb up from Cagnes-Ville is strenuous; fortunately, the free no. 44 minibus runs up there daily every 15 minutes year-round from Square Bordet in the town center. When on top, where you can enjoy the view from **place du Château** and have lunch or a drink at a pavement cafe, before hitting the enchanting **Chateau-Musée Grimaldi**.

Cros-de-Cagnes, the seaside part of Cagnes-Sur-Mer, is known for its 4km (2½ miles) of pebble beach, the **Plages de Cros-de-Cagnes**. On the seafront, **Location Rosalie** (www.locationrosalie.com; ✆ **06-34-67-28-61**) rents four-person pedal bikes (think of an Indian rickshaw with more wheels) with which to explore the promenade. Prices are 18€ per hour. The rental outfit also hires mountain bikes (15€ per day) and vintage *vélos* (12€ per hour). New cycle tracks make it possible to pedal to either Antibes or Nice.

Chateau-Musée Grimaldi ★ ART & CULTURE MUSEUM   Built in the 14th century by the Grimaldi family, this medieval castle dominates the lofty village of Haut-de-Cagnes. Such grandeur wasn't enough for Jean-Henri Grimaldi, who transformed the castle into a rococo show home back in 1620. The glorious palace can now be wandered around at leisure. It also hosts an olive museum, as well as temporary art exhibitions and classical music concerts.

Place du Château. ℭ **04-92-02-47-30.** Admission 4€ adults, free for adults and children 26 and under. May–Oct daily 10am–noon and 2–6pm; Nov–April Wed–Mon 10am–noon and 2–5pm.

Musée Renoir ★★★ ART MUSEUM   Just outside of town, Cagnes-sur-Mer's cultural highlight is the museum and former home of Impressionist painter Pierre Auguste Renoir. Reopened in 2013 after lengthy renovations, the artist's home and gardens have been restored to their original layout. Some 17 new sculptures and two new paintings are on display, too. For inspiration, gaze out of Renoir's windows towards Haut-de-Cagnes and the Cap-d'Antibes. It's easy to see where the Frenchman culled his inspiration from—although a few villas have been added to the picture since he painted these bucolic scenes. Renoir was at his creative best in the villa's endless gardens of citrus, pine, and rose. Park yourself on a bench amid the olive groves and enjoy the view.

19 chemin des Collettes. ℭ **04-93-20-61-07.** Admission 6€ adults, free for adults and children 26 and under. April–Sept daily 10am–1pm and 2–6pm (closed Tues in April and May); Oct–March Wed–Mon 10am–noon and 2–6pm.

NICE

NICE ★★★

929km (576 miles) S of Paris; 32km (20 miles) NE of Cannes

The largest city on this fabled stretch of coast, Nice is known as the "Queen of the Riviera." It's also one of the most ancient, founded by the Greeks, who called it Nike (Victory). By the 19th century, Russian aristocrats and the British upper class—led by Queen Victoria herself—were sojourning here. These days, however, Nice is not as chi-chi as Cannes or St-Tropez. In fact, of all the major French resorts, Nice is the most down-to-earth, with an emphasis on fine dining and high culture. Indeed, it has more museums than any other French city outside Paris. In late 2013 it inaugurated a new city center urban park, one of the largest public spaces in the South of France.

Nice is also the best place to base yourself on the Riviera, especially if you're dependent on public transportation. You can go to San Remo, a glamorous town over the Italian border, for lunch and return to Nice by nightfall. From Nice airport, the second busiest in France, you can travel by train or bus along the entire coast to resorts such as Antibes, Juan-les-Pins, and Monaco. Indeed, visitors may step off a direct flight from either New York or Montreal, then hop on an airport shuttle bus and be relaxing in their hotel 30 minutes later.

Because of its brilliant sunshine and liberal attitude, Nice has long attracted artists and writers, among them Dumas, Nietzsche, Flaubert, Hugo, Sand, and Stendhal. Henri Matisse, who made his home in Nice, said, "Though the light is intense, it's also soft and tender." The city averages 300 sunny days a year.

Essentials

ARRIVING **Trains** arrive at the city's main station, Gare Nice-Ville, avenue Thiers. From here you can take trains to Cannes for 6.80€, Monaco for 3.80€, and Antibes for 4.50€, with easy connections to Paris, Marseille, and anywhere else along the Mediterranean coast.

Buses (www.lignesdazur.com; ✆ 08-10-06-10-06) to towns east, including Monaco (no. 100) depart from place Garibaldi; to towns west, including Cannes (no. 200) from Jardin Albert I.

Transatlantic and intercontinental flights land at **Aéroport Nice–Côte d'Azur** (www.nice.aeroport.fr; ✆ 08-20-42-33-33). From there, municipal bus nos. 98 and 99 depart at 20-minute intervals for the Port and Gare Nice-Ville, respectively; the one-way fare is 6€. **Taxis** are not cheap. A ride from the airport to the city center costs between 35€ and 40€ each way. Trip time is about 20 minutes.

Ferryboats operated by **Trans-Côte d'Azur** (www.trans-cote-azur.com; ✆ 04-92-00-42-30), on quai Lunel on Nice's port, link the city with Île

Ste-Marguerite (see p. 161) from June to September and St-Tropez from June through August.

VISITOR INFORMATION Nice maintains three **tourist offices.** The largest is at 5 promenade des Anglais, near place Masséna (www.nicetourisme.com; ℂ 08-92-70-74-07). Additional offices are in the arrivals hall of the Aéroport Nice–Côte d'Azur and outside the railway station on avenue Thiers.

CITY LAYOUT The city is divided into five main neighborhoods: the Italianate Old Town; the vintage port; the commercial city center between place Masséna and the main train station; the affluent residential quarter known as the Carre d'Or, just inland from the promenade des Anglais; and hilltop Cimiez. All are easy to navigate on foot, with the exception of Cimiez. For more, see "Exploring Nice," p. 186.

SPECIAL EVENTS The **Nice Carnaval** (www.nicecarnaval.com), known as the "Mardi Gras of the Riviera," runs from mid-February to early March, celebrating the return of spring with 3 weeks of parades, *corsi* (floats), *veglioni* (masked balls), confetti, and battles in which young women toss flowers at the audience.

The **Nice Festival du Jazz** (www.nicejazzfestival.fr) runs for a week in mid-July, when jazz, funk, and reggae artists perform in the Jardins Albert I near the seafront. Recent performers have included Herbie Hancock and George Benson.

Getting Around

ON FOOT Nice is very walkable, and no point of interest downtown is more than a 10-minute walk from place Massena, including the seafront promenade des Anglais, Old Town, and harbor.

BY BICYCLE & MOTOR SCOOTER Like many French cities, Nice has its own bike-sharing scheme, **Vélo Bleu** (www.velobleu.org). You can register directly at one of Nice's 175 bike stands (difficult) or online (much easier); fees range from 1€ for 1 day to 5€ for a week. Alternatively, you can rent bikes (from 12€ per day) and scooters (from 26€ per day; driver's license and deposit required) from **Holiday Bikes,** 23 rue de Belgique (www.holiday-bikes.com; ℂ 04-93-16-01-62).

BY CAR A novel addition to the Nice transport scene is **Auto Bleue** (www.auto-bleue.org; ℂ 09-77-40-64-06). The scheme allows visitors to rent an electric Peugeot car from one of 50 vehicle stands around Nice for 45€ per day, inclusive of electricity, parking, and insurance. Sign-up online in advance. Cooler cats may rent an E Type Jaguar or Ford Mustang from **Rent A Classic Car** (www.rentaclassiccar.com; ℂ 09-54-00-29-33) from 189€ per day.

BY TAXI **Taxis Niçois Indépendants** (www.taxis-nicois-independants.fr; ℂ 04-93-88-25-82) will pick up within 5 minutes across town. Alternatively, call a **Cyclopolitain** (nice.cyclopolitain.com; ℂ 04-93-81-76-15) electronic tricycle for a ride around town (until 7pm, maximum two passengers, from 5€ per ride).

BY PUBLIC TRANSPORT Most local buses leave from the streets around place Masséna. Municipal buses charge 1.50€ for rides within the entire Alpes-Maritime province, even as far as Monaco or Cannes. The same ticket can also be used on Nice's tramway, which connects the Old Town with Gare Nice-Ville and northern Nice. Tickets, day passes (5€), and week passes (15€) can be bought directly onboard buses (although not trams) or at electronic kiosks around the city. For further information, see www.lignesdazur.com.

Nice

12

Nice

NICE

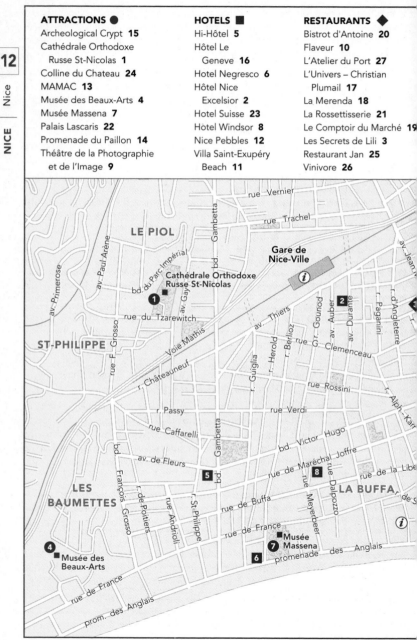

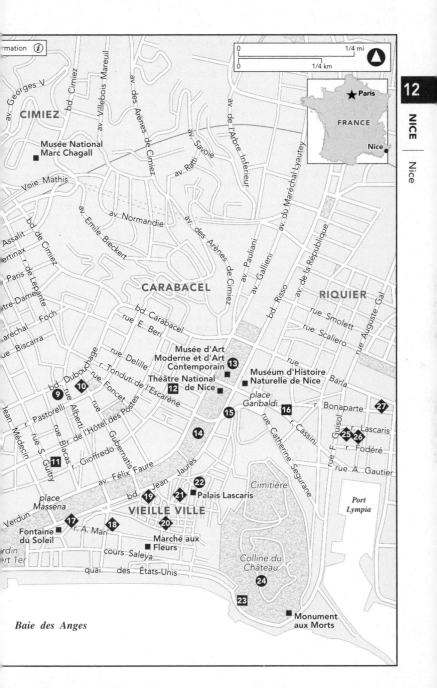

rmation (i)

1/4 mi

1/4 km

★ Paris

FRANCE

Nice

av. Georges V

bd. Cimiez

av. Villebois Mareuil

av. des Arènes de Cimiez

av. Savoie

av. de l'Arbre Inférieur

av. du Maréchal Lyautey

CIMIEZ

Musée National
Marc Chagall

Voie Mathis

av. Emile Bieckert

av. Normandie

av. Ratti

av. des Arènes de Cimiez

av. Pauliani

av. Gallieni

bd. Risso

av. de la République

Assalit

bd. de Cimiez

rtinax

... de Lepante

Paris

tre-Dame

Foch

réchal

Biscarra

CARABACEL

bd. Carabacel

rue E. Beri

RIQUIER

rue Smolett

rue Scaliero

rue Auguste Gal

rue Delille

r. Tonduti de l'Escarène

Musée d'Art
Moderne et d'Art
Contemporain ❶❸

Théâtre National ❶❷
de Nice

Muséum d'Histoire
Naturelle de Nice

rue ___ Barla

bd. Dubouchage

rue Foncet

❾ ❿

r. Pastorelli

r. Alberti

rue S. Guitry

r. Biscas

r. de l'Hôtel des Postes

Gubernatis

place
Garibaldi

❶❺

❶❻

r. Catherine Segurane

r. Bonaparte

r. Cassini

r. Guisol

r. Lascaris

❷❼

❷❺ ❷❻

Jean Médecin

r. Gioffredo

av. Félix Faure

❶❹

r. Fodéré

rue A. Gautier

❶❶

place
Masséna

bd. Jean Jaurès

❷❷

❶❾ ❷❶ ■ Palais Lascaris

Cimitière

Port
Lympia

Verdun

❶❼ ❶❽

r. A. Mari

VIEILLE VILLE

❷❾

Fontaine
du Soleil

rdin

rt 1er

cours Saleya

Marché aux
Fleurs

quai des États-Unis

Colline du
Château

❷❹

❷❸

Baie des Anges

Monument
aux Morts

[FastFACTS] NICE

ATMs/Banks Nice is home to dozens of banks; **LCL Banque,** 15 av. Jean Médecin (ℭ **04-93-82-84-61**), is one of the most central.

Dentists SOS Dentaire (ℭ **04-93-01-14-14**).

Doctors & Hospitals Hôpital Saint-Roch, 5 rue Pierre Dévoluy (www.chu-nice.fr; ℭ **04-92-03-33-33**).

Embassies & Consulates U.S. Consular Agency Nice, 7 av. Gustave V (ℭ **04-93-88-89-55**); **Consulate of** **Canada,** 2 place Franklin (ℭ **04-93-92-93-22**).

Internet Access As of 2013, various public squares and streets (such as the cours Saleya) throughout Nice offer free Wi-Fi. Look for the network "NiceGOWEXFREEWiFi."

Local Information The **"Riviera Times"** (www.rivieratimes.com) and the **"Riviera Reporter"** (www.rivierareporter.com) both cover news, art, culture, and events in and around Nice. Alternatively, **"Angloinfo** **French Riviera"** (http://riviera.angloinfo.com) is an invaluable resource.

Mail & Postage La Poste, 6 rue Louis Gassin (ℭ **36-31**).

Pharmacies Pharmacie Masséna, 7 rue Masséna (ℭ **04-93-87-78-94**).

Safety Nice is generally a very safe place. However, as in any big city, it's important to keep an eye on your valuables, in particular anywhere that's crowded. Avoid poorly lit streets at night, including in Nice's Old Town.

Where to Stay
EXPENSIVE

Hôtel Negresco ★★ For more than a century, the Negresco has been Nice's most iconic hotel. Its flamingo-pink dome crowns the promenade des Anglais, its Belle Epoque façade turned towards the sea. Guestrooms—a mix of Louis XIV antiques and state-of-the-art bathrooms—have hosted each era's most noted celebrities, from the Beatles and Salvador Dali to Michael Jackson. Public areas are decorated with works from an exceptional collection of private art, including the shimmering Nikki de St-Phalle sculpture welcoming guests at the hotel's entrance. Dining ranges from the exquisite (the double-Michelin-starred **Chantecler** and its 15,000-bottle wine cellar) to the playful (the kooky merry-go-round-style brasserie, **La Rotonde**).

37 promenade des Anglais. www.hotel-negresco-nice.com. ℭ **04-93-16-64-00**. 117 units. 165€–600€ double; 620€–2,500€ suite. Parking 28€. **Amenities:** 2 restaurants; bar; babysitting; exercise room; massage; room service; free Wi-Fi.

MODERATE

Hi-Hôtel ★★ Tucked into a residential neighborhood, yet just minutes from the beach, this seven-story, former 1930s boardinghouse is a tribute to contemporary architecture. Designed by Matali Crasset, a one-time colleague of Philippe Starck, the hotel's 10 high-tech room concepts are utterly unconventional. They range from Indoor Terrasse, a vision of wooden decking and bamboo, to the brand-new Utop-Hi, sleek with polished concrete and a glass cube shower. Onsite there's an organic restaurant, a REN spa, Turkish baths, and a rooftop swimming pool with its own honesty bar. The Hi's nearby beach club, **Hi-Beach** (p. 191), is a hip hangout in its own right.

3 av. des Fleurs. www.hi-hotel.net. ℭ **04-97-07-26-26**. 38 units. 99€–469€ double; 159€–679€ suite. Parking 24€. **Amenities:** Restaurant; 24-hr. bar and snack bar; outdoor swimming pool; Turkish bath; free Wi-Fi.

182

APP happy

Dozens of iPhone and Android apps bring the Riviera's largest city to life. Download **Nice Code** for the city's most salubrious addresses, **SNCF TER** for local train times, **Vélo Bleu** to track the free bike share stations around Nice, or the **Brad in Nice** app for an insider's guide to local monuments. Remember to turn off your cellphone's international data roaming and use your hotel's Wi-Fi for downloads instead, or else those 'free' apps might cost a whole lot more.

Hôtel Suisse ★★ A score of artists have set up their easels on the promenade in front of the Hôtel Suisse. As if to prove it, a reproduction canvas of a sea view scene by Raoul Dufy is surrounded by a bevy of amateur iPhone photographers, all hoping to snap the same panorama. The view from the recently renovated hotel rooms above is stupendous, and arguably the best in town. Deferential service in the lobby-cum-breakfast room is all very well, but for more color (and less cash) guests are advised to source their croissants and coffee on the nearby cours Saleya instead. Look online for the Suisse's heavily discounted winter and advance booking rates.

15 quai Rauba Capeu. www.hotel-nice-suisse.com. ✆ **04-92-17-39-00.** 38 units. 114€–337€ double. Public parking nearby. **Amenities:** Bar; babysitting; room service; free Wi-Fi.

Hôtel Windsor ★★★ The coolest, funkiest, and most friendly hotel in Nice is also one of its best-value lodgings. This *maison bourgeoise* was built by disciples of Gustav Eiffel in the 1890s and has remained a family-run hotel for three generations. Current owner Mme Payen-Redolfi has ushered in an artsy era where a different acclaimed artist decorates another guest room each year. The hotel currently has 31 contemporary-art rooms, including one painted entirely in gold leaf by Claudio Parmigiani. Art and color stream outside into the bamboo garden—**WiJungle**—where alfresco breakfasts are also served. Back indoors, **WiLounge** serves dinner and chilled rosé. **WiZen** is the fifth-floor health club, hammam, sauna, and meditation zone.

11 rue Dalpozzo. www.hotelwindsornice.com. ✆ **04-93-88-59-35.** 57 units. 89€–225€ double. Parking 15€. **Amenities:** Restaurant; bar; babysitting; health club; outdoor pool; room service; sauna; free Wi-Fi.

INEXPENSIVE

Hôtel Le Geneve ★ The newly-hip place Garibaldi area, between the Port and Nice Old Town, sorely lacked a good hotel, until this discount gem opened in 2014. Guestrooms are achingly modern, if a touch Spartan. But the French bistro bar and restaurant downstairs—where breakfast is also served—is loads of fun. Nice's MAMAC art museum and gay-friendly rue Bonaparte zone are just seconds away.

1 rue Cassini. www.hotel-le-geneve-nice.com. ✆ **04-93-56-84-79.** 16 units. 89€–169€ per double. **Amenities:** Bar; restaurant; room service; free Wi-Fi.

Hôtel Nice Excelsior ★ What a steal. This mansion dating from 1898 was updated as a hip hotel in 2013. Decor is inspired by a belle époque gentleman's Mediterranean tour: the lobby is strewn with antique packing cases, travel literature, and tropical plants. The panoply of different rooms (stretching up to family-sized) are similarly styled. Yet the leafy location, within walking distance from Nice train station, keeps rates are low. Those visitors booking far in advance can sometimes secure rooms for 80€ per double for a 3-night reservation. The Excelsior also has a cozy rear garden where guests may nibble on a picnic or sip a glass of rosé.

19 avenue Durante. www.excelsiornice.com. ☏ **04-93-88-18-05.** 42 units. 110€–240€ per double. **Amenities:** Bar; garden; library; room service; free Wi-Fi.

Villa Saint Exupéry Beach ★ Just outside Nice's Old Town, this upscale hostel makes an ideal base for budget travelers of all ages. Accommodation ranges from dormitory-style beds to private twin rooms, and includes an abundant free buffet breakfast. Also onsite is a communal kitchen, gym with sauna, daily happy hour, and quality meals at backpacker prices. Its award-winning sister hostel, **Villa Saint Exupéry Gardens,** 22 ave Gravier (☏ **04-93-84-42-83**), is located in a converted monastery just north of the city center. A former chapel with stained-glass windows now serves as its buzzing bar.

6 rue Sacha Guitry. www.villahostels.com. ☏ **04-93-16-13-45.** 60 units. 25€–80€ per person in a single or twin-bedded room; 16€–40€ per person for dormitory bed. Rates include continental breakfast, sheets and towels. **Amenities:** Bar, cooking facilities, computers, luggage room, TV lounge; free Wi-Fi.

ALTERNATE ACCOMMODATIONS

Nice Pebbles ★★★ A short-term rental of one of these holiday apartments allows you time to truly immerse yourself in local life, from cooking up morning-market bounty to sipping sunset aperitifs on your private terrace. More than 150 carefully selected properties (from studios to 10-bed homes) are dotted throughout the city's central neighborhoods, including the Old Town and harbor and along the promenade des Anglais. Apartments boast first-class amenities (iPod docks, high-def TVs, and designer bathrooms are common), yet weigh in at just a fraction of the price of a hotel room. Demand is high, so book well in advance. Sister agency **Riviera Pebbles** (www.rivierapebbles.com) manages additional properties along the coast.

20 rue Gioffredo. www.nicepebbles.com. ☏ **04-97-20-27-30.** 90€–350€ per apartment per night. **Amenities:** Babysitting; free Wi-Fi.

Where to Eat

The Riviera boasts more Michelin commendations (45 stars over 36 establishments as of 2014) than almost anywhere else on the planet. The regional capital of Nice teems with exquisite restaurants, from the high end to the downright local. Excellent eateries are scattered across the city—although beware of many of the Old Town's careless offerings, keen to lure in tourists for a single night only. In addition to the suggestions below, the portside **Le Bistrot du Port,** 28 quai Lunel (www.lebistrotduportdenice.fr; ☏ **04-93-55-21-70**), is where the Orsini family has been dishing up top-quality fish and creative seafood concoctions for over 30 years.

EXPENSIVE

Flaveur ★★ MODERN FRENCH Brothers Gaël and Mickaël Tourteaux (whose last name, almost unbelievably, translates as "cake") are a pair of very talented chefs. They may be relatively young—39 and 35 respectively—yet they've already spent decades in the kitchens of the Riviera's top restaurants. Little surprise, then, that in 2011 their contemporary bistro, Flaveur, earned its first Michelin star. A childhood growing up on the tropical islands of Réunion and Guadeloupe means their modern French cuisine is laced with exotic flavors: Plump scallops are seasoned with Japanese *gomasio;* artistically displayed lemongrass and bubbles of lemon caviar sit atop risotto.

Meals are variations on fixed-price menus only; there's no ordering à la carte, although lunchtime menus allow for gourmet bites on a relative budget.

25 rue Gubernatis. www.flaveur.net. © **04-93-62-53-95.** Reservations required. Fixed-price lunch 40€–68€; fixed-price dinner 52€–85€. Tues–Fri noon–2pm and 7:30–11pm; Sat 7:30–11pm. Closed early Jan.

MODERATE

L'Atelier du Port ★★ NIÇOIS   A design-heavy restaurant that mixes sleek contemporary furniture with an open kitchen and indoor citrus garden…and gets it completely right. Two of this guidebook's authors live around the corner from this new establishment and are devoted regulars. Chalkboard menus chart locally sourced daily delights including squid from the Italian border, lemons (for various desserts) from Menton, and stuffed ricotta tortelli from Nice Old Town's finest pasta store, **Barale** (7 rue Saint Réparate). Home-made terrines, pâtés, and tarts are also a joy, as are the fairly priced Provençal wines by the *pichet*.

45 rue Bonaparte. © **09-83-03-88-44.** Main courses 14€–21€. Daily noon–3:30pm, 7–11pm.

Le Comptoir du Marché ★ TRADITIONAL FRENCH   A fabulous addition to the local dining scene since 2012, Le Comptoir du Marché sits snugly within Nice's atmospheric Old Town. Dishes make use of hearty ingredients, yet chef Lois Guenzati has a light touch. The ever-changing menu may include seared tuna with coco beans, baby artichokes stewed with lardons, or grilled duck breast. There's an authentic vintage feel to the place. Request a table in the back room, where you'll have clear views into the open kitchen action. Le Comptoir's sister restaurant, **Bistrot d'Antoine,** 27 rue de la Préfecture (©) **04-93-85-29-57**), is also superb, although it books up far in advance.

8 rue du Marché. © **04-93-13-45-01.** Reservations recommended. Main courses 16€–33€. Tues–Sat noon–2pm and 7–10:30pm.

La Merenda ★★ NIÇOIS   Top chef Dominique Le Stanc left the world of *haute cuisine* far behind to take over this tiny, traditional, family-run bistro. And how lucky we all are. La Merenda is now one of most authentic and unpretentious eateries along the French Riviera. Market-fresh specials are scribbled on a small chalkboard; depending on the season, they may include stuffed sardines, tagliatelle drenched in delicious basil pesto, or a delectable *tarte au citron.* Note that the restaurant has no phone, so you'll need to make reservations in person.

4 rue Raoul Bosio. www.lamerenda.net. No phone. Reservations required. Main courses 14€–29€. No credit cards. Mon–Fri noon–2pm and 7:30–10pm.

Restaurant Jan ★★★ MODERN MEDITERRANEAN   This new Franco-South African gourmet restaurant is 2014's hottest meal ticket. Situated in the city's new dining district a block behind Nice Port, both décor and service (under the watchful eye of Maître d' Philippe Foucault, formerly of the Negresco and Grand Hotel du Cap Ferrat) are akin to being a guest in a French Presidential retreat. The inventive cuisine of South African chef Jan Hendrik van der Westhuizen blends regional ingredients (line-caught sea bass, Charolais beef) with African spice (Madagascar vanilla, rooibos jelly) and Italian style (Parmesan shavings, prosciutto chips). Dishes may include slow-roasted pork belly with scallops and sweet potato puree, and soya tuna with capers and crispy onion rings.

12 rue Lascaris. www.restaurantjan.com. © **04-97-19-32-23.** Reservations recommended. Main courses 20€–32€; fixed-price lunch 22€. Wed–Fri noon–3pm, Tues–Sat 7:30–10:30pm.

L'Univers – Christian Plumail ★ MODERN PROVENÇAL Modern market flavors are perfected by head chef Christian Plumail at this Michelin one-star restaurant. Over two set menus, he turns regional delights into classy, contemporary acts: menu items may include turbot fillet with fennel ice cream, or steamed grouper with oyster tartare. Be aware that the dining salon is formal—if you want cutting-edge, we recommend Flaveur or Vinivore instead. Fine dining becomes a bargain with a weekly-changing, market-inspired 23€ lunch menu. Choose a 6€ glass of wine to accompany this gourmet giveaway.

54 Boulevard Jean Jaurès. www.christian-plumail.com. ✆ **04-93-62-32-22.** Reservations recommended. Main courses 25€–36€; fixed-price lunch 23€; fixed-price dinner 46€ –75€. Tues–Fri noon–2pm and 7:30–9.30pm; Sat and Mon 7:30–9:30pm.

Vinivore ★★ MODERN FRENCH This vibrant eatery, located just behind the port, mixes fresh Provençal ingredients with Cantonese flair. Each day, Hong Kong–born chef Chun Wong's changing menu features just four appetizers, four main courses, and four desserts. Recent highlights include beef *tataki* with garlic flowers, wild rice risotto with grilled scallops, and vanilla-infused candied pineapple. Québécois sommelier Bonaventure Blankstein has handpicked some 200 vintages—carefully noted on the large chalkboards—from mostly organic wineries across southern France. In 2013 the small **Vinivore wine bar** opened next door to the main restaurant.

10 rue Lascaris. www.vinivore.fr. ✆ **04-93-14-68-09.** Reservations recommended. Main courses 11€–18€; fixed-price lunch 18€; fixed-price dinner 45€. Tues–Fri noon–2pm, Tues–Sat 7:30–10:30pm.

INEXPENSIVE

La Rossettisserie ★ ROTISSERIE GRILL Local boy Jean-Michel Caruana presides over one of the most fun restaurants on the French Riviera. The young proprietor-chef has replaced his establishment's 17th-century oven with a state-of-the-art rotisserie grill. Guests are seated just meters from the revolving spit roast or in the atmospheric vaulted basement. Choose from five simple starters, then select a joint of chicken, pork, beef, or lamb, which is popped into the rotisserie oven. It's that simple. The restaurant is sited a few steps away from place Rossetti in Nice Old Town, where innovative and inexpensive establishments like this one are hard to come by.

8, rue Mascoïnat. www.larossettisserie.com. ✆ **04-93-76-18-80.** Reservations required. Main courses 13.50€–14.50€. Mon–Sun noon–2pm and 7:30–10:30pm.

Les Secrets de Lili ★ CANTONESE Nice has welcomed immigrants from Algeria, Senegal, Vietnam, and many other French colonies besides. For authentic ethnic dining, take a walk alongside the Eglise Notre-Dame off avenue Jean Médécin. But none of the restaurants can top bona fide Cantonese favorite Les Secrets de Lili, just north of the church. The Wong parents govern a searing kitchen, while daughter Lili tends to the humming interior and three tiny outdoor tables. Even visiting Chinese tourists scour its Mandarin and French chalkboard for sautéed ray wings and steamed bok choy.

8 rue de Suisse. ✆ **04-93-88-11-48.** Main courses 8€–14€. Daily noon–2pm and 6–10pm. Closed mid-Feb–mid-March.

Exploring Nice

In 1822, Nice's orange crop had an awful year. The workers faced a lean time, so the English residents employed them to build the **promenade des Anglais ★★**, today a wide boulevard fronting the bay that stretches for 7km (4¼ miles), all the way to the airport. Along the beach are rows of grand cafes, the Musée Masséna, and the city's most glamorous hotels.

Crossing this boulevard in the tiniest bikinis are some of the world's most attractive bronzed bodies. They're all heading for the **beach.** Tough on tender feet, *le plage* is made not of sand, but of pebbles (and not small ones, either).

Rising sharply on a rock at the eastern end of the promenade is the **Colline du Château** (see p. 188). Once a fortified bastion, the hill has since been turned into a wonderful public park complete with a waterfall, cafés, and a giant children's play area, as well as an incredibly ornate cemetery.

Continuing east of the Colline, you reach the **Vieux Port,** or harbor, where the restaurants are filled with locals. While lingering over a drink at a sidewalk cafe, you can watch the ferries depart for Corsica and the yachts for St-Tropez. Just inland, the neighborhood around rue Bonaparte and place Garibaldi has become one of the hippest in town: head here for authentic eateries, organic food stores, fashion boutiques, and hip bars.

The **Vieille Ville ★★**, or Old Town, begins at the foot of the Colline and stretches to place Masséna. Sheltered by red-tiled roofs, many of the Italianate facades suggest 17th-century Genoese palaces, including the free museum **Palais Lascaris** (see p. 188). The Old Town is a maze of narrow streets teeming with local life, flower-strewn squares, and traditional *boulangeries:* sample a Niçois-style onion pizza *(pissaladière)* here. Many of the buildings are painted a faded Roman gold, and their banners are laundry flapping in the sea breeze.

From Tuesday through Sunday (8am–1pm), the Old Town's main pedestrianized thoroughfare, the **cours Saleya,** is crowded with local producers selling seasonal fruits and vegetables, cured meats, and artisanal cheeses. At the market's western end is the **Marché aux Fleurs.** A rainbow of violets, lilies and roses, the market operates Tuesday to Sunday from 8am to around 6pm. On Monday (8am–6pm) the cours Saleya is occupied by a superb **antiques market,** with vendors carting wares in from across France and Italy.

Nice's centerpiece is **place Masséna,** with rococo buildings and bubbling fountains, as well as the new **Promenade du Paillon** parkway that stretches from the **MAMAC** art museum (see p. 188) down to the **Jardin Albert-1er.** With palms and exotic flowers, this pedestrian-only zone is one of the prettiest places in town. During renovations, the city authorities discovered an **Archeological Crypt** near place Garibaldi, place Jacques Toja (nice.fr/culture; ℭ **04-92-00-41-90;** 5€, 2.5€ children under 16; closed Tuesdays). The site can now be visited on a 60-minute guided tour daily at 10am, 11am, 2pm, 3pm, and 4pm (closed Tuesdays).

Cathédrale Orthodoxe Russe St-Nicolas à Nice ★ CATHEDRAL Ordered
built by none other than Tsar Nicholas II, this recently renovated cathedral is the most beautiful religious edifice of the Orthodoxy outside Russia. It dates from the Belle Epoque, when some of the Romanovs and entourage turned the Riviera into their stomping ground. Everyone from grand dukes to ballerinas arrived on the—recently reinstated—direct train from Moscow, and then paraded their tiaras on the promenade. The cathedral is richly ornamented and decorated with icons. You'll spot the building from afar because of its collection of ornate onion-shaped domes.

Av. Nicolas II (off bd. Tzaréwitch). www.cathedrale-russe-nice.fr. ℭ **04-93-83-94-08.** Free admission. Tues–Sun 9am–noon and 2–6pm. From the central rail station, bus no. 71, or head west along av. Thiers to bd. Gambetta, and then go north to av. Nicolas-II.

Colline du Chateau ★★ RUINS AND PARK   This towering city park is where Nice locals go to escape the city crowds. Join them by hiking one of four sets of stone stairs (or take the 1.10€ elevator from the Tour Bellanda) to its 92m- (302ft) high plateau. The setting is so romantic that the two authors of this book met and fell in love here in 2005. Five centuries ago, the hill was a fortified citadel bristling with cannons. It won the city's eternal gratitude by holding out against an Ottoman bombardment in 1543 when local heroine Catherine Ségurane allegedly bared her generous posterior at the Turkish invaders, causing them to flee in fear. Gentle sea breezes and a score of leafy enclaves make it a perfect place to picnic or play *pétanque*. A vast hilltop cemetery is testimony to the French reverence for their ancestors, with wonderfully ornate gravestones.

Above Nice Old Town. Free admission. Daily 8am–dusk.

Musée d'Art Moderne et d'Art Contemporain (MAMAC) ★★★ ART MUSEUM   Nice's Modern and Contemporary Art Museum (or MAMAC as it's locally known) is a visionary display of art, architecture, and color. The building itself is boldness personified. It comprises two stone blocks clad in shimmering Carrara marble, with a glass walkway winding along the top: Loop around it in winter to see snow on the Alps to the north, as sunshine glitters on the Mediterranean to the south. Of the ten main salons, three permanent collections stand out. The first is the American Pop Art display featuring Tom Wesselmann, Robert Indiana, and Andy Warhol, which includes the latter artists' rejection letters from the New York MoMA. The second is the European New Realist display of César, Arman, and Niki de Saint Phalle. The third unique collection is the School of Nice room of locally acclaimed artists including Sacha Sosno and Ben.

Place Yves Klein (adjoining place Garibaldi). www.mamac-nice.org. ☎ **04-97-13-42-01.** Free admission. Tues–Sun 10am–6pm.

Musée Masséna ★★★ MUSEUM   Riviera aficionados will adore this astounding history museum. Located within an imposing Belle Epoque villa, it exhibits a quirky range of objects charting local life in Nice and its surrounds, from the first Victorian visitors through the roaring 1920s. Elegantly printed menus, train tickets from London to Nice, period maps, and snapshots of the promenading rich on vacation bring the past to life. Of additional note are the paintings and *objets d'art* donated by the Masséna family, a noble set of locals who constructed the villa. Botanist Edouard Ardre, who also designed the verdant greenery in front of the Casino de Monte-Carlo, landscaped the museum's neatly manicured gardens.

65 rue de France or 35 promenade des Anglais. ☎ **04-93-91-19-10.** Free admission. Wed–Mon 9am–6pm.

Palais Lascaris ★ MUSEUM HOUSE   Fifteen 'palaces' grace Nice's 300-year-old Vieux Ville. The Palais Lascaris is arguably the finest of these medieval mansions, and the only one open to the public. It was built by the noble Vintimille-Lascaris family—and boy did they live in style. Expect suits of armor, frescoed ceilings, and outdoor courtyards aplenty. The most celebrated floor is the *étage nobile*, where visitors are wowed by some serious rococo bling.

15 rue Droite. www.palais-lascaris-nice.org. ☎ **04-93-62-72-40.** Free admission. Wed–Mon 10am–6pm.

Théâtre de la Photographie et de l'Image ★ PHOTOGRAPHY MUSEUM
Nice's most overlooked exhibition space houses world-beating photography displays.
Shows are displayed over its six belle époque salons. Recent exhibitions have included
homages to Riviera photographer Jean Gilletta and Paris chronicler Brassaï, as well as
images from Nice in the roaring 1920s. The most famous collection is that of Charles
Nègre, who photographed the city in its pre-tourism splendor in the 1860s. In 2014,
the Théâtre held an acclaimed retrospective of National Geographic photographer
Steve McCurry, whose most captivating image is a piercingly green-eyed Afghan refu-
gee girl taken in 1984.

27 boulevard Dubouchage. www.tpi-nice.org. ✆ **04-97-13-42-20.** Free admission. Tues–Sun
10am–6pm.

Outlying Attractions in Cimiez

In the once-aristocratic hilltop quarter of Cimiez, 5km (3 miles) north of Nice, Queen
Victoria wintered at the Hôtel Excelsior. Half the English court traveled down from
Calais with her on a luxurious private train. Be sure to stroll over to the adjacent
Monastère de Cimiez (Cimiez Convent), which offers panoramic views over Nice and
the Baie des Anges; artists Matisse and Dufy are buried in the cemetery nearby. To
reach this suburb and its attractions, take bus no. 15 from bd. Dubouchage.

Musée Matisse ★★ ART MUSEUM   In 1963, this beautiful old Italian villa was
transformed into a museum honoring Henri Matisse, one of the 20th century's greatest
painters. Matisse came to Nice for the light and made the city his home, living in the
Hotel Beau Rivage and on the cours Saleya, and dying in Cimiez in 1954. Most of the
pieces in the museum's permanent collection—including "Nude in an Armchair with
a Green Plant" (1937) and "Blue Nude IV" (1952)—were created in Nice. Artworks
are interspersed with Matisse's personal possessions, such as ceramic vases and
antique furniture, as well as scale models of his architectural masterpiece, Vence's
Chapelle du Rosaire (p. 174).

164 av. des Arènes de Cimiez. www.musee-matisse.nice.org. ✆ **04-93-81-08-08.** Free admission.
Wed–Mon 10am–6pm.

Musée National Message Biblique Marc Chagall ★★ ART MUSEUM   Surrounded by pools and a garden, this handsome museum is devoted to Marc Chagall's
treatment of biblical themes. Born in Russia in 1887, Chagall became a French citizen
in 1937 and painted with astonishing light and color until his death in St-Paul-de-
Vence in 1985. This museum's focal set of artworks—12 large paintings, illustrating
the first two books of the Old Testament—was originally created to adorn the central
cathedral in Vence. The church's high humidity nixed the artist's original plans, and
Chagall assisted in planning this purpose-built space instead. The 200 additional artworks include gouaches, a mosaic, sculptures, and prints.

Av. du Dr. Ménard. www.musee-chagall.fr. ✆ **04-93-53-87-20.** Admission 8€ adults, 6€ students,
free for children 17 and under. May–Oct Wed–Mon 10am–6pm; Nov–April Wed–Mon 10am–5pm.

Organized Tours

BUS TOURS   One of the most enjoyable ways to quickly gain an overview of Nice
is aboard a **Nice–Le Grand Tour** (www.nicelegrandtour.com; ✆ **04-92-29-17-00**)
double-decker bus. Between 10am and 6pm year-round, one of a flotilla of this company's buses departs from a position adjacent to the Jardin Albert I. The panoramic

90-minute tour takes in the harbor, the museums of Cimiez, the Russian church, and the promenade. Per-person rates for the experience are 21€ adults, 18€ students, and 5€ children 4 to 11. Participants can get off at any of 11 stops en route and reboard any other buses, which follow at 30- to 60-minute intervals, depending on the season. Advance reservations aren't necessary, and commentary is piped through to headsets in seven different languages. Tickets are valid the entire day of purchase.

Another easy way to see the city is by the small **Train Touristique de Nice** (www.trainstouristiquesdenice.com; ℂ **06-08-55-08-30**), which also departs from the promenade des Anglais, opposite Jardin Albert I. The 45-minute ride passes many of Nice's most-heralded sites, including place Masséna, the Old Town, and the Colline du Château. Departing every 30 minutes, the train operates daily 10am to 5pm (until 6pm April–May and Sept, until 7pm June–Aug). The round-trip price is 8€ adults and 4€ children 4 to 12.

WALKING TOURS   The Office du Tourisme organizes a "Discover the heart of Nice" English-language walking tour of Nice Old Town every Saturday morning at 9.30am. It departs from the Tourist Office at 5 promenade des Anglais, and costs 12€, or [6] for children. It winds through markets, artists' residences, and along the ancient streets.

CYCLING TOURS   Energetic guests may join **Nice Cycle Tours** (www.nicecycletours.com; ℂ **06-19-99-95-22**), 3-hour bike voyages around the city. Tours cost 30€ per person, and the friendly team also run food tours and cycle expeditions.

BOAT TOURS   Nice owes its soul to the sea. In 1993, the nations of France, Italy, and Monaco teamed together for protect an 87,500km^2 (33,784 square miles) sanctuary for giant pelagics. To spot dolphins, turtles, and the Riviera's seasonal pod of migrating whales, take a trip into the blue with **Fastboat** (www.dolphins-whales-watching-med.com; ℂ **06-12-73-73-90**; departures from Nice Port and Beaulieu-sur-Mer). The 4-hour adventure costs 120€, or 70€ for children ages 11 and under. Fastboat's experienced captain is extremely respectful of local mammals and sea life.

ALTERNATIVE TOURS   Possibly the coolest way to get around Nice is by Segway, the two-wheeled electronic scooters. Tours are run by **Mobilboard**, 2 rue Halévy (www.mobilboard.com; ℂ **04-93-80-21-27**). Children 14 (minimum age) to 17 must be accompanied by an adult. An hour-long tour of Nice costs 30€ per person. Alternatively, **2CV Escapade**, 7 place Ile de Beauté (www.2cv-escapade.com; ℂ **06-52-01-30-40**), in Nice Port, offers multilingual city tours in a classic Citroën convertible from 60€ per group of two or three people.

FOOD TOURS   Foodie visitors to Nice should pack a pair of plus-size shorts. Those not content with a personal market tour can join the professionals at **The French Way** (www.thefrenchway.fr; ℂ **06-27-35-13-75**), for a 3-hour market tour. Sample local delights like *tarte aux blettes* and *socca* chickpea pancakes en-route. Tours costs 65€ per person. In a similar vein **A Taste of Nice** (www.foodtoursofnice.com; ℂ **06-19-99-95-22**), run a highly regarded Niçois cuisine food tour. The 3 to 4 hour guided walk indulges in local specialties and wines. Prices are 60€ per person. The outfit's other tours include an organic wine tasting 'Tour de France', plus an electronic bicycle tour that, to quote, "even couch potatoes" can enjoy. Cordon Bleu-trained Canadian chef Rosa Jackson runs Niçois cooking school **Les Petits Farcis** (www.petitsfarcis.com; ℂ **06-81-67-41-22**). Rosa's market tour, followed by a cooking class and four-course gourmet lunch in her 17th-century Old Town apartment, costs 195€ per person.

Outdoor Activities

BEACHES   Along Nice's seafront, beaches extend uninterrupted for more than 7km (4¼ miles), going from the edge of Vieux-Port (the old port, or harbor) to the international airport. Tucked between the public areas are several rather chic private beaches. Many of these beach bars provide mattresses and parasols for 12€ to 22€. The coolest clubs include **Hi-Beach** (www.hi-beach.net; ✆ **04-97-14-00-83**), which has a sushi bar, blanket Wi-Fi, and family-friendly playpens; and **Castel Plage** (www.castelplage. com; ✆ **04-93-85-22-66**), a celebrity hangout in summer.

SCUBA DIVING   Of the many diving outfits in Nice harbor, **Nice Diving,** 13 quai des Deux Emmanuel (www.nicediving.com; ✆ **06-14-46-04-06**), offers bilingual instruction and *baptêmes* (dives for first-timers) around Nice and Cap Ferrat. A dive for experienced divers, equipment included, costs around 50€; appropriate diver's certification is required.

Shopping

CLOTHES   Nice's densest concentrations of fashionable French labels are clustered around **rue Masséna** and **avenue Jean-Médecin.** For more high-end couture, the streets around **place Magenta,** including **rue de Verdun, rue Paradis,** and **rue Alphonse Karr** are a credit card's worst nightmare. A shop of note is **Cotelac,** 12 rue Alphonse Karr (✆ **04-93-87-31-59**), which sells chic women's clothing. Men should try **Façonnable,** 7–9 rue Paradis (www.faconnable.com; ✆ **04-93-88-06-97**). This boutique is the original site of a chain with several hundred branches worldwide; the look is conservatively stylish. For more unusual apparel, **Lucien Chasseur,** 2 rue Bonaparte (✆ **04-93-55-52-14**), is the city's most fabulous spot for Italian-designed shoes, scarves, and soft leather satchels.

BEACH CLUB babylon

The beach clubs of Cannes are seriously showy. Those of St Tropez promise sand-in the-toes (and boobs-in-your-face) hedonism. Nice's beach clubs are for topping up your tan, not touting your wares. Simply pitch up, hand over between 15€ and 20€, then recline on a soft mattress next to the lapping waves for the day. Most outfits offer waiter service, beach toys, and fixed-price menus no more expensive than those offered at restaurants in town.

Our favorites include **Hi-Beach** (www. hi-beach.net/en; ✆ **04-97-07-26-26**). It promises organic shakes, sushi lunches, and four-person swing chairs by the sea. It also boasts an architecture library, weights room, and children's play area.

Florida Beach (✆ **04-93-44-72-86**), is gourmet chic, although waiters are sometimes too cool to take your order. **Beau Rivage Plage** (www.plagenice beaurivage.com; ✆ **04-42-00-46-80**) is a beach stalwart. The largest and most professional of *les clubs,* it offers white sun loungers shaded by white linen drapes. For solid dining, **Castel Plage** (www.castelplage.com; ✆ **04-93-85-22-66**) combines fine food, a party atmosphere, and old-school glamour in equal measure.

Not feeling flush? Pitch up to almost any beach club at sunset to order a 20€ bottle of rosé on a seashore table to share between your friends.

FOOD   The winding streets of the Old Town and the locals-only streets around rue Bonaparte behind Nice Port are the best place to source foodie purchases. If you're thinking of indulging in a Provençale *pique-nique*, **Nicola Alziari,** 14 rue St François de Paule (www.alziari.com.fr; ✆ **04-93-62-94-03**), near the Old Town's Opera house will provide everything from olives, anchovies, and *pistous* to *aiolis* and tapenades. For an olive-oil tasting session—and the opportunity to buy the goods afterward—check out **Oliviera**, 2 rue Benoit Bunico (www.oliviera.com; ✆ **04-93-11-06-45**), run by the amiable Nadim Beyrouti. **Maison Barale**, 7 rue Sainte-Réparate (www.barale-raviolis. com; ✆ **04-93-83-63-08**), is generally regarded as the finest fresh pasta maker in Nice, if not on the entire French Riviera. With 120 years of experience, they makes a mean ricotta ravioli. **Caves Caprioglio,** 16 rue de la Préfecture (✆ **04-93-85-66-57**), is the go-to place for rare Provençal wines and big name Bordeaux vintages. In the port, **Confiserie Florian,** 14 quai Papacino (www.confiserieflorian.com; ✆ **04-93-55-43-50**), has been candying fruit, chocolate-dipping roasted nuts, and crystalizing edible flowers since 1949. Tastes become even more offbeat in the rue Bonaparte area. **Le Péché Mignon**, 41 rue Bonaparte (✆ **04-93-89-75-56**), is where three generations of Niçois have gone for high-end patisserie and picnic goodies. **Boulangerie Lagache**, 20 rue Arson (✆ **04-93-19-04-83**), is often the holder of the annual best baguette in Nice award. Italian-operated **O'Quotidien**, 2 rue Martin Seytour (www.oquotidien.fr; ✆ **04-93-55-43-50**), is an all-organic local food store: Customers (and lunchtime diners; set menu 16€) can sample, then purchase their weekly wine from huge vats.

CONCEPT STORES   For antiquarian books, contemporary art, kitsch, and comic books, wander north from place Garibaldi to **rue Delille and rue Defly,** just past the MAMAC modern art gallery. Hairdresser-cum-clothes atelier **My Cut Concept,** 11 rue Delfy (✆ **04-93-01-53-19**), is a typical local combination. On the same street, **l'Ara**, 2 rue Delfy (✆ **04-93-87-65-86**), sells vintage Scandinavian furniture and *objets d'art*. For more offbeat gifts, **Chambre Cinquante-Sept,** 16 rue Emmanuel Philibert (✆ **04-92-04-02-81**), stocks beautifully unique Art Deco delights. More vintage is for sale at **Deux Pièces,** 2 rue Antoine Gautier (✆ **06-68-86-23-00**), including '60s sunglasses and '80s sneakers. In the Old Town, **Caprice Vintage**, 12 rue Droite (✆ **09-83-48-05-43**), purveys Dior scarves, Zegna silk ties, and '70s Bakelite telephones. A few blocks away, **Pour Vos Beaux Yeux**, 10 rue Alexandre Mari (www.pourvosbeauxyeux. com; ✆ **04-93-01-69-25**), translates as 'For Your Beautiful Eyes'. Optician-proprietor Charles Mosa stocks a selection of original prescription glasses and shades, divided into sections dating from the '50s to the '90s. Steve McQueen would most heartily approve.

SOUVENIRS   The best selection of Provençal fabrics is at **Le Chandelier,** 7 rue de la Boucherie (✆ **04-93-85-85-19**), where you'll see designs by two of the region's best-known producers of cloth, Les Olivades and Valdrôme. Nearby at **Atelier des Cigales**, 13 rue du Collet (✆ **04-93-85-85-19**), expect top-class, hand-painted pottery and ceramics from across the province.

ANTIQUES   Nice's **antique quarter** (www.nice-antic.com) on the western side of Nice Port is second only to Paris in terms of serious collecting. Over 100 *antiquaires* line the streets of rue Foresta, rue Ségurane, and rue Antoine Gautier. Goods range from '50s Milanese furniture to Tibetan art and Dresden ceramics. Must-visits are **Harter**, 35 rue Ségurane (www.hartergalerie.com; ✆ **04-93-07-10-29**), for mid- to late 20th-century furniture, art, and lighting, and **Hierro des Villes**, 4 rue Antoine Gautier

market time IN NICE

Guests who are picnicking, self-catering, or hunting for antique bargains are in for a treat. The **cours Saleya street market** (Tues–Sun 7:30am–1pm) is the Old Town's fruit and vegetable go-to. The impossibly pretty piles of peaches, strawberries, olives, and jams have been painted by Henri Matisse, plus a thousand other amateurs who squat beside the stalls with their easels to this day. An entire section is been given over to organic goods (look out for the "*Agriculture biologique*" signs above each stall) and locally sourced items. One vendor even claims that his chickens have a panoramic view of the Mediterranean Sea. Tour groups have become a fixture in recent years, as has occasional overcharging, so count your change carefully.

The same space hosts an exceptionally offbeat **antiques market** every Monday (9am–6pm). The daily **flower market** (Tues–Sun 9am–6pm) takes place at the western end of the cours Saleya.

You will seldom spot another tourist at the **Libération fruit and vegetable market** (Tues–Sun 7:30am–1pm). The Riviera's finest street market is as authentic as they come. Some 150 stalls purvey artisanal breads, whole roast chickens, nuts, seeds, flowers, fish, and a thousand other items besides. Some stalls, invariably manned by a weathered local, sell one fruit only, a seasonal local delight. Like the Cours Saleya market, dozens of restaurants, wine shops, and cafés line the market route.

(www.hierrodesvilles.com; ✆ **04-97-12-15-15**), for far-out modern art and furnishings. Less expensive than bona fide antique stores are Dépôt Ventes. These warehouses are stocked with house clearance goodies and are veritable museums to Nice's wealthy past. The richest families seem to have shoveled all their Chanel homeware into **Mademoiselle,** 41 rue de France (www.mademoiselle-nice.fr; ✆ **06-88-54-22-00**), a Dépôt Vente Luxe near the Negresco Hotel.

Nightlife

Nice has some of the most active nightlife and cultural offerings along the Riviera. Big evenings out usually begin at a cafe or bar, take in a restaurant, opera, or film, and finish in a club. The website **riviera.angloinfo.com** lists all the week's English-language movies in VO, or *version originale.*

The major cultural center on the Riviera is the **Opéra de Nice,** 4 rue St-François-de-Paule (www.opera-nice.org; ✆ **04-92-17-40-00**), built in 1885 by Charles Garnier, fabled architect of the Paris Opéra. It presents a full repertoire, with emphasis on serious, often large-scale operas, such as "Tristan and Isolde" and "La Boheme," as well as a *saison symphonique* dominated by the Orchestre Philharmonique de Nice. The opera hall is also the major venue for concerts and recitals. Tickets are available right up until the day of performance. You can show up at the box office (Mon–Thurs 9am–5:30pm; Fri until 7:45pm; Sat until 4:30pm) or buy tickets in advance online. Tickets run from 10€ to 80€.

A chic gaming spot is the **Casino in the Palais de Mediterranée,** 15 promenade des Anglais (www.casinomediterranee.com; ✆ **04-92-14-68-00**), which offers a similar experience daily from 10am for slot machines, 8pm for gaming tables.

ROYA VALLEY & THE MERCANTOUR
national park

The timeless Roya Valley and the Mercantour forests (one of only seven National Parks in mainland France) are a train hop away from Nice. The entire area was once the private hunting ground of Italy's Turin-based kings. It only became part of France in 1947, and the Italianate train stations and tumbling hill villages remain. Thankfully, there's a lot of wildlife left too, in the form of wolves, marmots, ibex, eagles, and deer.

The **Train de Merveilles** (www. tendemerveilles.com) climbs up into the Roya Valley from Nice-Ville station up to six times daily. A stunning stop is **Sospel**, 45 minutes from Nice. This age-old village is sliced in two by a raging river, and is a center for mountain biking, horseback riding, and alpine hikes.

Further north up the valley, the village of **Breil-sur-Roya** has stolen a few hearts too. It lies at the nexus of several hiking paths, one of them leading downhill to Sospel.

The large ex-Italian town of **Tende**, 2 hours from Nice, is the train's final stop. The names above its stores, on its churches, and in its rococo graveyard are distinctly non-French. It's is also the gateway to the **Mercantour National Park** (www.parc-mercantour.eu). Before partaking in the park's 100 hiking routes, make a visit to Tende's **Musée des Merveilles** (www.museedesmerveilles.com; ✆ **04-93-04-32-50**), which highlights the area's prehistory, cave paintings, and fairytale geography.

Lovers of *la bella italia* may continue on to Cuneo in Italy using a locals-only train that runs from Tende towards Turin several times each day.

The Old Town's most happening spot is **Villa,** 7 rue Raoul Bosio ✆ **04-93-87-99-45**), whose house aperitif is the wickedly named Putain de le Palais: crushed strawberries topped with Champagne. Within the cool-kitsch decor of a former garage in the port area, talented staff serves up fruity cocktails and organic local wines at **Rosalina,** 16 rue Lascaris (✆ **04-93-89-34-96**). Around the corner, gay-friendly **Comptoir Central Électrique**, 10 rue Bonaparte (✆ **04-93-14-09-62**), has been the place Garibaldi neighborhood's epicenter of cool since opening in 2013. Also on the same street, **Deli Bo,** 5 rue Bonaparte (✆ **04-93-56-33-04**), is a hip dining spot for ladies who lunch.

The party spirit is best lapped up in the alfresco bars on the **cours Saleya.** Otherwise, head 1 block inland to **Wayne's Bar,** 15 rue de la Préfecture (www.waynes.fr; ✆ **04-93-13-46-99**), where dancing on the tables to raucous cover bands is the norm. For excellent house tunes, nonstop dancing, and heaps of understated cool, head to **Bliss,** 12 rue de l'Abbaye (✆ **04-93-16-82-38**).

RIVIERA SKI RESORTS ★★

913km (566 miles) S of Paris; 9.5km (6 miles) S of Cannes

The Eden-like French Riviera isn't only blessed with beaches, casinos, sunshine, and glamor. This fabled corner of France also boasts three international ski stations. What's more, each resort is set up for spoiled day-skiers from Cannes, Nice, and Monaco. Which means that outside of weekends and school holidays, the *pistes* are almost empty. So close are the ski slopes to the coast that visitors may swim in the Mediterranean just 90 minutes after pulling off their boots.

Like the coastline itself, the history of the Riviera ski resorts shows a pioneering spirit. In 1889, Niçois nobleman Chevalier Victor de Cessole went searching for his own slice of Europe's latest aristocratic activity: skiing. He was in luck. Over 80% of the Alpes-Maritimes province (the region that stretches from Cannes to Menton) is covered by towering peaks. For four decades, De Cessole pioneered downhill runs in an upland area that still revels in 300 days of sun per year.

De Cessole's trend caught on. In 1937, the Riviera resort of Auron received its first ski lift—the third in all of France. By the 1970s, French celebrities like Jacques Chirac and Sacha Distel were schussing down the slopes at the nearby ski stations Valberg and Isola 2000. Some 500km of ski runs and 100 ski lifts now link these three resorts. Activities from ice-climbing to snow-shoeing, not to mention mountain-biking and bird-watching in summer, now attract tens of thousands of visitors year-round. And even better: This being socialist France, resort prices are kept low for the public good. A return bus ticket to the slopes costs just 8€ flat.

Essentials

ARRIVING   All three ski resorts are connected by the **100% Neige Ski Buses** from Lignes d'Azur (www.lignesdazur.com; ℭ **08-10-06-10-06**). From December until April, the lines no. 740 (to Auron), no. 750 (to Isola 2000), and no. 770 (to Valberg) swing past Nice-Ville train station every morning for the 90-minute ride to the slopes. Each bus returns from its respective ski resort to Nice at around 5pm. Tickets cost 4€ one-way, and should be booked in advance (in English) online. Note that each route also calls at Nice Airport. Visitors traveling from Cannes, Antibes, or any other coastal resort can hop on here. **Local buses** shuttle between each ski resort for 1.50€ one-way.

To **drive** to the ski stations from Nice, follow the M6202 then the M2205 inland from Nice Airport. Trip time is approximately 80 minutes for Isola 2000, 90 minutes for Auron, and 80 minutes for Valberg.

VISITOR INFORMATION   Each ski station maintains its own excellent Internet portal. Here guests may reserve accommodation, equipment, and a lift pass, as well as downloading a map of the *pistes*. In Isola 2000, the **Office de Tourisme** is in the resort's center (www.isola2000.com; ℭ **04-93-23-15-15**). In Auron the **Office de Tourisme** is inside the wood-timbered Maison d'Auron Riou (www.auron.com; ℭ **04-93-05-84-72**). In Valberg, the **Office de Tourisme** is located on place Charles Ginesy (www.valberg.com; ℭ **04-93-23-24-25**). Note that each resort's website flips from 'winter' to 'summer' mode twice-yearly to promote that season's outdoor activities. Each resort offers ski schools for adults and juniors for around 30€ per lesson from the **Ecoles du Ski Français**, the official *French Ski School* (www.esf.net; ℭ **04-93-23-02-53**).

Isola 2000 ★

92km (57 miles) N of Nice

The Riviera's youngest ski resort is sited on what was Italian territory until 1947. The Italian military—who occupied the French Riviera in World War II—had built a number of mountain roads through the snowy hills. In the 1960s, the area was stumbled upon by former British Army officer and Olympic skier, Peter Boumphrey. The Englishman built up Isola into a 2,000m- (6,562ft) high world-beating ski resort. A *piste* still bears his name.

Today, a highly acclaimed 'snowpark' makes it the slickest ski resort near the coast. Its proximity to Nice, coupled with guaranteed snow (thanks to 430 snow cannons) makes it the busiest too. Boarders come from afar to sample the 2,300m- (7,546ft) high dedicated park, which contains a Jib Zone, Half Pipe, and Big Air. There's a mountain-top sound system to boot. A smaller wooden-built 'biopark' is more family-friendly, with towering totems and sculptures of local wildlife.

SKIING ISOLA 2000

Ski passes start at 32€ per day with deep discounts for family passes and stays of 3 days or more. Day passes cost 27€ for children aged 17 and under. **Snowpark passes** for serious boarders cost 20€ per day. **Ski Gliss St Pierre** (isola-2000.skimium.fr; ✆ **06-15-78-22-40**), rents boards, boots, and skis in the center of the village.

Being Isola 2000, non-ski activities are pretty hardcore. **AT2000** (www.sports loisirs.net; ✆ **04-93-23-91-32**) operate an ice karting circuit. Or try snowmobiling with their team for 100€ per hour.

WHERE TO EAT & STAY

In front of the ski lift, **Le Cow Club** (www.cowclub.com; ✆ **04-93-23-12-01**), does a fine line in banked raclette cheese, reblochon cheese fondue, and flaming Parmesan pasta. Unlike Auron or Valberg, Isola 2000 was built in the 1970s so hotels lack individual charm. Double rooms at the **Hôtel Le Druos** (www.hoteldruos.com; ✆ **04-93-23-12-20**) cost from 95€ to 160€, with promotional prices for half-board and longer stays.

SUMMER on the slopes

When the ski stations close down for the season in late April, the websites of Auron, Valberg, and Isola 2000 flip to 'summer' mode. Each resort keeps customers coming back until the next snowfall with a host of outdoor activities. It's also a great way to escape the coastline's heat and hustle.

Cycling and **mountain biking** are the three resorts' largest attractions. The Tour de France has passed through Isola 2000 twice, while nearby Auron has hosted the French Mountain Biking Championship. In the latter resort,

visitors are encouraged to hire a mountain bike, ride a gondola up a mountain, then hurtle down 50km (32 miles) of slopes. Auron also offers **hiking, archery, rock climbing, and horse riding**, as well as some of the cleanest summer air in France.

Valberg comes into its own each summer as a serious **hill-walking** destination. Some 20 hiking routes depart directly from the Office de Tourisme into the Mercantour National Park. Local mountain guides are available for more strenuous walks.

Auron ★

A road first linked Nice with the ski resort of Auron back in 1931. A ski lift followed a few years later, although it only moved at the stately pace of 2 meters (around 6.5 feet) per second! Much of the resort was built in the 1950s, rendering Auron the most traditional ski resort in the Alpes-Maritimes. A medieval church, horse-drawn carriages, a cozy village center, and several wellness boutiques make it the most family-friendly local ski station too.

Auron boasts 42 runs over 135km of slopes. It's a fine place to relax in a restaurant, take in the view, or meander down a blue run—posers head instead to Isola 2000. A wooden children's snowpark and sociable ski school makes it a boon for families. The resort is also justly famous for snowshoeing and wildlife hikes.

SKIING AURON

Ski passes start at 32€ per day with cheaper rates for family passes and longer stays. Daily passes cost 27€ for children aged 17 and under. Friendly proprietor Ziggy rents ski equipment at **Zen Altitude** (✆ **04-93-03-27-23**).

A number of experienced **showshoe guides** offer tours of the wintery mountain trails. All are listed on the official Auron website (www.auron.com), as are hikes to the **wolf sanctuary** on the edge of the Mercantour National Park.

WHERE TO EAT & STAY

Auron's delightful chalet restaurants all overlook the main *piste*, where skiers of all abilities rush past in time for lunch. Ski straight into **L'Alisier** (www.lalisier.com; ✆ **04-93-23-34-83**), pile up a tray of budget-friendly *daube* beef stew and potato soup, then dine out on the sun terrace. It's genuinely hard to pick the resort's most charming hotel. But the wooden-built **Hôtel le Savoie** (www.hotelsavoie.com; ✆ **04-93-23-02-51**) dates from the 1950s and offers half-board deals including five-course dinners and lift passes. Regular double rooms cost between 140€ and 170€ per night.

Valberg ★

Tucked inside the Mercantour National Park, Valberg's watchword is sustainability. This small, laid-back resort is as charming and as family-focused as they come. The oldest of the Riviera ski stations, it inaugurated its very own ski jump in 1930. By 1938, leaps of 58m (190ft) were being made, although modern Olympians manage jumps of more than twice that distance.

Valberg packs an enormous amount into its 53 runs over 90km of skiable *pistes*. A big draw is the snowboard zone, which boasts a Big Air Bag, an inflatable cushion were freestylers can flop into if they don't pull off their trick. As befits a resort in a protected environmental area, snowshoeing and Nordic skiing are major activities.

SKIING VALBERG

Daylong **ski passes** at Valberg start at 30.60€ per day, or 22.70€ for children aged 12 and under. Expect discounts for family passes and stays of 2 days or more. For equipment hire, try **Chalet Canadien**, at 1 Avenue de Valberg (chaletcanadiensport.voila.net; ✆ **04-93-02-50-21**).

FRENCH SOCIALISM on the slopes

France being France, the pursuits of yachting, skiing, or seeing Picasso paintings up close are not considered elite pastimes. To ensure access for all, the local government runs **daily ski buses** to the slopes for just 4€ one-way. By Googling local equipment hire, the price of your ski stay can be brought down further, especially if you visit on a weekday, when the resorts tend to be empty.

Some 25km of cross-country, or **Nordic skiing**, trails run throughout the Mercantour National Park. *Piste* access costs 8.60€ per day. Equipment hire and guides are available locally.

WHERE TO EAT & STAY

Find traditional mountain fare opposite the village church at **L'Etable** (✆ **04-93-02-68-20**). Raclettes and grilled river trout are the order of the day. In the village center, **L'Adrech de Lagas** (www.adrech-hotel.com; ✆ **04-93-23-12-20**) has a sauna, spa, and in-house masseur. Double rooms cost from 84€ to 194€.

NORTHERN CORSICA ★★★

286km (178 miles) SE of Marseille; 137km (108 miles) SE of Nice

Corsica is where residents of Provence and the French Riviera go on holiday. The Mediterranean island is breathtakingly beautiful: Google its empty coastline, its sky-topping mountains, or its Italianate piazzas and we can guarantee that you will be at a loss for words.

Not only does Corsica boast what are generally regarded as three of the Top 10 beaches in the world (plage Saleccia, plage Rondinara, and place Palombaggia), its spiny mountain center is also crossed by the GR20, arguably the most awesome hiking trail in France. Little wonder that ferries shuttle out of Marseille and Nice harbors to the Northern Corsican towns of Calvi and Bastia all year round.

Quite reasonably, Corsicans have long been keen to protect their language, culture, and environment. Even Corsica-born Napoleon Bonaparte didn't manage to definitively incorporate the island into the French state. After France's capitulation in World War II, Corsica was placed under Nazi rule. The ferocity of the local resistance fighters—known as the *maquis* after the fragrant scrub where they hid—ensured that the occupiers only held onto a tiny coastal strip. After liberation, the island was nicknamed *USS Corsica* as it hosted a dozen or so American Air Force runways, as the Allies flew sorties over southern France.

In recent decades Corsicans have received more autonomy from France. The once-banned Corsican language (a relative of Italy's Tuscan dialect) is now practiced at Corsica's only university, the *Università di Corsica Pasquale Paoli*, in the island 'capital' of Corté. Locals still like to let off steam by defacing or shooting French-language road signs. But such sentiments are directed at the disinterested government in Paris, and not towards the tourist industry that forms islanders' main form of income. With only 320,000 residents (the same population as Nice) spread over 8,680km2 (3,350 square miles), Corsica has an empty stretch of sand for everyone. Better still, the slow cruise over from France is a holiday in itself. Note that we haven't included restaurant recommendations along the northern coast. Dropping into unnamed beach shacks, local markets, and fisherman-run restaurants is all part of the charm.

Essentials

ARRIVING   The regular ferries that run from Marseille to Bastia, and from Nice to Bastia and Calvi, put guests in the holiday mood with sun decks, plunge pools, and fabulous food. **Corsica Ferries** (www.corsicaferries.com; ✆ 08-25-09-50-95), operate weekly routes from Nice to Bastia and Corsica from 19€ one-way for advance bookings. Frequency ramps up to near daily sailings in July and August. Journey time is 4 hours. **SNCM** (www.sncm.fr; ✆ 32-60) run a daily service from Marseille to Bastia. Sailing time is 7 hours. Tickets start from 30€ one-way when booked in advance.

Island airline **Air Corsica** (www.aircorsica.com; ✆ 08-25-35-35-35) also flies from Marseille-Provence Airport and Nice Cote d'Azur Airport from 59€ one-way. The hop across the Mediterranean takes just 40 minutes.

VISITOR INFORMATION   The official Visit Corsica portal (www.visit-corsica. com) offers information on beaches, guided tours, and activities. In Calvi, the **Office de Tourisme** (www.balagne-corsica.com; ✆ 04-95-65-16-67), resides inside the town's petite train station. Bastia's **Office de Tourisme** (www.bastia-tourisme.com; ✆ 04-93-54-20-40), is on the grand place Saint Nicolas.

GETTING AROUND   A bucolic **train line** (www.train-corse.com; ✆ 04-95-34-09-15), links Bastia to Calvi and serves as a lifeline for coastal communities. Be aware that it's dated, busy, and stops every 5 minutes, but the beach and mountain scenery en-route is spectacular. Many visitors arrive with their own **mountain bike** or **motor-scooter**, both of which can be rented locally for around 15€ per day and 30€ respectively. Try **Garage d'Angeli** in Calvi (www.garagedangeli.com; ✆ 04-95-65-02-13), or **Cycles 2**0 (www.cycles20.fr; ✆ 04-95-32-30-64), in Bastia. A local **hire car** is essential for exploring the Cap Corse peninsula, but not for touring around the towns of Bastia or Calvi.

Calvi and Around ★★

112km (70 miles) W of Bastia

Few destinations in France boast such an awesome emplacement. Calvi's **15th century citadel** pokes proudly into the Mediterranean, and offers sweeping views across the Corsica's northern coast. And what a view it is. A dozen of the island's famous beaches taper eastwards like a quicksilver necklace. Down below the scene is similarly timeless. Fresh fruit is unloaded from the Bastia train, and fishing boats haul in the daily catch, even if they are dwarfed by the occasional Corsica Ferry that putters across from the mainland.

Like most Corsican towns there's no "must-see" in Calvi; it's more a place to simply be. Sipping espressos on the quay, snorkeling beneath the citadel, or sunbathing on the endless beach sum up the town's sunny charms.

Heading westwards to Bastia the scene becomes even more relaxing. Visitors may drive, cycle, ride the train, or even walk to the secret sandy stretches of **Plage de l'Arinella** and **Plage Restitude**. One of the final stops before the Désert des Agriates (see p. 201) is **Algajola**. A cute walled town with an impossibly sandy beach, it is one of the train stops on the Calvi-Bastia line: Simply alight in your swimming trunks and

UNESCO-PROTECTED scandola nature reserve

It takes a lot for UNESCO to inscribe a natural region to its prestigious World Heritage List. That's why the **Scandola Nature Reserve**, just south of Calvi, really does astound. UNESCO claims that: "The site includes a coastline of astonishing beauty studded with offshore islets and sea pillars rising out of translucent waters." We'd certainly agree with that.

A local law prohibiting environmental destruction from 1930 predates the UNESCO listing by over 40 years. Since then, the Nature Reserve has slowly returned to its feral state. Osprey and Peregrine falcons circle above, as Cory's shearwaters and Audouin's gulls bob on the waves. A colossal amount of wildlife enjoys the serenity under the surface, including spiny lobsters and giant groupers, all safe from human intrusion. There are 450 varieties of seaweed

alone. The real star is the coastline itself. Blood red cliffs rise for 900m (2,952 feet), cracking open to reveal sandy beaches, basalt pillars, and tiny islands of pure porphyry volcanic stone.

Lucky are those visitors with their own private boat. The rest of us may indulge on a boat trip with **Colombo Line** (www.colombo-line.com; ✆ **04-95-65-32-10**), in Calvi Port. But make sure you book their full 5-hour trip, which includes a stop at Girolata, in order to get as far into the Nature Reserve as possible. Otherwise take a less expensive tour from Porto, a resort due south of Calvi, on the good ship **Explorateur** (www.promenade-en-mer-porto.com; ✆ **07-77-81-50-14**). Tours cost 42€ per person, and some voyages stop for snorkeling trips en-route. Passengers may even spot a pod of dolphins on the trip home.

walk into the sea. Beach restaurants, lazy hotels, and an additional small naturist beach make up the fun.

Those visitors craving a cultural break may drive up to the artsy village of **Pigna** high above Algajola. Looking out to sea from 500m (1,650ft) on high, its leafy pedestrian-only streets offer a bucolic break from the coastal heat. It's also the place to nibble Corsica's inland delights, including Calenzana goat's cheese, chestnut beer, and cured pork and liver *figatellu* sausage.

WHERE TO STAY

The **Hotel Corsica** (www.bestwestern.fr; ✆ **04-95-65-03-64**), is the pick of Calvi's hotels. It has free shuttle bus to cover the mile-long walk to the citadel and town center. Double rooms cost from 149€ to 349€. As accommodation is limited in town, many visitors source a homestay using **Airbnb** (www.airbnb.com). Down the coast in Algajola, the **Hotel Stella Mare** (www.stellamarehotel.com; ✆ **04-95-60-71-18**), is a luxurious 16-room villa set amid tropical flower-strewn grounds. Double rooms range from 70€ to 140€.

Bastia & Around ★

112km (70 miles) E of Calvi

Bastia is Corsica at its most elegant, cosmopolitan, and classy. As the capital of the Northern Corsica (or *Haute-Corse*) region it's blessed with vast piazzas, countless

CORSICA'S LOST WORLD: désert des agriates

Some of the world's best beaches skirt rugged moonscapes far removed from Europe's more gentrified shores. The **Désert des Agriates**—15,000 hectares (37,000 acres) of cactus, olives, wild figs, and even wilder donkeys—is one of them. The brave can hike the 3-day *sentier littoral*, or coastal trail, that runs along the northern Corsican coast. Less hardy visitors may sail into the park on day ferry **Le Popeye** from the resort of St-Florent (www.lepopeye.com; *C* 06-62-16-23-76) instead. Tickets cost 20€, or 12€ for children aged 10 and under. Launches deposit their spellbound passengers at the peerless **Plage du Lodu**. The heart-stoppingly beautiful beach of **Plage Saleccia** is a 45-minute hike from here.

But Plage Saleccia was nearly placed off-limits in the 1970s. The adjoining Désert des Agriates was once Corsica's breadbasket, but over-intensive production over the centuries had reduced this grain producing area to wasteland. When mainland officials were searching for France's next nuclear test site, they stumbled on this blank spot on the map. Fortunately, near atomic disaster was averted. The beach's potential as a film set backdrop was proved by the filming of WWII movie "*The Longest Day*" (although the actors no doubt had to bring their own water and parasols, as guests must still do today). With no commerce for miles around, the beach's movie set looks remain intact today.

churches, and over 100 **pavement cafés**. Like Calvi, it's immersed in year-round sunshine. Yet it adds boutiques, boat trips, and a fabulous weekend market to the mix. We dare you to drink a *pastis* on **place Saint Nicolas** at sundown and not wonder why the rest of Europe isn't sitting at the adjoining table.

But Bastia is a tale of two cities, not one. Step through the winding lanes south of place Saint Nicolas and into the **Vieux Port**. This icon of Corsica's past is stuffed with flamboyantly painted fishing boats of every size. Their daily catch is loaded onto the restaurant tables that occupy every spare inch around the quay. A kaleidoscope of towering townhouses forms an amphitheater of color around the harbor. It's a postcard-perfect sight.

Corsica's wild side is most assuredly **Cap Corse**. This spiny peninsula thrusts north from Bastia. It's a land of wild herbs, empty beaches, and tough locals, who cling to traditional mountain life with seemingly no intention of ever leaving. One solitary coastal road rings this endless spit of land. It would be considered courageous to drive around it by car, brave by motorbike, and foolhardy by bicycle, but each journey will deliver memories to last a lifetime.

WHERE TO STAY

Once again, holiday rental sites like **Airbnb** (www.airbnb.com) overcome Bastia's general lack of good hotels. One exception is the charming **Hotel Central** (www.centralhotel.fr; *C* 04-95-31-69-72) near the main place Saint Nicolas. Double rooms feature period fittings and antique floors, and range from 77€ to 180€. On Cap Corse, the stunning **Hotel Brando** (www.castelbrando.com; *C* 04-95-30-10-30) should not be missed. Soak up the pool and Jacuzzi, or wander to the beach over the road. Double rooms cost from 99€ to 199€.

MONACO & THE CORNICHE COAST

13

VILLEFRANCHE-SUR-MER ★★

935km (580 miles) S of Paris; 6.5km (4 miles) E of Nice

Just east of Nice, the coastal Lower Corniche sweeps inland to reveal Villefranche, its medieval Old Town tumbling downhill into the shimmering sea. Paired with a dazzling sheltered bay set against picturesque Cap Ferrat beyond, it's little wonder than countless artists made this beachy getaway their home—or that it's served as the cinematic backdrop for numerous movies including "Ronin" with Robert de Niro, "Dirty Rotten Scoundrels" with Steve Martin, and "Never Say Never Again" starring Sir Sean Connery.

All in all, Villefranche is tailor-made for a romantic wander. Coastal trails run from the marina and beach of Plage Darse to the sandy town beach underneath the train station. Serious strollers may now walk all the way to Nice (with a short hop up to the lower corniche road halfway along), thanks to a newly inaugurated coastal trail.

Essentials

ARRIVING **Trains** arrive from all the Côte d'Azur's coastal resorts from Cannes to Monaco every 30 minutes or so. For rail schedules, visit www.voyages-sncf.com or call ✆ **36-35. Lignes d'Azur** (www.lignesd azur.com; ✆ **08-10-06-10-06**) maintains a **bus** service at 5- to 15-minute intervals aboard line no. 100 from Nice to Monte Carlo via Villefranche. One-way fares cost 1.50€. Buses deposit passengers just above the Old Town, almost directly opposite the tourist information office. Many visitors **drive** via the Basse Corniche (Lower Corniche).

VISITOR INFORMATION The **Office de Tourisme** is on Jardin François-Binon (www.villefranche-sur-mer.com; ✆ **04-93-01-73-68**).

[FastFACTS] VILLEFRANCHE

ATMs/Banks **LCL Banque,** 6 av. du Maréchal Foch (✆ **04-93-76-24-01**).

Internet Access **Chez Net,** 5 place du Marché (www.cheznet.com; ✆ **04-89-08-19-43**).

Mail & Postage **La Poste,** 6 av. Albert 1er (✆ **36-31**).

Pharmacies **Pharmacie Laurent,** 2 av. du Maréchal Foch (✆ **04-93-01-70-10**).

Where to Stay

Hôtel de la Darse ★   If your South of France accommodation needs are satisfied by a balcony, a sea view, and a minibar stocked with your own supermarket rosé, then book now. Euro-for-euro, there are few better hotels in the area than this simple delight. The larger three- and four-person rooms plus several of the doubles boast terraces, while smaller rooms look onto the rear gardens. Granted, breakfast is basic and there is no elevator. But the town center of Villefranche and the locals-only beach of Plage Darse are both a 5-minute stroll away. Parasols and beach towels are also available for hire.

32 avenue du Général de Gaulle. www.hoteldeladarse.com. ✆ **04-93-01-72-54.** 21 units. 79€–98€ double. **Amenities:** Bar; babysitting; free Wi-Fi.

Hotel Villa Patricia ★   This petite seaside hotel really does offer some of the Riviera's cheapest double rooms during in the height of summer. A 5-minute stroll from the water, it also boasts a shared garden sheltered by lemon trees. As one might expect for the price, some rooms are small, while others are oddly shaped, but all are stylish, smart, and exceptionally clean, and share a large lounge area complete with book swap, outdoor sofas, and a piano. It's a gentle 10-minute stroll from Villefranche, Beaulieu, and Cap Ferrat.

310 Avenue de l'Ange Gardien. www.hotel-patricia.riviera.fr. ✆ **04-93-01-06-70.** 10 units. 65€–89€ double; 89€–119€ triple; 80€–119€ suite. Free parking. Closed Dec—Jan. **Amenities:** Free Wi-Fi.

Hôtel Welcome ★★   Villefranche's most prestigious hotel, the Welcome sits in the center of town and has been home to Riviera artists since the 1920s, including author and filmmaker Jean Cocteau (in room 22). Every one of the modern hotel's midsize-to-spacious rooms possesses a balcony and sea views. The on-site **wine bar** spills out onto the quay in warm weather. The hotel also rents out *Orphée,* its eight-person private sailboat, for daily cruises; prices from 650€ per half-day with crew.

3 quai Amiral Courbet. www.welcomehotel.com. ✆ **04-93-76-27-62.** 35 units. 145€–358€ double; 220€–525€ suite. Parking 45€. **Amenities:** Bar; babysitting; room service; free Wi-Fi.

Where to Eat

L'Aparté ★ MODERN FRENCH   One of Villefranche's most acclaimed restaurants is a step back in time, as it's sited on rue Obscure, a medieval street that dates back to the year 1260. Conversely, cuisine is breathtakingly modern. Flambéed duck breast is served with a courgette frappe, herb-crusted rack of lamb with pea purée. Top service combine with fair prices to produce a memorable meal.

1 rue Obscure. ✆ **04-93-01-84-88.** Main courses 18€–24€. Tue-Sun 7:30-10pm.

Le Cosmo ★★ MEDITERRANEAN   This friendly sidewalk cafe has been pulling in punters for a decade—and with good reason. Prices are reasonable, the creative menu is perfectly executed, and the setting is sublime: The restaurant's terraced seating overlooks Cocteau's Chapelle St-Pierre and the seafront beyond. Sample sautéed scallops with aubergine caviar, or *salade Cosmo,* topped with avocado, shrimp, grapefruit, and hearts of palm. Dozens of fantastical ice cream creations (think yogurt ice cream piled high with strawberries and raspberry puree, or a tower of praline ice cream, whipped cream, and chocolate sauce) are also on offer.

11 pl. Amélie Pollonais. www.restaurant-lecosmo.fr. ✆ **04-93-01-84-05.** Main courses 14€–25€. Daily 7:45am–2am.

Exploring Villefranche

Villefranche's long arc of golden sand, **plage des Marinières,** is the principal attraction for most visitors. From here, **quai Courbet** runs along the sea to the colorful Old Town past scores of bobbing boats; it's lined with waterside restaurants.

Old-town action revolves around **place Amélie Pollonnais,** a delightful square shaded by palms and spread with the tables of six easygoing restaurants. It's also the site of a **Sunday antiques market**, where people from across the Riviera come to root through vintage tourism posters, silverware, 1930s jewelry, and ex-hotel linens. Villefranche has several other great markets, too. An **artisanal market** occupies place Amélie Pollonnais every day except Sunday. In front of Jardin François Binon at the top of the village, an **antiques bazaar** takes place each Sunday. Each Saturday the same spot is dedicated to the sale of **organic local delicacies**, including olive tapenade, local cheeses, and paella.

The painter, writer, filmmaker, and well-respected dilettante Jean Cocteau left a fine memorial to the town's inhabitants. He spent a year (1956–57) painting frescoes on the 14th-century walls of the Romanesque **Chapelle St-Pierre,** quai Courbet (✆ **04-93-76-90-70**). He presented it to "the fishermen of Villefranche in homage to the Prince of Apostles, the patron of fishermen." In the apse is a depiction of the miracle of St. Peter walking on the water, not knowing that an angel supports him. Villefranche's busty local women, in their regional costumes, are honored on the left side of the narthex. Admission is 3€, free for children under 15. In spring and summer, it is open Wednesday to Monday 10am to noon and 3 to 7pm; fall and winter hours are Wednesday to Monday 10am to noon and 2 to 6pm. It's closed from mid-November to mid-December.

A short coastal path leads from the car park below place Amélie Pollonnais to the **16th-century citadelle.** This castle dominates the bay, and its ramparts can be wandered around at leisure. Inside the citadel sits a cluster of small, locally focused **museums** (✆ **04-93-76-33-27**), including the **Fondation Musée-Volti,** a collection of voluptuous female sculptures by Villefranche artist Volti (Antoniucci Voltigero) and **Le Musée Goetz-Boumeester**, featuring around 50 artworks by Dutch artist Christine Boumeester. Opening hours are July and August Monday and Wednesday to Saturday 10am to noon, Wednesday to Monday 3pm to 7pm; June and September Monday and Wednesday to Saturday 9am to noon, Wednesday to Monday 3pm to 6pm; October and December to May Monday and Wednesday to Saturday 10am to noon, Wednesday to Monday 2pm to 5pm. Admission is free.

ST-JEAN-CAP-FERRAT ★★

942km (584 miles) S of Paris; 9.5km (6 miles) E of Nice

Of all the oases along the Côte d'Azur, no other place has the snob appeal of Cap-Ferrat. It's a 15km (9¼-mile) promontory sprinkled with luxurious villas and outlined by sheltered bays, beaches, and sun-kissed coves. In the charming port of St-Jean, the harbor accommodates yachts, fishing boats, and a dozen low-key eateries.

It's worth mentioning that Cap-Ferrat is seriously wealthy. As in seriously, seriously rich. Stars like David Niven and Gregory Peck called 'Le Cap' home before a new generation of Russian oligarchs and Hollywood A-listers moved in. The world's most expensive property, Villa Leopolda, went on sale here a few years back for a cool half-billion dollars. In 2012, the BBC confirmed that the peninsula is the second most

LEARNING FRENCH on the riviera

Studying Europe's most beautiful language on the continent's most stunning shoreline is surely a bonus. Either way, it sure beats Rosetta Stone. Villefranche's **Institute de Français** (www.institutde francais.com) is widely regarded as the finest French language school in the region. The classroom overlooks the Mediterranean and a local breakfast and lunch are included in the program. That said, it's far from a vacation. So much is packed into the daily program that attendees start dreaming in French by the end of their month-long course—if they have any time for sleep at all. The high fees of 2,910€ per month from December to April and 3,520€ per month from May to November reflect the high achievement levels of the course. Local accommodation can be arranged by the school.

The **Alliance Française** (www.alliance-francaise-nice.com) in Nice is more low-key. Its 2-week courses are popular with youngsters and start at 110€ for 2 hours per day for 2 weeks, rising to around 450€ for more intensive 2-week classes.

As the Riviera is a trilingual destination with a century-old legacy of tourism, finding a flexible **private language tutor** for your stay is a cinch. Search the classified advertisements on local listings board AngloInfo (riviera.angloinfo.com), or post a message yourself. Individual tuition prices hover between 20€ and 30€ per our.

expensive location in the world (since you ask, Monaco came first). A wonderful coastal path loops past many of the world's richest residents' private homes.

Essentials

ARRIVING   **Trains** connect Beaulieu with Nice, Monaco, and the rest of the Côte d'Azur every 30 minutes. Many visitors then take a **taxi** to St-Jean from Beaulieu's rail station; alternatively, it's a 30-minute walk along Cap-Ferrat's promenade Maurice Rouvier to St-Jean village. For **rail** information, visit www.voyages-sncf.com or call ℂ **36-35. Bus** line no. 81 connects Nice with St-Jean every hour. One-way fares costs 1.50€. For bus information and schedules, contact **Lignes d'Azur** (www.lignesdazur. com; ℂ **08-10-06-10-06**). By **car** from Nice, take D6098 (the *basse corniche*) east.

VISITOR INFORMATION   St-Jean's **Office de Tourisme** is on 59 av. Denis-Séméria (www.saintjeancapferrat.fr; ℂ **04-93-76-08-90**).

[FastFACTS] ST-JEAN

ATMs/Banks   **Banque Populaire Côte d'Azur,** 5 av. Claude Vignon, St-Jean 06230 (ℂ **04-89-81-11-42**).

Mail & Postage   **La Poste,** 51 av. Denis Séméria, St-Jean 06230 (ℂ **36-31**).

Pharmacies   **Pharmacie Pont Saint Jean,** 57 bd. Dominique Durandy, St-Jean 06230 (ℂ **04-93-01-62-50**).

Where to Stay

Grand Hôtel du Cap-Ferrat ★★★   Put simply, this grande dame of a hotel is the greatest building on Europe's richest peninsula. It's sumptuous, stylish, and incredibly sexy. Set on 17 acres of tropical trees and manicured lawns, it's been the exclusive retreat of the international elite since 1908. The **Le Spa** wellness centre spills outside into curtained cabanas, where massages and other treatments can be indulged in. Aside from the modernist guestrooms, the coolest place to hang out is the seaside **Club Dauphin** beach club (nonguests can gain access for 90€ per day). It's reached by a funicular rail pod that descends from the hotel. The children of many visiting celebrities, including the Kennedys and Paul McCartney, have learned to swim in the Olympic-size infinity pool.

71 bd. du Général-de-Gaulle. www.ghcf.fr. © **04-93-76-50-50.** 73 units. 285€–1,120€ double; 700€–5,100€ suite. Closed Jan and Feb. Amenities: 3 restaurants; bar; babysitting; beach club; bikes; Olympic-size heated outdoor pool; room service; spa; tennis; free Wi-Fi.

Hôtel Brise Marine ★   An Italianate villa constructed in 1878, the Brise Marine is tucked into a quiet residential neighborhood south of St-Jean. Rooms are simply furnished and sunny, with enchanting sea views. Breakfast on the rose-twined terrace, and you can almost imagine you're aboard one of the luxury super-yachts bobbing off nearby Paloma Plage.

58 av. Jean-Mermoz. www.hotel-brisemarine.com. © **04-93-76-04-36.** 16 units. 160€–203€ double; 190€–233€ triple. Parking 15€. Closed Nov–Feb. **Amenities:** Bar; room service; free Wi-Fi.

Where to Eat

Le Cap ★★ FRENCH/INTERNATIONAL   The Grand Hôtel du Cap-Ferrat's acclaimed gourmet restaurant is overseen by head chef Didier Aniès. His Michelin-starred cuisine is heavy on caviar, oysters, and luxurious French classics, while the wine list includes every vintage of the esteemed Château d'Yquem label since the 1890s. Some Michelin starred restaurants listed in this guidebook welcome guests wearing Birkenstocks, shorts, and an eager smile. Le Cap is not one of them. Expect stiff formality as bow-tied waiters open silver cloches to reveal Wagyu beef with oysters and grapefruit, and slow-baked John Dory with citron confit.

71 bd. du Général-de-Gaulle. www.ghcf.fr. © **04-93-76-50-26.** Reservations required. Main courses 86€–108€; fixed-price menu 158€–198€. Daily 7:45–9:45pm. Closed Oct–March.

Capitaine Cook ★ PROVENÇAL/SEAFOOD   Perhaps the peninsula's most beloved eatery, Capitaine Cook is run by husband-and-wife team Lionel and Nelly Pelletier. Dine outdoors on the leafy terrace or indoors within the ruggedly maritime dining room. The menu is particularly strong on hearty yet imaginative fish dishes, from stuffed sardines to salmon ravioli.

11 av. Jean-Mermoz. © **04-93-76-02-66.** Reservations recommended. Main courses 18€–30€; fixed-price menu 27€–32€. Fri–Tues 12:30–2pm; Thurs–Tues 7:30–10:30pm. Closed mid-Nov–Dec.

Exploring St-Jean

One way to enjoy the area's beautiful backdrop is to stroll the public pathway that loops around Cap-Ferrat from Beaulieu all the way to Villefranche. The most scenic section runs from chic **plage de Paloma,** near Cap-Ferrat's southernmost tip, to **pointe St-Hospice,** where a panoramic view of the Riviera landscape unfolds. Allow around 3 hours to hike from St-Jean to family-friendly **plage Passable,** on the northwestern "neck" of the peninsula.

Villa Ephrussi de Rothschild ★★★ HISTORIC HOME/MUSEUM   The winter residence of Baronne Béatrice Ephrussi de Rothschild, this Italianate villa was

CAP-FERRAT'S HOMES OF THE rich & famous

The global aristocratic, business, and cultural elite have long favored Cap-Ferrat. As you wander around, keep your eyes out for these four key villas. **Lo Scoglietto** is a rococo pink edifice looking out towards Monaco from the promenade Maurice Rouvier coastal path. Once owned by Charlie Chaplin, it later passed to fellow British actor David Niven. More famous still is **Villa Mauresque** at the Cap's southern tip. In 1928 it was acquired by British author Somerset Maugham. The writer took up residence again after World War II to find that the liberating Allies had bombed his ornamental garden and the occupying Italians had raided his wine cellar. More modernist is **Villa La Voile**. This yacht-shaped mansion has 'sails' that draw across the property each day to diffuse the Riviera sun. To lend an idea of Cap-Ferrat's worth, that particular project was overseen by Lord Norman Foster, the architect responsible for the world's biggest airport (in Beijing). Peek over the fence between Villefranche and Cap-Ferrat at the **Villa Nelcotte**. Once owned by Count Ernst de Brulatour, a secretary of the American embassy in France, then by Samuel Goldenberg, a wealthy American survivor of the Titanic, it was rented in 1971 by reprobate rocker Keith Richards. That summer the Rolling Stones recorded the album *Exile on Main Street* in the villa's sweaty basement. John Lennon and Eric Clapton dropped by, as did half the personalities of the Riviera underworld.

completed in 1912 according to the finicky specifications of its ultra-rich owner. Today the pink edifice preserves an eclectic collection, gathered over her lifetime: 18th-century furniture, Tiepolo ceilings, tapestries from Gobelin, a games table gifted from Marie-Antoinette (Ephrussi's hero) to a friend, and tiny seats for her beloved poodles. The nine themed gardens, from Florentine to Japanese, are a particular delight. An attractive tea salon overlooks the Bay of Villefranche.

1 av. Ephrussi de Rothschild. www.villa-ephrussi.com. ℂ **04-93-01-33-09.** Admission 13.5€ adults, 9.50€ students and children 7–17, free for children 6 and under. July–Aug daily 10am–7pm; March–June and Sept–Oct daily 10am–6pm; Nov–Feb Mon–Fri 2–6pm, Sat–Sun 10am–6pm.

Villa Santo Sospir ★★ HISTORIC HOME/MUSEUM   As the story goes, in spring 1950 socialite Francine Weisweiller invited Jean Cocteau to her Cap-Ferrat villa for dinner. The Riviera artist ended up staying for 13 years. Cocteau proceeded to fresco nearly every wall of the property, while Greta Garbo, Marlene Dietrich and Coco Chanel partied within. Picasso sojourned here too, and ended up painting a few surfaces while on the scene. Weisweiller's former property manager Eric Marteau now acts as a caretaker to this rare property, which may only be booked by private groups (both small and large) in advance. The chance to step into any Cap-Ferrat villa, let along one adorned by Jean Cocteau, makes it worth the call.

14 avenue Jean Cocteau. www.villasantosospir.fr. ℂ **04-93-76-00-16.** Admission 12€. Open all year but visits by appointment only.

BEAULIEU-SUR-MER ★

941km (583 miles) S of Paris; 9.5km (6 miles) E of Nice

Cradled on the mainland just east of Cap-Ferrat, the Belle Epoque resort of Beaulieu-sur-Mer has long attracted *bons vivants* with its casino and fine restaurants. Its genteel environs once sheltered Sir Winston Churchill. Its palm-backed beaches and alfresco restaurants now welcome visiting celebrities from Bono to Sylvester Stallone.

Essentials

ARRIVING **Trains** connect Beaulieu with Nice, Monaco, and the rest of the Côte d'Azur every 30 minutes. For **rail** information, visit www.voyages-sncf.com or call 𝄢 **36-35. Bus** line no. 100 from Nice to Monte Carlo passes through Beaulieu. One-way fares costs 1.50€. For bus information and schedules, contact **Lignes d'Azur** (www.lignesdazur.com; 𝄢 **08-10-06-10-06**). By **car** from Nice, take D6098 (the *basse corniche*) east.

VISITOR INFORMATION Beaulieu's **Office de Tourisme** is on place Georges Clémenceau (www.beaulieusurmer.fr; 𝄢 **04-93-01-02-21**) adjacent to the Train Station.

[FastFACTS] BEAULIEU

ATMs/Banks **Banque Populaire Côte d'Azur,** 40 boulevard Marinoni (𝄢 **04-89-81-10-56**).

Mail & Postage **La Poste,** place Georges Clemenceau (𝄢 **36-31**).

Pharmacies **Pharmacie Internationale,** 38 boulevard Marinoni (𝄢 **04-93-01-01-39**).

Where to Stay

Le Havre Bleu ★ You could easily spend a fortune on a luxury hotel. Or you could check into this Riviera stalwart that underwent a design overhaul in 2013 and blow your money in boutiques and beach clubs instead. Le Havre Bleu has a variety of rooms, some with terraces and patios, which never rise above 100€ per night all year. Breakfast (10€) is served on the sunny communal terrace, where guests may sip a rosé or a café au lait any time of the day. The establishment also offers what vies to be the least expensive parking in the South of France.

29 bl Maréchal Joffre. www.lehavrebleu.com. 𝄢 **04-93-01-01-40.** 19 units. 70€–95€ double. Parking 8€. **Amenities:** Bar; free Wi-Fi.

Royal Riviera ★ At last, a bona-fide Riviera luxury hotel with all the trappings, yet none of the pretention. The palatial splendor of the Royal Riviera's interior is paired with contemporary elegance inside the light, airy guestrooms. Rooms and suites inside the ancient Orangerie annex are even cooler, calmer, and quieter. Two factors mark the Royal Riviera out from other hotels in the area: location and facilities. Guests may take a short stroll into Beaulieu, Villefranche, or St-Jean-Cap-Ferrat, or simply wander along the private beach and through the flower-filled gardens. The hotel's low-key friendliness extends to kids too, who may enjoy treasure hunts, waterskiing lessons, and pottery workshops while grown-ups lounge at the gigantic pool.

3 av Jean Monnet. www.royal-riviera.com. ✆ **04-93-76-31-00.** 94 units. 170€–850€ double; from 630€ suite. Parking 15€. **Amenities:** 2 restaurants; bar; babysitting; concierge; exercise room; indoor pool; outdoor pool; private beach; spa; room service; free Wi-Fi.

Where to Eat

The African Queen ★ FRENCH/INTERNATIONAL   A lively mix of yachties, celebrity patrons, and excellent cuisine makes this portside restaurant perennially popular. Wood-fired pizzas are superb; the finely chopped *salade Niçoise* is dressed at your table; the sole *meunière* is a buttery classic. Service can be erratic, but both the menu and the atmosphere are a delight. Celebrity-spotting opportunities abound all summer long.

Port de Plaisance. www.africanqueen.fr. ✆ **04-93-01-10-85.** Reservations recommended. Pizzas 12€–28€; main courses 12€–80€. Daily noon–midnight. Closed some holidays.

Pignatelle ★ FRENCH   A neighborhood favourite that spills out from a rustic dining room onto a simple, sunny terrace. La Pignatelle's à la carte selection and bargain fixed-price menus don't do pretention. Solid yet sublime starters include smoked salmon crêpes, frog's legs with parsley sauce, and garlic-laced escargot. Mains won't earn a Michelin star but have already won the hearts of local French diners: think roast rabbit with Dijon mustard, and cod with aïoli Provençal.

10 rue de Quincenet. www.lapignatelle.fr. ✆ **04-93-01-03-37.** Main courses 17€–28€; fixed-price lunch 15.50€; fixed-price menu 24€–36€. Thurs-Tues noon–2pm and 7–10pm (Nov–March closed Wed & Thurs).

Exploring Beaulieu

All of Beaulieu's (admittedly low-key) action takes place between two almost entirely public beaches: **Plage des Fourmis** near Cap-Ferrat and **La Petite Afrique** to the east of town. The rococo resort's ancient casino, age-old cafés, and daily market lie in between. Beaulieu's luxury marina is a fine place for a stroll. Its long line of alfresco harbor restaurants get progressively cheaper as you wander eastwards towards the sands of La Petite Afrique.

Villa Kérylos ★★ HISTORIC HOME/MUSEUM   This replica ancient Greek residence, constructed between 1902 and 1908, was painstakingly designed by archaeologist and devoted Hellenophile Theodore Reinach. Both indoors and out, the villa is a fastidiously flawless copy of a second-century Greek home. All period furniture was re-created using traditional Greek methods, while various rooms incorporated 20th-century conveniences, such as running water in the villa's *balaneion*, or thermal baths. The bucolic waterside gardens are dotted with olive and pomegranate trees and offer sweeping vistas over nearby Cap-Ferrat.

Impasse Gustave Eiffel. www.villa-kerylos.com. ✆ **04-93-01-01-44.** Admission 11.50€ adults, 9€ students and children 7–17, free for children 6 and under. July–Aug daily 10am–7pm; March–June and Sept–Oct daily 10am–6pm; Nov–Feb Mon–Fri 2–6pm, Sat–Sun 10am–6pm.

EZE & LA TURBIE ★★

942km (584 miles) S of Paris; 11km (6¾ miles) NE of Nice

The hamlets of Eze and La Turbie, 6.5km (4 miles) apart, are picture-perfect hill villages that literally cling to the mountains. Both have fortified medieval cores overlooking the coast, and both were built during the early Middle Ages to stave off raids from Saracen pirates. In Eze's case, it's now tour buses that make daily invasions into town. Impossibly cute streets contain galleries, boutiques, and artisans' shops. La Turbie is much quieter, offering a welcome respite from the coast's summertime heat.

Essentials

ARRIVING   **Trains** connect Eze-sur-Mer with Nice, Monaco, and the rest of the Côte d'Azur every 30 minutes. You may take a taxi from here up (1,400 ft.) to Eze; alternatively, bus no. 83 connects the rail station with the hilltop village. For rail information, visit www.voyages-sncf.com or call ✆ 36-35. **Bus** line no. 82 runs between Nice and Eze around every 90 minutes, while five to seven daily buses (no. 116) connect Nice and La Turbie. Both journeys take 40 minutes. One-way fares cost 1.50€. For all bus information and schedules, contact **Lignes d'Azur** (www.lignesdazur.com; ✆ **08-10-06-10-06**). By **car** from Nice, take the spellbindingly pretty D6007 (the *moyenne corniche*) east.

VISITOR INFORMATION   Eze's **Office de Tourisme** is on place du Général-de-Gaulle, Eze-Village (www.eze-tourisme.com; ✆ **04-93-41-26-00**). La Turbie's small **tourist information point** is at 2 place Detras, La Turbie (www.ville-la-turbie.fr; ✆ **04-93-41-21-15**).

[FastFACTS] EZE & LA TURBIE

ATMs/Banks   **Société Générale,** place de la Colette, Eze 06360 ((✆ **04-92-41-51-10**); **BNP Paribas,** 6 av Général de Gaulle, La Turbie 06360 ((✆ **08-20-82-00-01**).

Mail & Postage   **La Poste,** av. du Jardin Exotique, Eze 06360; **La Poste,** place Neuve, La Turbie 06360; both ((✆ **36-31**).

Pharmacies   **Pharmacie Lecoq,** place Colette, Eze 06360 ((✆ **04-93-41-06-17**); **Pharmacie de La Turbie,** 6 av Général de Gaulle, La Turbie 06360 ((✆ **04-93-41-16-50**).

Where to Stay

Château de la Chèvre d'Or ★★★   No hotel better sums up the glamour and grace of the French Riviera than La Chèvre d'Or. This resort hotel is built into and around the elegant hilltop town of Eze. Each sumptuously decorated suite is a grand apartment with a panoramic view of the coastline. It's a habitual favorite of royalty and A-listers, and recent makeovers have made it popular with vacationing families and young hipsters as well. The 38 terraced gardens drip down the hill towards the Mediterranean to ensure absolute privacy—indeed there's a ratio of one garden and three staff members to each room or suite. The best thing about La Chèvre d'Or? That would be the eponymous double-Michelin-starred **restaurant** overseen by top chef Ronan Kervaree (set menus 80€–230€). Experimental dishes include a vegan square decorated with an edible garden of herbs and flowers; San Remo shrimp wrapped in oyster-infused gossamer-thin pasta; and baby lamb shot through with parsley and violet.

Rue du Barri. www.chevredor.com. ✆ **04-92-10-66-66**. 37 units. 300€–610€ double; suites from 740€—2,600€ suite. Parking 15€. Closed Dec–Feb. **Amenities:** 4 restaurants; bar; babysitting; exercise room; outdoor pool; room service; sauna; free Wi-Fi.

Where to Eat

Gascogne Café ★ FRENCH/ITALIAN   On the main road just outside of Eze's fortified Old Town, this bustling eatery is a friendly spot to sample authentic local fare. The menu ranges from traditional flavors (homemade lasagna, sea bass on a bed of ratatouille) to more creative offerings (Asian-style rolls stuffed with snails and garlic cream). Tasty pizzas are also available. Ambience is decidedly casual.

151 av. de Verdun, place de la Collette, Eze 06360. www.gascogne-hotel-restaurant.fr. *©* **04-93-41-18-50.** Main courses 10€–24€; fixed-price menus 17€–29€. Daily 12:30–3pm and 7:30–10pm.

Hostellerie Jérôme ★★ FRENCH/ITALIAN   The village of La Turbie is a den of fine dining. One could do far worse than try Corsican delights at **A Stretta Corsa**, 10 place Detras (*©* **04-93-17-72-18**), or cheese specialist **Le Coin**, 9 place Banville (*©* **04-93-57-52-19**). But nowhere compares to Jérôme. Michelin-starred head chef Bruno Cironi presides over a magic show of 10 to 15 dishes on each set menu. Nor does his team shy away from less revered regional delights like pigeon, chickpeas, and zucchini flowers. Not only that, but his allegedly self-taught wife oversees an enviable wine cellar. The establishment also purveys **five classy bedrooms** (doubles 98€ to 140€) and manages the altogether-simpler **Café de la Fontaine** next door, which has a daily market-inspired set menu for 30€ per person.

20 rue Comte de Cessole, La Turbie. www.hostelleriejerome.com. *©* **04-93-41-18-50.** Main courses 34€–53€; fixed-price menus 75€–130€. Wed–Sun 7:30–10pm. Closed Nov–mid-Feb.

Exploring Eze & La Turbie

Aside from its pretty lanes, the leading attraction in Eze is the **Jardin d'Eze** ★, 20 rue du Château (*©* **04-93-41-10-30**). Here exotic plants are interspersed with feminine sculptures by Jean Philippe Richard, all perched atop the town at 1,400 feet. Admission is 6€ adults, 2.50€ students and ages 12 to 25, and free children 11 and under. In July and August, it's open daily 9am to 7:30pm; the rest of the year it opens daily at 9am and closes between 4 and 7pm, depending on the time of sunset.

La Turbie boasts an impressive monument erected by Roman emperor Augustus in 6 B.C., the **Trophée des Alps (Trophy of the Alps)** ★. Still partially intact today, it was created to celebrate the subjugation of the French Alpine tribes by the Roman armies. The nearby **Musée du Trophée d'Auguste,** cours Albert-1er de Monaco (*©* **04-93-41-20-84**), is an interactive mini-museum containing finds from digs nearby, a historical 3D film, and details about the monument's restoration. Both the ruins and the museum are open Tuesday to Sunday mid-May to mid-September 9:30am to 1pm and 2:30 to 6:30pm, and mid-September to mid-May 10am to 1:30pm and 2:30 to 5pm. Admission to both sites is 5.50€ adults, free children 17 and under.

MONACO ★★★

939km (582 miles) S of Paris; 18km (11 miles) E of Nice

This sunny stretch of coast became the property of the Grimaldi clan in 1297, when one Francesco Grimaldi tricked his way into the fortress protecting the harbor. The dynasty has maintained something resembling independence ever since. In recent decades the clan has turned Monaco into the world's chicest city-state, with its own mini-airport (with direct helicopter links to Nice and St-Tropez, no less).

Monaco

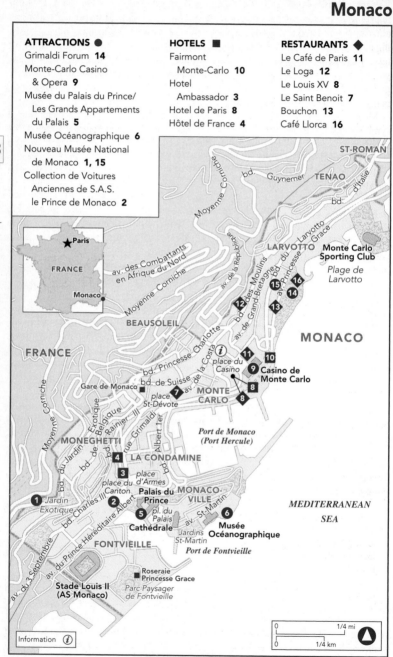

ST-ROMAN

TENAO

LARVOTTO   Monte Carlo
Sporting Club

*Plage de
Larvotto*

BEAUSOLEIL

MONACO

place du
Casino

Casino de
Monte Carlo

Gare de Monaco

*place
St-Dévote*

MONTE
CARLO

FRANCE

Moyenne Corniche

MONEGHETTI

LA CONDAMINE

*place
d'Armes*

*Port de Monaco
(Port Hercule)*

Palais du
Prince

MONACO-
VILLE

*MEDITERRANEAN
SEA*

*Jardin
Exotique*

*pl. du
Palais*

Cathédrale

*Jardins
St-Martin*

Musée
Océanographique

FONTVIEILLE

Port de Fontvieille

Roseraie
Princesse Grace

*Parc Paysager
de Fontvieille*

Stade Louis II
(AS Monaco)

Information ⓘ

0   1/4 mi
0   1/4 km

FRANCE

★ Paris

FRANCE

Monaco

Hemmed in by France on three sides and the Mediterranean on the fourth, this feudal anomaly harbors the world's greatest number of billionaires per capita. And as almost everybody knows, the Monégasques do not pay taxes. Celebrity exiles—including tennis player Rafael Nadal and racing driver Lewis Hamilton—are attracted by the tax regime too. Nearly all of Monaco's revenue comes from banking, tourism, and gambling. Better still, in an astute feat of cunning, local residents aren't allowed to gamble away their inheritance, so visitors must bring a passport to play on the Principality's famed poker, roulette, and blackjack tables.

Monaco, or, more precisely, its capital of Monte Carlo, has for a century been a symbol of glamour. The 1956 marriage of Prince Rainier III to actress Grace Kelly enhanced its status. She met the prince when she was in Cannes to promote "To Catch a Thief." Their daughter Caroline was born in 1957; a son, Albert, in 1958; and a second daughter, Stephanie, in 1965. The actress's life and times were recently relived on the silver screen in "Grace of Monaco." Starring Nicole Kidman as Grace Kelly, the movie opened at the 2014 Cannes Film Festival.

Prince Rainier was nicknamed the "Builder Prince" as he expanded Monaco by building into the Mediterranean. Prince Albert took over from his late father in 2005 and burnishes his "Eco-Prince" credentials with pride. Newer, more environmentally conscious land-reclamation schemes near the Fairmont Hotel were announced in 2014, and work starts on this man-made yacht-lined peninsula soon. The Principality also has its own green car manufacturer, Venturi—although this marquee specializes in a typically Monégasque market for all-electric supercars.

Fortunately for the Grimaldi line, Albert married his girlfriend, South African swimmer Charlene Wittstock, in July 2011, now Her Serene Highness The Princess of Monaco. Despite rumors of a pre-wedding fallout, the couple are idolized in the Principality. Following a hasty course in both Monégasque dialect and European court protocol, Princess Charlene is now a familiar sight at society events. The royal couple's official portrait has pride of place in every bar, hotel, and bakery in the land.

Essentials

ARRIVING   Monaco has rail, bus, highway—and helicopter—connections from other coastal cities, particularly Nice. There are no border formalities when entering Monaco from France. The 19km (12 miles) **drive** from Nice takes around 30 minutes and runs along the N7 Moyenne Corniche. The pretty D6098 coast road takes a little longer. **Lignes d'Azur** (www.lignesdazur.com; ✆ **08-10-06-10-06**) runs a **bus** service at 15-minute intervals aboard line no. 100 from Nice to Monte Carlo. One-way bus transit from Nice costs 1.50€. **Trains** arrive every 30 minutes from Cannes, Nice, Menton, and Antibes. Monaco's underground railway station *(gare)* is on place St. Devote. A system of pedestrian tunnels, escalators, and elevators riddle the Principality, and such an underground walkway links the train station to Monte Carlo. The scheduled **chopper** service to Nice Airport costs 120€ via **Heli Air Monaco** (www.heliairmonaco.com; ✆ **92-05-00-50**). By **bus** it's just 20€ (www.niceairportxpress.com; ✆ **04-97-00-07-00**).

> ### Earth Calling Monaco
>
> To call Monaco from within France, dial 00 (the access code for all international long-distance calls from France); followed by the **country code, 377;** and then the eight-digit local phone number. (Don't dial 33; that's the country code for France.)

VISITOR INFORMATION The **Direction du Tourisme et des Congrés** tourist office is at 2A bd. des Moulins (www.visitmonaco.com; ☏ **92-16-61-16**).

CITY LAYOUT The second-smallest state in Europe (Vatican City is the tiniest), Monaco consists of four parts. The Old Town, **Monaco-Ville,** on a rocky promontory 60m (197 ft.) high. It's the seat of the Prince's Palace and the government building, as well as the Oceanographic Museum. To the west, **La Condamine** is at the foot of the Old Town, forming its ritzy harbor and port sector. This area also has an open-air daily market. Up from the port (Monaco is seriously steep) is **Monte Carlo,** the playground of royalty and celebrity, and the setting for the casino, the Tourist Office, and various luxurious hotels. The fourth part, **Fontvieille,** is a neat industrial suburb housing the Monaco Football club, which was purchased by Russian billionaire Dmitry Rybolovlev. Thanks to the Russian's financial backing, the club was promoted to the French premier league in 2013, and topped the table several times in 2014.

SPECIAL EVENTS Two of the most-watched **car-racing events** in the world take place here in January (**Le Rallye**) and May (the **Grand Prix**); see www.acm.mc and www.formula1monaco.com. The coolest place to watch both events is on the top deck of the **Yacht Club de Monaco**, a liner-shaped restaurant, bar, and club designed by Lord Norman Foster, which opened in summer 2014. The **Monte-Carlo Masters** ATP tennis tournament (www.monte-carlorolexmasters.com) takes place in April. The **Monte-Carlo International Fireworks Festival** lasts all summer long. The skies above the harbor are lit up several times a week as millions of euros go up in smoke, courtesy of those who can assuredly afford it.

[FastFACTS] MONACO

ATMs/Banks Among many others, there are several banks along boulevard Albert 1er behind the Port of Monaco.

Internet Access **Bilig Café,** 11 rue Princesse Caroline (☏ **97-98-20-43**).

Mail & Postage **La Poste,** place de la Mairie in Monte-Carlo (☏ **36-31**).

Pharmacies **Pharmacie Internationale,** 22 rue Grimaldi (☏ **04-93-50-35-99**).

Getting Around

BY FOOT Aside from two very steep hills, the world's second-smallest country is **pedestrian-friendly.** Hardy local Jean-Marc Ferrie at **Monaco Rando** (www.monaco-rando.com; ☏ **06-30-12-57-03**) organizes **guided hikes** around his hometown from 10€ per person with an interpreter in-tow.

BY TAXI Taxis wait outside Monaco train station, or call ☏ **08-20-20-98-98.**

BY PUBLIC TRANSPORT CAM (www.cam.mc; ☏ **97-70-22-22**) runs buses inside the Principality. Lines nos. 1 and 2 link Monaco-Ville with the casino area. CAM's **solar-powered shuttle boat** hops between the banks of Monaco's port every 20 minutes. The ride is great for kids and connects the casino area with foot of Monaco-Ville. All CAM tickets cost 2€.

BY OPEN-TOP BUS **Monaco–Le Grand Tour** (www.monacolegrandtour.com; ☏ **97-70-26-36**) open-top minibuses allows visitors to hop-on and hop-off at the Principality's 12 main sights. Day passes cost 18€ adults; 7€ children between 4 and 11; free children under 4.

BY ELECTRIC CAR It may be the land of the gas-guzzling Grand Prix, but Monaco is a global pioneer in green technology and is justly proud of its eco-credentials. Join the club with a rented two-person **Renault Twizy** (a super-tiny electric car; 50€ for 4 hours) or an **Estrimo Brio** (an even cuter electric buggy; same rates) from **MC Eco Rental** (www.mc-eco-rental.com; ✆ **06-80-86-54-09**). These electric cars enjoy complimentary parking anywhere in Monaco. Guests renting either vehicle for more than 2 hours may have them delivered to their hotel for free.

BY LUXURY CAR Of course, nothing shouts Monaco more than a rented **Ferrari California** (1,500€ per day) or a **Porsche 911** (790€ per day). Reserve your ride with **Elite Rentacar** (www.eliterent.com; ✆ **97-77-17-37**).

Where to Stay

Fairmont Monte Carlo ★★ This five-star hotel is easily Monaco's most fun. It combines fine-dining restaurants, a spa, and a rooftop pool with an unstuffy attitude; albeit one backed by a legion of ever-smiling, mostly Italian, staff. Of course, this vision of modern opulence is also one most valuable pieces of real estate on the Côte d'Azur. It dips into the Mediterranean from behind the Casino de Monte-Carlo—indeed, a private passageway runs to the casino's rear entrance—and guests may combine the endless breakfast with the best sea views in the Principality. Formula 1 fans should also note that the fastest part of the Monaco Grand Prix zips right beneath the basement. The Fairmont also has a partnership with four local beach clubs, where families are dropped off with towels, mineral water, and sun spray, then picked up on demand. Diners are in for a treat too. Choose between bistro **Saphir**, Japanese atelier **Nobu** (opened in 2013), and rooftop Italian restaurant **Horizonte** (newly opened in 2014).

12 av. des Spélugues. www.fairmont.com/montecarlo. ✆ **93-50-65-00.** 602 units. 279€–879€ double; from 889€ suite. Parking 50€. **Amenities:** 3 restaurants; 2 bars; babysitting; concierge; health club; 1 outdoor pools; room service; spa; Wi-Fi (20€/day or free if you enroll in the Fairmont President Club at no charge at check-in).

Hôtel Ambassador ★ A 5-minute stroll from the main Monaco action, the Ambassador makes a bargain base from which to explore the Principality. Elegant guestrooms benefit from a recent style overhaul. Dimensions are tiny however (but heh, the entire country occupies less than one-square-mile, so little wonder). A buffet breakfast (included in the price) is offered next door in the cheap and tasty **P&P** restaurant and pizzeria.

10 avenue Prince Pierre, Monaco. www.ambassadormonaco.com. ✆ **97-97-96-96.** 35 units. 110€–225€ double. Parking 18€. Amenities: bar, free Wi-Fi.

Hôtel de France ★ Not to be confused with the Hôtel de Paris below, which is up to ten times the price, this cute two-star option awoke from a thorough renovation in 2012. The location is superb, just minutes from the Port, Monaco-Ville, and the Nice-Menton bus route. The downsides? Well, there's no elevator. And bedrooms and bathrooms are very, very small. However, this is Monaco, where real estate hovers around €20,000 per square meter. Those seeking a bargain should take the train to Nice.

6 rue de la Turbie, Monaco. www.monte-carlo.mc/france. ✆ **93-30-24-64.** 26 units. 95€–145€ double; 115€–170€ triple. Amenities: Bar, free Wi-Fi.

Hôtel de Paris ★★★ Never has so much history and glamour been suffused into 182 effortlessly chic guest rooms. La Prairie products and free access to the **Thermes Marins spa** (p. 220) come as standard in all of them. Accommodation culminates in two splendid super-suites, one of which, the "Churchill," overlooks the harbor and features Sir Winston's furniture. The former British Prime Minister used to sneak along a secret rooftop passageway to **Le Grill,** one of three award-winning restaurants in the hotel (see also the Louis XV; p. 217). If that isn't enough, the Hôtel de Paris boasts several sister hotels, including the five-star family friendly **Monte-Carlo Beach Hotel** (www.monte-carlo-beach.com; ✆ **93-28-66-66**)—whose **Restaurant Elsa** received the region's first 100% organic certificate in 2013—and the imposingly elegant **Hôtel Hermitage** (www.hotelhermitagemontecarlo.com; ✆ **98-06-40-00**), just around the corner.

Place du Casino, Monaco. www.montecarloresort.com. ✆ **98-06-30-00.** 182 units. 475€–1,400€ double; from 775€ suite. Valet parking 40€. Amenities: 3 restaurants (see "Where to Eat," below); bar; babysitting; concierge; exercise room; large indoor pool; room service; sauna; Thermes Marins spa offering thalassotherapy; Wi-Fi (free in lobby, or 20€/day).

Where to Eat

Pinch yourself. This postcard-sized Principality boasts a total of seven Michelin stars, and includes the most highly rated eatery on the entire Mediterranean, Le Louis XV.

Bouchon ★ TRADITIONAL FRENCH A refreshing new addition to the Principality's über-hip dining scene, Bouchon purveys classic bistro cuisine at distinctly un-Monaco prices. Art Deco *objets d'art* hand-selected from the flea markets of Paris and Nice set the scene. Breakfast kicks off with eggs and *viennoiseries.* Lunch continues with salade Niçoise and *moules marinières.* Dinner is slightly grander, although dishes like *filet de boeuf* or seared tuna won't break the bank when ordered with a *pichet* of wine.

11 ave Princesse Grace. www.bouchon.mc. ✆ **97-77-08-80.** Main courses 17€–38€; fixed-price lunches 18€ –20€, fixed-price menu 38€. Daily 7:30am–11pm.

Café Llorca ★ MEDITERRANEAN Super-chef Alain Llorca recently opened the very restaurant that Monaco lacked: an affordable contemporary eatery overlooking the shimming sea. Café Llorca is a bargain. Daily lunch mains at press time included crab spring rolls and Niçois beef stew, red mullet terrine and sautéed kidneys, and mackerel marinade and Provençal aioli. Call ahead for dinner—the establishment is often booked up for events.

11 ave Princesse Grace. www.cafellorca.mc. ✆ **99-99-29-29.** Main courses 16€–19€; fixed-price lunch 22€. Daily 11am–3pm.

Le Café de Paris ★ MODERN FRENCH Pricey, pretentious, and ever-popular, this Parisian-style restaurant-café on place du Casino has a location to die for. The menu has taken on an even more classic edge under head chef Jean-Claude Brugel, who trained alongside several top Riviera chefs including Roger Vergé and Joël Garault. Simple starters like garlic escargot and *croque-monsieur* share the menu with more innovative mains like filet of plaice (a North Sea fish) with pumpkin purée or steak tartare. From October to March, a special seafood stall dispenses Oléron oysters, sea urchins, and platters of chilled crab to passersby.

Place du Casino. ✆ **98-06-76-23.** Reservations recommended. Main courses 15€–49€; fixed-price menu 35€. Daily 8am–2am.

Le Loga ★ MEDITERRANEAN   This locals-only find is one of the best—not to mention cheapest—places to find *barbajuans*, the Monagasque national dish of ravioli stuffed with ricotta and chard. A tea room-cum-bistro, it's ever popular with ladies who lunch (and shop) on the boulevard des Moulins. Le Loga's Italian chef busts out home-made saffron gnocchi, brésaola pressed beef, and classic Milanese schnitzel. Dine inside the hipster tearoom interior or outside on the south-facing street terrace.

25 boulevard des Moulins. ✆ **93-30-87-72.** Main courses 11€–21€; fixed-price lunch 22€; fixed-price menu 38€. Mon, Tues, Thurs–Sat noon–2:30pm and 7–11pm, Wed noon–2:30pm. Closed middle 2 weeks in Aug.

Le Louis XV ★★★ MEDITERRANEAN   In the Hôtel de Paris, the Louis XV offers one of the finest dining experiences on the Riviera, and thus the world. Superstar chef Alain Ducasse oversees the refined but not overly adorned cuisine. The restaurant's head chef, Franck Cerutti, can be seen in Nice's market buying local cheeses or wandering through the corridors of the Hôtel de Paris carrying white truffles purchased from Italy. Everything is light and attuned to the seasons, with intelligent, modern interpretations of Provençal and northern Italian dishes. You'll find chargrilled breast of baby pigeon with sautéed duck liver, and a specialty known as Provençal vegetables with crushed truffles, all served under a magnificent frescoed ceiling, which includes the portraits of Louis XV's six mistresses. The restaurant celebrated 25 years as the Principality's top eatery in 2013.

In the Hôtel de Paris, place du Casino. ✆ **98-06-88-64.** Reservations recommended. Jacket and tie recommended for men. Main courses 80€–160€; fixed-price lunch 145€, dinner 230€–310€. Thurs–Mon 12:15–1:45pm and 8–9:45pm. Closed first 2 weeks in March.

Le Saint Benoit ★ MEDITERRANEAN   A seafood specialist with an esteemed reputation and panoramic view over Monaco Port, the rock of Monte-Ville, and the Mediterranean—albeit one with charming staff and extremely honest prices. The two-course lunch—which may include foie gras ravioli in a cep sauce followed by roast turbot—must rank as one of Monaco's best bargains. *Sole meunière* and platters of oysters grace the more traditional à la carte menu. Come spring, Le Saint Benoit's canvas roof and glass walls are taken away to reveal a sun-kissed dining terrace. The only tricky thing is finding the place: follow our map and the restaurant's knee-height street signs, or ride the elevator up from avenue d'Ostende.

10 avenue de la Costa. ✆ **93-25-02-34.** Main courses 19€–38€; fixed-price lunch 22€; fixed-price menus 31€ –42€. Tues–Sat 10am–2pm and 7:30–10:30pm, Sun noon–3pm.

Exploring Monaco

Monaco's main sights—including its glamorous port, casino and hotels—are clustered around the pedestrianized Place du Casino Square. Its principal museums, including the Prince's Palace and Oceanographic Museum, are situated on the history-laden rock of Monaco-Ville.

Collection des Voitures Anciennes de S.A.S. le Prince de Monaco
MUSEUM   Petrolheads, racing enthusiasts, and big kids alike will love the vintage car collection of Prince Rainier III. His private collection encompasses more than 100 vintage autos, including a locally built electric Venturi supercar and the bulletproof Lexus that served as the wedding car for Prince Albert and Charlene Wittstock in 2011. Other items include a Mercedes McLaren SLR and a classic Lamborghini Countach.

Les Terrasses de Fontvieille. www.palais.mc ✆ **92-05-28-56.** Admission 6.50€ adults, 3€ students and children 8–14, free for children 7 and under. Daily 10am–6pm.

Les Grands Appartements du Palais ★ PALACE   The home of Monaco's royal family, the Palais du Prince dominates the Principality from the Rock. A tour of the Grands Appartements—with audio tour recorded by none other than Prince Albert himself—allows visitors to glimpse the Throne Room and artworks by Bruegel and Holbein. The palace was built in the 13th century, and some of it dates from the Renaissance. The ideal time to arrive is 11:55am, so you can watch the 10-minute **Relève de la Garde (Changing of the Guard).** Summer concerts by the **Monte-Carlo Philharmonic Orchestra** are held outside in the courtyard.

Place du Palais. www.palais.mc. ✆ **93-25-18-31.** Admission 8€ adults, 4€ children 8–14, free for children 7 and under. Daily April–Oct 10am–6pm. Closed Nov–March.

Musée Océanographique de Monaco ★ AQUARIUM   This mammoth ocean-front museum was founded by Albert I, great-grandfather of the present prince, in 1910. It's now a living, breathing science lesson covering the world's oceans by way of a Mediterranean aquarium, tropical tanks, and a shark reserve. A delight for budding marine scientists is the 18m-long (60-ft.) whale skeleton that washed up on a local beach a century ago. Equally as compelling are the scientific specimens brought up from the ocean depths over the past 100 years.

Av. St-Martin. www.oceano.mc. ✆ **93-15-36-00.** Admission 14€ adults, 7€ children 4–18, free for children 5 and under. April–June and Sept daily 10am–7pm; July–Aug daily 10am–8:30pm; Oct–March daily 10am–6pm.

All-Night Glamour

Museums are all well and good, but to survey the soul of Monaco you need a credit card, a suntan, and a late-morning wake-up call. Early-evening glamour revolves around the bars that surround the historic port. Here, locally based luxury yacht agencies like **Y.CO** (www.ycoyacht.com; ✆ **93-50-12-12**) charter 50m-long (262 ft.) sailing craft for around $200,000 per week. At sundown the action moves uphill to Casino Square, where **Buddha Bar** (✆ **98-06-19-19**) is bedecked with chinoiserie, Asian statues, and a raised DJ booth. For sheer class, the **Crystal Bar** (✆ **98-06-98-99**) inside the Hôtel Hermitage pulls out all the stops. Elegant dress, vintage Champagne, and the odd feather boa set the scene until 1am. **Le Bar Américain** (✆ **98-06-38-38**), in the Hôtel de Paris, is far more raucous, with chillingly expensive cocktails and nightly jazz. Across place du Casino, the timeless superclub **Jimmy'z** (✆ **98-06-36-**

36), open nightly 11pm to 5am, has attracted stars from Farrah Fawcett to George Clooney. But it's the mythical **Casino de Monte-Carlo** (www.monte-carlocasinos.com; ✆ **98-06-21-21**) that lends the square its name. Since 2012, the casino's marble-floored Atrium has been open—for free—to all comers from 2pm who wish to shoot slots or play blackjack in the hallowed Salle des Amériques or try their luck at roulette in the Salle Europe. For roulette, *trente et quarante*, and Texas Hold'em in the private areas of rococo Salon Touzet and Salon Médecin, gamers must pay a 10€ fee. Entrance to Les Salons Supers Privés is by invitation only (heh, they've got our number!) and requires smart dress and nerves of steel. Another great summer addition is the Casino de Monte-Carlo **alfresco** terrace. Here visitors may play roulette and poker overlooking the moonlit Mediterranean. Now *that's* glamorous.

Nouveau Musée National de Monaco ★★ ART MUSEUM   Over the past decade Monaco has touted its cultural credentials to attract a savvier, younger, and more artistically aware crowd. The new Villa Sauber and Villa Paloma museums are two stunning art spaces set in palatial former homes across the city from one another. Both bring in global culture vultures by the score by way of contemporary-art exhibitions and shows covering sculpture, architecture, photography, and the glamorous history of the French Riviera.

Villa Sauber, 17 av. Princess Grace; Villa Paloma, 56 bd. du Jardin Exotique. www.nmnm.mc. ✆ **98-98-16-82.** Admission to both 6€ adults, free entrance for visitors 26 and under. June–Sept daily 11am–7pm. Oct–May daily 8am–6pm.

Opéra de Monte-Carlo ★ OPERA HOUSE   Monaco takes music seriously. In 2014 Robbie Williams played live to sell-out crowds. The Principality's lavish Opera House sits next to the casino, where its Salle Garnier hosts rock, pop, classical and opera events—and even hosted the wedding reception of Prince Albert and Charlene Wittstock in 2011. For big-hitting pop and DJ events, try the **Grimaldi Forum,** 10 av. Princesse-Grace (www.grimaldiforum.com; ✆ **99-99-20-00**).

Place du Casino. www.opera.mc. ✆ **98-06-28-28.** Year-round admission prices 20€–120€ adults, reduced entrance for visitors 26 and under.

Outdoor Activities

BEACHES   Just outside the border on French soil, the **Monte-Carlo Beach Club** adjoins the **Monte-Carlo Beach Hotel,** 22 av. Princesse-Grace (www.monte-carlo-beach.com; ✆ **93-28-66-66**), a five-star sister establishment of the ultra-elegant Hôtel de Paris. Princess Grace used to frolic on the beach here, and today it's an integral part of Monaco social life. It now has an Olympic-sized swimming pool, a La Prairie spa, cabanas, a poolside fine dining restaurant called Le Deck, and a low-key

---

Attacking the Plastic

If you insist on the likes of Hermès, Gucci, and Lanvin, you'll find them cheek by jowl near the Hôtel de Paris and the Casino de Monte-Carlo. But the prize for Monaco's hippest store goes to **Lull,** 29 rue de Millo (✆ **97-77-54-54**), awash in labels like Dries Van Noten and Raf Simons. Almost next door, **Une Femme à Suivre** (✆ **97-77-10-52**) sells French classics from the likes of Tara Jarman and Mariona Gen. Just west of Casino Square, **Pretty You,** 5 place Saint James (✆ **97-70-48-08**), vends Oscar de la Renta and Elie Saab. Just east of this piazza, **Galeries du Métropole** is packed with high fashion and specialty stores. As well as Dunhill and Gant, try **McMarket** (✆ **97-77-12-12**). Serious

labels in this fashion emporium include Balenciaga, Louboutin, and Jimmy Choo. **FNAC** (✆ **08-25-02-00-20**) is recommended for English-language novels, Monaco history books, and the latest electronics. Heading east from Casino Square, **boulevard de Moulins** sells 'everyday' Monaco labels. We're talking **Baby Dior,** no.31 (✆ **97-25-72-12**) and swimwear-to-the-stars brand **Erès,** also at no.31 (✆ **97-70-76-50**). For Repetto ballet slippers and Michael Kors satchels try **La Botterie,** no.15 (✆ **97-25-80-55**). For real-people shopping, stroll **rue Grimaldi,** the Principality's most commercial street, near the fruit, flower, and food market at **place des Armes,** which is open daily 7:30am to noon.

Mediterranean restaurant called La Vigie. Sea Lounge is an afternoon and late-evening club featuring live DJs and *nargile* hubble-bubble pipes. Beach activities include donuts, jet skis, and parachute rides. As the temperature drops in late October, the beach closes for the winter. The admission charge of 60€ to 150€, depending on the season, grants you access to changing rooms, toilets, restaurants, and bar, along with use of a mattress for sunbathing.

More low-key swimming and sunbathing is also available at **Plage du Larvotto,** off avenue Princesse-Grace. Part of this popular man-made strip of sand is public. The other part contains private beach clubs with bars, snacks, and showers, plus a kids' club. A jogging track runs behind the beach.

CINEMA Even the silver screen is slicker in Monaco than anywhere else. From June to September, the **Monaco Open Air Cinema** (www.cinema2monaco.com) occupies an alfresco amphitheater below the Rock of Monaco. Nightly blockbuster screenings take place in English-language only at 10pm in June and July, and at 9:40pm in August and September. Tickets costs 11€, or 9€ for ages 20 and under. Year-round movies are screened at the **Sporting Cinema** opposite the Casino de Monte-Carlo in both English and French. Prices are the same as the outdoor cinema.

SPA TREATMENTS The century-old **Thermes Marins,** 2 av. de Monte-Carlo (www.thermesmarinsmontecarlo.com; ✆ 98-06-69-00), reopened in summer 2014. It embodies wellness at its most chic. Spread over four floors is a pool, Turkish *hammam* (steam bath), healthy restaurant, juice bar, tanning booths, fitness center, beauty center, and private treatment rooms. A day pass, giving access to the sauna, steam rooms, fitness facilities, and pools, is 90€. Therapies include an hour-long Dead Sea salt peel for 150€.

SWIMMING Overlooking the yacht-studded harbor, the **Stade Nautique Rainier-III,** quai Albert-1er, at La Condamine (✆ 93-30-64-83), a pool frequented by the Monégasques, was a gift from Prince Rainier to his subjects. It's open May to October daily 9am to 6pm (until 8pm June–Aug). Admission costs 5.30€ per person. Between November and March, it's an ice-skating rink.

TENNIS & SQUASH The **Monte Carlo Country Club,** 155 av. Princesse-Grace, Roquebrune-Cap Martin, France (www.mccc.mc; ✆ 04-93-41-30-15), has 21 clay and 2 concrete tennis courts. The 43€ fee provides access to a restaurant, health club with Jacuzzi and sauna, putting green, beach, squash courts, and well-maintained tennis courts. Guests of the hotels administered by the Société des Bains de Mer (Hôtel de Paris, Hermitage, Monte Carlo Bay, and Monte Carlo Beach Club) pay half-price. It's open daily 8am to 8 or 9pm, depending on the season.

ROQUEBRUNE & CAP-MARTIN ★

Roquebrune: 953km (591 miles) S of Paris, 7km (4½ miles) W of Menton, 58km (36 miles) NE of Cannes, 3km (1¾ miles) E of Monaco. Cap-Martin: 4km (2½ miles) W of Menton, 2.5km (1½ miles) W of Roquebrune.

Roquebrune village is a Disney-like redoubt, which hangs above the Mediterranean from on high. Its sea views rival the village of Eze, and stretch all the way into Italy. Artists' ateliers and boutiques line rue Moncollet.

Brave visitors can hike down the hill from Roquebrune to Cap-Martin (and Ironmen can hike back up—a 45-minute long slog). This cape is a pine-covered peninsula, long associated with the rich and famous since the empress Eugénie wintered here in the 19th century. Artists and painters moved in during the 1920s. Among them were designer Eileen Gray (whose seaside cabin is set to open in late 2015) and architect Le Corbusier (after whom the coastal path that loop around the peninsula is named). Sir Winston Churchill regularly set up his easel here too. The long, pebbly plage de la Buse lies underneath Roquebrune-Cap-Martin train station. Its tranquillity is disturbed only by the occasional paraglider hurtling down to the beach from Roquebrune village.

Essentials

GETTING THERE   To **drive** to Roquebrune and Cap-Martin from Nice, follow N7 east for 26km (16 miles). Cap-Martin has **train** and bus connections from the other cities on the coast, including Nice and Menton. For **railway** information and schedules, visit www.voyages-sncf.com or call ✆ **36-35**. To reach Roquebrune, you'll have to take a **taxi** or follow the hiking signs for 30 minutes uphill. For bus information, contact the Gare Routière in Menton (✆ **04-93-28-43-27**).

VISITOR INFORMATION   The **Office de Tourisme** is at 218 av. Aristide-Briand, Roquebrune (www.roquebrune-cap-martin.com; ✆ **04-93-35-62-87**).

Where to Stay & Eat

Les Deux Frères ★ ITALIAN   A tried and tested gourmet restaurant looking out to sea from Roquebrune's old town square. Exceptional service is matched by professionally prepared classics from the four quarters of France. Expect Normandy lobster in Cognac, Mediterranean tuna with sesame and pesto, Provençal lamb with a lavender honey glaze, and confit de canard duck from the Languedoc. Best value is the 28€ lunch, which includes a half-bottle of Cotes du Ventoux red wine. Les Deux Frères also offers ten charming guestrooms (doubles from 75€ to 110€), some of which overlook the Mediterranean below.

1 place des Deux Frères. www.lesdeuxfreres.com. ✆ **04-93-28-99-00**. Main courses 18€–34€. Fixed-price lunch 28€; fixed-price menu 48€. Tue 7:30–9:30pm. Wed–Sat noon–2pm and 7:30–9:30pm, Sun noon–1:30pm.

Hôtel Victoria ★★   Cap-Martin's understated glamor is exemplified by the Hôtel Victoria. Both rooms and public spaces have been newly styled in homage to local artistic greats Le Corbusier, Pablo Picasso, and Eileen Gray. Modern interiors, which feature giant showers and funky rugs, are a designer dream. Half look out to sea; half overlook the leafy peninsula. All are a 60-second stroll to the pebbly public beach. Sip a 'Rio' house cocktail (a blend of cachaça, banana syrup, and coconut) on the sunny seaside terrace and raise a toast to the hotel's Anglo-Brazilian owners. The establishment also serves as an inexpensive base from which to visit Monaco, which is a 5-minute drive (or 1-hour walk for hardcore hikers) away.

7 promenade du Cap. www.hotel-victoria.fr. ✆ **04-93-35-65-90**. 32 units. 89€–345€ double. Parking 15€. **Amenities:** Bar; concierge; room service; free Wi-Fi.

Exploring Roquebrune

Exploring Roquebrune will take about an hour. You can stroll through its colorful streets, which retain their authentic feel. **Château de Roquebrune** (✆ **04-93-35-07-22**), was originally a 10th-century Carolingian castle; the present structure dates in part from the

THE SENTIER LE CORBUSIER coastal trail

Cap Martin is the fabulously rich spit of land between Monaco and Menton. Not as glitzy as Cap Ferrat or as fabled as Cap d'Antibes, its beauty lies in a 2-hour-long coastal trail that loops past the gardens of countless billionaires. This seaside path is as historical as it is beautiful. It was named after Le Corbusier, the zany French architect who built an urban utopia in Marseille (Unité d'Habitation) before constructing a coastal retreat here.

The **Sentier le Corbusier** path extends between Pointe du Cap-Martin to the eastern frontier of Monaco. If you have a car, you can park it in the lot at avenue Winston-Churchill, and begin your stroll. A sign labeled PROMENADE LE CORBUSIER marks the path. As you hike along, you'll take in a view of Monaco set in a natural amphitheater. In the distance, you'll see Cap-Ferrat and, high above, Roquebrune village.

The final stages of the path run past Corbusier's **Cabanon** log cabin, which was created by the architect to showcase his love of low-impact, prefabricated living spaces. Guided visits can be arranged with the Roquebrune Tourist Office (www.roquebrune-cap-martin.com; ℭ **04-93-35-62-87**, admission 10€ adults, 6€ children ages 12–18, free for children 11 and under). Almost next door is the **Villa E-1027**. This modernist beach home was designed in 1924 by the famed Irish architect Eileen Gray and is due to reopen to the public in 2015.

The scenic path ends at Monte-Carlo Beach and passes several secret sandy coves en-route. Walkers may then take the line no. 100 bus back to their rough starting point. An alternative is to return on foot from either Monte-Carlo Beach or Roquebrune-Cap-Martin train station, following the walking signs back through the Parc des Oliviers, which occupies the central spine of Cap Martin.

13th century, although it was jazzed up by its wealthy British owner, Sir William Ingram, nearly a century ago. From the towers, there's a panoramic view along the coast. The interior is open in February to May daily 10am to 12:30pm and 2 to 6pm; June to September daily 10am to 1pm and 2:30 to 7pm; and October to January daily 10am to 12:30pm and 2 to 5pm. Admission is 5€ for adults, 4€ for children aged 16 and under.

Rue du Château leads to place William-Ingram. Cross this square to rue de la Fontaine and take a left. This leads you to the **Olivier millénaire** (millenary olive tree), one of the oldest in the world—it's at least 1,000 years old. The tree allegedly exudes a peaceful aura. Why not give it a light hug for yourself?

Roquebrune and Cap-Martin have some truly exceptional **guided walking tours**. Each uncovers an attraction that few visitors will see. The most popular of the three is a 90-minute guided tour of the old town and castle, priced at 8€ for adults and 4€ for children ages 7 to 18, and free for children 6 and under. Tours depart whenever there are enough (at least five) participants to justify it. More esoteric (and conducted for the most part exclusively in French) are tours of the municipality's wealth of public buildings, one of them a rather humble cabin, **Le Cabanon**, designed by world-famous architect Le Corbusier. It's offered every Tuesday and Friday at 9:30am. Prices are 10€ for adults and 6€ for children aged between 13 and 18, and free for children 12 and under. Call the Tourist Office to book your place.

MENTON ★★

963km (559 miles) S of Paris; 30km (19 miles) E of Nice

Pack your shades. For the belle époque resort of Menton is the sunniest place in all France. It's no surprise that this balmy locale hosts both a winter lemon festival and the finest botanical gardens in the country. Liberal sprinklings of sun, sand, and citrus also attracted artists by the dozen, among them Picasso, Matisse, and Jean Cocteau. The brand-new Musée Cocteau dedicated to the latter artist makes the town worth visiting alone.

The aptly named Promenade du Soleil runs in front of Menton's Old City, Port and Casino. Game guests may follow this seaside boulevard all the way into Monaco—provided they have a spare 90 minutes and a sturdy set of legs.

Essentials

ARRIVING   **Trains** run to Menton from Nice, Monaco, the rest of the Côte d'Azur en route, and right into Italy every 30 minutes. For **rail** information, visit www.voyages-sncf.com or call ✆ **36-35. Bus** line no. 100 to Nice runs every 15 minutes until 8pm. One-way fares costs 1.50€. For bus information and schedules, contact **Lignes d'Azur** (www.lignesdazur.com; ✆ **08-10-06-10-06**). By **car** from Nice, take D6098 (the *basse corniche*) east.

VISITOR INFORMATION   The **Office de Tourisme** occupies a magnificent belle époque building near the Train Station at 8 avenue Boyer (www.tourisme-menton.fr; ✆ **04-92-41-76-76**).

[FastFACTS] MENTON

ATMs/Banks   **Crédit Mutuel,** 24 rue de la République (✆ **32-25**).

Internet Access   For free Wi-Fi, hit Menton Tourist Office, which maintains its own wireless Hotspot.

Mail & Postage   **La Poste,** 2 cours George V (✆ **36-31**).

Pharmacies   **Pharmacie Otto,** place St Roch (✆ **04-93-35-70-16**).

Where to Stay

Hôtel Napoléon ★★★   It's hard to find a hotel this perfect on the entire French Riviera. Guestrooms at this Cocteau-themed delight were designed by Jean-Philippe Noel, an artist usually found creating 7-star hotels in Dubai. Yet prices at the Napoléon couldn't be keener for such a stunning beachfront location. The hotel also boasts a private beach club, a solar-powered heated swimming pool, and a leafy rear garden. The hotel enjoyed a thorough renovation throughout 2013 and 2014. Leaving such a cocoon of fine linen and original art for anything less is a painful experience.

29 porte de France. www.napoleon-menton.com. ✆ **04-93-35-89-50.** 44 units. 89€–345€ double. Parking 10€. **Amenities:** Bar; concierge; swimming pool; free Wi-Fi.

Hôtel Palm Garavan ★   The prize for the friendliest hotel in Menton goes to the Palm Garavan. Superior rooms boast cracking views over the resort's botanical gardens, while guests may also gaze at Italy in their bathrobes. The spotless modern accommodation boasts touch-sensitive lights and ice-white decor. A top touch is the 3.50€ express breakfast, offering early-bird guests a croissant and cappuccino before they hit the resort's gardens, art museums, and beach.

3 porte de France. www.hotel-menton-garavan.fr. ☏ **04-93-78-80-67.** 19 units. 75€–160€ double. Parking 10€. **Amenities:** Bar; free Wi-Fi.

Hôtel Riva ★   The sun-kissed Riva faces due south from near the new Cocteau Museum. Guests may even follow this seaside promenade out front westwards to Monaco or east to the Italian border. Hip, colorful furniture is found on the outdoor terrace, in the funky lobby, and inside the otherwise rather standard guest rooms. The top floor sun deck is for hotel guests and spa visitors only.

600 promenade du Soleil. www.rivahotel.com. ☏ **04-92-10-92-10.** 41 units. 102€–144€ double. Parking 12€. **Amenities:** Bar; concierge; fitness room; library; sauna; spa; free Wi-Fi.

Hôtel Royal Westminster ★   A grand hotel without the grand prices, the venerable Westminster has a plum emplacement, facing due south towards the shimmering Mediterranean in the epicenter of town. Attracting an older clientele, guests may relax in the genteel front gardens or in the various lobby bars. The hotel boasts a library and billiards room too.

28 avenue Félix Faure. www.hotel-royal-westminster.com. ☏ **04-93-28-69-69.** 92 units. 80€–215€ double. Parking 12€. **Amenities:** Bar; concierge; library; restaurant; free Wi-Fi.

Where to Eat

A mere mile from the Italian border, Menton does pizza and pasta with aplomb. For more exotic fare laced with Menton lemons and offerings from the Ligurian fishing fleet, sail in to one of the eateries below.

A Braijade Meridiounale ★ MODERN PROVENÇAL   Not only is A Braijade situated on rue Longue, the atmospheric Old Town street that once connected Provence with Rome. It also serves the most wow-factor cuisine in the area. Dishes are mostly based around a brochette vertical flambée—or flaming vertical kebab. Sample skewers of seabass with aioli, prawns with pesto, and marinated lamb from the Provençal hills. The myriad of set menus (five at last count) combine wine, dessert, coffee, and palate-cleansing sorbets between courses. Bags of fun.

66 rue Longue. www.abraijade.fr. ☏ **04-93-35-65-65.** Reservations recommended. Main courses 18€–28€. Fixed-price menus 28€–50€. Daily 12:15–2pm and 7:15–11pm.

La Cirke ★★ ITALIAN   For a combined package of value, taste, and service La Cirke beats all-comers. Chef-owners Agostino and Eva welcome guests to this sunny corner emplacement above Menton Port. Their set menus, with aperitif included, are to die for. Read smoked swordfish, *bouillabaisse Mentonnaise*, and langoustine-laden paella. Italian sourced seafood is also a specialty: try salt-baked seabass, *calamari fritti*, and giant shared platters for two. Wine by the *pichet* (jug) brings prices down further. Although the 20€ or so bottles of sparkling Prosecco, crisp white Orvieto, and full bodied red Il Roggio will surely tempt.

1 place Victoria. ☏ **04-89-74-20-54.** Main courses 12€–19€. Fixed-price menus 24€–36€. Daily noon–2pm and 7–11pm.

La Pergola ★ MEDITERRANEAN   Open since 1902, it's doubtful as to whether La Pergola has changed its menu over the last century. And that's no bad thing. Vast platters of *fritto misto* seafood, grilled fish, salt-baked sea bream, and *paella de la mer* are heaved from the kitchen to the sand-in-the-toes tables. Local wines by the jug and hotlist of ten daily specials make for a beach blowout that won't break the bank—a rarity on the French Riviera. This beach bar also possesses a line of sun loungers, which can be rented for a post-prandial siesta all year round.

4 promenade de la Mer. ℰ **04-93-35-44-72**. Main courses 12€–26€. Fixed-price menus 40€. Daily noon–3pm and 6–11:30pm.

Restaurant Mirazur ★★★ MODERN MEDITERRANEAN   The awards have rolled in for Mirazur's young Argentine chef Mauro Colagreco. Two Michelin stars. A place on San Pellegrino's World's 50 Best Restaurants list. His multiple set menus (which range from a moderately priced lunchtime 'Déjeuner' to the wallet-crunching 'Carte Blanche') combine experimentation with élan. Expect tuna carpaccio with raspberries and almonds, plus a heady volley of desserts topped off with homemade marshmallows. Other gems include a deconstructed savory egg on a steaming bed of hay, oysters with edible flowers, and a tapenade-stuffed bread pillow. Cheeses are sourced from Fromagerie Moulinet in Menton market, breads from Pain du Four in rue Piéta in the village centre, and some of the seafood from the fishermen of Menton port. Graceful service and a panoramic sea view over Menton Port complete this priceless picture.

30 avenue Aristide Briand. www.mirazur.fr. ℰ **04-92-41-86-86.** Reservations recommended. Main courses 39€–58€; fixed-price menus 49€–135€. Wed–Sun noon–2pm 7:30–10pm. Closed mid-Nov–mid-Feb.

Al Vecchio Forno ★ ITALIAN   As authentic as a Neapolitan scooter, this established eatery serves Menton's Italian neighbors from just across the border. If the dress and dialect of its patrons shouts 'Godfather', the pizza is just as genuine. Seasonal artichokes and *funghi* come from Italy, as does the mozzarella and sea bream. The latter is seared crisp alongside the pizzas in the wood-fired oven.

39 quai Bonaparte. ℰ **04-92-10-04-78.** Main courses 6€–19€. Daily noon–2pm and 7–11pm.

Exploring Menton

Mentonnaise are lucky devils. They can choose to hang out in the historic Old Town, on a very long beach, or on the seaside boulevard (the Promenade du Soleil). The resort's world-famous gardens all lie just behind this ocean walk. Meanwhile, Jean Cocteau's artist legacy is spread out along the seafront.

Jardin Serre de la Madone ★★ GARDEN   A garden so enchanting that it's protected as a French National Monument. Like many of Menton's gardens the Serre

MENTON'S villages perchés

Three breathtakingly beautiful *villages perchés* (or perched villages) hover high above Menton. Each one is linked to the French Riviera by a winding mountain road. Better still, precipitous hiking trails run between each settlement.

At 360m (1,181 ft.) in altitude, **Gorbio** is the lowest of the three. Beloved of artists seeking sanctuary from the coastal bustle, it boasts several colorful churches and a panoramic sea view.

At 750m (2,461 ft.) high, **Sainte-Agnès** is the loftiest. Cobbled streets

and country restaurants set the scene. The village once formed part of the Maginot Line fortifications built to protect France from Nazi Germany (not that it did much good). Remnants of the military bastion remain.

Around 6km (4 miles) from Menton, **Castellar** perches above the Mediterranean like a fairytale redoubt. It's cute, quiet, and both the GR51 and GR52 walking trails pass through its medieval streets.

de la Madone was planted by an eccentric Englishman, this time Lawrence Johnston who created Britain's Hidcote Manor. Fountains and pergolas are shaded by strawberry trees and umbrella pines. Caught the garden bug? Menton's more private botanical gems include **Jardin Maria Serena** (by guided tour only, Monday 10am and Friday 2:30pm, 6€), **Fontana Rosa** (by guided tour only, Monday and Friday both at 10am, 6€), and **L'Orangeraie** (open Thursday 10am–4pm only, 6€).

Route de Gorbio. www.jardins-menton.fr. ✆ **04-93-35-86-72.** Admission 8€ adults, 6€ for children 12–18, free for children 11 and under. April–Oct Tues–Sun 10am–6pm, Dec–March Tues–Sun 10am–5pm.Closed Nov. Bus no. 7 from Menton town center.

Jardin Val Rahmeh ★★★ GARDEN   Even if you loathe botanical gardens, and even if you only visit one in Menton (although the resort boasts five), we beg you to come here. Menton's microclimate has reared a leafy wonderland within its protective walls. Fragrant paths weave past giant Amazon waterlillies, Buddha's Hand citruses from Thailand, and flowering *toromiro* trees from Easter Island. The scene is most magical within the black bamboo plantation, where sunlight dapples a babbling brook.

Route St Jacques. www.jardins-menton.fr. ✆ **04-93-35-86-72.** Admission 6€ adults, 4.50€ for children 16 and under. April–Sept Wed–Mon 10am–12:30pm and 3:30–6:30pm, Oct–March Wed–Mon 10am–12:30pm and 2–5pm.

Musée Jean Cocteau ★★★ MUSEUM   When not judging the Cannes Film Festival or chasing ballet dancers from the Monaco stage, *bon viveur* Jean Cocteau turned his artistic hand to painting on a grand scale. In 2011 many of his finest works were displayed in this oceanfront museum. Most of the 1,800 exhibits were donated by Belgian-American collector Séverin Wunderman. These include canvases by Cocteau's friends Picasso, Modigliani, and Miró, plus movies shot by the Frenchman at the Villa Santo Sospir on Cap Ferrat. Architect fans may note that the curvy, light-filled building that houses the Musée Jean Cocteau was designed by Rudy Ricciotti, who also styled the new MuCEM Mediterranean Museum in Marseille (see p. 117). A few blocks away, Cocteau's lifesize love scenes inside Menton's **Salle des Marriage**s (marriage office, Place Ardoïno, adults [2eu], free to children under 18, open Mon–Fri 8:30am–noon and 2–4:30pm) earned him honorary citizenship of the town in 1958. Three years after Cocteau's death in 1963, the **Musée du Bastion** (Tues–Sun 10am–noon and 2–6pm) opened on Menton's seafront to showcase his final period of work.

2 quai de Monléon. www.museecocteaumenton.fr. ✆ **04-89-81-52-50.** Admission 8€ adults, free for children 18 and under. Wed–Mon 10am–6pm.

Outdoor Activities

BEACHES   The all-public Plage du Soleil pans west from Menton to Cap Martin. Private beach clubs are found on Plage du Garavan just east of town. All-day sun-loungers at **Terenga Plage** (✆ **04-93-28-27-56**) and **Napoléon Plage** (✆ **04-92-10-92-60**) cost around 12€ per day.

SAILING   From the end of April until October visitors may bob around the Bay of Menton on a paddleboard, kayak, or sailing dinghy available for rent from the **Centre Nautique de Menton** (www.voile-menton.fr, ✆ **04-93-35-49-70**), located beside beach bar La Pergola.

BIKING   The verdant hills around Menton are the training ground for several Tour de France cyclists. Lesser mortals may still peddle along the seafront from Italy to Monaco on a rented mountain bike (from 14€ per day) or electric bike (from 35€ per

THE SECRET PATH TO italy

Thanks to European Union law, you don't need a visa to wander from Menton into Italy. In fact, thousands of locals—from vegetable grocers to taxi drivers—commute between the two countries every day. The seaside stroll from Menton Port to the now derelict border post runs seaward past the Jardin Maria Serena botanical gardens (✆ **0184 38 113**). A few hundred meters after the Italian border is the **Museo Preistorico dei Balza Rossi** (Museum of Prehistory, ✆ **39-01-84-38-11-13**, admission 2€ adults, 1€ children aged 16 and under, open Tues–Sun 8:30am–7:30pm). This petite museum highlights the 20,000-year-old civilization that once lived in the caves set back from the waterfront. In the late 19th century, three prehistoric graves were found in the rocks. One of the cavemen was wearing a ceremonial headdress adorned with shells and deer's teeth—a ritzy outfit entirely fitting with this classy Riviera location. Walking on into Italy you'll cross the small beach of Balzi Rossi, which becomes a private beach club in summer. Further on the path loops over the Nice to Genoa train track towards the Italian town of Ventimiglia. Hikers may also follow another path up to the Italian village of Grimaldi, perched directly above the coast

day) from **Bike Trip**, 1 avenue Carnot (www.rent-bike.fr, ✆ **04-94-96-48-93**), which also offers self-guided tour maps of the Menton Riviera.

Shopping

Menton has an Italian heart, with the taste buds to match. The best place to start is the pedestrian-only **rue Saint Michel**. Try **Maison Larnicol** at no.28 (✆ **04-93-97-80-92**) for chocolates, **Famille Mary** at no. 10 (✆ **04-92-09-19-43**) for flowery honey, or Menton-based **Oliviers & Co** at no.5 (✆ **04-89-74-19-76**) for olive oil tastings. The town's most venerated product, its home-grown lemons, are served by two rival stores at no. 22 and no. 27. From the former, **Au Pays du Citron** (✆ **04-92-09-22-85**), purchase lemon soap and citrus liqueur. From the latter, **Coté Citron** (✆ **04-89-74-19-76**), find limoncello and marmalade. One of Menton's most charming stores is **Maison Herbin**, 2 rue Vieux Collège (www.confitures-herbin.com, ✆ **04-93-57-20-29**). Visitors can see local citrus turned into jams, chutneys, and candies in their adjoining sweet factory.

Nightlife

Sunny Menton hosts the highest number of retirees in France, so the resort doesn't exactly dance until dawn. However, the town buzzes all August during the **Menton Music Festival** (www.festival-musique-menton.fr), where evening classical concerts occupy over almost every Old Town square. Gamblers may also test their luck at the **Menton Casino,** at 2 avenue Félix Faure (www.lucienbarriere.com; ✆ **04-92-10-16-16**). It boasts a traditional poker room as well as a vast sea view gaming terrace.

PLANNING YOUR TRIP & USEFUL PHRASES

14

Of almost any destination in the world, flying into Provence and the French Riviera is one of the most effortless undertakings in global travel. Direct flights run to both Marseille and Nice from North America, and from all over the world. There are no shots to get and no particular safety precautions, and more and more locals now speak English. With your passport, airline or train ticket, and enough money, you just go. In the pages that follow, you'll find everything you need to know to plan your trip: finding the best airfare, deciding when to go, getting around the country, and much, much more. At the end of the chapter, we've included some useful phrases and terms to help ease communication.

GETTING THERE

By Plane

Nice Côte d'Azur (airport code: NCE; www.nice.aeroport.fr) is France's second airport. It's served by direct flights from New York and Montreal, as well as up to 30 daily flights from both Paris and the U.K. Dozens of other destinations cover Europe the Middle East. This being France, the airport greets passengers with free Wi-Fi plus a fleet of free bikes and electric share-cars. See the Nice chapter for details.

Marseille Provence (airport code: MRS; www.mrsairport.com) is midway between Marseille and Aix-en-Provence. Since 2013 it's been served by direct flights from New York, adding to its scores of daily routes from around France and Europe.

Most airlines charge their lowest fares between November and mid-March. The shoulder season (Oct and mid-March to mid-June) is a bit more expensive, but we think it's the ideal time to visit France.

By Train

Marseille, Avignon, Aix-en-Provence, and Nice are four of France's busiest rail junctions, with trains departing across France every few minutes. If you are Italy or Spain, our recommendation would be to travel to the South of France by train; and the journey is even a treat if coming from as far as the U.K. or Germany.

Eurostar (www.eurostar.com; ℂ **800/387-6782** in the U.S.) trains even run directly from London to Avignon each summer from as little as $179 round-trip; journey time is just under 6 hours. Easier still, trips from London can be booked online on the Eurostar to any major station in southern France, with a short station change in Paris enroute. For the best deals, book as tickets become available exactly three months in advance. Highly recommended is train and accommodation specialist **Railbookers** (www.railbookers.com; ℂ **888/829-3040** in the U.S.). Their specialized team can plan bespoke rail journeys throughout the region.

By Car

The major highway from Paris to the South of France is the A7. It's called the *Autoroute du Soleil*, which poetically translates as the "Highway to the Sun." From Marseille and Aix-en-Provence, drivers may take the A8, *La Provençale*, eastwards towards Cannes, Nice and Monaco.

SPECIAL-INTEREST TRIPS & TOURS

Academic Trips & Language Classes

The **Alliance Française** (www.alliancefr.org; ℂ **01-42-84-90-00**), is a nonprofit French-language teaching organization with a network of 1,040 establishments in 136 countries. See p. 205 for more details.

Just outside Nice, the **Institut de Francais,** 23 av. Général-Leclerc, Villefranche-sur-Mer 06230 (www.institutdefrancais.com; ℂ **04-93-01-88-44**, see p. 205), offers highly acclaimed month-long French immersion courses.

Other language schools include **Actilangue** (www.actilangue.com; ℂ **04-93-96-33-84**), in Nice, **Centre Internationale** (www.cia-france.com; ℂ **09-70-40-57-06**), in Antibes, and French immersion specialists **CREA** (www.crealangues.com; ℂ **001-32-51-31-97-42**), in the nearby Gorges du Verdon.

Cruising

LUXURY CRUISES Dozens of major cruise lines call at Marseille, Nice, Villefranche, Monaco and at many points between. Google each destination for a list of who goes where (it's a big list!) but the major players include **MSC** (www.msc-cruisesusa.com; ℂ **877/655-4655**), and **Celebrity** (www.celebritycruises.com; ℂ **302/341-0205**).

RIVER CRUISES Before the advent of rail, many crops, building supplies, raw materials, and finished products were barged through the South of France on a series of rivers, canals, and estuaries. Many of these waterways retain their old-fashioned locks and pumps, allowing shallow-draft boats easy access through idyllic countryside.

Go Barging (www.gobarging.com; ℂ **800/394-8630**) operates 6-night river cruises departing from Paris along the River Seine, as well as trips through the Canal du Midi, Arles & Avignon, and Provence. Fares range from 3,360€ to 5,500€ per person (double occupancy) including all meals and drinks.

Viking River Cruises (www.vikingrivercruises.com; ✆ **800/304-9616**) leads 1-week tours along the Rhône, taking in Arles and Avignon en route. For double occupancy, prices start at $1,860.

Wellness Trips

The newly renovated **Thalazur** (antibes.thalazur.fr; ✆ **08-25-82-70-94**), complex in Antibes offers wellbeing stays of 1 to 7 nights, which may include cocooning, salt water therapy, and seaweed wraps.

For serious Provençal pampering just outside of Gordes, the five-star **Les Bories Hotel & Spa** (www.hotellesbories.com, ✆ **04-90-72-00-51**), offers two- to five-day treatment programs at their on-site spa, La Maison d'Ennea. Facials, massages, and wraps use locally sourced essential oils, such as lavender and sweet orange.

There are plenty of excellent **yoga** and **meditation** retreats dotted around the region. A few popular places include **Dévi Yoga Retreats** (www.deviyogaretreats.com) across the South of France, **Kaliyoga/France** (www.kaliyoga.com) in Provence's Lubéron, and **LuxYoga** (www.luxyoga.com) on the French Riviera.

Food & Wine Trips

Dozens of gourmet tours have set up shop in Provence and the French Riviera in recent years. Ideas range from market tours, to shopping with chefs, to wine-tasting by bike. See individual chapters for more details.

Guided Tours

BIKE TOURS   Some of the best cycling tours of France are offered by **VBT** (www.vbt.com; ✆ **800/245-3868**), which offers a 7-day trip around Avignon, St Rémy, and the Pont du Gard. Prices start at $2,545 per person, with airfare packages also available.

Cycling for Softies (www.cycling-for-softies.co.uk; ✆ **44/161-248-8282**) is ideal for easy-going travelers with little cycling experience. Tours cover most of Southern France, in particular the Lubéron Natural Park. Prices vary according to type of tour (both self-guided and small groups are available); buffet breakfasts and gourmet dinners are included.

Cycle Cote d'Azur (www.cyclecotedazur.com) in Nice is run by former cycling pros. The personal knowledge its staff allow for near unlimited packages through the region from 2 to 14 days. Their 4-night Nice packages takes in parts of the Tour de France route from $699 per person; as does their longer self-guided Mont Ventoux and Provence tour, from $800 per person.

BUS TOURS   Most larger cities in Provence and the Riviera offer hop-on, hop-off bus tours, including Nice, Monaco, and Marseille. They are ideal for scoping out the lay of the land on arrival. See specific chapters for details.

GETTING AROUND

Within most major cities—including Nice, Marseille, and Avignon—public transportation is efficient, comprehensive, and cheap. Distances between each destination are too short to be covered by air, but are the perfect length to zip among by high-speed train. Indeed, no two towns in the region are much further than 3 hours apart by rail. In smaller towns, such as Cannes, Arles, or Antibes, it's easy to navigate the city center on foot. See each chapter for specific details.

By Car

The most charming châteaux and country hotels always seem to lie away from the main cities and train stations. Renting a car is a good way to travel around the Southern French countryside, especially in the Lubéron area, the vineyards north of Avignon, and in rural Provence. Day car-hire is inexpensive, so visitors may want to rent a vehicle just for a day en-route if they wish. After all, driving around the Monaco Grand Prix route sure is fun.

Driving schedules in Europe are largely a matter of conjecture, urgency, and how much sightseeing you do along the way. Driving time from the most westerly town in this book, Arles, to the most easterly, Menton, is just over 2½ hours by car.

RENTALS   To rent a car, you'll need to present a passport, a driver's license, and a credit card. You will also have to meet the company's minimum age requirement; 21 or above at most rental agencies. The biggest agencies have pickup spots all over Southern France, including **Budget** (www.budget.com; ✆ **800/472-3325**); **Hertz** (www.hertz.com; ✆ **800/654-3001**); and **Europcar** (www.europcar.com; ✆ **877/940-6900** in the U.S. and Canada).

Note: The best deals are always booked online, in advance. Rental companies won't generally mind if you drive your car into, say, Italy. After all, the border is only a five-minute drive from Menton, the most easterly town covered in this guide.

In France, **collision damage waiver (CDW)** is usually factored into the overall rate quoted, but you should always verify this before taking a car on the road. At most companies, the CDW provision won't protect you against theft, so if this is the case, ask about purchasing extra theft protection. Automatic transmission is a luxury in Europe. If you prefer it to stick-shift, you must specifically request it—and you'll pay extra for it.

GASOLINE   Known in France as *essence,* gas is expensive for those accustomed to North American prices, although the smaller cars common in Europe use far less fuel. Depending on your car, you'll need either leaded (*avec plomb*) or unleaded (*sans plomb*).

Note: Sometimes you can drive for miles in rural France without encountering a gas station; don't let your tank get dangerously low.

DRIVING RULES   Everyone in the car, in both the front and the back seats, must wear seat belts. Children 10 and under must ride in the back seat.

In France, you drive on the right. Drivers are supposed to yield to the car on their right (*priorité a droite*), except where signs indicate otherwise, as at traffic circles.

If you violate the speed limit, expect a big fine. Limits are 130kmph (80 mph) on expressways, 110kmph (68 mph) on major national highways, and 90kmph (55 mph) on country roads. In towns, don't exceed 50kmph (31 mph).

Note: It's illegal to use a cellphone while you're driving in France; you will be ticketed if you're stopped.

MAPS   While most French drivers are happy with Google Maps, traditional motorists opt for the large **Michelin maps** of the country and regions (www.viamichelin.com) on sale at all gas stations. Big travel-book stores in North America carry these maps as well. GPS navigation devices can be rented at most car-hire stations.

BREAKDOWNS/ASSISTANCE   A breakdown is called *une panne* in France. Call the police at ✆ **17** (if calling from a landline) or ✆ **112** (if calling from a mobile phone) anywhere in France to be put in touch with the nearest garage. Most local garages offer towing.

By Train

The world's fastest trains—known as *Train à Grande Vitesse,* or TGVs—link all the major cities and resorts in the South of France, allowing you to travel within the region at speed. First class travel by TGV is an experience in itself, with at-seat dining, picture windows, and train interiors courtesy of fashion designer Christian Lacroix. Booked in advance, it's not much more than second class. SNCF (French National Railroads; www.voyages-sncf.com, or call ℂ 36-35 in France) also runs local trains that connect rural areas, as well as along the resort-heavy French Riviera. It also operates trains running into the mountains above Nice, and over into the Italian border.

For information or reservations, go online (www.voyages-sncf.com). You can also visit any local travel agency. If you have a chip credit card and know your PIN, you can use your card to buy your ticket at the easy-to-use *billetteries* (ticket machines with an English-menu option) in every train station.

RAIL PASSES Rail passes as well as individual rail tickets are available from **Rail Europe** (www.raileurope.com; ℂ **800/622-8600** in the U.S.). Options include a 5-day rail pass usable within France for a 1-month period for $322. **Eurail** (www.eurail.com) offers regional rail passes throughout Europe, including a France-and-Italy combined pass for $540, allowing 6 days of first-class travel within a 2-month period.

By Bicycle

Over the past few years, most cities and towns throughout Provence and the French Riviera have initiated bike-sharing schemes. You can register online or directly at one of the city's dozens of bike stands; in most cases, you'll need a credit card and a mobile phone. Average fees range from 1€ for 1 day to 7€ for a week, and entitle you to use any of the city's hundreds of bikes for up to 30 minutes at a time. When you're finished, just slot the cycle back into any allocated bike stand around town. Among many others, Avignon, Aix-en-Provence, Marseille, and Nice all offer citywide bike-sharing. Monaco, being the showiest town in the South of France, introduced an all-electric bike-share scheme in 2014. See each chapter for specific details.

On Foot

France's ancient **Sentiers de Grande Randonnée** (www.grsentiers.org), or "GR" walking routes link many of the country's prettiest towns. Close to two centuries old and stretching over 112,000 miles (180,000 km), these footpaths ripple through vineyards and along the coastline, crisscrossing picturesque towns and mountain passes en route. Regional favorites include the GR 51, looping above coastal Provence, the GR 52A, in the Mercantour National Park, and the challenging GR 20, a mountainous trail along Corsica's spine. Keep an eye out for the routes' red and white way-markings. A new section of the GR network, the GR 653A, connects the towns of Menton and Arles with the Santiago de Compostela pilgrim's route in Spain.

THE VALUE OF THE EURO VS. OTHER POPULAR CURRENCIES

Euro (€)	US$	C$	UK£	A$	NZ$
1	1.36	1.49	0.82	1.53	1.63

[FastFACTS] FRANCE

Business Hours Business hours in France can be erratic. Most banks are open Monday through Friday from 9:30am to 4:30pm. Many, particularly in small towns in Provence, take a long lunch break. Hours are usually posted on the door. Most museums close 1 day a week (often Mon or Tues), and they're generally closed on national holidays. Usual hours are from 10am to 7pm. In Marseille or other big French cities, stores are open from around 10am to 7pm, with or without a lunch break (up to 2 hr.). Some shops, delis, cafes, and newsstands open at 8am and close at 8 or 9pm.

Disabled Travelers Facilities for travelers in the South of France, and nearly all new or modern hotels, provide disabled access. The TGVs (high-speed trains) are wheelchair accessible; older trains have compartments for wheelchair boarding. **Handiplage** (handiplage.fr) has a detailed map and breakdown of every French beach that offers accessible to disabled visitors.

Doctors Doctors are listed in Pages Jaunes (Yellow Pages; www.pages jaunes.fr) under "Médecins: Médecins généralistes." The minimum fee for a consultation is about 23€—for this rate, look for a doctor who is described as "secteur 1." The higher the "secteur," the higher the fee. **SOS Médecins** (www.sos medecins.fr; ℰ **36-24**) can

make house calls. See also "Emergencies" and "Health" later in this section.

Drinking Laws As well as bars and restaurants, supermarkets and cafes sell alcoholic beverages. The legal drinking age is 18, but persons under that age can be served alcohol if accompanied by a parent or guardian. Drinking and driving is illegal, and incurs a heavy fine. Drinking wine on the beach, however, seems *de rigueur.*

Drugstores Spot French *pharmacies* by the green neon cross above the door. If your local pharmacy is closed, there should be a sign on the door indicating the nearest one open. Alternatively, **Pharmacies de Garde** (www.pharmaciesde garde.com or www.3237.fr; ℰ **32-37**) can direct you to the nearest open pharmacy.

Electricity Electricity in France runs on 220 volts AC (60 cycles). Adapters or transformers are needed to fit sockets, which you can buy in branches of Darty or FNAC.

Embassies & Consulates If you have a passport, immigration, legal, or other problem, contact your consulate. Most countries have representatives in Paris, although a few maintain a presence in either Marseille or Nice. Many are open Monday to Friday, approximately 10am to 5pm. However, call or check online before you visit to confirm.

Australian Embassy: 4 rue Jean-Rey, 15e Paris (www. france.embassy.gov.au; ℰ **01-40-59-33-00;** Métro: Bir Hakeim).

Canadian Embassy: 35 av. Montaigne, 8e Paris (www. amb-canada.fr; ℰ **01-44-43-29-00;** Métro: Franklin-D-Roosevelt or Alma-Marceau). Regional consulate at 2 place Franklin, Nice (ℰ **04-93-92-93-22**).

Irish Embassy: 4 rue Rude, 16e Paris (www.embassyof ireland.fr; ℰ **01-44-17-67-00;** Métro: Argentine).

New Zealand Embassy: 7ter rue Léonard de Vinci, 16e Paris (www.nzembassy.com/ france; ℰ **01-45-01-43-43;** Métro: Victor Hugo).

UK/British Embassy: 35 rue du Faubourg St-Honoré, 8e Paris (http://ukinfrance.fco. gov.uk; ℰ **01-44-51-34-00;** Métro: Concorde or Madeleine). Regional consulate at 24 avenue du Prado, Marseille (ℰ **04-91-15-72-10**).

United States Embassy: 2 av. Gabriel, 8e Paris (http:// france.usembassy.gov; ℰ **01-43-12-22-22;** Métro: Concorde). Regional consulate at place Varian Fry, Marseille (ℰ **04-91-54-92-00**).

Emergencies In an emergency while at a hotel, contact the front desk. If the emergency involves theft, go to the police station in person. Otherwise, call ℰ **112** from a cellphone. The fire brigade can be reached at ℰ **18.** For an ambulance, call ℰ **15.** For the police, call ℰ **17.**

Etiquette & Customs

French value pleasantries and take manners seriously: Say "Bonjour, Madame/ Monsieur" when entering an establishment and "Au revoir" when you depart. Always say "Pardon" when you accidentally bump into someone. With strangers, people who are older than you and professional contacts use *vous* rather than *tu* (*vous* is the polite form of the pronoun *you*).

Health For travel abroad, Non–E.U. nationals should consider buying medical travel insurance. For U.S. citizens, Medicare and Medicaid do not provide coverage for medical costs incurred abroad; check your health insurance before leaving home. U.K. nationals need a **European Health Insurance Card** (**EHIC;** www.ehic.org. uk) to receive free or reduced-cost medical care during a visit to a France.

If you take regular medication, pack it in its original pharmacy containers, along with a copy of your prescription.

Holidays Major holidays are New Year's Day (Jan 1), Easter Sunday and Monday (late March/April), Labor Day (May 1), VE Day (May 8), Ascension Thursday (40 days after Easter), Pentecost/Whit Sunday and Whit Monday (seventh Sun/Mon after Easter), Bastille Day (July 14), Assumption Day (Aug 15), All Saints Day (Nov 1), Armistice Day (Nov 11), and Christmas Day (Dec 25).

Hospitals For hospitals in other major French cities, see individual chapters.

Hotlines SOS Help is a hotline for English-speaking callers in crisis ☎ **01-46-21-46-46** (www.soshelpline. org). Open 3 to 11pm daily.

LGBT Travelers France is one of the world's most tolerant countries toward gays and lesbians. Indeed, its tourism bureaus welcome LGBT travelers with open arms. Nice in particular boasts a large gay population, with many clubs, restaurants, organizations, and dedicated services. For local information, visit www.gay-provence.org. Gayvox (www.gayvox.fr) has updated listings about the gay and lesbian scene.

Mail Most post offices in France are open Monday to Friday from 8am to 5pm and every Saturday from 8am to noon. Allow 5 to 8 days to send or receive mail from home. Stamps are also sold in *tabacs* (tobacconists). For more information, see www.laposte.fr.

Mobile Phones You can use your mobile phone in France, provided it is **GSM** (Global System for Mobile Communications) and tri-band or quad-band; just confirm with your operator before you leave.

Using your phone abroad can be expensive, so it's a good idea to get it "unlocked" before you leave. This means you can buy a French SIM card from one of the three main French providers, **Bouygues Télécom** (www. bouyguestelecom.fr)**, Orange** (www.orange.fr)**, or SFR** (www.sfr.fr). Or do like the locals do and use **Skype** (www.skype.com) for long-distance calls.

Money & Costs Frommer's lists exact prices in the local currency. The currency conversions quoted above were correct at press time. However, rates fluctuate, so before departing, consult a currency exchange website such as www.oanda.com to check current rates.

It's always advisable to bring a mix of cash and credit cards on vacation. Before you leave home, exchange enough petty cash to cover airport incidentals, tipping, and transportation to your hotel. Alternatively, withdraw money upon arrival at an airport ATM. In many international destinations, ATMs offer the best exchange rates. Avoid exchanging money at commercial exchange bureaus and hotels, which often have the highest transaction fees and terrible exchange rates. ATMs are widely available in France.

Newspapers The most popular French newspapers are **Le Monde** (www. lemonde.fr), **Le Figaro** (www.lefigaro.fr), and left-leaning **Libération** (www. liberation.fr).

The English-language **International New York Times** (international. nytimes.com), based in Paris and published Monday to Saturday, is distributed all over France.

Packing Tips Remember that the bulk of hotel rooms in France are small indeed. Try to adhere to the old traveling maxim, "pack half of what you think you need." You will *always* actually need far less than you imagine. And you can easily purchase any missing items—along with the copious souvenirs you'll pick up too—along the way.

Passports Citizens of the U.K., New Zealand, Australia, Canada, and the United States need a valid passport to enter France. The passport is valid for a stay of 90 days.

Police In an emergency, call 𝄐 **17** from a landline or 𝄐 **112** from a mobile phone anywhere in France.

Safety The most common menace, especially in large cities, is the plague of *pickpockets*. Take precautions and be vigilant at all times: Don't take more money with you than necessary, keep your passport in a concealed pouch or leave it at your hotel, and ensure that your bag is firmly closed at all times. In cafes, bars, and restaurants, it's best not to leave your bag under the table, on the back of your chair, or on an empty chair beside you. Keep it between your legs or on your lap. Never leave valuables or luggage in a car, and never travel with your car unlocked.

In general, the South of France is a safe region and it is safe wander from restaurants to bars late at night, though it is always best to not drawn attention to the fact you are foreign by speaking loudly in English. Use common sense when taking public transport at night.

Although there is a significant level of discrimination against West and North African immigrants, there has been almost no harassment of African-American tourists to France in recent decades. However. **S.O.S. Racisme,** 51 av. de Flandre, 19e (www.sos-racisme.org; 𝄐 **01-40-35-36-55**), offers legal advice to victims of prejudice and will even intervene to help with the police.

Female travelers should not expect any more hassle than in other major cities, and the same precautions apply. Avoid walking alone at night and never get into an unmarked taxi. If you are approached in the street or on public transportation, it's best to avoid entering into conversation, and walk into a well-lit, populated area.

Senior Travel The South of France is stocked with retirees. It's little surprise that Menton, the sunniest town on the southern coast, has the most number of seniors in the country. Many discounts are available countrywide to men and women over 60. National trains have senior discounts. Check out www.voyages-sncf.com for more information. Frommers.com offers more information and resources on travel for seniors.

Smoking Smoking is banned in all public places in France, including cafes, restaurants, and nightclubs. It's permitted (dare we say popular) on outdoor and semi-enclosed terraces.

Student Travel Student discounts are less common in France than from other countries, but simply because young people 25 and under are usually offered reduced rates. SNCF also offer discounts for 25-and-unders traveling on national trains (www.voyages-sncf.com).

Taxes As a member of the European Union, France routinely imposes a value-added tax (VAT in English; TVA in French) on most goods. The standard VAT is 20%, and prices that include it are often marked TTC (*toutes taxes comprises,* "all taxes included"). If you're not an E.U. resident, you can get a VAT refund if you're spending fewer than 6 months in France, you purchase goods worth at least 175€ at a single shop on the same day, the goods fit into your luggage, and the shop offers *vente en détaxe* (duty-free sales or tax-free shopping).

Telephones Public phones can still be found in France. All require a phone card (known as a *télécarte*), which can be purchased at post offices or *tabacs*.

The country code for France is 33. To make a local or long-distance call within France, dial the person or place's 10-digit number. If you're calling from outside of France, drop the initial 0 (zero).

Time France is on Central European Time, which is 1 hour ahead of Greenwich Mean Time. French daylight saving time lasts from the last Sunday in March to the last Sunday in October, when clocks are set 1 hour ahead of the standard time. France uses the 24-hour clock (so 13h is 1pm, 14h15 is 2:15pm, and so on).

Tipping By law, all bills in **cafes, bars, and restaurants** say *service compris*, which means the service charge is included. However, it is customary to leave 1€ or 2€, depending on the quality of the service; in more upscale restaurants leave 5€ to 10€. **Taxi drivers** usually expect a 5% to 10% tip, or for the fare to be rounded up to the next euro. The French tip **hairdressers** around 15%,

and if you go to the theater, you're expected to tip the **usher** about 2€.

Toilets If you're in dire need, duck into a cafe or *brasserie* to use the lavatory. It's customary to make a small purchase if you do so. France still has some hole-in-the-ground squat toilets. Try not to lose your change down the pan!

Visas E.U. nationals don't need a visa to enter France. Nor do U.S., Canadian, Australian, New Zealand, or South African citizens for trips of up to 3 months. Nationals of other countries should make inquiries or

look online at the nearest French embassy or consulate.

Visitor Information Before you go, your best source of information is the **French Government Tourist Office** (www.france-tourism.com).

Water Drinking water is generally safe. If you ask for water in a restaurant, it'll be served bottled (for which you'll pay), unless you specifically request *une carafe d'eau* or *l'eau du robinet* (tap water). Your waiter may ask if you'd like your water *avec gas* (carbonated) or *sans gas* (without bubbles).

USEFUL TERMS & PHRASES IN FRENCH

It's often amazing how a word or two of halting French will change your hosts' dispositions in their home country. At the very least, try to learn a few numbers, basic greetings, and—above all—the life raft, *"Parlez-vous anglais?"* As it turns out, many French do speak passable English and will use it liberally if you demonstrate the basic courtesy of greeting them in their language. So, it's not essential to speak French when visiting the French Riviera—indeed, some expats living along the Côte d'Azur manage to get by for years or even decades without bothering to learn the language! However, as you explore further into Provence, you'll find that the more French you know, the better your progress. And in the furthest reaches of Haute-Provence, you'll struggle to make yourself understood without some proficiency in French. In any event, any stay in France will be immeasurably enhanced if you speak French, and your linguistic effort will predispose you well to the locals.

Go on, try our glossary out, and don't be bashful. *Bonne chance!*

Basics

English	French	Pronunciation
Yes/No	Oui/Non	**wee/nohn**
Okay	D'accord	**dah-*core***
Please	S'il vous plaît	**seel voo *play***
Thank you	Merci	**mair-*see***
You're welcome	De rien	**duh ree-*ehn***
Hello (during daylight hours)	Bonjour	**bohn-*jhoor***

English	French	Pronunciation
Good evening	Bonsoir	**bohn-swahr**
Goodbye	Au revoir	**o ruh-vwahr**
What's your name?	Comment vous appellez-vous?	**ko-mahn voo za-pell-ay-voo?**
My name is . . .	Je m'appelle . . .	**jhuh ma-pell . . .**
Happy to meet you	Enchanté(e)	**ohn-shahn-tay**
Miss	Mademoiselle	**mad-mwa-zel**
Mr.	Monsieur	**muh-syuh**
Mrs.	Madame	**ma-dam**
How are you?	Comment allez-vous?	**kuh-mahn tahl-ay-voo?**
Fine, thank you, and you?	Très bien, merci, et vous?	**tray bee-ehn, mare-ci, ay voo?**
Very well, thank you	Très bien, merci	**tray bee-ehn, mair-see**
So-so	Comme ci, comme ça	**kum-see, kum-sah**
I'm sorry/excuse me	Pardon	**pahr-dohn**
I'm so very sorry	Désolé(e)	**day-zoh-lay**
That's all right	Il n'y a pas de quoi	**eel nee ah pah duh kwah**

In Your Hotel

English	French	Pronunciation
We're staying for . . . days	on reste pour . . . jours	**ohn rest poor . . . jhoor**
Is breakfast included?	petit déjeuner inclus?	**peh-tee day-jheun-ay ehn-klu?**
Are taxes included?	les taxes sont comprises?	**lay taks son com-preez?**
Room	une chambre	**ewn shawm-bruh**
Double room	une chambre double	**ewn shawm-bruh doo-bluh**
Twin room	une chambre aux lits simples	**ewn shawm-bruh o lee sam-pluh**
Triple room	un triple	**uh tree-pluh**
Family room	une chambre familiale	**ewn shawm-bruh fam-ee-lee-al**
Family suite	une suite familiale/un appartement familial	**ewn sweet fam-ee-lee-al/uhn apart-a-mahn fam-ee-lee-al**
Interconnecting rooms	des chambres communicantes	**day shawm-bruhs com-you-nee-kohnts**
Suite	une suite	**ewn sweet**
Extra bed	un lit supplémentaire	**uh lee sup-lay-mon-tair**
Cot	un lit bébé	**uh lee bay-bay**
Balcony	un balcon	**uh bahl-cohn**
Key	la clé (la clef)	**la clay**
Bathroom	une salle de bain	**ewn sal duh ban**
Bathtub	une baignoire	**ewn bayn-nwar**
Shower	une douche	**ewn dooch**
Sink	un lavabo	**uh la-va-bow**
Shower room	une salle de douche	**ewn sal duh dush**
Hot and cold water	l'eau chaude et froide	**low showed ay fwad**

English	French	Pronunciation
Babysitting	le babysitting/garde d'enfants	**luh bay-bay sitting/gard den-fons**
Swimming pool (heated/indoor)	une piscine (chauffée/couverte)	**ewn pee-seen (show- fay/coo-vair)**

Getting Around/Street Smarts

English	French	Pronunciation
Do you speak English?	Parlez-vous anglais?	**par-lay-voo ahn-*glay*?**
I don't speak French	Je ne parle pas français	**jhuh ne parl pah frahn-*say***
I don't understand	Je ne comprends pas	**jhuh ne kohm-*prahn* pas**
Could you speak more loudly/more slowly?	Pouvez-vous parler un peu plus fort/plus lentement?	**poo-vay-voo par-lay un puh ploo for/ploo lan-te-*ment*?**
Could you repeat that?	Répetez, s'il vous plaît?	**ray-pay-*tay*, seel voo *play***
What is it?	Qu'est-ce que c'est?	**kess kuh *say*?**
What time is it?	Qu'elle heure est-il?	**kel uhr eh-*teel*?**
What?	Quoi?	**kwah?**
How? or What did you say?	Comment?	**ko-*mahn*?**
When?	Quand?	**kahn?**
Where is . . . ?	Où est . . . ?	**ooh eh . . . ?**
Who?	Qui?	**kee?**
Why?	Pourquoi?	**poor-*kwah*?**
Here/there	ici/là	**ee-*see*/lah**
Left/right	à gauche/à droite	**a goash/a drwaht**
Straight ahead	tout droit	**too drwah**
I'm American/Canadian/British	Je suis américain(e)/canadien(e)/anglais(e)	**jhe sweez a-may-ree-*kehn*/can-ah-dee-*en*/ahn-glay (*glaise*)**
Fill the tank (of a car), please	Le plein, s'il vous plait	**luh plan, seel voo *play***
I'm going to . . .	Je vais à . . .	**jhe vay ah . . .**
I want to get off at . . .	Je voudrais descendre à . . .	**jhe voo-*dray* day-son-drah ah**
I'm sick	Je suis malade	**jhuh swee mal-*ahd***
airport	l'aéroport	**lair-o-*por***
bank	la banque	**lah bahnk**
bridge	pont	**pohn**
bus station	la gare routière	**lah gar roo-tee-*air***
bus stop	l'arrêt de bus	**lah-*ray* duh boohss**
by means of a bicycle	en vélo/par bicyclette	**ahn vay-low/par bee-see-*clet***
by means of a car	en voiture	**ahn vwa-*toor***
cashier	la caisse	**lah *kess***
cathedral	cathédral	**ka-tay-*dral***
church	église	**ay-*gleez***
dead end	une impasse	**ewn am-*pass***
driver's license	permis de conduire	**per-mee duh con-*dweer***

English	French	Pronunciation
elevator	l'ascenseur	**lah-sahn-*seuhr***
stairs	l'escalier	**les-kal-*yay***
entrance (to a building or a city)	une porte	**ewn port**
exit (from a building or a freeway)	une sortie	**ewn sor-*tee***
fortified castle or palace	château	**sha-*tow***
garden	jardin	**jhar-dehn**
gasoline	du pétrol/de l'essence	**duh pay-*trol*/de lay-*sahns***
highway to . . .	la route pour	**la root por**
hospital	l'hôpital	**low-pee-*tahl***
museum	le musée	**luh mew-*zay***
no entry	sens interdit	**sehns ahn-ter-*dee***
no smoking	défense de fumer	**day-*fahns* de fu-may**
on foot	à pied	**ah pee-*ay***
1-day pass	ticket journalier	**tee-kay jhoor-nall-ee-ay**
one-way ticket	aller simple	**ah-*lay* sam-pluh**
police	la police	**lah po-*lees***
rented car	voiture de location	**vwa-*toor* de low-ka-see-on**
round-trip ticket	aller-retour	**ah-*lay*-re-*toor***
slow down	ralentir	**rah-lahn-*teer***
store	le magasin	**luh ma-ga-*zehn***
street	rue	**roo**
subway	le Métro	**le *may*-tro**
telephone	le téléphone	**luh tay-lay-*phone***
ticket	un billet	**uh *bee*-yay**
ticket office	vente de billets	**vahnt duh bee-*yay***
toilets	les toilettes/les WC	**lay twa-*lets*/lay vay-say**

In Provence

English	French	Pronunciation
Bull/horse farm	une manade	**ewn man-ad (Camargue)**
Bullfighting festival	la féria	**lah fair-ree-ah**
Cave	une grotte	**ewn grot**
Coastal/cliff-clinging road	une corniche	**lah kor nee-sh**
Country house	une bastide	**ewn bah-steed**
Farmhouse	un mas	**uh ma**
Mediterranean fjord	une calanque	**ewn ca-lahnk**
Olive mill	un moulin à huile	**uh moo-lan a oh-ee-le**
Scrubland (with aromatic plants)	la garrigue/le maquis	**lah ga-reeg/luh ma-key**

Necessities

English	French	Pronunciation
I'd like . . .	Je voudrais . . .	jhe voo-*dray* . . .
a room	une chambre	ewn *shahm*-bruh
the key	la clé (la clef)	la *clay*
I'd like to buy . . .	Je voudrais acheter . . .	jhe voo-dray ahsh-*tay* . . .
aspirin	des aspirines/des aspros	deyz ahs-peer-*eens*/deyz ahs-*prohs*
condoms	des préservatifs	day pray-ser-va-*teefs*
dictionary	un dictionnaire	uh deek-see-oh-*nare*
dress	une robe	ewn robe
envelopes	des envelopes	days ahn-veh-*lope*
gift (for someone)	un cadeau	uh kah-*doe*
handbag	un sac	uh sahk
hat	un chapeau	uh shah-*poh*
magazine	une revue	ewn reh-*vu*
map of the city	un plan de ville	unh plahn de *veel*
matches	des allumettes	dayz a-loo-*met*
necktie	une cravate	eun cra-*vaht*
newspaper	un journal	uh jhoor-*nahl*
phone card	une carte téléphonique	ewncart tay-lay-fone-*eek*
postcard	une carte postale	ewn carte pos-*tahl*
road map	une carte routière	ewn cart roo-tee-*air*
shirt	une chemise	ewn che-*meez*
shoes	des chaussures	day show-*suhr*
skirt	une jupe	ewn jhoop
soap	du savon	dew sah-*vohn*
socks	des chaussettes	day show-*set*
stamp	un timbre	uh *tam*-bruh
trousers	un pantalon	uh pan-tah-*lohn*
writing paper	du papier à lettres	dew pap-pee-*ay* a *let*-ruh
How much does it cost?	C'est combien? / Ça coûte combien?	say comb-bee-*ehn*?/sah coot comb-bee-*ehn*?
That's expensive	C'est cher/chère	say share
That's inexpensive	C'est raisonnable/C'est bon marché	say ray-son-*ahb*-bluh/say bohn mar-*shay*
Do you take credit cards?	Est-ce que vous acceptez les cartes de credit?	es-kuh voo zaksep-*tay* lay kart duh creh-*dee*?

Numbers & Ordinals

English	French	Pronunciation
zero	zéro	zare-*oh*
one	un	uh
two	deux	duh

English	French	Pronunciation
three	trois	**twah**
four	quatre	*kaht*-**ruh**
five	cinq	**sank**
six	six	**seess**
seven	sept	**set**
eight	huit	**wheat**
nine	neuf	**nuf**
ten	dix	**deess**
eleven	onze	**ohnz**
twelve	douze	**dooz**
thirteen	treize	**trehz**
fourteen	quatorze	**kah**-*torz*
fifteen	quinze	**kanz**
sixteen	seize	**sez**
seventeen	dix-sept	**deez**-*set*
eighteen	dix-huit	**deez**-*wheat*
nineteen	dix-neuf	**deez**-*nuf*
twenty	vingt	**vehn**
twenty-one	vingt-et-un	**vehnt**-ay-*uh*
twenty-two	vingt-deux	**vehnt**-*duh*
thirty	trente	**trahnt**
forty	quarante	**ka**-*rahnt*
fifty	cinquante	**sang**-*kahnt*
sixty	soixante	**swa**-*sahnt*
sixty-one	soixante-et-un	**swa**-*sahnt*-et-*uh*
seventy	soixante-dix	**swa**-*sahnt*-*deess*
seventy-one	soixante-et-onze	**swa**-*sahnt*-et-*ohnze*
eighty	quatre-vingts	**kaht-ruh**-*vehn*
eighty-one	quatre-vingt-un	**kaht-ruh-vehn**-*uh*
ninety	quatre-vingt-dix	**kaht-ruh-venh**-*deess*
ninety-one	quatre-vingt-onze	**kaht-ruh-venh**-*ohnze*
one hundred	cent	**sahn**
one thousand	mille	**meel**
one hundred thousand	cent mille	**sahn meel**
first	premier	*preh*-**mee-ay**
second	deuxième	*duhz*-**zee-em**
third	troisième	*twa*-**zee-em**
tenth	dixième	*dees*-**ee-em**
twentieth	vingtième	*vehnt*-**ee-em**
thirtieth	trentième	*trahnt*-**ee-em**
one-hundredth	centième	*sant*-**ee-em**

The Calendar

English	French	Pronunciation
Sunday	dimanche	**dee-*mahnsh***
Monday	lundi	***luhn*-dee**
Tuesday	mardi	***mahr*-dee**
Wednesday	mercredi	***mair*-kruh-dee**
Thursday	jeudi	***jheu*-dee**
Friday	vendredi	***vawn*-druh-dee**
Saturday	samedi	***sahm*-dee**
yesterday	hier	**ee-*air***
today	aujourd'hui	**o-jhord-*dwee***
this morning/this afternoon	ce matin/cet après-midi	**suh ma-*tan*/set ah-preh-mee-*dee***
tonight	ce soir	**suh *swahr***
tomorrow	demain	**de-*man***

GLOSSARY OF BASIC MENU TERMS

Note: To order any of these items from a waiter, simply preface the French-language name with the phrase *"Je voudrais"* (jhe voo-dray), which means "I would like . . ." *Bon appétit!*

Meats

English	French	Pronunciation
beef stew	du pot au feu	**dew poht o *fhe***
marinated beef braised with red wine, served with vegetables	du boeuf à la mode	**dew bewf ah lah *mhowd***
chicken	du poulet	**dew *poo*-lay**
rolls of pounded and baked chicken, veal, or fish (often pike), usually served warm	des quenelles	**day ke-*nelle***
chicken with mushrooms and wine sauce	du coq au vin	**dew cock o *vhin***
chicken wings	des ailes de poulet	**dayz ehl duh poo-lay**
frogs' legs	des cuisses de grenouilles	**day cweess duh gre-*noo*-yuh**
ham	du jambon	**dew jham-bohn**
kidneys	des rognons	**day *row*-nyon**
lamb	de l'agneau	**duh lahn-*nyo***
lamb chop	une cotelette de l'agneau	**ewn koh-te-lette duh lahn-*nyo***
rabbit	du lapin	**dew lah-pan**
sirloin	de l'aloyau	**duh lahl-why-*yo***
steak	du bifteck	**dew beef-*tek***
pepper steak	un steak au poivre	**uh stake o *pwah*-vruh**
double tenderloin	du chateaubriand	**dew *sha*-tow-bree-ahn**
sweetbreads	des ris de veau	**day *ree* duh voh**

English	French	Pronunciation
veal	du veau	**dew** *voh*
Fried ravioli (Monaco)	barbajuan	**bah-ba-joo-an**
Garlic mayonnaise	de l'aïoli	**duh lie-oh-lee**
Niçoise pancake	socca	**soh-ka**
Salad Niçoise in a bap	pan bagnat	**pan bay-nee-ay**

Fruits/Vegetables

English	French	Pronunciation
cabbage	du choux	**dew** *shoe*
eggplant	de l'aubergine	**duh loh-ber-***jheen*
grapefruit	un pamplemousse	**uh** *pahm***-pluh-moose**
grapes	du raisin	**dew ray-***zhan*
green beans	des haricots verts	**day ahr-ee-coh** *vaire*
green peas	des petits pois	**day puh-tee** *pwah*
lemon/lime	du citron/du citron vert	**dew cee-***tron***/dew cee-tron** *vaire*
orange	une orange	**ewn o-***rahnj*
pineapple	de l'ananas	**duh lah-na-***nas*
potatoes	des pommes de terre	**day puhm duh** *tehr*
potatoes au gratin	des pommes de terre dauphinois	**day puhm duh tehr doh-feen-wah**
french fried potatoes	des pommes frites	**day puhm** *freet*
spinach	des épinards	**dayz ay-pin-***ards*
strawberries	des fraises	**day** *frez*

Beverages

English	French	Pronunciation
beer	de la bière	**duh lah bee-***aire*
milk	du lait	**dew** *lay*
orange juice	du jus d'orange	**dew joo d'or-***ahn***-jhe**
water	de l'eau	**duh lo**
red wine	du vin rouge	**dew vhin** *rooj*
white wine	du vin blanc	**dew vhin** *blahn*
Anise-flavoured liqueur	pastis	**pah-steess**
coffee	un café	**uh ka-***fay*
coffee (black)	un café noir	**uh ka-fay** *nwahr*
coffee (with cream)	un café crème	**uh ka-fay** *krem*
coffee (with milk)	un café au lait	**uh ka-fay o** *lay*
coffee (decaf)	un café décaféiné (slang: un déca)	**un ka-fay day-kah-fay-***nay* **(uh** *day***-kah)**
coffee (espresso)	un café espresso (un express)	**uh ka-fay e-***sprehss***-o (un ek-***sprehss***)**
tea	du thé	**dew** *tay*

Index

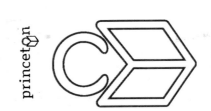